D1194416

CRIMINAL WOMEN

JOYCELYN M. POLLOCK

SOUTHWEST TEXAS STATE UNIVERSITY

anderson publishing co.
2035 Reading Road
Cincinnati, OH 45202
800-582-7295

Criminal Women

Copyright © 1999
Anderson Publishing Co.
2035 Reading Rd.
Cincinnati, OH 45202

Phone 800.582.7295 or 513.421.4142
Web Site www.andersonpublishing.com

Library of Congress Cataloging-in-Publication Data

Pollock, Joycelyn M., 1956-
    Criminal women / Joycelyn M. Pollock.
        p.   cm.
    Includes bibliographical references (p.   ) and index.
    ISBN 0-87084-715-5 (pbk.)
    1. Female offenders--United States. 2. Criminal behavior--United States. I. Title.
    HV6046.P63   1999
    364.3 ' 74--dc21
                                                            98-36919
                                                            CIP

Cover design by Tin Box Studio/Cincinnati, OH
Cover photo credit: Brad Smith/PhotoSmith

EDITOR Gail Eccleston
ASSISTANT EDITOR Elizabeth A. Shipp
ACQUISITIONS EDITOR Michael C. Braswell

Dedication

*To Lee Bowker, from whom I learned the importance of
comprehensive and critical research;*

*To Hans Toch, from whom I learned the importance of and respect
for the worldview of those studied; and,*

*To Meda Chesney-Lind, from whom I learned that without passion
and purpose, research is merely an empty exercise.*

—Joycelyn M. Pollock

Preface

Almost 50 years ago, Otto Pollak published *The Criminality of Women*, an exhaustive survey of the preceding literature on female criminals. Although it has been criticized by practically all subsequent treatments of the subject, little bits and pieces of his theories can be identified even in the work of those theorists who criticized his work. At the very least, one may commend him for directing attention to a subject that the field of criminology continued to ignore for another 20 years. Hopefully it will not be considered too presumptuous to consider this book as a type of half-century update on Pollak's work. I confess I have felt some affinity to his work through the years because of the similarity of our names.

It is now completely inaccurate to allege that little is written on the female criminal. One need only look at the sources for this book (or ask my graduate assistant who filled out the interlibrary loan cards). Rather, what continues to be true is that most new theories of crime or revisions of older theories start with little or no explanation of how the theory explains patterns of female criminality, and then a host of later "tests" of the theory apply it to female samples. Since theories are usually created for men and use male definitions, often the application to females is at best weak and/or convoluted.

In this book we accept only broad, consistent, and longstanding findings regarding women's crime rates. What we know for sure is that across cultures and across time, women have participated in dramatically less violent crime and moderately less property crime, except for certain "consumer" crimes where there seems to be little or no sex differential. This is the fact that must be explained by any crime theory. Our examination of which theories are better able to explain this fact proceeds from the earliest to the most recent, and includes the most classic to the most controversial.

This book is meant to be used in upper-level to graduate-level criminology classes, rather than in freshman or sophomore criminology classes. Students who have not had a basic criminology course would find the treatment of major theories too abbreviated to understand them fully. However, this book can be used as a companion volume to a standard text on criminology, in addition to being appropriate for use in an advanced criminology class, a special topics class, or a women in criminal justice class. There is a presumption that the reader is at least somewhat familiar with the major theories of crime. Further, the instructor would probably also need to supplement the treatment of feminist theory with additional readings. Notes at the end of each chapter are provided to aid in readability. Readers will find more detail and cites to additional sources in these notes.

Acknowledgments

I view this work as a merging of my two research trajectories throughout the years—ethics and women's issues. Many friends and colleagues have shaped my thinking, helped in the writing of this book, or provided me with opportunities that influenced the development of some of the ideas herein; although I hasten to add that many will definitely *not* agree with some of the conclusions reached herein. Specific individuals I wish to thank include: Alida Merlo, Meda Chesney-Lind, Lee Bowker, Donna Hale, Frankie Bailey, Jill Rosenbaum, Verna Henson, Barbara Owen, Barbara Bloom, Ellen Halbert, Tim Flanagan, Michael Braswell, Rita Warren, and Dorothy McClellan. There are also individuals whom I have not had the pleasure of knowing personally, but whose work has greatly influenced my thinking in these matters: Carol Smart, Dorie Klein, Pat Carlen, Clarice Feinman, Pat Heidensohn, Carol Gilligan, Deborah Denno, Freda Adler, Rita Simon, Gary Jensen, Darrell Steffensmeier, Joanne Belknap, Kathleen Daly, Nicole Rafter, Cathy Widom, and Merry Morash. Finally, I should thank Otto Pollak who provided the originating concept for this book.

I must thank Tim Flanagan, Jerry Williams, and Jim Alexander for giving me the opportunity to teach criminology at the Law Enforcement Management Institutute. Teaching criminology to skeptical law enforcement administrators helped to solidify my thoughts and test certain arguments in a forum quite different from a typical college criminology class. Gina Sewell assisted with research, making countless trips to the library to pick up interlibrary loans. Interlibrary loan librarians generously did not cut me off, even though I probably exceeded my and 10 other faculty member's allowance of IL monies. Greg Garvelli picked up where Gina left off after her graduation. Walter DeKeseredy, Susan Griffith, Frankie Bailey, and Donna Hale read the manuscript and provided suggestions. Although I did not follow all of their suggestions, I am sure the manuscript is better because of their assistance. Finally, my thanks to Tess Sherman at Southwest Texas and Gail Eccleston at Anderson for their careful attention to detail in editing the manuscript. This book would not have been completed in a timely manner without the able and dedicated work of Tess Sherman. I would also like to thank Ahti Laitinen, Petri Sjöblom, and others at the University of Turku Law Faculty, who helped me overcome the difficulties of finishing this project in a different country (Finland).

I also thank those close to me who have, over the years, helped me with my small son. My safety net of mother-substitutes includes friends, college students, secretaries, and neighbors. These women (and men) have stepped in when necessary in the inevitable crises that occur in the life of a single working mom, as well as taken over parenting when I needed to work on this (and other) book(s) during school vacations or weekends. They have shared in and contributed to the growth and development of my son and I thank them for it: Jan Bullock (and Dave Bullock), Cherry Seaton, Verna Henson, Pam McKay (and Ron Becker), Linda Medellin, Linda Staats, Rae Josey, and Susan Griffith (and Jim Langabeer).

Our beliefs, research interests, and interpretations of knowledge do not exist in a vacuum. I confess that I became much more interested in the issue of women prisoners as parents when I became a parent myself. I changed from being a die-hard sociologist believing in "nurture" rather than "nature," to one who accepts inherent sex differences after I observed my toddler son compared to his female best friend. I am perhaps more sensitive to Mike Gottfredson's and Travis Hirschi's portion of the general theory of crime that postulates low self-control as the reason for large family size because I come from a family of six siblings and might criticize my mother for other things, but would never describe her as someone with little self-control; further, as someone who has no self-control myself (over chocolate chip cookies anyway), I cannot accept the theory that it is the same factor that causes someone to drive drunk or to kill a store clerk in a robbery. I am sensitive to the arguments for and against the potential detrimental influences of divorce and single-parent households on children, especially boys, since I acquired that role myself. One general theme that runs through this work is that truth is relative and knowledge is personal; therefore, I make no claims that this book presents the truth; I only offer it as my version of understanding the criminality of women.

Table of Contents

Introduction: Framing the Questions

1

Objectives

- Understand the post-modernists' critique of positivism.

- Identify the problems with measuring crime and measuring the factors associated with crime causation.

- Recognize alternative methods of understanding criminal behavior.

This is a book about women's criminality; however, it is also a book about men's criminality because one cannot hope to explain women without also understanding men. In the past, the criminality of men was explored through the use of studies that excluded women. Feminist critiques in the 1970s argued that such attempts could not possibly explain human behavior because they excluded one-half of the population. Later, efforts were offered that explained women's criminality through the use of unique theories of female behavior—arguably, these theories also are deficient because of their exclusion of men. Women and men are different, but if we are ever to understand human behavior, in this case, criminal behavior, it must be through an understanding of both women and men. Thus, this book revisits the standard criminological theories one would find in any criminology textbook, but does so with a focus upon how well they explain the gender differences in criminal behavior. Newer theories are also discussed, many of which continue to virtually ignore the central issue focused upon in this work—the gender difference in criminal behavior.

This is also a book about the criminological enterprise. The approach taken is critical of past and recent attempts to develop and test theories of crime. The book's topic—the criminology of female offenders—can be used to illustrate and illuminate larger and more fundamental problems in the attempt to "explain" criminal behavior. In this first chapter, we frame the questions to be asked and addressed in the remainder of the book. Before we do that, however, there are a number of issues to discuss that call into question the legitimacy of positivism as it relates to social science.

> **Positivism**: knowledge construction that employs the methods of the natural sciences—collection of data, testing of hypotheses, and searching for measurable causal factors.
>
> **Post-modernism**: critical theory emerging in the twentieth century that questions the objectivity of science and the ability to measure reality or explain causation.

POSITIVISM, POST-MODERNISM, AND CRIMINAL THEORY

"Crime rates are decreasing."

"Arrest reduces the future incidence of battering."

"African-Americans are more likely than caucasians to commit violent crime."

"Drug use causes criminality."

Are these facts? The definition of a fact is something that can be proven, but within the realm of social science, what we think we know about human behavior is subject to doubt. What if it is impossible to isolate objective reality from one's biases, values, and distorted perceptions of reality? This is the premise of post-modernism. Post-modernism, like feminism, has many definitions and perspectives. No attempt will be made here to describe and categorize types of post-modernism or present the array of criticisms leveled against it.[1] Basically, the relevance of post-modernism to criminology is the critique it offers against any attempt to define "truth" through positivistic methods. In fact, post-modernism rejects the legitimacy of any particular "truth" at all. Thus, while it has been linked to radical or critical criminology or feminist criminology, it goes further than either of those perspectives because while they offer an alternative "reality" vis-à-vis power relations and definitions of crime, post-modernism "deconstructs" the very nature of reality.[2]

A fundamental premise of this book will be that *all* social science research is rife with hidden or not-so-hidden biases, preconceptions, and ethnocentric and/or androcentric values that make it impossible to measure, much less explain, the reality of crime.[3] This premise is obviously not original, nor even very controversial. Many radical and feminist critiques, as well as more mainstream text treatments, of traditional criminology clearly illustrate how early theorists confused stereotypes with facts and carried out research accepting time- and culture-specific views of women, minorities, and economic classes as truth. The premise simply applies the critique to the critiquers. In other words, it is assumed here that no one person has a "corner on the truth" and while (for instance) feminist critiques of traditional criminology theories were enlightening, the feminist perspective may be no more than another biased, value-ridden approach presented as objective research. In fairness, this possibility is recognized and accepted by many who define themselves as feminists. Schwartz and Friedrichs explain the value of the post-modernist approach:

> The guiding premise here is that a postmodernist approach enables us to comprehend at a more appropriate level our knowledge of a dynamic and complex human environment. It looks to different layers of "texts," which are interrelated with each other as the locus of social reality, and discounts the notion of some separate, "factual" reality [footnotes omitted].[4]

Two specific issues related to the weakness of positivism will be discussed below. The first identifies problems of criminal theory; in other words the influence of values and the fallacy of "objectivity" or "neutrality" in social science; and, the second concerns the difficulty inherent in measuring subjective realities such as crime.

Problems of Criminal Theory: Values and Paradigms

The belief that criminologists are objective scientists who have no biases or preconceptions regarding crime or human behavior is patently untenable. All of us have preconceptions regarding the nature of humans and the origins of crime. Whether human behavior originates from free choice or whether human behavior is "determined" by biological, social, and cultural factors is a bias that one possesses before any theory is constructed, and before a test of any theory is undertaken. The premise that humans are fundamentally social and altruistic or, the alternative premise that humans are inherently egocentric and must be controlled, is implicit in all criminal theory. Similarly, whether men and women have fundamental differences beyond reproductive capabilities is a belief that colors everyone's reading of sex difference research. This is not to say that researchers cannot approach data with an attempt to keep an open mind, but the presumption that they are not influenced by their biases is to presume that they are not human.

Even the construction of theory itself holds a presumption—specifically, that a theory can explain a behavior such as crime through linear causality. Williams and McShane provide a wonderfully concise and clear treatment of traditional criminological theory, but in their critique of theories, they evidently assume that a legitimate theory must be able to predict all behavior.[5] In their discussion, they refer to theories that identify broken homes, hanging around with the wrong crowd, and poor upbringing as deficient because: "If they were correct, then everyone whose life has these causes would be criminal (or delinquent) and, of course, we know that that is not true." Why? Why assume that a theory must have perfect predictive power? Everyone who smokes tobacco does not get cancer, everyone who has a genetic predisposition to a degenerative disease does not contract that disease, and everyone who eats too many Twinkies does not get fat. Medical science has come to terms with probabilities. No one seriously doubts the link between smoking tobacco and cancer despite the fact that some people can smoke tobacco for 50 years and not die from lung cancer; this merely illustrates the awesome variation in human physiology. Why would we assume that social science could be more accurate than medical science in its ability to predict? That is the first value that colors the exploration of criminal theory—that a theory must be able to explain all behavior, or at least a good portion of it, otherwise it is not a valid explanation of any behavior.

Another problem of criminal theory is the lack of clarity when testing or discussing different levels of causation. Consider the following quote:

> [Referring to a female offender] She had a record of juvenile delinquency, including membership in a female gang. When discussing her family, she took the blame for her criminality, explaining that she came from a "good" family; that they had clothes to wear and were made to go to school. With further discussion of her upbringing, however, she described a mother who was totally under the control of a strict, authoritarian husband. The father controlled the household with fear and intimidation and the girl was punished severely for not living up to his standards in dress, academic performance, or behavior. One incident she recalled was when she was 10 years old and went to a friend's house after school, instead of coming home. When she did return, her father beat her, called her a slut and locked her out of the house, telling her she was no longer his daughter. She was let back into the house, but her childhood became a pattern of engaging in increasingly more delinquent behaviors with consequential beatings and punishments from the father.[6]

How does one explain this woman's criminality? The woman herself understood her criminality in one way; her counselors probably have "diagnosed" her in another way; the interviewer came away from this interview with yet another understanding of why she engaged in increasingly more serious criminality. And even if one can figure out how to measure the content of her life, those factors identified may or may not be recognized as correlated with crime in the aggregate or help us to understand societal levels of crime. One might argue that the influence of life factors cannot be broken down to objective, measurable parts—that somehow in that process of abstraction, the meaning and influence of an individual's life circumstances are lost.[7]

There are at least two levels of criminological explanation. Crime is explained at a societal level (for instance, theories that explain why crime rates go up or down), and also at an individual level (for instance, theories as to why a particular person might commit crime). Societal factors, such as unemployment, the percentage of women employed, urbanization, and so on, are examined to determine their relationship to crime rates—a completely different level of causation from the individual level. The problem is when the two levels of abstraction are confused, or the problem of ecological fallacy is not fully exposed.

> **Ecological Fallacy:** a fallacy (misstatement) that occurs when one infers something about an individual based upon some factor that is associated with a group in which the individual is a member. For instance, assuming that an individual is criminal because he or she lives in a poor area of town, or is a member of a minority group.

Williams and McShane[8] present a logical premise that societal crime rates are probably more influenced by social factors, while individual predictions of crime are probably better served by looking at personality characteristics. That makes sense, but it is also important to be cautious in transferring the importance of one factor to the other level. For instance, the increase of broken homes can be postulated as a "cause" of crime—on an individual level, one tests this by counting the number of criminals who come from broken homes and comparing them to a control group. Applying this to the societal level, one may make the prediction that an increase in broken homes will create an increase of crime. That may be true, but it may be true because (for instance) homes are left unattended and all criminals (whether they come from a broken home or not) burglarize more often because it is easier to commit burglary when more houses are empty (an environmental or opportunity factor). Or, broken homes may lead to more youths living in poverty which, in turn, affects their motivation to commit burglary (an individual or causation factor). Or some other factor may be at work. The point is that societal changes may or may not be helpful in understanding individual criminal offending; and individual reasons may or may not be relevant to societal-level changes in crime rates.

Today, criminologists are in the curious position of trying to explain the apparent decrease in crime rates. It is interesting to observe the scramble to explain this decrease when the previously proposed explanations for the increase in crime, i.e., broken homes, lack of supervision of children, societal disorganization, or lack of social support, have not appreciably changed. The decrease may be real, or it may be a reflection of reporting changes or changes in official actions. It could be due to increased imprisonment, better economy, demographic changes, community policing, changes in reporting, or normal statistical fluctuations (what goes up has to come down) over time. The very attempt to explain crime rate changes, however, may be fallacious without a recognition that the researcher has some suspicions as to why crime goes up or down, and these biases influence the questions asked, the tests constructed, and the interpretation of the answers.

Even the view of crime itself is colored by the researcher's values and preconceptions. Feminist critiques of traditional theorists exposed their approach as one that viewed crime as dynamic and "fun," thus women were uninteresting and passive because they were not as criminal as the "boys."[9] The implicit premise that crime was more interesting than goodness fundamentally affected the construction of the theory, the choice to ignore women, and the interpretation of data. But feminism has its own blinders. There is almost a wistful and/or combative premise in some feminist writings that women are (or can be) just as criminal as men.

Feinman identifies "images" of women that have existed throughout history and which continue to influence perceptions of women. *Photo credit: Mark C. Ide.*

Feminist critiques were also scathing in their criticism of early theories of female delinquency and the presentation of delinquent girls as more "needy" emotionally who tended to come from more disturbed family backgrounds.[10] The criticism directed at these researchers implied that the researcher operated under sex role stereotypes and was wrong in the view that female delinquents had different motivations related to their entry into delinquency. However, reading the findings of these early researchers, one senses that they might have had a better understanding of the girls they studied than the later critiques acknowledge. The researchers, employing phenomenological methods, used quotes from girls that illustrated their emphasis on friends and boys, and the deep pain they felt stemming from family abuse or neglect. Obviously such information was interpreted through the lens of personal values and biases, but why could it not be true that female delinquents did care more about boys than anything else? That they did have worse family backgrounds? That they did emphasize relational goals more than did their male counterparts? The latter day feminist interpretation that girls and boys are essentially the same is not necessarily any more the "truth" than the earlier supposition that girls were fundamentally different from boys.[11]

Feinman identifies "images" of women that have existed throughout history and which continue to influence perceptions of women: the "good" image of women as pure, submissive, moral, and passive can be compared to the "bad" image of woman as "worse than man," vicious, and sexually rapacious.[12] These images have little empirical support, but the point made here is that whatever images hold power in any given time period will influence the collection of empirical data; thus, one cannot be too smug about any current knowledge because it is likely to be influenced by current paradigms.[13]

Fads of scientific "fact" concerning women are almost amusing in their cyclical nature. Women are more evil than men (1800s), women are more moral (early 1900s), women—at least terrorist women—are more evil (1960s), women are the same as men (1970s), women have a different moral voice (1980s), women are equal (1990s). We have come a long way in over-coming sex-sterotypes but we also run the risk of stubbornly ignoring real differences between men and women in our attempt to avoid stereotyping. Wonders discusses the idea that people "do gender," that there is no objective reality of "woman" (or "man"), that woman is constructed specific to cultural time and place.[14] But one might argue that this premise is itself a bias and value that influences the researchers' interpretation of research.

Sex Differences: Those differences determined to be biological in nature, i.e., women's ability to give birth and lactate; also those average differences in musculature, height, and weight. More controversial are those differences in intellectual predispositions (spatial versus verbal skills) and aggressiveness (thought by some to be inherently biological in nature and thought by others to be a product of socialization).

Gender Differences: Those differences determined to be a product of socialization, i.e., what is female or male is thought to be largely determined by cultural definitions and proscriptions and prescriptions of behavior inculcated in the individual from birth onward.

One basically chooses between at least two fundamentally different paradigms or perceptions of reality: (1) that women and men are essentially the same *except for* reproduction, and all observed differences are socially and culturally influenced; or, (2) that women and men are essentially different in the natural function of reproduction and *that* contributes to an array of behavioral and emotional predispositions that stem from biological differences and, then, influenced and reinforced by the social and cultural expectations of each sex. If one presumes the first, certain anthropological evidence is cited to prove sex differences are almost nonexistent and observed differences between men and women are purely the effect of socialization. Those who give more credence to socialized differences point to converging behavior patterns between men and women as evidence that differences are largely culturally induced. If one presumes the second, socio-biological sources are utilized to show how physical differences affect behavior and perception. Those who give more credence to biological differences between women and men would point out there is nothing subjective or "fictive" about pregnancy, childbirth, or lactation, or the effects these phenomena have on the body.

There are also biases and scientific "fads" regarding the causes of crime. While early researchers, such as Sheldon and Eleanor Glueck, identified family factors as causal in the development of delinquent children, these theories were largely discarded in the 1970s and 1980s in favor of social and subcultural factors, such as social disorganization or economic disparity.[15] Current "discoveries" that parental practices, after all, might have something to do with delinquency are debated, but the point is that social organization, subcultures, economic disparity, or demographics need not necessarily eliminate the explanatory power of parental practices or vice versa.

Biological theories have been scorned and derided as either irrelevant or downright facist in their proposition that criminal behavior may be influenced by physical and/or genetic factors. Those who review biological theories, but obviously reject them, usually present such theories in a most superficial way, with the inevitable association with Lombroso and other early-century theorists.[16] There is also a tendency to present such theories in an all-or-nothing fashion. For instance, Akers, has this to say about biological theories:[17]

> . . . a theory which proposes that criminals are biologically deficient and that deficiency explains their criminal behavior cannot also claim that family socialization is the basic cause of criminal behavior.

Why not? If the biological deficiency is a reduced ability to absorb stimuli, it can create learning disabilities and a person that seeks a high level of excitement; these traits, together with poor socialization, act as pre-determiners to create the probability of delinquency. Those who happen to come from strong socializing families may overcome their biological deficiencies. For instance, autism is a biological predeterminer that drastically restricts and predetermines the behavior and future of the individual born with it, but there are also examples of families in which parents have accomplished tremendously more than predicted by "experts" because of time, love, and commitment. The same is true of other biological predispositions. Alcoholism is almost surely influenced by genetic factors, but not all individuals who inherit the predisposition become or remain actively alcoholic. The current biological theories describe the relationship between crime and genetic inheritance as so attenuated and diffuse that it is hard to argue against, unless one chooses to argue the whole concept of genetic transmission. Thus, those who criticize biological explanations of crime bring out Lombroso, the XYY studies, and PMS.[18] Again, the point is that all researchers are influenced by their personal beliefs about such issues as biological causation and sex differences. Their reviews of criminological theory are influenced by such preconceptions.

Finally, most treatments until recently ignored the dynamics of race and class and how these factors intermixed with gender to influence criminal behavior patterns. One lives a different reality depending on whether one is white or black, and to be poor adds yet a different texture. These factors form social realities in women's and men's lives, constricting and guiding their behavioral choices apart from, but related to, their sex and/or gender. White, male researchers can attempt to understand the world of other groups, but they must first recognize the point that there are different realities, and paper and pencil tests or measurements they create based on their perceptual world may not be adequate to describe, much less understand, the worlds of others.

One might object at this stage and point out that this text is also a version of "truth" and that the author has her own paradigms that will shape her review and description of the criminology of women. That is correct and the only solution available, it seems, is to present one's values and biases at the outset to at least let the reader know what they are. Thus, one should be aware that:

- The reviewer has a distrust of sophisticated quantitative methods as being able to help us understand the choice of criminality. The higher the level of abstraction, the less confidence exists that the measurements accurately reflect "truth."

- The reviewer believes sex differences exist beyond reproduction. Further, this review is influenced by a cautious belief that biological factors can help us understand criminal choices.

- The reviewer believes that in addition to sex differences, there are also gender differences that are created by social and cultural pressures.[19]

Now, at least, the reader knows the biases, values, and paradigms that will influence the discussion that follows.

Problems of Measurement

In order to test any theory of crime, one must be able to measure the dependent variable (crime) and the independent variables (i.e., poverty, drug use, attachment to parents, and so on) presumed to *cause* or at least be *correlated* with the dependent variable. If one can identify a statistical relationship between the two that meets predetermined levels of "significance," one can say that the two are correlated. If the independent variable occurs with the appropriate pattern (consistently before the dependent variable) and one can eliminate all alternative hypotheses (i.e., other factors that may influence one or both factors), then one can cautiously conclude that there is a causal relationship between the two factors. But Akers[20] points out: "To be a cause, X must be both a 'necessary condition,' the absence of which means that Y will not occur, and a 'sufficient condition,' so that Y always occurs in the presence of X. No criminological theory can meet these two traditional causation criteria of necessary and sufficient conditions." A different question is why would a factor that causes criminal choice by one individual necessarily need to be the cause of all criminal choices by all individuals? Why would human behavior be predictable in the same manner as physical phenomena?

The scientific method described above works fairly well (one assumes) in a laboratory with chemical compounds. The laws of chemistry and the laws of physics tend to hold few surprises.[21] Whether scientific method is helpful or even appropriate to utilize in understanding human behavior depends, to a large degree, on the accuracy of the measurements used to test theories.

Measuring Crime

Measures of crime are notoriously problematic. Textbooks in criminology often start with the difficulties of measuring crime. Included in this discussion are the weaknesses of the official data sources, such as the Uniform Crime Reports (UCR), as well as problems with self-reports. Difficulties of even agreeing on a definition of crime are sometimes offered as well. While we all know these problems, tests of criminal theory proceed regardless, perhaps with the blithe assurance that these data sources are "all we have" or the "best available."

The difficulties, however, are fundamental to the enterprise of criminology. How can one explain a social behavior (crime) when there is no agreed upon definition of what it is? Do criminal theories presume to explain, in addition to "street crime" such as robbery, the causes behind toxic waste dumping and/or spousal abuse? Income tax evasion? Speeding? Bribery of public officials? Price-fixing? Gaybashing? Given a theory of crime, will it explain the crime of drug use? Did it explain such behavior also when it was not a crime? And, did it explain abortion when it was a crime—but now does not because it is no longer a crime, at least in the first trimester? Does this theory of crime explain prostitution—except in Nevada? Gambling—except gambling that is legalized? Radical and critical criminologists make it perfectly clear that crime is a dynamic relationship between those who perform a behavior and those who define such behavior as criminal.

In later chapters we will explore criminological theories; note that most of them do not explicitly define what crime they seek to explain, although, implicitly theory is usually directed to "street crime." Robbery, homicide, assault, burglary, and theft/larceny are categories of crime that underlie, however indirectly, the enterprise of criminology. Admittedly there is increasing attention to white-collar and corporate crime, and some attempt to explain the motivations behind such crimes. Gottfredson and Hirschi's "general theory of crime" is one of the few theories that does make explicit the range of behavior addressed.[22]

Thus, the very definition of what will be explained in criminology is often left unresolved. Then, to compound the problem, we measure crime through means that capture only a portion of "reality." "Crimes reported" leave the vast area of the "dark figure of crime" unexplored. Through victim reports (i.e., the National Crime Survey) we know a little bit more about how much crime is out there and unreported, but this knowledge is subject to the accuracy of victimization studies. When we say that 90 percent of rapes are unreported, we must assume that the victimization survey samples used to generate the number of individuals who were raped, but did not report it, are representative of the general population, that they answered honestly, that they all had a shared understanding of what rape is, and that there were no errors or intentional malfeasance or misfeasance of the survey takers.[23]

Another issue is the "naming" of crime. Reporting practices pigeonhole human behavior into preconceived categories that can be counted; but life is usually not so simple. Police officers respond to a domestic call where an ex-husband has come back for his stereo equipment that was stolen by his ex-wife, because she did not agree that it was his. She is now brandishing a gun and shoots in his general direction while he is busting out her front plate glass window with a tire iron and, in the heat of the moment, he swings at and hits the arriving police officer. What *crime* should be counted in this event? The wife's theft; her assault, his destruction of property, or assault on a police officer? Obviously, some crimes are more simple; one burglar committing one burglary is not complicated to count. It is also easier to see how criminal theory might possibly "explain" why someone would commit a burglary, as opposed to a theory that might "explain" the theft or assault or destruction of property described in the first event.

How much crime in official reports is more similar to the first event than the one-burglar, one-burglary variety? How much crime has been pushed and prodded into crime categories, and, in so doing, bears little resemblance to the textual reality of its occurrence. In a vacuum, we mentally construct a reality of assault, theft, homicide, or rape. In other words, when one reads a news report that says assaults are down or rapes have increased, there is a presumption of what assault means and what rape means. These constructions are then used in criminal theory. We should pause to remember, however, that the *measures* of crime are distinct from the original reality.

Even the most serious of crimes—homicide—may present a variety of realities. A homicide might be any of the events below:

- A drive-by shooting where an innocent victim is killed though the target was a rival gang member.

- An abusive husband is killed by his wife in the middle of an abuse episode when he hands her the gun and says, "shoot me or I'm going to kill you."

- A barroom brawl that started over a football game and ends in the one starting the fight getting hit, striking his head on a barstool, and dying.

- An ex-husband who searches for his ex-wife for six months, finally finds her, lies in wait, and empties a gun into her, and then kills their children and himself.

- An out-of-work manual laborer who agrees to kill a businessman for $3,000, and does it.

All of these are homicides; can all be explained by any single theory of crime?

More egregious problems occur in the measurement of crime. For instance, using prisoner samples as representative of criminals obviously ignores the influence of social class and race (and perhaps sex) in imprisonment decisions. Prisoners do not statistically represent all criminals because not all criminals get caught, nor do all who get caught go to prison. Any use made of prisoner samples to explain crime should be subject to criticism. One particularly troublesome example of this error is the practice of using prisoner populations to illustrate changes in crime. For instance, a reduction in the percentage of women who are in prison for a violent crime is presented as if that means there has been a reduction of violent crime by female offenders. It could mean that, or it could mean that there has been a huge increase in the number of women incarcerated for drug offenses that reduces the percentage of those in prison for violent crimes, because the number of women committed for violent offenses has not changed. Demographic profiles of prisoners say as much about official crime control policies as they do about the behavior patterns of those who are incarcerated.

Measuring Causal Factors

Criminological theory seeks to identify the causes of crime, thus the problems of measuring crime as described above are compounded by problems in measuring the independent variables being studied. There are problems when attempting to measure any of the variables historically associated with crime. Even factors that are, by nature, quantitative, such as poverty or socio-economic status (SES), pose difficulties. What is the poverty line? Are all individuals equally affected by any given income level; that is, do they feel deprivation equally? What if an individual has access to another's wealth? If one had no income, but had access to a parent's, spouse's, or friend's income, would he or she behave differently from someone who had no such access? Even unemployment measures are notoriously subject to political expediency. Should summer college students be counted? Should those who have given up looking for work be counted? Should adjustments be made for seasonal fluctuations in such industries as construction? Intelligence has also been identified by many as a causal factor; yet, there continues to be a vociferous debate on the difficulties or even the ability to measure intelligence. All correlates of crime, even those that seem simple, must be measured. The measurement of such factors creates a constructed reality distinct from the factor itself—an IQ score is only a partial reality of intelligence, an unemployment rate is only a partial reality of the level of need in a society.

Some theory testing uses old data sets. The advantage of such sets is that they are already collected and just waiting in the computer for researchers to run statistical tests on them. The argument (one supposes) for the validity of such an enterprise is that if one is testing a factor's influence on criminality, it should be robust and operate even in data that is 20 or 30 years old. However, one might also argue that such archived bits of reality are probably not very helpful to understand criminal behavior today; family patterns have changed, social roles are different, and any given factor influences an individual differently today than it did 20 years ago. Broken homes, for instance, were counted in data sets of 20 and 30 years ago, but a divorce meant something entirely different in the 1960s than it does today; why would we expect it to influence the individuals involved in the same way? Any other factor runs the same risk of non-comparability.

What makes perfect sense intuitively may be devilishly hard to measure and "prove" as causal. For instance, control theory postulates that various bonds to society act to insulate young people from delinquency. One bond is "attachment." What is it and how does one measure it? The original research measured it using answers on a paper and pencil test given to high school students.[24] Attachment to parents was measured by several questions that asked such things as how often the youth ate dinner with his or her parents, or how close they felt they were to their parents. Can one truly measure—through answers to simple questions—such a concept? Think of how many "constructions of reality" have been enacted here—first, the researcher develops the idea of attachment, he or she operationalizes it through some questions, the students read the questions adding their own constructions to the ideas and concepts embedded in such questions, the theorist then adds up "scores" that presume to measure the concept of attachment, and then the statistical relationship between the score and some other measure (i.e., crime or delinquency) is examined.

Earlier works at least provide more detailed explanations of their terms. In some criminological tests of theory today, one has to read the footnotes to discover the elements used to define a major construct. The fundamental problem of measuring constructs is often ignored in debates pitting two theories against each other, so that the reader is presented with a *fait accompli*; i.e., the reader should be satisfied that self-control (or self-esteem, or attachment, or economic deprivation) has been measured, counted, and computed and the only issue is which factor is causal to crime. When one steps back and examines all the major theories in criminology, it does not take a postmodernist to see that there might be some question as to the legitimacy of the measurements of such factors as "goals of society," "strain," "masculinity," "social support," or "stigma." Methodologists criticize a theory if the terms cannot be operationalized; post-modernists criticize the belief that any concept can be operationalized at all.

Measurements of crime (despite their difficulties) and measurements of independent variables (despite their difficulties) are then analyzed using increasingly sophisticated statistical tools. In fact, if one is deficient in statistical expertise, it is tempting to leave it to the experts and skip to the conclusion in any article or research report. After all, if multiple regression analysis says so, it must be true. Might it be possible, however, that the sophisticated statistical techniques were never designed for the content of the data used in criminology? Measures of correlation presume integer level data; that is, to be able to measure correlation there must be quantitative and equal units of measurement in the two variables. This presumption is routinely violated by forcing data into numerical measurements. Using the example of the "attachment" variable described above; is it possible to measure attachment and assume that one's measurement is composed of equal parts, i.e., that one person is exactly twice as attached as another person and therefore has less probability of being delinquent? Can human emotions be placed on a Likert scale?[25]

Of course we do seek to measure everything, including human emotions, and a Likert scale is as good as any measurement to quantify stress or liking for parents or any other thing. The most problematic element of the criminological enterprise, however, is not that measurements are perhaps only partial realities, or that the statistical tests used may not be appropriate for the type of data; rather, it is the unquestioning acceptance of such research as the "truth." In criminological texts, it is not unusual to see a statement regarding a relationship or lack of a relationship between some factor and crime indicating it is fact, with two or three sources cited to support such an assertion. Denzin is one post-modernist who discusses the common practice of establishing "proof" by referring to previous texts that referred, in turn, to previous texts.[26] Truth is established through (if nothing else) multiple citations.

Measurements and statistical tests are used to describe a reality—for instance, there is no correlation between poverty and crime; there is no racism in the criminal justice system; or broken homes are correlated with delinquency. However, there are different realities; an African-American man who is stopped several times a week because he drives a nice car would probably not accept the statistical reality of no racism in the criminal justice system; a correctional counselor who sees that almost all of his or her clients are poor, unskilled, and without education would probably not agree that SES has nothing to do with crime. Our literature reviews, however, are filled with neat categorizations of reality—these factors have statistical significance; those do not. These theories have been tested and are supported by data; those are not. Bitter arguments are carried out in print between two theories or types of methodologies, centering on methodological or theoretical issues, with little attention on either side to the more fundamental difficulties in the very nature of the enterprise.[27] It is no wonder that students, practitioners, and the public view much of criminology as irrelevant to the very real problem of crime.

Applications to the Criminology of Women

Each of the issues above is relevant to the research on female criminality. Regarding the problems of values influencing criminal theory, the feminist critiques that will be fully explored in a later chapter laid waste to the theories developed in the early part of the twentieth century that proposed to explain female criminality. Writers mixed up gender (the sex-role identity that one is socialized to have) and sex differences (biological, not socialized differences), assumed cultural patterns of behavior as the norm, and viewed women through the sexist and classist notions of the time. Even theorists in the 1950s and 1960s were exposed as assuming culturally prescribed behaviors of women were "natural" and believing the "nature of women" to fit predetermined patterns evidenced by their socio-economic position in society.[28] So much for objective research.

Regarding the measurement of crime, Otto Pollak in 1950 was not the only, or even the first, researcher to point out that official sources underreport crime; he then concluded that it was more likely that females committed the largest percentage of unreported crime because they engaged in more deceitful methods. His explanation of who commits unreported crime illustrates how easy it is to construct a reality that fits our stereotypes. Pollak believed that women were not less criminal than men, therefore he utilized the difficulties of measurement to advance that view. Pollak's sexist views are obvious to us only because of the passage of time and social changes that have occurred since 1950. Later, in the 1970s, researchers argued that women may not have been as criminal as men in the past, but were now becoming more criminal.[29] These conclusions were then disputed by a closer look at the statistics. How can we be sure that any theorizing conducted today on the nature of crime will not be viewed as culturally biased, sexist, or racist 50 years from today?

Steffensmeier and Streifel discuss problems of the Uniform Crime Report (UCR) and why official statistics may not be accurate measures of any changes observed in the criminality of women. Their first point is that official reports are a measure of law enforcement practices as clearly as a measure of behavior; for instance, decreases of prostitution, public drunkenness, and increases of DWI do not illustrate changes in behavior as much as changes in official processing of such crimes. Other possible factors in changes in women's crime rates are:[30]

- less chivalrous attitudes toward females and increased pressure to administer law in a neutral way;

- increased awareness of female crime leading to greater suspicion and surveillance;

- police arresting and charging women despite having a peripheral role so they can then coerce them into being informants;

- improvements in police recording practices;

- changes in sanctioning policies on the part of welfare or retail leading to more prosecution;

- white-collar crime (with large participation rates by women) traditionally was underinvestigated, but recently has been focused
  on by police departments, resulting in more arrests.

Thus, changes in offense rates may indicate changes in criminality, or the numbers may be affected by the changing practices of the system—or both! The difficulty of trying to explain female criminality has issues of defini- tion unique to so-called crimes of women, including such actions as prostitu- tion and killing an abusive spouse. Can these behaviors be explained by any available criminal theory? Historically, female criminals were defined almost exclusively through their sexuality.[31] Even later theorists were inordinately interested in a woman's sexuality because, at the time, it was hard to perceive deviance in a woman in any way other than through sexuality. While the lit- erature on prostitution is filled with theories of why women turn to prosti- tution, many also recognize the political elements inherent in the definition and enforcement of prostitution as a crime.

Women who killed their abusers historically were defined as criminal and usually ended up in prison (for the most part). Today, they may be acquitted. The perceived social reality of domestic abuse has changed the definition of criminality for those women; thus, we must ask not only whether women are more or less violent today (as some research asks), but also, have definitions of their criminal violence changed?[32]

The research on domestic violence illustrates, again, the difficulties of measurement and the influence of values on so-called neutral research. Most of the early literature on domestic violence illustrated it as largely a problem of abusive men physically assaulting female partners. Researchers explored why women stayed in such a relationship, they explored why men were vio- lent, and they explored the effects on children. Then, "new" research emerged that "proved" women were just as violent as men. Two facts supported such a conclusion: first, that domestic homicides were symmetrical, that is, there were almost as many women killing their male partners as there were men killing their female partners. Second, a paper and pencil violence index was created that showed that women self-reported as much, in fact in some appli- cations of the research, more violence than did males.[33] Domestic violence was redefined in this research as not a problem of females being abused, but rather violent people swinging at each other. Yet, the emergency room per- sonnel who observed almost exclusively female victims, and the shelter per- sonnel who heard so many similar stories of abuse and emotional terrorism that they could come up with early markers that identified which men were more likely to become abusers, were not persuaded by this "new evidence."

Then, others reviewed the evidence and observed that homicides by women were more likely to be in self-defense; and the so-called violence index survey did not distinguish motivation (self-defense versus first strike aggression) or intensity, so a woman pushing away a spouse who was threat- ening her was counted as equally violent as a man who swings and breaks the jaw of his spouse.[34] The point of this example is not that researchers intentionally misled, but that they do not have a "corner on the truth" and our measurements of reality are woefully inadequate to accurately describe any particular person's *truth*. The shelter personnel and those in the field who did not accept the statistical reality of symmetrical violence, and believed that domestic violence was largely a problem for women, possess a "truth" just as valid as the statisticians' numbers. Wonders, in a discussion of another issue, makes this point: "Truth . . . is never absolute, uncontested, transhistorical, or transcultural. Instead reality is at best a complex composite of different stories being lived and told by different people."[35]

An ironic problem regarding the problems of measuring crime today is the continuing practice of ignoring women. Some fairly recent large-scale research efforts have continued to sample only men despite the scathing criticism of such practices offered by feminists in the 1970s and 1980s. The argument that crime is largely an activity engaged in by men, so the best use of finite research dollars is to oversample or only sample men ignores the fact that crime is *human behavior*, not *male behavior*. If indeed, the "*x factor*"—the factor that is most instrumental in crime causation—occurs more commonly with men, to men, or by men, by only sampling men, researchers will never see it. Of course, there is no "*x factor*," but one can understand the skepticism that meets such research efforts if they are presented as theories of criminal behavior instead of theories of male criminal behavior.

Alternative Methods of Knowing

The above criticism of criminology does not necessarily lead to a conclusion of futility or resignation that understanding is impossible, but it does promote the need for alternative methods of study. One of the contributions of feminist criminology, as well as post-modernism, is the importance given to subjective, qualitative methods of research. The phenomenological world of the individuals studied is every bit as important, and perhaps more important, than the numbers and levels of statistical significance that characterize quantitative method, yet qualitative methods meet resistance and are not considered as "scientific" as quantitative methods. Make no mistake, qualitative methods carry just as much reality constructing as do quantitative methods, but usually the researcher is at least a little more aware of the possibility and more humble regarding the results.

Any survey of criminological theory will uncover the lack of integration between such theory and almost all other fields of inquiry. Fields such as psychology or socio-biology are ignored or given very short treatments in most texts, with the clear message that they hold little relevance in the understanding of crime. Other fields as well, such as child development and social work are usually ignored, despite the obvious connections between such fields and criminology. The field of inquiry is, then, artificially circumscribed to very narrow treatments of identified factors that are presumed to be correlated with crime. Crime is seen as the only or most important feature of the lives of those studied. This ignores real lives: real criminals and real victims are influenced and live with housing problems, family, poverty, television, peers, hopelessness, gangs, and so on. More sophisticated research efforts measure more factors, but the post-modernist critique is that the act of measuring changes the nature of reality; thus, in addition to counting, measuring, and applying statistical analysis, one must utilize narrative, storytelling, and other methods of understanding.

FRAMING THE QUESTIONS: THE CRIMINOLOGY OF WOMEN

Keeping in mind the critique of criminological inquiry offered above, this book will proceed to explore criminological theories and the evidence gathered to support or rebut them. We will cover the information we have available on men's and women's criminality. However, this work will not chronicle why all other theories are wrong; rather, the approach will be that there is more agreement than disagreement in criminological theorizing, that disagreements are sometimes exaggerated and exceed the capability of data to support them, that most disagreements about theories are a matter of emphasis more so than association, and that almost all theories today result in similar policy implications anyway.

So, then, what are the questions? Otto Pollak and his work in 1950 will be taken as a milestone marker in the criminology of women. His review of theories in the first one-half of the century was comprehensive, if flawed, and his observations of female criminality were provocative, if hopelessly biased. However, it is also humbly accepted that just as it is easy to criticize Pollak as being influenced by his own sexism and classism, this review (and reviewer) may be criticized as well, if not today, then almost certainly 50 years from now for her own biases and preconceptions and the way those biases influenced and colored interpretations of data.

The principles one can draw from Pollak's work are as follows. These seem to be a good place to begin a general inquiry of women's crime; thus, his conclusions will become our questions.

- **Women and men are equally criminal.** (Are women and men equally criminal?) – The "gender differential" in crime will be explored through crime statistics because these are available, with attention to how these numbers may be influenced by definitional differences, official practices, and misinterpretations. Patterns of crime for both adults and juveniles will be reviewed.

- **Women's crimes are different. Women utilize more deceit, thus their crimes are hidden, and harder to detect.** (Are women's and men's crimes different?) – The crime patterns of men and women will be explored. Other methods of knowledge, such as narratives, will also be used to construct a reality of women's offense patterns.

- **Women's crimes are associated with her housewife or sexual object role, and less subject to formal censure; and, because of female traits of passivity and helplessness, women more often play the part of instigator rather than active player in a criminal event.** (Do women play an instigator role rather than act as a direct player in crime?) – Again, crime patterns will be explored, as well as possible changes in official processing of women.

- **The system is chivalrous toward women and decision-makers are less likely to arrest, convict, or send women to prison.** (Is the system chivalrous?) – The so-called chivalry hypothesis will be explored in Chapter 3.

We will add several other questions to those suggested by Pollak's propositions. These questions concern the vast literature that has accumulated in the almost 50 years since Pollak wrote his book. Much of the new literature is either directly concerned with female criminality or includes women in the theory and theory testing. Thus, our additional questions are:

- **Is women's crime changing, specifically are women becoming more criminal?** – Now that the problems of definition have been revealed, it is clear that this question is much more complicated than it seems. How does one define crime? Have official definitions changed? Has official treatment of women changed?

- **Can the traditional theories of crime help us to understand why some women commit crime?** – Traditional theories will be covered in Chapter 4. They are almost exclusively concerned with the criminality of men and they have been reviewed and criticized by feminist criminologists for such androcentrism. However, some theories seem to be more helpful than others in understanding female criminality, even if they were not originally designed to explain it.

- **Do other theories exist that help us to understand female criminality?** – Specific "female" theories that have been developed will also be reviewed, as well as the contributions of feminist inquiry to criminology. More recent "integration" theories will also be explored, as well as some theories that might be described as out of the mainstream, such as socio-biological theories and moral development. As mentioned before, this reviewer's biases and values regarding all theories have been revealed, thus the answers to the questions asked above are presented only as this reviewer's particular truths.

- **So what?** – It seems that this question is one that is rarely asked in criminological inquiry. This review will conclude with an examination of this question: so what? If factors are identified as being correlated with crime, so what? What are the policy implications of these findings?

With this introduction, we now proceed to present the accumulated knowledge concerning female criminality, starting with a picture of crime patterns, changes in crime patterns, and a discussion of the chivalry hypothesis. Then, theories are explored, starting with traditional theories, moving through women-specific theories, and concluding with the most recent theories developed in the criminology field. The concluding chapters will present an integrated theory of criminality that is offered to understand both women's and men's criminality, as well as a discussion of what policy implications exist if one accepts such an explanation.

NOTES

[1]   For a good discussion of post-modernism, see Rosenau (1992); and for the application of post-modernism to criminology, see Arrigo (1995).

[2]   Schwartz and Friedrichs (1994, 222) provide, in a remarkably clear and jargon-free discussion of post-modernism, a number of contributions that post-modernist theory can offer criminology:

   (1) A method that can reveal starkly how knowledge is constituted, and can uncover pretensions and contradictions of traditional scholarship in the field. This method further provides an alternative to linear analysis;

   (2) A highlighting of the significance of language and signs in the realm of crime and criminal justice;

   (3) A source of metaphors and concepts (e.g., "hyperreality") that capture elements of an emerging realtiy, and the new context and set of conditions in which crime occurs.

[3]   Whether there is an objective reality I will leave for philosophers to ponder.

[4]   Schwartz and Friedrichs (1994, 225).

[5]   Williams and McShane (1988, 2).

[6]   Pollock (1998, 51).

7 The Gluecks (1934) and other early researchers collected "life stories" of delinquents and criminals. These stories were presented, sometimes in their entirety, as well as the researchers' attempts to isolate and count factors and identify patterns in the stories. One might argue that these stories tell us something qualitatively different from the numbers themselves.

8 Williams and McShane (1988, 3).

9 Cohen (1955) is used as the best example of this observation; see, for instance, Naffine (1987) or Leonard (1982).

10 As examples of this, see Konopka (1966) and Morris (1964); for examples of criticism of this early research, see, for instance, Naffine (1987) and Smart (1976).

11 Understandably, feminist critiques were and are critical of the paternalistic treatment of women in the juvenile justice system, and there was good reason to object to different treatment for women when it was more harmful, i.e., girls but not boys being locked up for sexual promiscuity. However, often the feminist approach also tends to ignore real differences between men and women, such as consistent evidence that indicates female juveniles come from more disturbed backgrounds.

12 Feinman (1980).

13 Lynch et al. (1992) illustrates the insidious nature of presumptions of truth. Their critique of the "cultural literacy" approach includes the way such reviews systematically ignore and thereby discredit feminist works. Even the treatment of women in introductory criminology textbooks illustrates the bias that women are not worthy of study or important in the study of crime. While we might understand why Wilson and Rigby's (1975) study more than 20 years ago showed women to be the subject of a miniscule portion of criminology texts (an average of 2.5% of texts were devoted to discussing female criminality), it is harder to understand why today the percentage has increased to only four percent (Wright, 1992). Criminology textbooks do not review truth, they are engaged in a dynamic construction of their version of truth.

14 1996, 616.

15 Gluecks (1934); see, for instance, Barkan (1997, 62).

16 While it may be perfectly appropriate to begin a review of biological theories with Lombroso (1894), it does current researchers a grave disservice to imply that their methodology is similar or that they approach criminal causation in the same manner that Lombroso did. His work will be reviewed in a later chapter.

17 1997, 6. Akers presents an excellent critique of criminological theories (discussing elements such as logical consistency, scope, parsimony, testability, validity, usefulness, and policy implications), thus it is unfortunate that he does not take the time to review biological theories as carefully as he reviews the other theories.

18 These will be reviewed in more detail in a later chapter. XYY studies attempted to show that those individuals who carried an extra Y chromosome had observable and predictable effects of such a genetic abnormality—one of which was a higher than normal level of criminality. Premenstrual syndrome (PMS) is a medically defined syndrome with a constellation of physical symptoms, and has been correlated with a higher than average level of aggressiveness for women. Both of these examples of biological theories are highly controversial, rife with methodological problems, and explain very little crime by men or women even assuming they have some level of truth. They are usually used to discredit biological approaches, but even biological researchers do not argue against the problems of these studies.

[19]   The most appropriate label to attach to this review (and reviewer) would be "cultural feminist," that is a belief that there are fundamental sex differences, but that societal features do oppress women in economic and social spheres and that social and economic equality should but does not exist.

[20]   1997, 6.

[21]   Although it is also true that even in the "hard" sciences one may surpass the simple laws of nature to a realm where prediction is more problematic; at a certain point even physics becomes metaphysics and there are more questions than answers.

[22]   Gottfredson and Hirschi (1990). In fact, some might argue that the very breadth of their theory is its greatest weakness because it is difficult to see any similarity of causation between a person who drinks too much and/or commits income tax evasion, and a person who commits armed robbery. This theory will be discussed in more detail in Chapter 7.

[23]   For instance, if one asks "Have you been raped in the last six months?" or "Have you been forced to have sex in the last six months against your will?," it is conceivable that the answers might be different because of the individual interpretation of each question. Non-consensual sex may not be defined as rape by many people, even if it fits the legal definition.

[24]   Hirschi (1969).

[25]   It is, of course, true that there are non-parametric statistical tests that supposedly are able to utilize non-integer data. In fact, there are statistical tests arguably for every conceivable purpose and type of data. However, the basic argument here that is subject to question is whether such mathematical manipulations provide us with "truths." The explanation of "statistical significance" and the practice of setting it at a variety of levels is one such example of the constructed reality of statistical truths.

[26]   Denzin (1990).

[27]   See, for example, Jensen (1996), and the corresponding articles, or Akers (1996) and Hirschi's (1996) response.

[28]   Pollak (1950) is one example of such research and more will be presented in Chapter 4.

[29]   See, for instance, Adler (1975) or Simon (1975a, 1975b).

[30]   Steffensmeier and Streifel (1992, 77).

[31]   For instance, theorists such as Lombroso (1894) believed all criminal women were prostitutes because criminal women were throwbacks to an earlier evolved state and all primitive women were prostitutes.

[32]   See, for instance, DeKeseredy, Saunders, Schwartz, and Alvi (1997).

[33]   See, for instance, Straus et al. (1980); McLeod (1984); Straus and Gelles (1986).

[34]   See DeKeseredy, Saunders, Schwartz, and Alvi (1997).

[35]   1996, 614.

Crimes Committed by Women: Violent and Property Crime

2

Objectives

- Become familiar with crime statistics regarding violent crime committed by women.

- Become familiar with crime statistics regarding property crime committed by women.

In this chapter we will thoroughly explore crimes committed by women. The questions asked at the conclusion of the first chapter form the outline for this and the next several chapters: Are women and men equally criminal? Are women's and men's crimes different? Do women play an instigator role rather than act as a direct player in crime? Is women's crime changing, specifically, are women becoming more criminal? Does the system treat women more "chivalrously."

We will examine the evidence as to the extent and types of crimes women commit, the percentage of total crime in all crime categories account-ed for by women, and changes in crime patterns over time, as well as other issues. Accepting the difficulties of gathering and interpreting such evidence, after exploring all crime data available, certain conclusions can be reached:

- Women account for a small percentage of total crime relative to men's participation in violent crime, but the "gender or sex dif-ferential" (the relative difference in participation between men and women in their contribution to total crime) is most extreme in violent crimes and almost disappears in some property crimes.

- "Women's crimes" continue to be largely the traditional con-sumer crimes that they have always committed, such as larceny, theft, and fraud.

Recall that the four sources of knowledge we can utilize to know what crimes are committed and by whom are: crime reports to police, official arrest statistics, self-reports, and victim surveys. Of these sources, only arrest statistics and self-reports tell us much about the criminal because the other two (crime reports and victim surveys) require the victim to know something about the offender. If it is a violent, personal crime then the victim is presumed to know or at least have seen the offender, but the vast majority of crime is property crime and the victim may not know the age, sex, or race of the offender.

Arrest statistics are measures of official activity as well as offender activity; first, they account for only those crimes where an arrest is made. Clearance rates are fairly high in crimes such as homicide or aggravated assault, but low in crimes such as burglary and larceny/theft. Thus, the "dark" figure of crime (crimes not cleared by arrest) is a problematic issue when using arrest statistics. Also, changes in official arrest statistics may indicate changes of policy, changes of definition, or changes of efficiency, instead of or in addition to changes in offender behavior.[1]

In this section we will look at crimes committed by adult women, broken into general crime categories of violent crime and property crime.

VIOLENT CRIMES

Violent crimes include homicide, aggravated assault, simple assault, robbery, arson, rape, and other sex crimes using force. The most extreme gender differentials are seen when comparing the relative contributions of men and women to total arrests for crimes of violence. There is little doubt that women commit violent crime significantly less often than do men. Pollak's assertion in 1950 that women's choice of victims (family members) and choice of method (more likely to use poison than firearms) hid much of their crime is unsupported by any data available. In other words, there does not seem to be a large "dark" figure of women's crimes disproportionate to men's crimes. Recent figures from the Uniform Crime Reports (UCR) indicate that women continue to be responsible for about 15 percent of all violent crime (10% of murder and non-negligent manslaughter; 1% of forcible rape; 9% of robbery; 18% of aggravated assault; and 16% of arson).[2]

The idea of criminally violent women is such an anomaly that many works on the subject do not even address the small numbers of women who commit violent crime. Toch[3], for instance, doesn't even include women in the index of his exploration of the social psychological elements of violence. The themes he discusses as relating to violence: respect, fear, and power are written as largely male concerns. Both Toch and Katz[4] look at the individual's justification for the violence, but neither author satisfactorily explains why particular individuals feel violence is pleasurable, why it is necessary to earn respect, or why power (gained through violent means) is important. In these authors' works, there is more than a little suggestion that those men who engage in violence to preserve respect, enjoy the violence and engineer incidents that will allow them to use it.

Theories of violence are largely socio-psychological. For instance, Toch proposes that violence-prone persons are deficient in verbal and other social skills, and, therefore, resort to violence because they do not have other skills to attain their needs.[5] Another theory is that violence is learned—both by modeling and by reward structures. Children who get what they want and are rewarded for aggressiveness will continue to utilize aggression to get what they want. Both of these theories provide tenable explanations for women's lesser aggressiveness: women are less violent, perhaps because they are in general more verbal, and also perhaps because they have been socialized to be so:

> Females are socialized to be less aggressive, are more closely super-
> vised, and are more strictly taught to conform to rigid standards,
> whereas males are rewarded for aggressive behaviors.[6]

Another reason women may be less violent is simply that it is not rational to be violent; that is, the general differences in strength between men and women make violent, aggressive actions on the part of women—at least toward males—unrewarding since they are unlikely to win such encounters.[7]

One theme that runs through popular media accounts of violent women, as well as some academic analyses, is that violent women are somehow "more terrible" than violent men. Lombroso, in 1894, and others writing in the early part of the twentieth century claimed that violent women were more blood-thirsty, and more heartless than violent male criminals. They used vignettes drawn from dime-store novels to illustrate the terrible crimes of some female criminals and presumed that these crimes "proved" their assertion that the violent female criminal was much worse than her male counterpart. Inter-estingly, one continues to see this thread of thought even in more modern academic treatments of the subject matter, such as this quote: "Women ter-rorists have consistently proved themselves more ferocious and more intractable in their acts than their male counterparts."[8]

Some recent studies call into question the truism that women are nonvi-olent.[9] In studies by Baskin and Sommers, interview data from 23 women arrested for violent felony offenses and 65 women incarcerated for such offenses were analyzed. They found a high correlation between crimes of vio-lence and drug use. The violent female offenders they interviewed were also involved with other types of crime, especially prostitution (77% of the total sample). They describe an early onset group and a later entry group of vio-lent female offenders. The group of women who engaged in violent crime early also participated in a range of other criminal activities and deviant lifestyle activities. The group of women who committed violent crimes later did so with drugs being a larger contributory factor.

These authors argue that traditional theories of women's crime empha-sizing gender roles does not explain current involvement in violent crime.[10] The authors argue that the same forces that affect male offenders are influencing women's commission of violent acts, specifically, neighborhood effects, drug use, and opportunity structures in city ghettos.

While this study helps us understand the violent female offender, it is important to note the limitations of such an approach. The sample consisted of those women who were convicted of violent crimes (defined by the researchers). The research obtains a rich data set of the women's criminal history, criminal motivation, and circumstances of the crime(s). Conclusions regarding the data set are valid and important, specifically that violent female criminals incarcerated in New York State are likely to be drug-involved and have prior records if they have engaged in assaults or robberies. However, one cannot extrapolate from this data set to "explain" or "prove" an increase of violent female offenders. First, recent information indicates that the arrest rate of women (and men) for violent crimes is decreasing, not increasing. In the 1995 Uniform Crime Reports, it is reported that City Arrest Trends show declines in women's commission of homicide, rape, and robbery. Only aggravated assaults show an increase, but because it is impossible to know what percent of these crimes represent domestic and what percent represent predatory street crime, the authors' assumption of an increase in women's "street crime" in this nation's cities seems premature.[11] One example of an alternative explanation for assault rate increases, for instance, is that police department policies today to arrest both spouses in domestic violence cases have increased the numbers of those arrests for women. This seems just as likely as the possibility that women's assault rate increases are due to "predatory" street crimes.

Thus, the incarcerated women whose lives are examined in this study may or may not represent the larger numbers of women who commit crimes. In fact, we could expect there to be differences between this sample and those women arrested for violent offenses that subsequently did not result in a prison sentence. One simply cannot assume that the profile of a sample, especially an incarcerated sample, is reflective of a larger population represented by an arrest statistic, and the theory that women are influenced by the economic and social pressures that influence violent offending by males still cannot explain the fact that in 1995, women only accounted for about 10 percent of all homicides, and nine percent of all robberies.[12] Other studies that utilize similar methodology tell us about the violent female criminal, but not necessarily anything about whether the numbers of violent female criminals are increasing.[13]

Arson

Arson is included in the Uniform Crime Reports as a violent crime, although there is some question about whether it should be categorized as such. Very little information is available on the small number of women who commit arson. If one small study is representative of other female arsonists, it seems that female arsonists present a different profile than male arsonists.[14] This study examined 27 female arsonists in New York State and concluded that they were older than male arsonists tended to be, they did not gain sexual excitement from the fire, nor did they commit arson for economic reasons (insurance); rather, they set fires to retaliate against individuals they felt had harmed them or with whom they wanted to get even. The women exhibited alcohol and drug abuse problems and, often, mental illness such as personality disorder or schizophrenia. The fire was not premeditated and was simply a way to strike out, the women could have just as easily committed a violent assault to achieve their goal of injury and retaliation.

Homicide

Blum and Fisher's[15] review of female murderers revealed that sexist notions of women who kill are pervasive in historical accounts. Female killers are portrayed as more evil than men and are also described as being excessively masculine. The good woman versus bad woman dichotomy is very apparent in descriptions of women who kill. Seemingly because the idea of women killing is so foreign to the female sex role and cultural stereotypes, the few women who do kill must be "monsters," and extreme in their lack of femininity and lack of humanity.

However, historical accounts of female criminals also describe influences that are very similar to those that affect women's decisions to kill today. Jones'[16] journalistic account of women who kill, from colonial times to today, describes women as killing intimates more often than strangers. Jones recounts tales of women who killed batterers, who killed their unwanted babies, who killed for money, and who killed because of jealousy or other reasons. These motivations are not at all different from the female homicide offenders of today.

Wilbanks examined crime patterns for female homicide offenders across the United States in 1980. Some of his findings include the following:

- Women were more likely to kill sexual partners than men when they killed (45% of women's homicides involved sexual partners compared to 10.1% of men's). Note that this does not mean that women were more likely than men to kill their sexual partners (there were 1,492 victims of male offenders compared to 1,089 victims of women).

- Women were also more likely to kill family members than men (14.5% versus 8.8%, respectively of the total homicides for men and women).

- Male offenders were 16 times more likely to commit robbery/ homicides than female offenders.

- Of all homicides in 1980, only two percent involved women killing women. The most common pairing was men killing men (65.2%), then, men killing women (20.4%), then women killing men (12.4%).

- Homicides rates for women varied across the country, from a low of less than one for South Dakota to a high of 5.57 per 100,000 in Nevada.[17]

A more recent study of homicide by women succinctly captures the research conducted in the past:

> About 80% of homicides by women involve the killing of intimates . . ., especially in long-term abusive relationships . . . and in pre- or post-partum periods. . . The homicides generally occur in the home . . . and are spontaneous rather than planned . . . The women tend to be socially conforming, to view themselves in the context of traditional sex roles, and to perceive themselves as under extreme life pressures that appear in many forms, especially depression . . . However, mental illness *per se* does not appear to be an important factor in the killings . . .[18]

Only one out of every 10 female victims of homicide are killed by another woman.[19] In her study of female homicide offenders, Mann[20] provides a description of a sample of women who killed other women:

> It was found that women who kill other women basically resemble the portrait depicted over the past two decades by previous researchers: they are young, black, undereducated, and unemployed. Anger, arguments, and fights which could take place at any time or any place were most often the precipitating factors that led to the killing of another woman, who, in many instances, instigated her own death. Possibly because of the victim's contributory role in her homicide, prison sentences were assigned in only 41.1% of the cases, and time to be served in prison averaged only 6.4 years.

In a New York study of female homicide offenders, it was found that in two-thirds of the cases (other than when the subject was not present at the crime), there were elements of victim precipitation. Drugs played a large role in homicide; four out of 10 offenders were high on a drug at the time of the offense, most commonly alcohol or crack. The researchers rated more than one-half (57%) of the homicides as "psychopharmacological drug-related," 12 percent as "economic-compulsively drug-related," and 11 percent as "systematically drug-related." Only about one-third were not related to drugs in any way.[21] The authors describe female homicide offenders in the following way:

> The lives of the women we studied were complex and filled with patterns of pain, prolonged abuse, and isolation. There does not

seem to be any one factor to which we could point and say, this is what led them to become involved in violence. Instead, a host of factors, including abuse, contributed to the wear and tear these women experienced with violence as an integral part of their everyday lives. To intervene in that cycle requires programs that address multiple needs and deficits of living.[22]

In a another, related study of homicide, all those convicted of homicides occurring in 1984 were identified; not surprisingly very few of them were women—13 out of the total sample of 430.[23] The authors described the homicides as follows:

> Only two of these nine were involved in domestic disputes with abusive partners. Another had accidentally killed her boyfriend during a dispute with a male acquaintance who had been harassing them. Still another had killed her brother during an argument over who got to smoke the last vial of crack. Another had killed a female acquaintance during a dispute over an unpaid debt. Two women killed men who were paying them for sex. Of the two who denied the involvement in the homicide, one was convicted for the murder of a stranger during a robbery and the other for killing a male acquaintance.[24]

The authors described these nine cases to illustrate that many killings take place outside of domestic abuse since only two involved domestic abuse, but the most telling theme that emerges from the narratives is the ever present influence of drugs. Every single case involved drugs and/or alcohol—women were either heavy users and attempting to get money to buy drugs, sellers, or the victims were drinking heavily. The authors offer drugs as the key to understanding the "changing pattern of lethal violence by women," meaning that women are becoming more likely to kill strangers than intimates, and for reasons other than self-protection from domestic violence.[25] While there is no question that drugs play a part in understanding the homicide committed by women (and men); the authors contention that women's homicide patterns are changing is more questionable since the studies used to support the contention were small samples and, for the most part, incarcerated samples. Still, it does not seem to be an unlikely proposition that drugs are playing an increasing role in homicide.

Serial Murder

There is very little information available on female serial murderers because, quite simply, there are very few female serial killers.[26] Some dispute the contention that the percentage of female serial killers is minuscule and believe that their participation probably is closer to their participation rates for all violent crimes (about 10%).[27] There seem to be differences in the moti-

Aileen Wuornos was labeled by the FBI as the nation's first "predatory" female serial killer. Today she sits on death row for the murders of seven men. A prostitute who was convicted in 1992, Wuornos claims the killings were in self-defense. *Photo credit: REUTERS/ CORBIS-BETTMANN.*

vations and methods of killing between male killers and those few female serial killers that have been prosecuted. Keeney and Heide report that there are differences in the amount of damage inflicted on the victim (men inflict more damage and "overkill" their victim), the use of torture (men are more likely to torture), the method of targeting (women "lured" while men "stalked"). Men were more likely to kill with their hands or use an object other than a gun to kill, whereas women were more likely to use poison. Men were more likely to have affective motives (emotional or psychological reasons for killing) whereas women in the sample were about equally divided between affective and instrumental motives for killing their victims. Women were more likely to abuse drugs and alcohol. Both women and men were likely to have come from dysfunctional families and to have suffered physical and sexual abuse. The majority of the sample was diagnosed with some form of pathology (antisocial personality, schizophrenia). Women were likely to stay in one location, while men were mobile, moving from city to city, state to state.[28] Although the study sample was small and the authors used secondary sources to arrive at their conclusions, it is instructive to note that there are major differences between female and male perpetrators.

Spousal Violence and Homicide

The issue of domestic homicide is unique from other crimes of violence since there is a real question as to whether some offenses are actually crimes of violence or acts of self-defense. Several good studies exist now that show many women convicted and incarcerated for murdering their husbands were perhaps only defending themselves.[29] Huling[30] reports that 59 percent of the women committed to prison in New York in 1986 for killing a partner were being abused at the time. Even those women who murdered outside of an episode of abuse have very different motivations for murder than other types of homicides.

Ironically, there is a series of research reports that indicate that men, not women, are the more likely victims of battery and that women are just as lethal as men in domestic relationships. Steinmetz,[31] for instance, surveyed 2,143 families and discovered that 3.8 percent of wives reported being hit but 4.5 percent of husbands reported being hit; therefore, she projected that across the United States, two million husbands are "battered" compared to only 1.8 million wives. Other studies also presented self-report survey evidence that showed women committed equal or greater amounts of violence toward intimate partners.[32] Thus, these researchers concluded that women in domestic relationships are just as violent as men even if they did not have the physical strength to inflict injuries that were as serious as those inflicted by men. This certainly came as a surprise to those who worked with battered women. Although there were a few cases, rarely did they see men needing protection from an abusive spouse. Obviously this "new" reality was shaped by the methodology. The "Conflict Tactics Scale" that measured violence did not distinguish intensity or motivation of violent acts and it included pushing, shoving, and slapping. Hitting or shoving away in self-defense is not the same as hitting in anger. A playful slap is not the same as a fist that sends the victim across the room with a broken jaw. This research was used to advance the idea that women were just as violent as men.

Rebuttals of such claims came quickly. Other researchers argued that the violence surveys overestimated and misinterpreted female violence.[33] Recent data continue to support the conclusion that domestic violence is largely a problem for female victims. The Bureau of Justice Statistics recently reported that women experience 10 times as many incidents of violence by intimates as do men.[34]

Yet, many have utilized the "symmetrical violence" data when describing domestic violence; for instance in this quote the author acknowledges different motivations: "A portion of women's abuse of their husbands may be 'protective reaction violence' where the wife strikes the first blow to protect herself from her spouse. . .'"; however, in the next sentence, she concludes that: "Men and women batter each other in the same way."[35]

Homicide rates are also used to support a symmetrical violence argument. Dawson, for instance, reported that females were the killers in 41 percent of spousal murders. African-American women were responsible for 47 percent of domestic homicides (African-American men, 53%), but white women were responsible for only 38 percent of domestic homicides (white men, 62%).[36] While the rates of domestic homicide between men and women may be closer than that for injury, simple numbers do not tell the whole story. Estimates of the number of women who kill because of self-defense are around 40 percent; thus, if one takes out the self-defense cases, the rates of women being victimized are higher than their rate of victimizing their male partners.[37]

Even more important, in more recent years, the number of women killing their partners has decreased. Browne and Williams[38] argued almost 10 years ago that those areas that offered resources for battered women showed a decline in female perpetrated domestic homicide. Evidently, their prediction was accurate if one considers the rapid proliferation of shelters across the country and the recent declines of domestic homicide by women. In a Bureau of Justice study on domestic homicide, it was reported that:

In 1977, 54 percent of the murder victims who were killed by intimates were female. By 1992, the ratio of female to male victims had
changed, with 70 percent of the victims being female. In other
words, the number of male victims fell from 1,185 in 1977 to 657
in 1992 and the number of female victims increased from 1,396 to
1,510 during the same period.[39]

Since then, the number of female victims has also declined slightly. From
1977 to 1995 the rate for husbands, boyfriends, or other male partners of
women killed by their partner declined by two-thirds (from 1.5 to .5 per
100,000); the decline of female victims was much less, from 1.6 to 1.3 per
100,000.[40] Thus, the acceptance of the so-called "battered women's syndrome" as a legal defense to homicide has not resulted in an "open season" on
husbands, as some dire predictions warned. In fact, the opposite has
occurred. With the rise of battered women's shelters, more social support,
and a recognition that domestic abuse is not the victim's fault, abusive male
spouses are now less likely to be murdered.[41]

Other research shows that not all domestic killings are due to abuse.
Mann, for instance, showed that in a sample of cases of female homicide
offenders who killed intimate partners, there was premeditation in about 58
percent of the cases, the motive was self-defense in only 59 percent of the
cases (leaving "other" as the motivation for 41% of the cases), although the
cases were categorized as "victim precipitated" in 84 percent of the cases.[42]
Almost all the cases in the sample were minority women (91%), most were
unemployed (63%), and most reported no alcohol or drug use during the
homicide (64% and 91%), although more than one-half of the victims (53.3%)
were reported to be drinking at the time of the offense.[43] The choice of
weapon was about equally distributed between firearms (52%) and knives
(44%). About one-half of the offenders had a prior record (49%), but most had
no violent history (70%). While most were initially charged with murder
(90%), that percentage decreased to 28 percent by the final charge. Only 37
percent of the women in the sample were sentenced to prison, and about
three-quarters of them served less than 10 years.[44]

Child and Elderly Abuse and Homicide

There is very little information available on violence perpetrated on family members other than spouses. The common belief is that women are more
likely to be perpetrators of intimate abuse, partly because they are disproportionately proximate to the victims of such abuse. One of the difficulties
with this area, also, is the likelihood that, except for domestic homicide, it is
vastly underreported. This fact leads some to presume that women are much
more violent than official arrest statistics indicate:

> It is difficult to judge how many women are the primary abusers of elderly people, but we can presume the number is high because there is a tendency for elderly parents to live with their daughters more often than with their sons and daughters-in-law. In the latter case, if the age-old stories about mothers-in-law have a modicum of truth to them, it is also conceivable that when a daughter-in-law is the primary caretaker of her husband's mother, mistreatment might result.[45]

This statement actually contradicts the one study the author reported that identified perpetrators of elderly abuse as more commonly male. While it is true that women are more likely to be primary care-givers of the elderly and children, and the amount of time spent in the presence of the elderly and children is vastly disproportionate between men and women; it is not at all clear that women are *more likely* to abuse these victims. It has been reported that 68 percent of those arrested for child abuse were women and 58 percent were men.[46] Another report indicates that 55 percent of those arrested for killing children were women.[47] When one considers the disproportionate time spent with children, the statistics do not support the idea that women are more likely to abuse those in their care than men.[48]

Dawson reported that domestic homicides represent 16 percent of all homicides: 6.5 percent of victims are killed by spouses, 3.5 percent are killed by parents, 1.9 percent are killed by children, 1.5 percent are killed by siblings, and 2.6 percent are killed by some other family member.[49] Fifteen percent of sibling murders were committed by women and 18 percent of parental killings were committed by women. Women were more likely to kill sons than daughters (64% versus 36%), while men showed no such disparity (52% versus 48%). Daughters were much more likely to kill fathers than mothers (81% versus 19%), while sons showed little difference (47% mothers versus 53% fathers).[50]

One British study that examined women who were incarcerated for killing or attempting to kill their children during the years 1970 through 1975 placed the female offenders in a typology that included batterers (36 cases), mentally ill (24 cases), neonaticides (11 cases), retaliating mothers (9 cases), women who killed unwanted children (8 cases), and mercy killings (one case).[51] There seemed to be quite a bit of overlap in some categories since 17 of the 36 battering mothers were diagnosed with personality disorders. Eighteen of the sample attempted suicide at the time of the offense or soon afterward. Some of these suicide attempts were linked with the homicide, that is, women would kill their children before attempting to kill themselves because "there would be no one to care for the children."[52] Interestingly this study showed a great deal of court tolerance for such crimes—for instance, of the 23 women who committed infanticide, 18 of the offenders were put on probation, two were sentenced to prison for less than three years, one was given a nominal one-day sentence, another was conditionally discharged, and a final woman was committed to a psychiatric hospital for a related mental illness.[53]

This certainly seems at odds with the current popular cry for the death penalty for teenagers who commit the same crime.

Reiss and Roth provide data for 1989 on the relationship between offenders and victims of violent assault and homicide. These rates are per 1,000 and show that women's rates are less than men's for every relationship except relatives. Unfortunately, the data do not indicate the nature of the relative, and the figures are likely to represent spousal homicide more so than child homicide or other family members.[54]

Table 2.1
Relationships of Offenders to Victims/Rate per 1,000

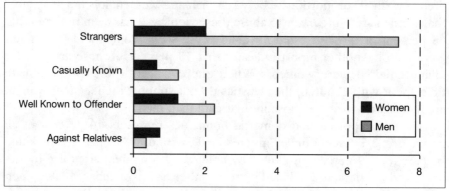

From Reiss and Roth, 1993, p. 3.

Robbery

The crime probably least associated with women is robbery, only 9.3 percent of all robbery arrests are of women.[55] Although there are some women who engage in this crime, either alone or with crime partners, the numbers are extremely small. When women do engage in this crime, it is often associated with gang membership. In one of the few studies reporting on robbery by women, it was found that they were less likely to have histories of robbery arrests and the robberies were often tied directly to prostitution.[56] In another study of female robbers, it was noted that women usually played an accessory role to a male robber. In this study it was found that they held a "career orientation" to robbery, but because the number of women interviewed was small (33), it is probably unwise to generalize from it.[57]

Katz discusses "stick ups" as an almost exclusively male activity. Robbery does not fit in with women's identity in the same way that it does for men, especially urban, African-American men, according to Katz. He analyzes the relative profit and risk of robbery versus other forms of criminal activity and concludes that, for some men, robbery is undertaken as part of a larger undertaking of self-definition. It is the ultimate proof of "manhood"; therefore, of course, the activity holds no relevance for women: "unless it is given sense as a way of elaborating, perhaps celebrating, distinctively male forms of action and ways of being . . . stickup has almost no appeal at all."[58]

Arguably, women do not engage in robbery because the risk of victims challenging a woman is greater than when the robber is a man. Even if the woman has a gun, perhaps male victims would assume they could wrest control of the gun away from the female robber. This does not explain why women would not choose female victims, however, and in fact, elderly women are likely targets of the few female robbers that are arrested. Thus, one might propose a psychological reason to explain why women do not engage in robbery (i.e., Katz's theory of robbers as the ultimate male), or a rational reason why they do not (weighing the risk of victims fighting back, it is not worth the trouble). There may be other reasons as well.[59]

Differences Between Violent and Nonviolent Offenders

There are not many studies that examine any differences that might exist between violent and nonviolent female offenders. One such study was done with an incarcerated population, thus the conclusions must be viewed with caution since the sample is not representative of all offenders, only those offenders who received prison sentences. In this study it was found that minority women were overrepresented in convictions for assaultive crimes. Women committed for homicide were less likely to have a criminal record than other offenders, but those committed for assault and robbery were more likely to have recidivistic records than homicide offenders. Interestingly, all violent criminals had fewer prior arrests than did property offenders. It was found that violent offenders were no more likely to come from broken homes than nonviolent offenders, but homicide and assault offenders were more likely to have problems with alcohol. Most of those women committed for homicide or assault acted alone, but those who committed robbery or burglary acted with others.[60]

A slightly different issue is a comparison of chronic versus non-chronic offenders; with the chronic offender defined as having five or more adult convictions. A study of incarcerated females showed that female chronics were quite similar to male chronic offenders in their likelihood of being a minority group member, single, a substance abuser, and having a history of spouse abuse. They were different from male chronic offenders in that they also showed significant differences in education (women completed more years of school), lower IQs, they were more likely to come from broken homes, and were more likely to have other family members with convictions and commitments.[61]

PROPERTY CRIMES

Most research indicates that the sex/gender differential is drastically reduced in property crimes. In 1995, it was reported that women were responsible for 27.3 percent of all arrests for property crime.[62] Property crimes include such crimes as burglary,[63] larceny/theft, forgery/counterfeiting, fraud, and embezzlement.

Burglary

In 1995 women comprised just 11.1 percent of all arrests for burglary.[64] Mann reviewed research on burglaries and reported that some studies indicated women's burglaries were hastily conceived and yielded smaller profits than burglaries committed by males. She reported on a study in California that indicated women committed nine percent of the burglaries, and that they were more likely to work in groups and commit burglaries at a greater distance from their residence.[65]

In a more recent study that compared female and male burglars, Decker et al. found that:

- Males were more likely to commit additional crimes besides burglary.

- Women were more likely to work with others (83% versus 39%).

- Female burglars were more likely than male burglars to be drug addicted.

- Male burglars started committing burglaries earlier than female burglars.

- Males committed more burglaries than females.

- Female burglars reported less contact with the criminal justice system.

- Both male and female burglars were equally likely to use drugs.[66]

Steffensmeier points out that women's rise in the percentage of total arrests for burglary may be due to changes in male patterns of offending and that males are decreasing their commission of this crime.[67] Also, women's participation in burglary may have increased because of the reduced risks the crime presents in today's society where large percentages of the population leave their house completely unattended during the day. Also, women may take advantage of other opportunities to commit burglary. For instance, Steffensmeier reports on a female offender who was working as a real estate agent who committed a burglary of a house she had shown to prospective homebuyers. She had the key, she knew there was loose money at the house, so she went back and illegally obtained entry to steal the money.

Larceny/Theft

In 1995 women were responsible for 33.3 percent of all larceny/theft arrests.[68] The most common type of larceny/theft for women and men is shoplifting, although it could also include stealing from one's place of employment or some other location. In this crime, women account for about one-third of all arrests and their contribution to total arrests has increased. Mann described three types of shoplifters: the adult occasional shoplifter or pilferer, the amateur shoplifter, and the "boosters" or professional shoplifters.[69] In one of the few studies of female shoplifters, it was reported that more than 90 percent had no prior records and they exhibited much smaller recidivism rates than did their male counterparts.[70]

Recall that Pollak in 1950 speculated that women were responsible for a vast amount of shoplifting and other thefts that were undetected and unreported. He did not allow for the possibility that men also were probably responsible for large amounts of such crime, therefore, he believed that this "dark" figure represented women's true criminal tendencies. It is important to recognize that statistics of shoplifting and other larceny/thefts are very much affected by official actions; many stores and places of business choose not to prosecute (or have chosen not to prosecute in the past). Policy changes affect arrest rates (if there is an increased willingness to report and prosecute, this will increase arrest figures). Also, stores have become increasingly sophisticated in their methods to detect and catch shoplifters, again leading to higher arrest figures.

Daly described the increase of larceny/theft among women as petty—examples included women in low-level sales and clerical jobs stealing a bit of money from the cash register, or poor or unemployed women defrauding state or federal government welfare programs or banks through credit card scams.[71] Chesney-Lind reviews early and more recent studies on shoplifting, concluding that women may be disproportionately arrested (directly contrary to Pollak's original assertion that they were underrepresented). The patterns of men and women differ—while women steal smaller items, men steal just one, more expensive, item. Women are less likely to be organized or professional in their shoplifting.[72]

Organized and White-Collar Crimes

Very little information is available on women's participation in organized crime. Block found few women in organized crime; although he noted that early in the twentieth century some women played an active role in crime gangs. Describing organized crime as a community enterprise, he recited a list of women from a variety of historical sources who served as more than prostitutes in organized crime activities. Women were madams, bookmakers, bankers, and loansharks. He describes recent descriptions of organized crime as completely ignoring women, and as almost "pathological" in its refusal to accept that women may play active roles in organized crime.[73]

White-collar crime includes embezzlement and fraud. In 1995 women accounted for 35.9 percent of all forgery/counterfeiting arrests, 41 percent of all fraud arrests, and 43.6 percent of all embezzlement arrests.[74] Early theories speculated that women would increase their participation in these crimes as they entered the workplace and gained access to opportunities.[75] It is unclear, however, to what extent this predication has been supported. While the rate of arrests has increased, the seriousness and type of crime and the motivations for such crime are largely still under debate.

Albanese found that there was a statistical association between the rise of women in managerial occupations and increased commission of "white-collar" crimes such as embezzlement, fraud, and forgery. In 1970 women constituted only 31.7 percent of managerial positions and accounted for roughly 25 percent of white-collar crime. In 1989 women accounted for 44.7 percent of all managerial positions and committed roughly 40 percent of white-collar crimes. While this seems to indicate support for the theory that women would embezzle once they reached the executive suite, Albanese agreed that there was no way to tell whether these women held high-level or low-level managerial positions; and, since crime figures do not indicate seriousness or amount of loss, the increase could represent the petty theft of clerks and office managers just as easily as it could a new type of crime by female executives.[76]

Zietz's study of female embezzlers is one of the very few that targets female white-collar criminals and illustrates that female offenders may continue to show different patterns, even though their arrest numbers may become more similar to those for men. In this study, she compares her sample of women to the typologies of male white-collar/property offenders developed by other theorists such as Donald Cressey. Zietz found that women, more often than men, stole money to maintain a love relationship or to fulfill a caretaking role rather than to pay for personal excesses. In essence, she concluded that the motivational pressures that created the crime were very different for men and women.[77]

Daly also studied white-collar crime by women. Her sample consisted of a group of federal offenders incarcerated for embezzlement, fraud, and forgery. Her findings included the following points:

- Females accounted for very little corporate or organizational crime.

- Females contributed close to 50 percent of bank embezzlement crimes as tellers.

- Women were more likely to commit their crimes alone.

- Women obtained less financial gain than men, on average about one-tenth the amount embezzled by men. In fact, Daly characterized almost all female crime as "petty."

- Motives for men and women were different, with women more often citing family responsibilities as a pressure to embezzle.[78]

Daly's study illustrates the possibility that women's and men's crimes, even when reported under the same crime category, may be different in the participation level, motivation, and extent of harm. Unfortunately, there are very few studies that look as closely at any other crime categories as Daly did.

CONCLUSION

It becomes clear that any discussion of women's contribution to crime must clearly differentiate violent crime from property crime to give the most accurate picture. While violent crime rates continue to show large differences in the relative rates of participation between men and women, property crime rates are converging. As Table 2.2 shows, the arrest rates of women vary tremendously, depending on crime categories.

Whether these relative percentages are influenced by official policies is not clear, nor is it clear exactly what the nature of the offending is within crime categories. Some evidence indicates that there are qualitative differences between crimes by men and women, i.e., women have different motivations and methods of crime commission. Our discussion of women's contribution to crime continues in the next chapter.

Table 2.2
Arrest of Women as Percentage of Total Arrests
Selected Crime Categories

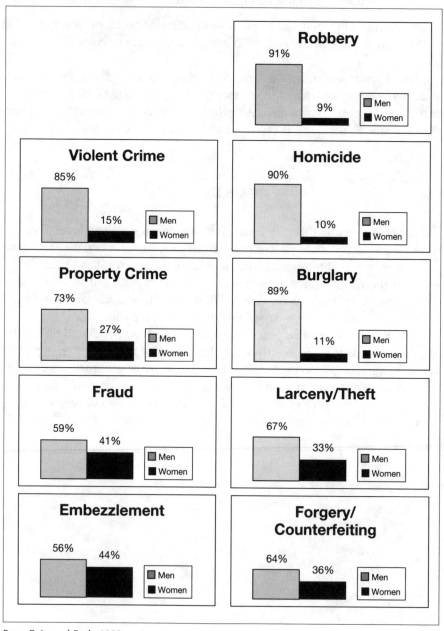

From Reiss and Roth, 1993, p. 3.

NOTES

[1]   One hypothesis, for instance, for the observed increase in juvenile women's arrest numbers is that officials are now more likely to arrest juvenile women than they were 10 or 20 years ago. This would be difficult to prove, but is an intriguing possibility. One alternative source that could shed light on the preceding hypothesis is the use of self reports. If, for instance, juvenile women reported about equal participation in crimes today as they did 10 or 20 years ago, but their official arrests showed an increase, this would tend to support the hypothesis that official actions had changed, rather than offender behavior. In fact, Chesney-Lind and Sheldon (1992) propose just such a hypothesis and support it through self-report data.

[2]   UCR (1995, 225).

[3]   1969/1992.

[4]   1988.

[5]   1992, 141.

[6]   Toch (1992, 191).

[7]   Felson (1996) proposes such a rational-choice theory in a study of size and physical strength differences and how these may affect choices for violence.

[8]   Mann (1984b, 29). Also, see Pearson (1997).

[9]   Sommers and Baskin (1992, 1993), Baskin and Sommers (1993, 1998) and Baskin, Sommers, and Fagan (1993).

[10] Baskin, Sommers, and Fagin (1993, 411), for instance, seem to argue against theories of female criminality that point to economic necessity, the influence of a male partner, or an abusive childhood. It is not clear, however, that they are disputing these claims, nor is it clear whether they believe that the authors they cite believe that these are the *only* means by which women engage in criminal choices.

[11] UCR (1995, 230).

[12] UCR (1995, 225).

[13] Alarid et al. (1996) examined the type of participation of female felons in violent and other crimes, i.e., whether their roles were primary or secondary in the criminal event. The sample was a prison (boot camp) sample of 104 female felons. Once again, researchers obtained a wealth of rich textual material concerning the women's crime, motivation, and meaning attached to the crime. However, the sample is not representative and cannot be used to generalize about other female felons. Women who have been incarcerated for a felony are already a biased sample—it is likely that those who acted as accomplices have already been partially screened out by probation sentences or "deals" with prosecutors. Boot camp participants are an unrepresentative sample of a prison population since they typically "skim" the top of the prisoner population for those offenders who are most amenable to treatment. Finally, the researchers asked for volunteers ensuring that some bias would be introduced into study results—what specific bias is introduced by a volunteer sampling is impossible to predict. Thus, while the study results are interesting and informative, they should not be used beyond their representativeness. Alarid et al. (1996) found that no woman in their sample committed robbery alone and in only one case was robbery initiated by a female accomplice. Aggravated assault was undertaken alone by 31 percent (5) of the women who were incarcerated for that crime

(but it is impossible to tell from this data how much of this was intimate violence) (1996, 441). Most crimes—violent or otherwise—were committed with accomplices (85% of the sample) (1996, 440).

14   Harmon et al. (1985).

15   1978.

16   1980.

17   Wilbanks (1980).

18   Ogle, Maier-Katkin, and Bernard (1995, 173 [cites omitted]). The authors develop a theory of homicide committed by women. They propose that women are under at least as much stress, and perhaps more stress than men in this society, partially due to the social, economic, and cultural oppression of women. Further, women with lower social status experience higher stress than women with higher social status. Women do not express anger in the same way that men do because they have been socialized to control it (this explains the general overall lower violent crime rate for women). Because they have not learned appropriate methods of expressing anger, when environmental stresses push them to the breaking point, they react with episodes of extreme uncontrolled violence and targets of this violence will likely be those close to them at the time (explaining the greater percentage of intimates).

    While interesting, this theory sounds suspiciously like those of Lombroso and others who postulated that women who committed violence were much worse than men and did so out of an excess of passion that overcame their biological passivity. There is no evidence to support the assumption in this theory that women kill in situations that men would not kill in because of an "explosion" of hitherto suppressed rage. It seems that a simpler theory of homicide would be to accept that women are typically less prone to violence, but that certain women because of individual factors will commit violence. These individual factors may be situational and similar to those motivations that might induce a man to kill, i.e., she kills a male partner in order to prevent herself from being killed; or personal, i.e., she is psychologically damaged by abuse and/or neglect during childhood, or she is born with mental defects that result in violent acting out, or simply that she is born with a statistically unusual temperament that includes higher levels of aggression and temper than most women.

19   Craven (1996, 1).

20   1993, 219.

21   Spunt, Brownstein, Crimmins, and Langley (1994).

22   Spunt, Brownstein, Crimmins, and Langley (1994, viii).

23   Brownstein, Spunt, Crimmins, Goldstein, and Langley (1994). The authors reported that there were 1,768 homicides in 1984, so it is unclear why there were only 430 potential respondents identified, i.e., whether there were multiple victims, the crimes were not cleared by arrest, the prosecutions resulted in acquittals, or for some other reason. We, therefore, do not know how many more women were part of the original contingent of offenders. The 13 potential respondents resulted in interviews conducted with nine women. The strength of this research study is that the authors captured almost all of the female offenders who were imprisoned for homicide in a given year; the weakness of the study is that even when published, the data described events of 10 years earlier, the number of women in the sample may or may not have been representative of the number of women who kill given the confusion regarding the initial homicide figures and potential respondents, and the small number in the sample.

[24]   1994, 102.

[25]   1994, 109.

[26]   Examples of the few studies that exist include Hickey (1997) and Levin and Fox (1993).

[27]   Keeney and Heide (1994).

[28]   1994 and 1995.

[29]   Browne (1987); Ewing (1987).

[30]   1991.

[31]   1978.

[32]   See, for instance, Straus, Gelles, and Steinmetz (1980), Straus and Gelles (1986), and McLeod (1984). See DeKeseredy and Schwartz (1996, 331-332) for a discussion of the methodology used in estimating violence by women as compared to men.

[33]   See, for instance, Schwartz (1987), and Dobash et al. (1992). Schwartz, in response to McLeod (1984), used data from the National Crime Survey for the years 1973 through 1982 to examine the claim that men were just as likely to be as seriously injured or more seriously injured than women. However, any discussion of the percentage of those report-ing certain types of injury was eclipsed by the realization that only 69 men reported vio-lent attacks against them by intimate partners compared to 1,166 women. He also report-ed that other studies replicate the percentage of men as comprising about 4-5 percent of domestic violence victims (Schwartz, 1987, 66).

[34]   1994b.

[35]   Mann (1984b, 25).

[36]   Dawson (1994, 1).

[37]   Schwartz (1987, 71).

[38]   1989.

[39]   Bureau of Justice Statistics (1994b, 3).

[40]   Craven (1996, 2).

[41]   A small study provides partial support for this idea—the study compared 21 incarcerated women who killed their abusive spouses and 273 women who sought shelter and pro-tection from abusive spouses. The researchers found that the women who killed appeared to be more isolated from social support systems and perceived more danger than those women who did not kill (Grant and Curry, 1993). Another, more complicated, macro-level study is much more difficult to interpret. Gauthier and Bankston (1997) pro-pose that as women obtain economic equality relative to men, the sex ratio of domestic homicide will decline (meaning more men will kill women than vice versa) due to a type of frustration-aggression theory, i.e., they feel they are losing the power rightly theirs according to cultural norms. They also propose that this association will take place only in those areas of general economic well being (although the authors do not entirely make clear why this would be so). Finally, the negative association will occur only within the Southern region because of cultural prescriptions that include more traditional sex-roles for men and women (1997, 582). The authors operationalized the constructs, i.e., using labor force and income figures for economic well being. To substantiate the idea of the South as holding more traditional sex-role beliefs, they cite several other studies. Analysis

of the FBI data on homicides for the years 1988 through 1992 provided support for the authors' hypotheses. However, whether their operationalization of constructs was valid, or the relationships that they found were due to the association they describe, some statistical artifact, or some other reason is more questionable. First, one might argue about whether the South holds more traditional sex-role beliefs than the rest of the country, especially in those large metropolitan areas that were studied. There is also a great deal of question whether any macro-level indictor of labor force participation or income level can capture "equality" between men and women. Finally, if the association the authors propose is true; it does not explain the overall (albeit small) decline of males killing female partners that has occurred in the last several years, if one is willing to grant that women's economic equality has continued to improve.

[42]   Mann (1988, 36).

[43]   1988, 43.

[44]   1988, 37, 48.

[45]   Mann (1984b, 25).

[46]   Mann (1984b, 26).

[47]   Dawson (1994).

[48]   Note the difference in these statements: The killers of children are more likely to be women than men. And: Women are more likely than men to kill their children. Is it simply semantics? The point made by the first statement is simply a statistical fact—women compose 55 percent of the group of killers of children. The second statement implies much more and is, in fact, wrong, since we do not know if women are more likely than men to kill their children until we control for opportunity and access. One cannot kill unless one has opportunity and access and the fact is that women are more often custodial parents and spend more time caring for children even in intact families.

[49]   1994, 1.

[50]   1994, 1.

[51]   d'Orban (1979, 560).

[52]   1979, 565.

[53]   1979, 567.

[54]   Reiss and Roth (1993).

[55]   UCR (1995, 225).

[56]   Kauffman (1993).

[57]   Mann (1984b).

[58]   Katz (1988, 247).

[59]   A female interviewee in a study of addicts explains why she would not resort to robbery, except for women also on "the stroll" (engaged in prostitution): "I don't think I'd bop a little ol lady walking down the block . . . could be my moms, but I might think about takin one of the other bitches off" (reported in Maher and Curtis, 1992, 231). One might argue that this is a qualitatively different reason than those already cited, one that points to affective motivations rather than rational.

[60]   Ward, Jackson, and Ward (1979).

[61]   Danner et al. (1995)

[62]   UCR (1995, 225).

[63]   Many researchers argue that burglary should be categorized as a violent crime since it involves more predation than other types of property offenses.

[64]   UCR (1995, 225).

[65]   Mann (1984b, 30).

[66]   Decker et al. (1993).

[67]   Steffensmeier (1993).

[68]   UCR (1995, 225).

[69]   1984b, 31.

[70]   Cameron (1964).

[71]   1989a, 790.

[72]   1997, 106.

[73]   Block (1980); also see Steffensmeier and Allen (1988).

[74]   UCR (1995, 225).

[75]   See, for instance, Simon (1975a, 1975b, 1976).

[76]   1993, 126.

[77]   1981.

[78]   1989a.

Crimes Committed by Women: Drugs and Delinquency

3

Objectives

- Become familiar with crime statistics regarding drug abuse violations by women.

- Become familiar with crime statistics regarding crimes "specific to women."

- Understand the issues involved in the efforts to punish prenatal drug use.

- Become familiar with crime statistics regarding female delinquency.

- Be aware of how race interacts with sex to influence crime rates.

In this chapter we continue to explore crimes by women, focusing on their participation in drug violations, as well as certain other crimes associated with female offenders. We also discuss female delinquency in a separate section. Finally, the interaction effects of race and sex are discussed. The reader should continue to keep in mind that most of what we know about women's contribution to crime comes from the UCR and other official sources. Data for juvenile crime often use self-report data and those studies may include more minor forms of wrongdoing, thus, comparisons between such findings should be made cautiously.

DRUG CRIMES

There are fundamental philosophical and political differences of opinion in the characterization of the "drug problem" in this country. Some argue that it is the scourge of this nation's young and that drugs are responsible for countless crimes and economic losses, not to mention personal tragedies. Others argue that the rate of use of psychotropic drugs has gone up and

down in the last 100 years, but that the focus on a "drug problem" and policies of prosecution and interdiction rather than treatment has been largely
responsible for the public's view of drugs as a major social problem. In other
words, it is the state reaction to drug use that is the problem, not the problem itself. These two views, at least insofar as they describe drug use and
addiction as a factor in crime, are not necessarily contradictory. The fact that
drug use and drug selling is a crime in this country means that drugs are
expensive to obtain (artificially so), dangerous to use, and create associations
with unsavory and criminal individuals. Further, if caught, drug use or selling
drugs may lead to criminal convictions and/or prison sentences that are obviously quite detrimental to one's life and livelihood. These elements of drug
use are present largely because of the illegality of drug use. Thus, in the following section we describe drugs as a major contributor to female criminality; in fact, drugs may account for the most dramatic changes in the profile of
female criminality in the last 50 years. However, to what extent these events
have been due to state action against drug use and sales, and to what extent
they are due simply to the choice to use psychotropic substances and what
effect these substances have on one's life, is impossible to say.

Data used to discover the link between drug use and crime include a number of different sources and types. DUF (Drug Use Forecasting) figures are collected by law enforcement agencies and reported by the National Institute of
Justice in annual reports and periodic updates. These data track whether
arrestees were under the influence of drugs at the time of arrest in several large
cities across the country. Drug crimes are obviously one of the Part II crimes
collected by the FBI and reported in the UCR. Phenomenological/ethnograph-
ic studies of drug users, sellers, and addicts are
available that describe the life of the addict,
including associations, patterns of use and selling, motivations, and criminal patterns as they
are associated with drug use. Prevalence rates
(the number of individuals in this country who
use drugs) and whether such use has increased
or decreased, are provided by a variety of sources
that employ random samples of the populace or
selected populations.

Drug use by the general population in this
country has declined by almost 50 percent
since 1979, although drug-related arrests have
increased.[1] In 1994, women committed 16.7 percent of drug abuse violations.[2] There is some evidence that indicates the number of females
arrested (for any crime) who test positive for
marijuana has increased, that females continue
to exceed males in the number who test positive
for cocaine upon arrest, and female arrestees are

Evidence indicates that drugs may be associated more with female criminality than with
male criminality. *Photo credit: Mark C. Ide.*

more likely than male arrestees to self-report cocaine use (70% compared to 54%). While, generally, opiate use has been stable among tested arrestees, the use of at least one type of drug among female arrestees has increased. However, among juvenile women, the number of arrestees testing positive for cocaine use has declined somewhat.[3]

Merlo explores the relationship between drugs and crimes in a review of the literature on female crime. She proposes that drugs may be a defining factor in any explanation of women's participation in criminality, as well as any increases or changes in the patterns of criminality for women. Reviewing the evidence, she concludes that drugs at least increase criminality if not cause it, and may be associated more with female criminality than with male criminality.[4] We will explore these conclusions using the available data. Several questions present themselves concerning women's criminal drug use:

- Are female and male addicts different in their motivations, entry, persistence, and desistance in drug use?

- Is women's drug use related to criminality, and if so, in what way?

- Is there an increase in women's drug use and/or is the criminality associated with drug use increasing?

An early description of the female addict provided the following information:

> What is known about female drug abusers is scattered and somewhat fragmented. The demographic data available indicate that female addicts appear to be getting younger, with black and other minority females usually younger than white female addicts. Yet female drug abusers tend to be older than male addicts, probably because they begin their drug careers later, in their middle twenties. Also, women addicts, especially heroin abusers, are more likely to be separated, divorced, or widowed (35%) than male addicts (15%) and are significantly more likely to have children. Female addicts are thought to have experienced more general disorganization and economic insecurity in their early family life than male addicts. As a part of this deprived family background incestuous assaults by their fathers or other male relatives are quite high, ranging from 20 percent in one study to 44 percent in another . . .[5]

Several phenomenological studies are available that describe the role of women in the subculture of drug use and sales. For instance, Rosenbaum interviewed 100 women who were on heroin. This sample was non-random—she obtained interviewees through a modified "snowball" method wherein users were identified who then led her to other female users. She cited crimes associated with heroin use as including prostitution, and a variety of property crimes. Her interviewees had tried a variety of crimes to support their habit: auto theft (3% of the sample admitted this activity), burglary

(18%), conning (6%), dealing drugs (61%), forgery (21%), pickpocketing (5%), pimping (1%), prostitution (60%), and shoplifting (28%).[6] She described how addiction changed criminal patterns of prostitution: high-class call girls, if addicted, would accept increasingly less money for their services because they needed the money to buy drugs and could not afford to reject a customer. As a result of continuing drug use, the women would "let themselves go," reducing their marketability and bargaining power further to create an ever-downward spiral of desperation. Thus, a woman who had been a call girl only accepting referrals, might eventually end up as a streetwalker, and instead of earning $500 for a "date," she may only be able to earn $20.

In her study, Rosenbaum identified a typology of pre-drug lifestyles, including "the hippie trip," "the outlaw world," and "the fast life"—all had in common reduced options and a general lack of optimism toward future opportunities.[7] Rosenbaum rejected the suggestion by other researchers who thought that women were brought into drug use by men.[8]

> In many earlier studies of addiction, it has been argued that women are generally initiated into heroin use through a man—a lover, spouse, boyfriend, "old man"; the image presented is that of a rather passive woman "turned on" to illicit activities by her man. My data indicate that this picture is far from accurate—particularly for women in the sample who are under 25 and, typically, were members of the social worlds previously described.[9]

However, she then describes women as wanting to get involved because heroin was around the house and/or the woman's boyfriend/husband was involved with the lifestyle. Rosenbaum provides no numbers of women who entered heroin use without a relationship connection and, in fact, her descriptions of the heroin world almost all refer to relationships. Only by changing the previous suggestion to one where a woman is *unwillingly* led into heroin use is her rebuttal of previous theories supported by her own evidence.

Like other researchers, Rosenbaum's interviewees describe the attraction of the drug world through explanations of "the life's" excitement and risk. Women described a feeling of being in a secret world—the drug itself as creating a rush akin to a sexual orgasm. Further, the risk involved in the drug lifestyle (including fears of arrest, bad dope, and violent drug deals), and the chaos and social nature of the lifestyles (parties and alcohol were ever-present) led to the attraction as well.[10]

According to Rosenbaum: "the most devastating aspect of the woman's time inundation by heroin is her inability to fulfill her mothering responsibilities."[11] Children posed the biggest problem for heroin addicted women. Some were able to handle mothering and meet their drug needs, but many could not: "women who are able to use heroin and take care of their children are respected in their heroin world, many can't because of withdrawing or having to hustle to make money for their habit."[12] The women themselves were tormented by their deficiencies as mothers and Rosenbaum noted that social norms, even in the drug world, expected more of women than men: "Men do not suffer the stigma of addiction as severely as women, especially in the area of interpersonal and sexual relationships."[13] She noted that addict women are usually not attractive to non-addict men, but the reverse is not necessarily as true. Women, therefore, almost always chose other addicts as mates and that made breaking free of the drug virtually impossible.

Inciardi used similar methodology with a sample of 149 women heroin addicts in Miami. Most had criminal histories and the most common crime was shoplifting, followed by drug sales and prostitution—in that order of frequency.[14] Interviews with Miami street girls and women show the devastation of crack cocaine in women's lives.[15] Women described differences in motivation for drug use—while men used crack for thrills or pleasure, women tended more often to use crack as a type of self-medication. Female crack addicts were more likely to have been victims of extensive physical and sexual abuse. This research also described "crack house" sex—the economic exchange of sex for drugs that occurs in crack houses by desperate female addicts.[16] Researchers point out that the women who sell themselves for drugs have destroyed the economic viability of street prostitution in those neighborhoods where crack is prevalent. Prostitutes then become involved in other types of crime, such as ripping off johns, to survive.

Researchers describe the life of the crack user as one characterized by poverty, chaos, and disordered family lives. Since drugs affect their self-identity as mothers, women are especially damaged by addiction.[17]

> I've been on dope for most of my life. Dope killed my momma, killed my two brothers, and it's gonna kill my little sister 'cause she out here in a crew that's out cold . . . we all gonna die, just wait and see . . . Crack is what makes us crazy, but it's the best high I know. This ain't the way I wanted things to work, but that's the way it is . . .[18]

Adler provides a "participative-observation" study since she explains that her husband and she were friends with the addicts described in her ethnography, partied with them, and used drugs with them.[19] The study covered several years and she was able to follow up and discover what happened to several of the addicts who were described during the study time period. Unlike those studies above, female addicts were not the central focus of this research, although they were part of the drug subculture and, therefore, were described by Adler in the study results. She mentions a few independent women dealers, wives of dealers who had varying participation in the drug world, and "dope chicks" who hung out with men attached to the drug world to gain access to drugs. Adler's narrative quotes and descriptions lead one to the conclusion (unlike Rosenbaum) that women usually entered the drug subculture through a relationship with a man. Even if they subsequently became independent dealers, their first entry and apprenticeships were conducted through a relationship, as the following female drug dealer describes:

> After my husband got busted I was left alone to support the kids. I
> had never wanted to deal but I knew a lot of people who did.
> When I started to get really hard up I decided to try to see if I could
> make some money off of knowing all these big dealers. It's not real-
> ly dealing—it's just putting together two connections, but the trick
> is to keep them apart so they don't know who each other are and
> they need you to complete the task.[20]

The roles of women included "mules" (those who carried the drugs across the
border) and those who were involved in "middling" (described in the above
quote).[21] Adler explains that not all men would do business with female dealers, some felt that women could not handle the dope trade and got too
"uptight" or nervous about the inevitable mess-ups that occurred. She also
described a type of chivalry in the dope trade whereby women were given
longer periods of time to repay in deals on credit—at least by some.[22] This
chivalry seems to have disappeared in more recent years in crack and cocaine
distribution systems.[23]

Maher and Daly describe an ethnographic study of women drug users
during 1989 through 1992 in New York City.[24] They present the claim by
some researchers that women are advancing and playing increasingly more
dominant roles in the drug underworld, but then dispute the claim using
other literature and their own research. Their findings indicate that women
continue to play fairly traditional roles in the drug subculture. A few of the
women they interviewed acted as "steerers" or "touts" who referred potential
customers to dealers. Some women were hired as low-level temporary street
dealers and many women "copped" for others (for instance, a white male
would enter the neighborhood, approach the woman and pay her to buy
drugs for him with or without a sexual exchange as part of the bargain as
well). Maher and Daly found that women were not hired as drug sellers
because they were perceived to be not "bad" enough—they could not deploy
and/or threaten violence to the same extent that men could (making collecting debts and protecting drugs problematic). Although women attempted to
run "shooting galleries" they were successful only when they had male partners to keep order and ward off interlopers. The authors suggest that even
the police department targeted female-owned "shooting galleries" for harass-
ment and shut them down.

Other reports from the same larger study describe how women tend to
hold lower-level distribution roles, although a few women in the study had
been lieutenants (who act as conduits for drugs and money, linking the street
dealers and higher level bosses or owners).[25] Women have also developed
special niches described by these authors, for instance, as "house distribu-
tors" (running crack houses or "freak houses" for a male partner or boss),
"freak house girls" (performing sexual services for money or crack), and
"smoking partners" (providing the drugs as well as company with which to
get high). This study presented a number of common themes of drug-using
women even though their individual backgrounds and current activities were

quite different. Most of the women had been involved in the drug world for a long time, predating the huge increase of crack use across the country; most had been active "street" people with extensive networks, and most had lost their children due to their drug involvement. Even so, many expressed the view that selling gave them a feeling of self-worth and success.[26]

Another phenomenological study interviewed 141 methamphetamine users/dealers in San Francisco, San Diego, and Honolulu.[27] These women users exhibited a range of roles in the distribution system of the drug economy. Most of the women in their study dealt drugs in order to have access to the drugs for personal use; drug selling also provided them with an income and some independence and control in their life, without having to resort to prostitution. Contrary to other studies, this one did not find that women were relegated to low-level positions, especially in the California sites.

The phenomenological studies above describe the drug subculture as one in which women are certainly present, but play a different role than men. Because each study presents a slice of reality we get different pictures of whether women's roles in the drug world have changed. Those researchers who talked to women who were independent dealers and were active and aggressive in their drug dealing describe a different world from those researchers who talked to women who did not engage in these activities. The advantage of the phenomenological method is the richness of the data; the weakness is not knowing whether one's informants are representative of others in the same world.[28]

By combining the results of a number of phenomenological studies we might conclude that women are seldom major dealers (although there are some), and they are usually connected to the drug world through a relationship with a man, at least initially. Their roles range from independent dealer, to equal partner (usually with a husband or boyfriend), to "mules" (peripheral players used to smuggle drugs into the country) and other small players such as "steerers," down to "dope chicks" or "crack ho's" who exchange sex for drugs. Children are more problematic for women than for men in the drug subculture. Many cannot handle the responsibilities of motherhood and many of them are tormented by their deficiencies.

Patterns of Use

It seems that female offenders may use drugs more often than male offenders. One should probably interpret this with caution, however, since the differences are not extreme and the comparisons made are with arrestees and incarcerated populations.[29] Most women in prison have used alcohol, but it seems that while imprisoned women are more likely to be heavier users of drugs than their male counterparts, the reverse is true for alcohol.[30] About one-third of sampled female inmates in California and Texas reported that crack or cocaine had been a problem in their life. Alcohol and heroin also were mentioned by up to one-third of the women as being a problem in their lives. All other drugs were reported less often as being a problem.[31] Women in prison have been multi-drug users—many have at least sampled all drugs even if they prefer certain types.

Drug Use Forecasting (DUF) figures indicate that female arrestees are more likely to test positive for drugs and self-report more drug use than male arrestees.[32] Thus, it seems probable that women in the criminal justice system can be described as heavier drug users, although the meaning of this fact is unclear. Some studies show little differences between male and female addicts in treatment settings;[33] while others describe female addicts as displaying significantly more sociopathy and psychological disturbance than male addicts.[34] While it is estimated that about two percent of the U.S. population has a drug problem necessitating treatment, 33 percent of the incarcerated population and 25 percent of all those on probation and parole are estimated to have such a problem—many of these offenders are women.[35]

Creating the Drug Criminal

Chesney-Lind calls the "War on Drugs" a war on women because of large percentage increases of women being arrested for drug crimes.[36] Between 1985 and 1994, women's drug arrests increased 100 percent while men's drug arrests increased only by about 50 percent. Bloom et al. report that the percentage of women admitted to prison for drugs increased from 14.2 percent of total admission in 1982 to 42.2 percent of the total in 1992.[37] About one in three women in U.S. prisons were there for drug crimes in 1991, an increase from one in 10 in 1979.[38] As stated in the section above, women in the criminal justice system seem to be heavier drug users than men.[39]

Whether drug use precedes criminality or whether criminality precedes drug use has been explored by several researchers and results have been mixed. Anglin and Hser reported that their sample of 328 Anglo and Chicana methadone users showed patterns of criminality that were exacerbated by drug use.[40] Although their interviewees committed property crimes before addiction occurred, the rate of narcotic use influenced the rate of crime commission after their drug use had been established. Crimes by women included prostitution, drug sales, and shoplifting, while crimes by men were more likely to include violent crime, burglary, and drug dealing. Anglo women were also somewhat less likely to have pre-drug criminal activity and somewhat more likely to engage in prostitution after drug use had been established as opposed to more serious crimes. Other research has also linked drug use to more frequent crime.[41]

Baskin and Sommers provide a summary of the research that addresses this question and then explore the connection with their own sample of violent arrestees and incarcerated women in New York. They describe the drug-crime connection as mixed: their "early onset" group (those women who engaged in crime early and consistently) committed criminal acts before drug use, but the "late onset" group (those women who had remained relatively crime-free until they were much older) were very likely to begin criminal activities after a period of drug use.[42]

Thus, drugs play an important role in the criminality of women. It seems that drugs may not be the sole and necessary cause of criminal choices by women, but that, once addicted, women are more likely to engage in crime and commit crimes much more frequently than those women who do not use drugs. Phenomenological studies give us different pictures regarding the role women play in drug subcultures. While women are undertaking higher-level roles in drug distribution networks, the numbers of women who do so seem to be relatively small and their participation seems to be influenced by the neighborhood and culture in which they live. It is clear that many women— at least one-third—caught in the criminal justice system are likely to have been drug users and require treatment.

SPECIAL CRIMES OF WOMEN

In this section we will address a few areas of criminality that have been and are uniquely associated with women. Historically, special crimes of women—scolding, infanticide, witchcraft—have existed. Legal processing, and the system's approach to women, has also been very different from that for men.[43] For instance, women have been subject to indeterminate terms for the purpose of rehabilitation long after specific lengths were assigned to men; the "crime" of incorrigibility was used to govern young women's sexuality; and, early female reformatories were used as a method of social control since women did not even need to commit a crime to be incarcerated within them.[44] Prostitution used to be a crime only when committed by a woman soliciting a man. Today that is no longer the case, at least formally—whether law enforcement practices follow the law is a different matter.

Although most sexually discriminatory laws have been struck down and discarded, there are still differences experienced by women in court processing. One thought is that they are the recipient of chivalrous treatment (this concept will be discussed in the next chapter). The other possibility is that women are subject to different laws than men, or existing laws are applied in a different manner.

Prostitution

It would be hard to publish a book on female criminality without at least some mention of prostitution; however, like drug crimes, any discussion of prostitution as a crime must first acknowledge the social, political, and philo-

Most studies indicate that female criminals, regardless of crime, often have a history of prostitution. *Photo credit: Mark C. Ide.*

sophical issues regarding the definition of the activity as a crime. Prostitution—at least when not associated with robbery, "viccing" (taking the money and running), or other forms of victimization—is considered by many to be a victimless crime. In fact, in some places it is not a crime at all. Thus, it is hard to view prostitution as similar to other crimes that are more clearly injurious to innocent victims. On the other hand, prostitution continues to be associated with the criminal subculture—prostitutes may victimize "johns," or be victimized themselves by "johns" or pimps; and, they may be part of a larger criminal organization that includes gambling and drugs.

Much of the research on prostitution is phenomenological and provides typologies of the different types of prostitutes, i.e., call girls, streetwalkers, bar girls, and so on. Rosenbaum, in a phenomenological study, explores how call girls develop their identity, the power relationships between call girls and their clients, motivations for entering "the life," and other elements of the prostitutes' world.[45]

There is a continuing debate in the literature over whether entry into prostitution is clearly and solely economic or whether there is a correlation between entry into prostitution and personal victimization, i.e., childhood sexual abuse or deprivation. Many point to the connection between teenage runaways and prostitution. Many teenage girls who run away do so because of dysfunctional families; once on the street they turn to prostitution to survive, or become emotionally attached to a man who then "turns her out" to prostitute for him.[46] Chesney-Lind also documents the link between sex work and drugs.[47] Many prostitutes use drugs; many prostitute to get money for drugs. Interestingly, in interviews some prostitutes explain that they need drug intoxication in order to engage in sex with a customer (as a type of self-medication); therefore, the relationship in some cases is circular—women use drugs to help themselves perform as prostitutes, but they also engage in prostitution in order to buy drugs.

Most studies indicate that female criminals, regardless of crime, often also have a history of prostitution although it is not clear which came first, the prostitution or other crime choices. Teenage runaways are recruited by street pimps, or engage in prostitution independently to survive. Other women are recruited or turn to sex work from compatible occupations (that emphasize women's sex role and attractiveness, i.e., dancing, massage, and bar service). Some women resort to prostitution only after becoming addicted to drugs, although for some, entry into prostitution may predate heavy drug use, however drug dependency develops and then makes exit more difficult or impossible.

The explanation of why women engage in prostitution can be psychological—life scripts that develop due to sexual abuse as a child. The explanation could be economic—it is simply one alternative to earning money, sometimes a great deal of money. Or, the explanation might be sociological—the sexualization of women in this society almost ensures the creation of a prostitute role and women are socialized to accept the role created for them by society. Finally, one might employ a political analysis—by a lack of other viable economic choices for women, society ensures that some women are forced to select prostitution in order to survive or maintain economic independence. James provided a list of reasons why women enter prostitution:

- There is no other occupation available to unskilled or low-skilled women with the potential income of prostitution.

- Sex work offers adventure and independence.

- It is consistent with women's traditional sex role.

- Some women are already labeled deviant because of their sexuality.

- There is a cultural importance placed on wealth and material goods, and sex work offers one avenue to attain these things.[48]

It is now accepted that both the female prostitute and the "john" are committing a crime. Law enforcement is more likely to engage in reverse "stings" whereby female officers pose as prostitutes. Certain communities employ tactics to reduce the demand for prostitution by taking photographs of the "johns'" license plates or publishing their names in the newspaper. Even with these changes in policy, however, it is interesting that there continues to be more attention to why women enter prostitution (as a concern of criminology for instance) than why men seek prostitutes.[49]

Pregnancy as a Crime?

Obviously pregnancy is not a crime, but being pregnant has precipitated differential definitions of criminality and court processing for women. Thus, for at least some women, being pregnant has become a punishable offense. Women's unique role in procreation arguably has been one cause for greater social control. Eugenics movements have utilized sterilization of men, but they also have usually employed sterilization or incapacitation of women and these methods have, at times and in some places, been accepted as legitimate methods of population control or genetic cleansing.[50] In this country, the eugenics movement was aided by family studies that identified the female as the transmitter of deviancy.[51] Forced sterilization has been directed to three groups of women: mentally retarded, chronic welfare recipients, and criminals. The only U.S. Supreme Court case on the matter upheld forced sterilization, although its current validity is questionable.[52] Most court decisions have allowed state laws that provide for nonconsensual sterilization of individuals not able to care for themselves (mentally retarded and handicapped).[53] What is at issue today is forced contraception for women who are deemed unfit mothers, criminalization of certain behaviors during pregnancy that pose a risk to the developing fetus, and differential sentencing based on the fact that the offender is pregnant.

Many authors have written on the trend of those in the criminal justice system to "criminalize" the actions of pregnant women who use drugs.[54] About 11 percent of babies are exposed to drugs *in utero*.[55] It is difficult to distinguish the effects of drug use from those of poor nutrition and lack of prenatal care, or the effects of smoking and drinking during pregnancy, however, one must accept that drug-using pregnant women do put their fetus at risk and, especially with the prevalence of crack, this problem certainly exists. Whether "crack babies" are an epidemic, as some popular media accounts would have us believe, whether the effect of drugs on babies is more of a problem today than it ever was, and whether the criminal justice system is best suited to respond to the problem are the questions debated in this field.

Some states have responded to drug use by pregnant women by either increasing and adapting their use of child-injury laws, using drug laws by redefining delivery, or by using the civil courts to deprive women of custody at birth.[56] Many states passed informant laws that required hospital or medical personnel to report positive toxicology tests. In order to use child-injury laws against pregnant women, the definition of "child" has to include the fetus. Under common law, the fetus was not protected by such statutes because it was not defined as a child. Although several attempts were made to do so, courts resisted such an expansion—probably because of the implications for therapeutic and early term abortion. Another method used, more successfully, against pregnant women was to charge her with delivery of a controlled substance. Under this legal theory, the woman was described as delivering drugs to the fetus in the short period of time after birth (to achieve the legal definition of person), but before the umbilical cord was cut (to meet the definition of delivery). The most commonly used method against drug using women was to employ the civil courts to wrest custody away from the mother after birth. Medical personnel often express resistance to mandatory reporting when it is tied to such sanctions since it discourages some pregnant women from seeking prenatal care.

A more subtle way the system punishes pregnant women is by sentencing such women to terms of incarceration or longer terms of incarceration *because* of her pregnancy and to protect the fetus from further drug use. In several reported cases, judges said on record they were incarcerating a woman because of her pregnancy. It is obviously unknown how many other judges do not express such reasoning in open court. One can agree that drug use during pregnancy is obviously a social problem and one that needs to be addressed, while at the same time agreeing that pregnant women who are charged with crimes unique to women, or sentenced disproportionally for crimes, compared to similar male offenders, are being sanctioned not for the crime but, rather, for the fact of committing the crime while pregnant.

This issue represents the construction of criminality. Attention is brought to bear on a social problem (the birth of babies exposed to drugs), statistics are presented to prove the seriousness of the problem (11% based on one study), a criminal is identified (the mother), and a solution is proposed (punish the mother). Unfortunately, reality is not quite so simple as is offered in the simplistic portrayal of "bad" mothers whose drug use is hurting an increasing number of babies. First, there are real questions about whether the percentage of babies born exposed to drugs has increased. The same few studies utilizing samples were used by many subsequent articles to "prove" the 11 percent figure. More importantly, the figures used indicated positive toxicology test results, not addiction. The fact that a baby is born with a positive toxicology test does not mean that the baby is addicted, nor does it necessarily mean that the baby will experience short- or long-term effects from the drug. Also, there is evidence to indicate that a far greater problem than drug exposure is the lack of prenatal care and that this social deficit is probably responsible for many more long-term problems for more infants than drug-using mothers. Finally, the criminalization of women may have resulted in exactly the opposite result desired. Once the word on the street was that medical personnel would report drug use to authorities and women who were reported were likely to lose their babies and also could face formal sanctions during pregnancy, many drug-using women simply stopped seeking prenatal medical attention, further endangering their developing fetus.

Feinman provides a whole collection of essays on the criminalization of a women's body, including discussions of abortion, surrogate motherhood, prenatal crack cocaine use, and other forms of prenatal harm.[57] One cannot ignore the fact that today, as in past decades, the law treats the pregnant woman as *sui generis*.[58] At times this is to her benefit (probably there have been many cases in which a pregnant woman has received probation instead of prison, and pregnancy discrimination laws provide partial protection to pregnant working women). At times, however, the system takes control of her body, criminalizes her conduct, and punishes her more severely than men, simply because of her pregnancy.

FEMALE JUVENILE DELINQUENCY

After reviewing the crime statistics relative to delinquency, certain conclusions can be made. First, juvenile women's contribution to the total number of arrests of juveniles has increased, but only moderately so, and juvenile women still account for only about one-quarter of total arrests. Second, the presence and problem of female gangs is one that is probably overstated by the popular media. Although they exist in certain cities, numbers are small and activities continue to be less violent and less criminal than those gangs composed of male juveniles.

The Uniform Crime Reports are used to show actual arrest numbers and the percentage of total arrests contributed by juvenile females. Girls account for about one out of every four (24%) juvenile arrests.[59] Table 3.1 shows modest increases in almost all crime categories for juvenile women between 1989 and 1994. Crime categories with modest increases include larceny/theft, aggravated assault, forgery/counterfeiting, motor vehicle theft, and vagrancy. Crime categories that showed decreased participation by women were homicide, forcible rape, fraud, embezzlement, and prostitution. The table indicates some increases, but they are hardly dramatic.[60]

Crime Patterns: The Same or Different?

Early literature on juvenile women reported that they were more likely to be arrested for sex crimes and running away; in fact, much of the early literature chronicled the system's predisposition to be almost solely interested in the girl's sexual activity (contrary to the general disinterest in boy's sexual activities).[61] Later works employed self-report studies and discovered that girls and boys showed far more similar patterns of activity than official arrest statistics indicated. Again, however, boys committed far more delinquency in almost every category.[62] Figueira-McDonough et al. reviewed earlier self-report studies and concluded that girls reported a broad range of behaviors. The difference between girls and boys was in the frequency of commission, not in the pattern of offenses committed. They concluded that girls did not "specialize" in sex crimes. They also found, however, that the gender differential increased with the seriousness of crime.[63]

In one study of 562 males and 557 females, it was found that neither group reported much delinquent activity, but there were fewer admitted delinquencies by girls than boys.[64] The study also examined the relevance of the "chivalry hypothesis," the idea that officials were less likely to arrest girls. By comparing self-reports to official arrests, but then by controlling for crime factors such as seriousness and number of prior police contacts, the apparent differential in arrest rates due to chivalry disappeared.

Table 3.1
Arrests of Females Under Eighteen—1989 and 1994

	1989			1994		
	Total	Female	%	Total	Female	%
Total	1,611,664	351,541	21.81	2,076,949	503,382	24.24
(Index Offenses)						
Homicide	2,086	131	6.28	3,016	178	5.9
Forcible rape	4,328	99	2.29	4,648	93	2
Robbery	29,234	2,472	8.46	46,268	4,258	9.20
Aggrav. assault	42,729	5,781	13.53	67,398	12,523	18.58
Burglary	105,513	8,450	8.01	110,678	10,568	9.55
Larceny/Theft	334,486	89,319	26.70	395,334	126,949	32.11
Motor vehicle theft	69,542	7,169	10.31	71,212	9,919	13.93
Arson	5,963	581	9.74	8,857	1,088	12.28
(Part II Offenses)						
Other assaults	105,667	24,154	22.86	165,192	43,612	26.40
Forgery/ counterfeit	5,584	1,755	31.43	6,690	2,436	36.41
Fraud	8,960	2,655	29.63	18,265	4,751	26.01
Embezzlement	1,059	485	45.80	790	282	35.70
Stolen property	31,873	2,901	9.10	34,616	3,913	11.30
Vandalism	90,206	8,094	8.99	116,771	12,033	10.30
Weapons	29,687	1,989	6.70	50,425	4,062	8.06
Prostitution	1,199	709	59.13	997	487	48.85
Other sex offenses	12,528	896	7.15	13,804	1,063	7.70
Drugs	82,944	9,565	11.53	127,225	14,898	11.71
Gambling	829	33	4.0	1,463	73	4.99
Offenses against family	1,837	656	35.71	3,823	1,373	35.91
DUI	13,911	1,930	13.87	9,990	1407	14.08
Liquor laws	107,943	29,958	27.75	88,545	25,421	28.71
Drunkenness	15,853	2,666	16.82	14,036	2,290	16.32
Disorderly conduct	91,004	17,863	19.63	129,759	30,274	23.33
Vagrancy	2,144	322	15.02	3,585	672	18.74
Curfew	61,928	15,888	25.66	101,816	29,434	28.91
Runaway	118,045	65,978	55.90	151,899	86,706	57.08
All other	234,132	48,525	20.73	329,845	72,619	22.02

Sources: FBI, Crime in the United States: Uniform Crime Reports. Washington, DC: U.S. Dept. of Justice, 1990, p. 181; and FBI, Crime in the United States: Uniform Crime Reports. Washington, DC: U.S. Dept. of Justice, 1995, p. 226.

Chesney-Lind and Sheldon also presented self-report data that showed more similarity in some behavior patterns than some official reports indicated. Both young men and young women reported almost equal participation in some use of drugs, disobeying parents, defying parental authority, running away from home, skipping school, disturbing the peace, smoking marijuana, drinking alcohol, engaging in sexual encounters, theft (less than $2), theft ($2-$50), and selling hard drugs, although for the last couple of offenses, the gender differential started to appear. In other words, the gender gap was smaller in self-report studies than in official statistics, but was still present.[65]

Finally, Triplett and Myers analyzed National Youth Survey data and concluded that there was a greater sex-ratio difference for serious offenses and women showed lower prevalence patterns than did male juveniles. However, for those female juveniles who did offend, they did so at levels about equal to those of male juveniles.[66]

The picture is not simply one in which girls track boys' crime patterns at a lower level. The gender differential is most extreme in violent crime, and almost disappears in some other types of delinquency. Because self-report studies of juveniles ask about a broad range of behaviors, many of which might be described as quite trivial, the gender differential appears to be reduced and researchers could argue that "patterns" of misbehavior were similar. But that is not entirely true; patterns of behavior showed that boys and girls both engaged in a variety of non-serious misbehaviors and delinquent acts, but boys were and are far more likely to be involved in violent crime and serious property crimes.[67]

Self-report studies can be compared to official arrest patterns. Girls are more likely than boys to be arrested for status offenses such as running away from home, incorrigibility, truancy, and in need of care and protection. The most common cause of arrest for boys and girls was larceny/theft, but the second most common cause for girls was running away; while for boys it was "other offenses" and then burglary (in 1985) or other assaults (in 1994).[68] As Table 3.2 shows, girls and boys are arrested for different offenses, and girls are much more likely to be arrested for status offenses. One of the reasons that girls' percentages of arrest for status offenses is so high is because they are arrested for fewer violent and property crimes and so, unlike boys, their total arrest figures are not distributed among these crimes as much as the boys' total arrest figures.

Table 3.2
Crimes as Causes of Arrest—Boys and Girls

Type of crime	1985	1994
Serious violent crime	4.9% of total arrests of males 2.1% of total arrests of females	6.6% of total arrests of males 3.4% of total arrests of females
Violent offenses (includes other assaults)	9.6% of total arrests of males 7.0% of total arrests of females	14.3% of total arrests of males 12.0% of total arrests of females
Status offenses	8.2% of total arrests of males 24.6% of total arrests of females	8.6% of total arrests of males 22.9% of total arrests of females

Adapted from Chesney-Lind, 1997, p. 13. Data from Federal Bureau of Investigation (1994) Crimes in the United States—1993, p. 222.

Chesney-Lind, using self-report and official data, concludes that both boys and girls participate in the type of activities that status offenses entail, yet girls are more likely to be arrested for such activities.[69] Alternatively, comparing official reports to self-reports, girls seem to be under-represented in official reports for other types of delinquency except for larceny/theft.[70]

An Increase in Crime?

There has been increasing public concern about a rise in juvenile crime, and part of the media's attention has been directed toward the female juvenile criminal. Determining exactly when this dramatic upswing in female juvenile crime is supposed to have occurred is somewhat problematic. By choosing certain years, it is certainly possible to identify large percentage increase figures, but looking at a longer span of time, one observes that the rise of female juvenile crime has been slow, inconsistent, and modest. Almost 20 years ago, Steffensmeier responded to alarm over the increase in female juvenile crime with a careful analysis of self-report data and official arrest statistics.[71] He concluded that females showed gains in larceny (shoplifting), liquor law violations, and runaways. He concluded that female gang membership had not affected female delinquency, that female delinquency showed no dramatic increase, and that what increase had occurred was consistent with traditional female sex roles.

Table 3.3
Female Juvenile Arrest Rates (per 100,000 Population, Ages 10-17)
Selected Offenses

Crime	1965	1975	1985	1989	1992
Homicide	*	1	*	*	1
Larceny/Theft	434	607	570	404	980
Aggravated assault	18	27	32	26	90
Robbery	7	17	13	11	29
Other assaults	53	73	111	109	n/a
Drugs	7	94	65	43	70

Years 1965 through 1989 adapted from Chesney-Lind, M., 1992, p. 13. Rates for 1992 from Poe-Yamagata, E. and J. Butts, 1996, pp. 6-7. Note: there may be problems with combining these two calculations of rates. Poe-Yamagata and Butts also report on arrest rates for 1983 that do not seem consistent with Chesney-Lind's data, i.e., larceny/theft-830; aggravated assault-45; robbery-19; drugs-98.

More recently, other authors note that there was a dramatic rise of female arrests between 1965 and 1975, but this increase fell off between 1976 and 1985.[72] This may account for the discrepancies in predictions and conclusions regarding any dramatic increase in female juvenile delinquency. While some reports, and popular media articles, issue dire warnings regarding a drastic rise in female crime, the numbers indicate a clear, but very moderate increase. Part of the confusion stems from what years are compared and how the comparison is made. In Table 3.4, one sees that arrest rates do not reflect large increases, and, in fact, have begun to show decreases.

One sees decreases in all Index crime categories between 1994 and 1995, except for aggravated assault. Although it is too soon to tell if this trend will continue, if it does, it flies in the face of most theories that predict increased female delinquency. Looking at Table 3.4, it is clear that official reports reflect official actions as well as offender behavior. Note, for instance, the very large increase in arrests for runaways. It seems unlikely that this large of an increase is due solely to a real increase of runaways; rather, it is probably at least partially due to policy changes that artificially increase the runaway figures (i.e., use of formal arrest or decision to count differently). Whether the decreases observed in Table 3.4 will continue, or whether they even reflect reality and are not an artifact of the measurement method, is difficult to say. However, it seems clear that any media claim to an epidemic of female juveniles seems, at best, overstated.

Girl Gangs

The very earliest gang research mentioned girl gangs, but the attention was slight and the analysis superficial.[73] More recent accounts diverge dramatically in their representations of girl gangs and the profile of the girl gang member. One view is that girl gang members are largely incidental contributors to the crimes committed by female juveniles and that girl gang members are no more criminal than non-gang juveniles.[74] Another view holds that girl gang members have become increasingly independent from their male gang members, more criminal, and more violent.[75] The differences in these two profiles may be due to methodology and definitional inconsistencies.

Girl gangs have always been seen as auxiliary gangs to boy gangs; girl gang members' contributions were seen as providing sex and as acting in minor ways to assist the violent and criminal activities of the male gang members. Campbell points out, however, that it is hard to tell what the role of the female gang member has been since most early writers were male and that probably affected their interpretation of female activities and membership.[76] Periodically there is a flurry of interest in girl gangs by the popular media. Girl gangs have been described as becoming more prevalent and violent than in years past, and acting no longer as just auxiliaries to male gangs, but undertaking violent and criminal actions on their own. Academic interest in girl gangs has also increased.

Table 3.4
Arrests of Females Under Eighteen—1994 and 1995

	1994	**1995**	**Change?**
Total	503,382	532,554	+
(Index Offenses)			
Homicide	178	158	–
Forcible rape	93	86	–
Robbery	4,258	4,078	–
Aggrav. assault	12,523	12,591	+
Burglary	10,568	10,092	–
Larceny/theft	126,949	125,871	–
Motor vehicle theft	9,919	9,215	–
Arson	1,088	948	–
(Part II Offenses)			
Other assaults	43,612	44,968	+
Forgery/ counterfeit	2,436	2,348	–
Fraud	4,751	4,868	+
Embezzlement	282	402	+
Stolen property	3,913	4,014	+
Vandalism	12,033	11,205	–
Weapons	4,062	3,507	–
Prostitution	487	504	+
Other sex offenses	1,063	894	–
Drugs	14,898	18,614	+
Gambling	73	61	–
Offenses against family	1,373	1,868	+
DUI	1,407	1,669	+
Liquor laws	25,421	25,448	+
Drunkenness	2,290	2,430	+
Disorderly conduct	30,274	32,055	+
Vagrancy	672	313	–
Curfew	29,434	34,011	+
Runaway	86,706	108,830	+
All other	72,619	71,184	–

Sources: FBI, Crime in the United States: Uniform Crime Reports. Washington, DC: U.S. Dept. of Justice, 1994, p. 226; and FBI, Crime in the United States: Uniform Crime Reports. Washington, DC: U.S. Dept. of Justice, 1995, p. 222.

Almost all the studies of female gangs have been phenomenological. That is, the studies have used observation and interview methods, providing a rich, textually complex picture of the life of the girl gang member. Descriptions of membership initiation, roles, rules, "colors," territoriality, discipline, specific philosophies, and feuds are some of the meanings provided in this type of study. One thing that these studies cannot do, however, is provide a good estimate of any increase in membership or changes in the violent activity of girl gang members.

One of the earliest descriptions of a girl gang was of the "Molls."[77] These girls were white, Catholic, and mostly Irish. They had extensive criminal records, starting at a very young age. Of the 11 members, five had been arrested. The most common charge was truancy, then theft (shoplifting) and drinking. Other female gangs studied showed more assaultive crimes than did the Molls, however and, compared to male gangs, no female gang was very criminal. The girls in this gang could not be described as "liberated." The gang was an auxiliary gang to a male gang and the girls evidently "gloried" in the idea that they were the property of boys.[78]

Quicker's study of Chicana gangs in East Los Angeles discussed 12 different gangs. Intensive interviews were conducted with 13 girls and less intensive interviews were undertaken with 30 more female gang members. In this study, gangs were described as substitute families for the girls. "Homegirls" provided the social support that families evidently could not provide, either because of poverty and overwork or because of neglect and abuse. Quicker found no instance of a completely independent girl gang and indicated that both boys and girls showed ambivalence regarding the appropriateness of girls being in a gang.[79]

There are evidently several ways to be initiated into the gang, somewhat related to whether the gang is associated with a boy's gang. One way is to be "jumped in," which meant the girl was pummeled by other gang members for a short period of time, either standing and taking it quietly, or fighting back. Other, less common, ways to be initiated were a "fair fight" where only one girl was selected to fight the initiate or getting "walked in," which occurred only by agreement. Another method of initiation, however, was getting "trained in," which means having sex with a number of boys in the gang. If the latter initiation occurs, researchers note that the girl is not respected and looked down upon as a tramp.[80]

Leaving the gang can be relatively passive, i.e., the girl simply stops hanging around with the gang; or, it could be through a "throw," meaning a fight with several girls.[81] Status changes such as marriage, pregnancy, or graduation from high school were the most common reasons for leaving. Others note that older girls and women may act as informal advisors or "ex-officio" members even though they are excused from playing a more active role after marriage or motherhood.[82]

Leadership tends to be more diffuse in girl gangs; the female gang seems more democratic with more decisionmaking by consensus rather than operating under a strict authoritarian structure.[83] Girls described how the gang was their family and their major interest and social outlet, because many of the members hated school.

The breakdown of the traditional Chicano culture was described by Quicker as partially responsible for the origin and growth of Chicana gangs. With fewer women accepting the traditional familial subservient role, there is a need to turn to peers for social support.

> Traditionally, women have found their major role and validation in their families as wives and mothers. Whereas boys were trained for the world, girls were trained for the home. . . . These traditional roles are undergoing modification within the Chicano family.[84]

Harris also described female gang members as challenging the Hispanic stereotype of the female as wife and mother.[85] The "homegirl" role provides the Latino girl more freedom, and more opportunity to engage in activities such as drinking and "hanging out." However, Latino girls still are controlled by the sex roles and stereotypes of their culture. Authors describe a sexual double standard whereby male gang members viewed girl gang members as tramps, even though they had relationships with them.[86] Far from being the vanguard of a new wave of women's liberation, most accounts of gang girls indicate that they hold very traditional views of sex roles, as do male gang members, as the following illustrates:

> To me a Queen [female gang member] is someone waiting for her man, to treat him like a King. If she has a kid, to take care of her kid. A Queen's job isn't to be out banging, it's to stay home and keep the house the way it was taught historically in the Latin race. There's no place for a girl in this. My Nation's business is none of her concern.[87]

Thus, females can join gangs, but they run the risk of being seen as merely a sexual object. Male and female juveniles continue to see the woman's role as homemaker, and gang membership continues to be less acceptable for female juveniles than for male juveniles.

Like a family, the gang also is a social control device. Almost all gang studies indicate that gang membership acts to control girls since they could only date boys in the associated gang.[88] The girls in the gang will police the sexual behavior of each other, especially if a girl begins to date outside the gang, dates a rival gang member, or is too predatory toward other girls' boyfriends.

Campbell's ethnological study of girl gangs in New York utilized an observation/interview method and covered six months with three different gangs in New York. The age ranges of the gang members were from 15 to 30.[89] Campbell offers the statistic that about 10 percent of all gang membership is female. Her estimates of the total number of female gang membership cover a range of 8,000 to 40,000, indicating the difficulty of determining membership at any one point in time, much less attempting to compare different time periods to determine any increase in gang membership. She offers the view that girls are not just auxiliaries anymore, but committing more of the crime associated with gang activity.

In her historical account of gangs in New York from the early 1800s forward, it becomes clear that females have always had a role in gangs and some females were very active in fighting and other criminal activity. Her more recent descriptions of female activities are typical—she describes girls as holding weapons, acting as lookouts, sometimes setting up a rival male gang member by agreeing to a date with him, and procuring younger girls for gang rapes. Reviewing other studies of gangs through the 1950s, 1960s, and 1970s, Campbell observed that some female gangs fought and enjoyed fighting, and some committed crimes. Thus, it is not clear whether girls' activities are changing, or whether researchers are beginning to see that the involvement of female juveniles in gang activity is more multifaceted than was first believed.

Campbell describes the female gang member as quite similar to the male gang member in some respects.

> The majority of gang girls, however, have a static class value orientation. They are not tortured by dreams of upward mobility and have a realistic view of their chances of success in society. They have not done well in school, and when they have money, they spend it. . . Like the boys in the neighborhood, they enjoy excitement and trouble, which break the monotony of a life in which little attention is given to the future. They like sharp clothes, loud music, alcohol, and soft drugs. They admire toughness and verbal "smarts."[90]

Campbell also offers a follow-up study of Hispanic girl gangs in New York.[91] Her description of their lives is bleak—almost all will have children, almost all will raise their children on welfare, and almost all will be socially controlled by men although not economically provided for by them. The gang is important for a short period of time before they settle into motherhood, it provides an escape from reality. The gang is largely a social outlet, providing fun by "hanging out" and/or partying with alcohol and drugs.

Lauderback et al. offer a description of an African-American female gang in San Francisco. These girls were engaged in crack sales and organized shoplifting ("boosting"), but gang membership also filled an emotional void in the lives of the girls. The authors also describe the girls' lives as hopeless with no opportunities and no expectation that they would be economically provided for by the fathers of their children.[92]

Joe and Chesney-Lind's study covers female gangs in Hawaii. They describe the gang in much the same way as that provided above. The gang provides escape from abuse and violence in the home, and offers an antidote to boredom and hopelessness. While fighting was a common pastime for boys, girls were more likely to dance than fight. Joe and Chesney-Lind describe the girl gang as smaller than those of boys, with the favorite activities listed as sports, drinking, and hanging out (for boys it was drinking, fighting, cruising, and looking for girls). About three-quarters of the girls had been physically abused (compared to 55% of the boys), and 62 percent of the girls reported sexual abuse. Most of the girls and boys had other family members in gangs. Joe and Chesney-Lind describe the gang as taking the place of family in these youngsters' lives. Both boys and girls tended to stay away from home because of abuse, neglect, or general disruption. Gangs provided the social support that was unavailable through the family. The researchers also observed that the presence of girls tended to suppress fighting by the male gang members, and the fighting engaged in by the girls should be understood within the larger context of Samoan and island culture where fighting was quite commonplace, outside or inside of a gang.[93]

Taylor provides yet another account of female gang membership.[94] This study was of young, African-American women in Detroit. Introducing new terminology into the literature, Taylor's interviewees spoke of their gangs as "posses" or "crews." Taylor's description echoed many of the points above, i.e., that the gang filled a void in members' lives, that the home life of gang members was dysfunctional and probably abusive. However, his portrayal of gang members' activities described a much more criminalistic outlook, more criminal activities, and more violent criminal activity. Taylor described a typology of different gang types, i.e., "scavenger gangs," which drift in and out of crime as opportunity presents itself; "territorial gangs," which hold power over geographic boundaries; "commercial gangs," which have a product and an organization to sell it; and "corporate gangs," which have an infrastructure not unlike any business in corporate America. Of these types, women were involved in all types, even the corporate (which meant that females ran fairly large-scale drug rings). Scavenger gangs were described as women and children banding together for begging and other hustles. Taylor's work stretches the definitional boundaries of youth gangs since many of his "posse" girls were in their late twenties and some of the descriptions indicated that the groupings were transitory and bore little resemblance to the highly structured male gangs in Los Angeles and New York City.

Chesney-Lind criticizes Taylor's work as reinforcing the idea that women are becoming more violent.[95] She points out that it is not clear how many gang members were interviewed, thus calling into question the representativeness of the sampled gang members. However, this criticism could be applied to most of the studies above. Phenomenological studies provide context and meaning, but they do little to shed light on prevalence or changes in gang activity over time. Another criticism that can be leveled at most of the studies above is the looseness of the definition of gang member; many gangs claim membership by individuals in their late twenties and even thirties. It stretches the definition of such groupings as youth gangs to the breaking point and calls into question the whole practice of trying to identify gangs (as opposed to groups of friends, clubs, loose associations of friends, etc.). While these definitional issues have been dealt with in the gang literature, the few studies available on female gangs have not utilized the stringent definitions that are beginning to be agreed upon in the law enforcement community and interested academics.

Sikes offers a journalistic account of girl gangs, covering San Antonio, Los Angeles, and Milwaukee. Sikes describes the double standard that girls feel, since girls are, in general, disparaged by male gang members:

> . . . feminine attributes are disparaged. "Bitch," "girl," or "faggot" are the worst insults one can sling at a man. The notion of femininity is complicated, even for gang girls. Although some feminine girls secure a role beyond that of a seductive informer or spy . . . inevitably their biology holds them back.[96]

Her descriptions also echo those above citing dysfunctional home lives of gang girls. Often abused or neglected, the girls tend to seek in the gang those attributes commonly associated with one's family—love, acceptance, and support.

Chesney-Lind and Sheldon reviewed previous research on girl gangs and concluded that older research found girl gangs existed as auxiliaries for boys, but also that members were more violent than non-gang members (although much less so than male gang members).[97] They carried weapons for male gang members, acted as spies, drank alcohol, and provided sexual favors. They also reported that more recent studies show more independence among female gangs. In a later review, Chesney-Lind comments that early studies such as Thrasher's 1927 study, Miller's 1958 study, and Cohen's 1955 study, ignored the girl gangs they studied in the early part of the twentieth century and, for the most part, the gang literature that is emerging today is also ignoring any female gangs discovered,[98] except for those studies that focus exclusively on female gangs.[99]

Curry et al. report that law enforcement estimates that 3.6 percent of all gangs are "girl gangs," and girls account for 13.6 percent of gang related property crime, 12.7 percent of drug crime, and 3.3 percent of violent crime.[100] Others estimate that 33 percent of all gang membership in Los Angeles is girls, although this is by far the highest estimate given in the literature, the average being about 10 percent.[101] Joe and Chesney-Lind report that about seven percent of Oahu's gangs were composed of females.[102] One definitional problem illustrated by their statistics, however, is the problem of describing these as "girls" since about 78 percent of female gang members were legally adults and 33 percent of them were older than 26.

We have no clear perception as to whether or to what extent there has been an increase in female gang membership. A different question is whether gang girls are participating in more crimes, and especially more violent crimes than in the past. Chesney-Lind found in a detailed study of girl gangs in Honolulu that the girls police identified as gang members showed a similar pattern of delinquency as non-gang-related girl delinquents; for both groups, the most common arrest was for larceny/theft. For male gang members, the arrest pattern represented more violent crime by gang members than delinquents not related to a gang. In a matched sample of gang and non-gang-related delinquents in Honolulu, Chesney-Lind found that gang-related girls were most likely to be picked up for status offenses, and for non-gang girls, the reason for formal intervention was "other assaults."[103]

There has been extensive media coverage of the "new" trend of girl gangs, describing them as "violent as the boys." *The New York Times, Wall Street Journal, Time,* and *Newsweek* all ran stories in the early 1990s on female gangs.[104] Television news shows and local news broadcasts also did stories complete with girl gang members profiled that sought to illustrate the "new" violent girl criminal. This is described by Chesney-Lind as virtually a repeat of the news splash in the early 1970s on the rise of female crime; the question is, does it reflect reality? Examining the evidence for such a trend, Chesney-Lind reports that there was an increase of 143 percent of girls arrested for "other assaults" between 1985 and 1994 and arrest rates for violent offenses do show double and triple digit increases over the last 10 years; however, boys' rates went up as well. Violent crime as a percent of total arrests showed very little change; the girls' percent of total arrests for violent crime went up from 11 percent to 14 percent between 1985 and 1994—hardly an earth-shattering increase.[105] One cannot even be sure how much of the assault and homicide figures are gang-related. For instance, there are differences in patterns of homicide with girls more likely to murder family members alone during a conflict and boys more likely to murder non-family members with accomplices.[106] The latter is obviously more likely to be gang-related, but it would be difficult to identify and isolate these factors in official statistics.

To conclude, there have always been a small number of girls involved in gangs. Usually these gangs have been auxiliaries to male gangs. It is unclear to what extent girls took an active role in gang crime historically; our descriptions are too fragmented and subject to researcher-bias in the extent and meaning attributed to the girls' role in gang activity. Today juvenile women do participate in some crime, including violent crime, although to a far lesser degree than that of their male counterparts. The role of the gang for girls may also be different than for boys. Her sexuality continues to be emphasized, indicated by initiation rituals, dating codes, the use of female members to "set up" rival male gang members, and the likely exit from gang life once she becomes a mother. Her membership is a double-edged sword; gang membership brings acceptance, some protection, and social support, but also she lives with a double standard and male gang members look down upon her. Only those few female gang members who can compete equally on a physical level with males and do not engage in multiple sexual relationships are exempt from this double standard.

A more important question is to what extent gang activity contributes to criminality. In the few studies that looked at this question directly, it is far from clear that gangs account for much female delinquency at all. The two views of female gang members described above (i.e., that they continue to be largely social outlets for drinking and socializing with boys; and the view that they are increasingly becoming independent from male gangs and more criminal) cannot be reconciled because they are derived from different ways of looking at reality. Those researchers who talked to girl gang members generally support the idea of increased membership and increased violence and criminality. However, their data are confined to those women who express support for violence and crime, who actively participate in criminal activities, and who follow criminal lifestyles. These young women are great persuaders that gang membership is growing more violent. But are they representative of all girls, or just as exceptional as the few violent female gang members in the early 1900s? Few studies attempt to look at self-report or official data to discover whether there are changes in gang-related crime for female juveniles. Until such studies are done, there is little cause to believe that female gang membership is a major problem across the country.

RACE AND CRIME

Statistics indicate that adult minority women and girls may present different crime patterns than white women and girls. Some studies indicate that minority women are more likely to commit serious crime. Recall that certain studies described above reported that Chicana female drug addicts were more likely to engage in more serious crimes than white female drug addicts[107] Studies of domestic homicide indicate that minority women are more likely to kill their partners than white women.[108] Minority women were also found to be more likely to be chronic (versus non-chronic) offenders among incarcerated female inmates in Florida.[109]

Other studies also indicate that minority women may be more likely than white women to engage in crimes of violence and that the gender gap between minority women and minority men is less than that between white women and men. One early collection of information on incarcerated African-American women showed that crime among African-Americans was less sexually differentiated, but also that the system may discriminate against African-American female defendants.[110] The study of female violent criminals in New York utilized arrest data and arrest histories of 266 women and concluded that Hispanic and African-American women exhibited higher rates of violent offending relative to white females.[111] Minority women's rates, in fact, paralleled those of white males.[112] The authors argue that this pattern is a product of "the effects of the social and institutional transformation of the inner city." Crime was described as a way of coping with the hopelessness and despair of city ghetto living. They also found that violence and drug involvement were linked and race was associated with drug involvement.[113]

Chilton and Datesman, after analyzing arrest figures for larceny for the years 1960 through 1980, present evidence that indicates that non-white women were largely responsible for the increase in property crimes (larceny), and that non-white women's rates of such crime paralleled white men's.[114] Thus, it seems to be the case that official statistics show that minority women are responsible for a disproportionate amount of crime in this country, and that they are even more likely to engage in crimes of violence than white women.

Why this might be so is a complicated subject that has been addressed by a number of excellent sources.[115] One potential explanation is differential treatment by the criminal justice system. There is certainly some evidence that indicates minority women do not receive any "chivalrous" treatment that may or may not exist in the system for white women.[116] Like African-Americans and Hispanics, Native American women contribute disproportionate numbers to prison populations. In South Dakota, for instance, where Native Americans are only seven percent of the population, Indian women represent 44 percent of the state's prison population. In Alaska, Native Americans make up one-third of prison populations, and in Montana, 28 percent of the prison population is Native American.[117] Whether these statistics tell us more about criminal behavior patterns or more about the system's differential treatment of minority versus white citizens, is a difficult question.

Even assuming higher rates of crime, the criminal choices of African-American, Chicana, Native American, and other minority women cannot be understood without also an understanding of the larger reality that surrounds those choices.[118] Chilton and Datesman present a number of alternative explanations to address the disproportional contribution of minority women to crime rates. They reject the masculinization hypothesis (that African-American women are socialized to be more masculine) and conclude that the best explanation for the criminality of minority women is their economic condition of poverty. African-American women are the most likely of all demographic groups to head a household under the poverty line. They are more likely than white women to be unemployed, and, if employed, their average wage is the lowest of any group (white men, white women, minority men all earn a higher average wage).[119]

Poverty leads to other realities. Maternal mortality rates for African-American women are almost four times higher than those of white women.[120] In the mid 1990s, about 65 percent of births in the African-American community were to unmarried mothers (compared to 20% for whites).[121] African-American women are twice as likely to be reported as white women to formal authorities for drug use (despite similar use rates), and 10 times more likely to be drug-tested in public hospitals than white women.[122] Native American women are, when compared to national averages, less educated, give birth at a younger age, have less income, and are a higher risk for motor vehicle accidents, homicide, and alcoholism.[123] Minority women are more likely than white women to be victimized sexually and physically—both as children and as adults. They are more likely to come from broken families and dysfunctional families where alcohol, drugs, and criminality affect their childhood. Minority women are probably more likely to join youth gangs for protection and social support. They may also be more likely to be part of criminal networks.[124]

Race and Juvenile Female Crime

Official statistics and self-report studies seem to indicate that African-American and Hispanic female juveniles commit more violent crimes than do Caucasian girls. For instance, African-American girls have higher rates of homicide and aggravated assault than white girls, and African-American girls participate in UCR violent offenses 5.5 times more often than white girls.[125]

Chesney-Lind and Sheldon report mixed findings from studies comparing race and gender; some show African-American females are more similar to white females, some show them more similar to white males. Offense patterns are slightly different—non-white females are more likely to engage in weapons and violent crimes, and white females are more likely to be involved in drugs, liquor, and family offenses (running away or defying parental authority).[126]

Other studies urge caution and find little or no difference in participation rates between white and non-white females. Since there are considerable differences in certain years, the selection of years one analyzes makes a great difference in the conclusions drawn regarding the relative rates of participation in crime of white and non-white women.

CONCLUSION

Crime is only one element in the reality of life for minority women and girls. To what extent race or poverty or both affect the meaning of crime and the choice of crime is a difficult and complicated question. To what extent race and poverty affect drug use which, in turn, affects criminality is also a complicated issue. The statistics that tell us that minority women contribute a disproportionate share of arrests of women cannot tell us the meaning behind those numbers. An even greater problem is that arrest numbers cannot tell us in any great detail about the crime committed—crime categories are somewhat arbitrary and arrest figures do not capture meaning, motivation, or extent of harm.

NOTES

[1]   The National Drug Control Stategy (1997, 10).

[2]   UCR (1995, 225).

[3]   DUF (1996).

[4]   Merlo (1995).

[5]   Mann (1984b, 39).

[6]   Rosenbaum (1981, 71).

[7]   1981, 20.

[8]   See Bowker (1978), Hser, Anglin, and Booth (1987b, 248), and Boyd and Mast (1993).

[9]   Rosenbaum (1981, 30).

[10]   1981, 31 and 51.

[11]   1981, 60.

[12]   1981, 97.

[13]   1981, 132.

[14]   Inciardi (1980).

[15]   Inciardi et al. (1993), also see Inciardi and Pottieger (1986).

[16]   This phenomenon was also described by Fullilove et al. (1992) and Chesney-Lind (1997); also see Maher and Curtis (1992) and Maher and Daly (1996).

[17]   Fullilove et al. (1992) and Inciardi et al. (1993).

[18]   Quote from Taylor (1993, 194).

[19]   1993.

[20]   P. Adler (1993, 4).

[21]   Huling (1995) also describes the role of "mules" in the drug world—these women are sometimes economically or physically coerced into such activity or duped to unwittingly smuggle drugs secreted in objects and clothing by friends who are dealers.

[22]   1993, 90.

[23]   Other authors such as Maher and Daly (1996), Dunlap, Johnson, and Maher, (1997), and Maher and Curtis (1992) describe situations in which women street dealers are beaten up for coming up "short," and even pregnant women are attacked if they steal from a dealer/boss.

[24]   1996.

[25]   Dunlap, Johnson, and Maher (1997).

[26]   One portion of the study reported on street-level sex work by crack addicts. Many of the addicts interviewed described how they were introduced to drugs by boyfriends, how they resorted to sex work because of no opportunities (for legal or illegal economic gain) other than prostitution, how sex work was not paying as well as it used to because women desperate for crack would underbid the street prostitutes, and that there was more violence—both by "johns," strangers who robbed them for their money or even clothing, and by other women working the street. Maher and Curtis (1992).

[27]   Morgan and Joe (1997).

[28]   Maher and Daly (1996) also point out that one-time interviews are less accurate in obtaining information than ethnographic studies, such as theirs, that cover a longer range of time and consist of multiple interviews over time with the same informants.

[29]   See, for instance, Snell and Morton (1994), Fletcher et al. (1993), or Pollock (1998).

[30]   See, for instance, Pollock (1998).

[31]   Bloom et al. (1994, 5) and Pollock (1998, 76).

[32]   DUF (1995).

[33]   Hser, Anglin, and Booth (1987), also see Anglin and Hser (1987).

[34]   Townes, James, and Martin (1981)

[35]   National Institute of Justice (1993, 5).

[36]   1997, 99.

[37]   1994.

[38]   Bloom et al. 1994.

[39]   Deschenes and Anglin (1992) and Hser, Anglin, and Chou (1992) report that women caught in the criminal justice system are more likely than men to have problems with drugs in the system.

[40]   Anglin and Hser (1987); also see Hser, Anglin, and Booth (1987).

[41]   Sanchez and Johnson (1987) interviewed 175 female inmates of Riker's Island. Although the sample was not random, findings described the women as heavy drug users (more than two-thirds used heroin or cocaine daily) (1987, 207). Most reported property crimes and drug sales as the type of crimes committed in the six-month period before incarceration—property crimes accounting for one-half of all crimes. Non-users reported an average of one crime during the previous six-month period; soft drug users reported an average of 105 crimes and cocaine or heroin users reported an average of 212 crimes (1987, 208). Fletcher et al. (1993, 49) also report that drug-addicted women commit three to five times the amount of crime as non-drug addicted women. Inciardi et al. (1993) report that while heroin and narcotics tend to be associated with prostitution and property crime, crack cocaine is more likely to be linked to violent crime, drug dealing, and sex trading.

[42]   Baskin and Sommers (1993, 572-573).

[43]   See, for instance, Kermode and Walker (1994).

[44]   See Mann (1984b), Chesney-Lind (1997), and Rafter (1985).

[45]   Rosenbaum (1980).

[46]   See Chesney-Lind and Sheldon (1992).

[47]   Chesney-Lind (1997).

[48]   James (1976).

[49]   This query is beyond the scope of this book; however, it is important to point out that even though there has seemingly been an increase of male prostitutes, especially teenage male prostitutes (in fact in 1994 there were more male juvenile arrests for prostitution than there were of female juveniles, 510 per 100,000 versus 487 per 100,000), these boys provide sexual services to men, rarely women. Thus, prostitution has been and continues to be a crime largely whereby sex is provided to men (UCR:1994, 226).

[50]   Blank (1993, 57-61).

[51]   Rafter (1980) and (1988).

[52] In *Buck v. Bell*, 274 U.S. 200 (1927), Oliver Wendell Holmes uttered the famous quote to support the holding: "three generations of imbeciles are enough . . ." (274 U.S. at 297 [1927]). One might wonder if he would have proposed the same rationale toward criminals.

[53] Blank (1993, 68).

[54] See Merlo (1993), Sagatun (1993), Humphries et al. (1992), Humphries (1993), Pollock-Byrne and Merlo (1991), Feinman (1992), Maher (1992), and Bagley and Merlo (1995).

[55] Bagley and Merlo (1995, 138)

[56] Pollock-Byrne and Merlo (1991).

[57] Feinman (1992).

[58] This is a legal term meaning uniqueness, it is applied to a case or circumstance that stands alone and is distinct from all others.

[59] UCR (1995, 226).

[60] As discussed in the first chapter, there are some troubling issues regarding the use of official statistics. At least the table represents clearly the contribution of women to total arrests unlike percentage increase figures that calculate an increase in each baseline number. For instance, Kelley et al. (1997, 2) report for 1991-1995 (almost the same time period represented in Table 3.1), an alarming 34 percent increase in violent crime Index arrests for young women, compared to only a nine percent increase for male juveniles. Yet looking at the table, the largest increase is for aggravated assault and female juveniles increased their participation from 13.53 percent of arrests for aggravated assault to 18.58 percent of total arrests—not exactly as dramatic as "nearly four times the male juvenile increase," but arguably much clearer.

[61] Chesney-Lind (1978).

[62] For instance, Weis (1976) found that the patterns of delinquency were similar for girls and boys, although boys committed significantly more delinquent acts. Datesman and Scarpetti (1980a, 1980b) also found that the patterns of delinquency for boys and girls were similar, noting that the general assumption that girls were more likely to engage in sexual deviance was probably more a function of official intervention than actual behavior.

[63] Figueira-McDonough et al. (1981, 21-22).

[64] Feyerherm (1981a, 1981b).

[65] Chesney-Lind and Sheldon (1992, 16).

[66] Triplett and Myers (1995).

[67] Kelley et al. (1997) report on a large self-report study conducted with female and male offenders in Denver and Rochester that asked about violent crimes. It is difficult to integrate these findings with others above because the purpose and data collection methods were different. Rather than random samples, researchers collected probability samples. Interviews were conducted face-to-face, which might have increased or decreased accuracy. Rather than a measure of all crime, measures of serious violence were obtained by asking youths about aggravated assault, robbery, rape, and gang fights. Overall, findings were consistent with other research that indicates females account for small percentages of total violent crime. However, there were some interesting differences. First, extreme differences in the self-reported delinquency between youths in cities sampled were obtained that exceeded, in some cases, the gender differential. For instance, while about

five percent of 13-year-old girls in Denver reported any violent delinquent acts, closer to 18 percent of 13-year-old girls in Rochester admitted such acts and this percentage exceeded that reported by 13-year-old boys in Rochester and Denver. Whether a juvenile has ever committed a violent act is a different issue than asking how many violent acts have been committed. In both cities that sampled female juveniles, it was found that juvenile women reported far less numbers of violent acts than did their male counterparts. Findings also indicated, however, that Rochester girls displayed violence rates of prevalence and incidence that were much closer to those of male juveniles and much higher than those of female juveniles in Denver. The meaning of these findings are not clear, however, they do point to the need for caution in extrapolating city self-report data to the rest of the country. Our views on the general nature of female juvenile violence would be different depending on if we only looked at the Rochester data or only looked at the Denver data.

[68]   Chesney-Lind (1997, 13).

[69]   (1997, 14), also see Chesney-Lind and Sheldon (1992, 20).

[70]   Chesney-Lind comments on other changes in official reporting of girls and boys delinquency and offers the possibility that decreases in the "gender gap" in some crime areas could be due to changes in official enforcement patterns as well as any real changes in boys and girls behavior.

[71]   Steffensmeier (1980).

[72]   Chesney-Lind and Sheldon (1992, 11).

[73]   See, for instance, Thrasher (1927).

[74]   Joe and Chesney-Lind (1993).

[75]   Taylor (1993), Campbell (1990).

[76]   1984, also see 1990.

[77]   Miller (1980).

[78]   Miller (1980, 243-245 and 248).

[79]   Quicker (1983, 10).

[80]   Qucker (1983, 14). Also see Portillos and Zatz (1995), and Campbell (1984).

[81]   Quicker (1983, 20).

[82]   Sikes (1997).

[83]   Quicker (1983, 22).

[84]   Quicker (1983, 41).

[85]   Harris (1988).

[86]   Moore (1991).

[87]   Sikes (1997, 199).

[88]   Quicker (1983). Also see Campbell (1984).

[89]   This calls into question the practice of discussing gangs as largely a problem of youth.

90   1984, 7.

91   1990.

92   1992.

93   1993.

94   1993.

95   Chesney-Lind (1997).

96   Sikes (1997, 253).

97   1992.

98   See, for instance, Jankowski (1991).

99   See, for instance, Campbell (1984 and 1990), Harris (1988) and Quicker (1983).

100 Curry et al. (1994, 8).

101 Moore (1991), also see Moore and Hagedorn (1995).

102 1993, 8.

103 Chesney-Lind (1993, 338). Qucker also pointed out that the vast majority of gang activity was not criminal (1983, 74).

104 Chesney-Lind (1997, 33).

105 Chesney-Lind (1997, 39).

106 Chesney-Lind (1997, 40).

107 Anglin and Hser (1987) and Hser, Anglin, and Booth (1987).

108 Dawson (1994).

109 Danner et al. (1995).

110 French (1978 and 1983).

111 Baskin, Sommers, and Fagan (1993) and Sommers and Baskin (1992, 1993).

112 Sommers and Baskin (1992, 191).

113 1992, 198.

114 Chilton and Datesman (1987).

115 See, for instance, Tonry (1995), Mann (1993), and Lewis (1981).

116 Chilton and Datesman (1987, 166).

117 Lujan (1995, 13).

118 Henriques (1995).

119 Chilton and Datesman (1987, 166-167).

120 Maher (1992, 57).

121 Merlo (1995, 123).

[122]   Maher (1992, 59).

[123]   Lujan (1995, 10).

[124]   Alarid et al. (1996) found, in a study of incarcerated women, that African-American women were more often members of female "deviant networks" than were Anglo or Hispanic women that engaged in a variety of criminal activities.

[125]   Simpson (1991, 117-118).

[126]   1992, 122.

An Increase in Crime or
a Decrease in Chivalry?

4

Objectives

- Become aware of the findings that indicate women are not dramatically increasing their participation in violent crime, but there have been increases in consumer crime categories.

- Become familiar with the evidence that indicates that preferential treatment might have existed in the past but the presence of differential sentencing for men and women is complicated by factors such as family circumstance, criminal history, and race.

- Note that the best studies of sentencing disparity look "behind the numbers" to determine what other factors are being used for judicial sentencing decisions.

This chapter addresses two related questions. First, has there been an increase in crime by women, and if so, has it been greater than a corresponding increase by men? Second, has the system treated women more chivalrously, and have there been changes in that chivalry?

CRIME TRENDS: ARE CRIMES BY WOMEN INCREASING?

In 1975 Freda Adler and Rita Simon both offered versions of a new social problem—the rise of female criminals. Adler proposed that women's liberation had opened the door to equal opportunity in illegitimate spheres, including what had been traditional male areas of crime, i.e., assault, robbery, and homicide. The emancipation theory or masculinity thesis, as Adler's theory came to be known, implied that women were becoming more like men, including developing a more aggressive nature that they exhibited in criminal activities.[1] Simon's hypothesis was similar, but she offered the explanation that women would not necessarily become more aggressive, but they would take advantage of employment opportunities to engage in such crimes as embezzlement and workplace fraud. Simon believed that women's involvement in violent crime would not increase because when women killed, it was usually out of frustration and anger and they usually killed a man. Increased economic and social independence would decrease "their feelings of being victimized and exploited. . . and their motivation to kill will become muted."[2]

Both theorists used percentage increases as their statistical support for the hypothesis that women were increasing their level of participation in criminal activities. And percentage increases were quite startlingly large. However, later criticism pointed out that percentage increases are a very poor method for studying actual participation in crime since women's small numbers affect the percentage increase number.[3] So while women's percentage increases looked huge, the base numbers were very small in relation to men's. Looking at women's percentage of the total arrest numbers, or looking at women's arrest rates (per 100,000) over time, are other ways to analyze changes in women's crime rates. These methods provided a different—less dramatic—picture of women's criminality. One thing was clear—women did not increase their percentage of violent crime during the years they should have been affected by the women's liberation movement.[4] Also, recent increases in women's percentage of arrests for aggravated assault are almost completely responsible for the increase in women's increased percentage of violent crime arrests, since their arrests for homicide and robbery, as a percentage of total arrests, have remained stable or decreased (See Tables 4.1 and 4.2). Women's participation in property crime, however, has risen and continues to rise, although there is some dispute about what type of crimes this increase represents. Tables 4.1, 4.2, and 4.3 provide some information regarding the increased arrest rates of women.

Table 4.1
**Women's Participation in Crime as Percentage of Total;
Violent Crime and Property Crime**

Year	Women as Percentage of Total Arrested for:	
	Violent Crime	**Property Crime**
1965	10.2	14.1
1970	9.6	18.7
1975	10.3	21.7
1980	10.0	21.0
1985	10.9	24.0
1990	11.3	25.3
1995	14.9	27.3

Violent crimes include: homicide, forcible rape, robbery, and aggravated assault.
Property crimes include: burglary, larceny/theft, and auto theft.
Adapted from Simon and Landis, 1991, p. 46. Years 1990 and 1995 added from UCR, 1990, p. 191 and 1995, p. 225.

Table 4.2
Male and Female Arrest Rates per 100,000 for 1960/61, 1975/76, and 1989/90

	Male Arrest Rates			Female Arrest Rates		
	1960/61	1975/76	1989/90	1960/61	1975/76	1989/90
Homicide	9	16	16	2	2	2
Aggravated assault	102	200	317	16	28	50
Robbery	65	131	124	3	10	12
Burglary	274	477	320	9	27	31
Larceny	291	749	859	74	321	403
Fraud	70	114	157	12	58	132
Public drunkenness	2,573	1,201	624	212	87	71
DWI	344	971	1,193	21	80	176
Drug violations	50	522	815	8	79	166
Gambling	202	60	14	19	6	2
Other/nontraffic	871	1,140	2,109	150	197	430
Total	7,060	7,850	9,211	831	1,384	2,122

Source: Steffensmeier and Streifel, 1993, p. 67.

Table 4.3
Females Arrested as Percentage of Total: Selected Crime Categories

Crime	Percentage of total arrests (female)/year			
	1965	1975	1985	1995
Homicide	15.4	14.9	12.4	9.5
Robbery	5.2	7.0	7.6	9.3
Aggravated assault	13.5	13.1	13.5	17.7
Burglary	3.7	5.4	7.4	11.1
Larceny	22.1	30.7	31.0	33.3
Auto theft	4.2	7.0	9.3	13.1
Embezzlement	17.2	31.1	35.6	43.6
Fraud	20.3	34.2	42.6	41.0
Forgery/ counterfeiting	19.8	28.9	33.2	35.9
Offenses against family	8.8	11.7	12.7	20.2
Drug laws	13.4	13.8	13.8	16.7
Prostitution	77.5	74.3	69.5	61.1

Adapted from Simon and Landis, 1991, pp. 46, 52. Year 1995 added from UCR, 1995, p. 225.

Adler continued in later work to utilize percentage increases to support the notion that female criminality was increasing at unprecedented rates, although she did accept that absolute numbers remained small.[5] She also enlarged the scope of inquiry to other countries. Developing countries, according to Adler, would see their women's crime rate rise in relation to the extent to which women participated in economic development and attained economic equality with their male counterparts.[6] Her hypothesis included the notion that: "Where the restraining influence of family control continues, female criminality remains at a low level."[7] The data collected to test this theory of economic development and women's criminality included economic indicators and official crime rates. As Table 4.4 shows, findings did not provide overwhelming support for the thesis. While there was a general trend in the direction predicted, some countries did not seem to fit the model and there were lower rates of arrests in some developed countries than one might expect.

Table 4.4
Regional Distribution of Crime Rates per 100,000 Population, 1970/75

Offender	Country					
	N. Africa/ Middle East	Asia	Eastern Europe	Latin America	Caribbean	W. Europe/ N. America
Male adult	624.0	537.4	427.2	121.1	1,498.6	1,051.3
Female adult	45.2	48.1	68.0	16.6	181.9	128.5
Male juvenile	7.4	32.6	53.3	7.8	116.6	154.6
Female juvenile	1.0	2.2	3.7	2.2	15.6	33.6

Report of the Secretary General on Crime Prevention and Control A/32/199. Reported in F. Adler (1981) *The Incidence of Female Criminality in the Contemporary World.* NY: New York University Press, p. 7.

Adler reiterated Pollak's idea that women's crime is hidden to explain why Western European rates are not as high as the theory of economic development would indicate.

> That female arrest and conviction rates (especially in the adult category) are not higher is attributed to the chivalry or courtesy factors, that is, hesitancy on the part of a predominantly male officialdom to apply the rigors of the law to women. Possibly, then, the dark figure of female criminality is higher than the male dark figure.[8]

It is unclear why chivalry would operate differentially throughout the years, which would be the only way it could affect the data to undercut the theory that economic development and greater equality for women affected the crime rates.[9] Steffensmeier, Allen, and Streifel also compared crime rates and various economic indicators across developing and developed nations and concluded that the data did not fit the "liberation" theory as well as they fit a theory that increased criminality by women came about through more opportunity for consumer crimes (i.e., more radios to steal), and a theory that proposed that developed countries use more formal means of social control that reduces differential treatment for women.[10]

Simon also maintained her original thesis was correct and in a later edition of her 1975 work, reiterated the thesis that women's liberation enabled women to take advantage of white-collar positions of responsibility to engage in crime.[11]

> The opportunity thesis posits that as the employment patterns of men and women become more similar, so too will their patterns of employment-related crimes. . . . As for violent acts, the argument advanced in the first edition claims that as women become more economically self sufficient (a function of their increased education and labor force participation), they will be less likely to play the role of victim. As they become less beholden to men for their economic and social status, they will gain self-esteem and confidence. In turn, such women will be more likely to extricate themselves from situations of verbal and physical abuse before they reach a level of desperation at which only the death of the abusive person can release them from their torment.

Simon and Landis, to support their thesis that women are engaging in more workplace-related crime, argue that women's larceny/theft arrests dramatically increased as a percentage of the total crimes committed by women.[12] One might argue, however, that percentage increases in any crime category as a percentage of women's total crime are not very helpful in answering the question of whether women overall are committing more crime.[13] In a similar manner, changes in men's activity in certain crime categories will affect the women's percentage of total arrests, i.e., if men committed fewer burglaries and burglaries committed by women held steady, there would be an apparent increase reflected for women since the percentage of total arrests of women would increase.

Further, arrest numbers do not tell us much about actual but unreported crime, how much was stolen, from where it was stolen, and so on. Steffensmeier agrees that the greatest difference in arrest profiles of women between 1960 and 1990 is the greater involvement of women in crimes such as larceny and fraud, but he is unpersuaded that these illustrate advances women have made in employment, arguing that the numbers come from crimes of shoplifting, passing bad checks, credit card fraud, theft of services, welfare fraud, and small con games.[14] Further, he compares self-report data and data from the National Crime Survey (victimization data) to official arrest numbers and proposes that these sources show a much less serious increase of women's crime over the years 1973 through 1990. He also points out that greater bureaucratization and more formal methods of policing have probably artificially inflated women's arrest numbers. For instance, he points out that today "unknown" is used less often on UCR forms asking for the sex of the offender. In the past, these were automatically counted as men and so some amount of crime by women was incorrectly attributed to men. He also points out that police practice today may be more likely to arrest a female crime partner in order to get her to inform on her male partner as part of a plea agreement.[15] While these possibilities may not account for large numbers, they do illustrate the multitude of factors that affect our crime numbers quite apart from an offender actually committing a crime.

Chesney-Lind reports on percentage changes in arrests between men and women for the years 1985 through 1994.[16] She finds the largest increases for women in aggravated assault (110%), other assaults (126%), drug abuse violations (100%), and offenses against family and children (265%). She also notes that in crime categories in which women showed an increase of activity, men also posted large increases, although not quite as large. Overall, women's crime increased about 36 percent and men's crime 15 percent. Some of the apparent larger percentage of women's arrests to men's arrests for certain crimes were due to major decreases in some men's areas, i.e., gambling for men showed a 44 percent decrease, vagrancy a 43 percent decrease.

Merlo, after noting the increases of women in many areas of crime, points out that other changes in society may be partially responsible. For instance, she observes that more women now are heads of single-parent households—57 percent of children who lived only with their mother were below poverty line. Further, the earnings of women do not equal those of men; in 1992, men averaged weekly earnings of $505, compared to $381 for women.[17] Steffensmeier also points to economic factors in the increase of crime by women.

> Rising rates of divorce, illegitimacy, and female-headed households, coupled with continued segregation of women in low-paying occupations, have aggravated the economic pressures on women and have left them more responsible for child care than they were two or three decades ago. Growing economic adversity increases the pressures to commit consumer-based crimes such as shoplifting, check fraud, theft of services, and welfare fraud.[18]

One final note: very few of the studies of crime trends cover more than 30 or 40 years. Mukherjee and Fitzgerald,[19] in a careful analysis of female crime trends in Australia, illustrate the dangers of making predictions based on too narrow of a time focus. In their study of 75 years of crime rates, they discovered that women's participation in crime was U-shaped, higher in the early part of the twentieth century, falling during the war years, and rising again in the 1950s through the 1970s. One might have assumed that the crime trend data were solidly supportive of any emancipation or liberation thesis if one looked only at the latter half of the twentieth century, but such a theory definitely would not explain why women's crime rates were also higher in the first part of the century when, arguably, they were at their most oppressed. Thus, it is important to take a longer view, if one intends to use crime rates to show patterns over time.

Another issue entirely, of course, is how well crime rates represent reality at all. Percentage increase figures are influenced by the size of the base number. Percentage of total figures are influenced by increases or decreases by male offenders in that crime category. Percentage of total women's crime figures are likewise influenced by increases or decreases in other crime categories. All of the above are influenced by the efficiency with which arrests are counted, since they all use UCR arrest figures. Arrest figures, of course, are influenced by formal or informal policies of arrest and changes in the clearance rate for crime categories. These influences presumably grow stronger when a longer time period is used to compare crimes rates because of reporting and system changes. Another issue that may affect arrest figures is the so-called chivalry hypothesis.

THE CHIVALRY HYPOTHESIS

Official records indicate that, except for a very few crimes, women are not arrested as often as men—in fact, only about 20 percent of all arrests are of women.[20] They are convicted even less often than male counterparts. In 1994, only 15 percent of all state convictions were of women (8% of all violent offenses, 19% of all property offenses, and 17% of all larceny offenses).[21] And, finally, women are even less likely to be sentenced to prison. About six percent of the national prison population in 1996 were women.[22]

Is there a double standard in the American criminal justice system whereby female offenders are treated with more leniency than male offenders? *Illustration credit: CORBIS-BETTMANN.*

Some, however, dispute the notion that women are less criminal and propose, instead, that decisionmakers treat women differently and are less likely to utilize formal processing—the so-called chivalry hypothesis. Pollak was not the first to speculate that women may be just as criminal as men, but he was perhaps the most quoted: "Men hate to accuse women and thus indirectly send them to their punishment, police officers dislike to arrest them, district attorneys to prosecute them, judges and juries to find them guilty."[23]

The so-called chivalry hypothesis has been studied by numerous researchers and after reviewing the burgeoning literature, the following conclusions can be made:

- The system does employ differential processing standards; the relevant factors seem to be issues such as childcare and differential culpability between male and female defendants.

- Later studies were much more sophisticated than early studies by controlling for such factors as prior record, injury, and other sentencing factors that may have affected decisionmakers besides, or in addition to, sex. When these factors are controlled, the apparent preferential treatment for women is reduced, but does not disappear.

- Certain authors' findings that women who deviate from normal sex roles are more harshly treated has not been replicated by many researchers.

- It seems to be the case that increased imprisonment rates for women are due to equalization efforts in the system, i.e., determinate sentencing and sentencing guidelines, that have impacted women more harshly than men.

Methodological Concerns

To test the chivalry hypothesis, one must compare sentences given to male and female defendants and find significant differences that are unaccounted for by all other factors. Many factors may affect sentencing, such as prior record, seriousness of crime, victim injury, offender culpability, and so forth. Many of these factors are correlated with the sex of the offender; women are less likely to have prior criminal records and they (typically) are less likely to play major roles in criminal activities. Therefore any study of chivalry must, at the outset, ensure that all these factors are controlled for before assuming that any sentencing differences are due to the sex of offender. Some studies are more successful at controlling for such factors than others.

More fundamental issues, however, undercut all studies of chivalry undertaken at the sentencing stage. The sentencing decision comes after many previous "decision points" in processing. A true test of whether the system treats women differentially would have to begin at the point of the arrest decision, carry through to formal booking, the decision to charge (and with what to charge), pretrial decisions such as bail or release on recognizance (ROR), convictions, and, finally, sentencing. Each of the prior decision points are important and may reflect differential processing. The earlier in the system, the more difficult it would be to study decisionmakers; for instance, how could a researcher determine whether police officers were more likely to arrest men than women in similar circumstances? These issues, of course, are the very same issues that are debated relative to the question as to whether the system is racist. Even if statistics indicate there is no racial bias at the point of sentencing, that does not tell us much about the other parts of the system—each step, beginning with the decision to stop and investigate, is part of the larger picture. In the following review of the literature, it is obvious that the weakest aspect of the research is the lack of attention to earlier stages in the formal processing of suspects and defendants.

Chivalry in the System?

Nagel and Weitzman found that women appearing in court on charges of assault and larceny were treated differently than male defendants. They were less likely to be in custody before trial, they were less likely to be convicted, and they were less likely to be sent to prison if convicted. White women received less harsh treatment than African-American women, but African-American women received less harsh treatment than white men.[24] Nagel and Weitzman's sample was 11,258 cases from all 50 states, but the nature of their sample did not allow for controlling for such variables as the seriousness or level of participation in each offense, nor criminal history. Both of these variables are obviously extremely important in sentencing decisions and, therefore, their study results have to be treated with a great deal of caution.

Simon and Sharma also did not control for these factors in a study of chivalry. Not surprisingly, in their analysis of California statistics during a period of 1960-1972, they found that women received more lenient treatment from the courts when comparing conviction rates and sentences for male and female defendants.[25] However, a later analysis of California sentencing data, controlling for race, offense and prior record, also found that women received more lenient treatment from the courts.[26] Again, though, this study failed to control for level of participation in crime or any other measures of culpability.

Wilbanks offered one of the few studies that looked at earlier points in the system, including arrest and charging decisions. Unfortunately, he was not able to control for such factors as seriousness of culpability or prior record. His findings indicated that women were not treated more favorably at the "front end" of the system, but they were at the sentencing stage, although the effect of sex was inconsistent across offense types. In other words, for some crimes women were treated more harshly than men, and in other crimes they were treated more leniently.[27]

Other studies also showed some leniency toward women in sentencing decisions in the 1970s and 1980s.[28] Nagel and Hagan, in a very thorough review of the chivalry research that had been conducted up to the early 1980s, concluded that sex appeared to affect decisions differently at different stages in the criminal justice process. At the pretrial stage, sex did affect the decision to release on recognizance (rather than set bail), but did not affect the amount of bail if bail was set. With regard to decision to prosecute, plea bargain, or convict they conclude that the evidence available did not clearly support a chivalry hypothesis. Sentencing studies, however, did show differential processing by sex, although the effect was small after controlling for other variables.[29]

Research on sentencing has continued to explore whether women enjoy differential sentencing.[30] Some studies conclude that "chivalry" is not supported by statistical analysis.[31] For instance, Hagan and O'Donnel, in a Canadian study, found no statistically significant differences in court decisions to dismiss, adjudicate, or incarcerate.[32] Others found that sentencing patterns were changing.[33] Farrington and Morris found that sex was highly interactive with offense seriousness and they found no independent effect of sex apart from offense seriousness on sentencing decisions.[34] Feyerherm also disputed the chivalry hypothesis based on his study of juveniles. Comparing self-reports of high school juveniles (562 males and 557 females) to official records, and controlling for frequency and seriousness of delinquency, he found no differential processing by police or the court system.[35]

Steffensmeier, Kramer, and Streifel studied sentences that departed from sentencing guidelines in Pennsylvania during the years 1985-1987. In 29 percent of cases of female defendants, judges departed from the guidelines, but they did so in only 15 percent of cases for men. The authors concluded that the reasons for the judges' decisions included a number of social/background factors that were related to the sex of the defendant. Their findings are summarized below:

- Sex had a small-to-moderate effect on the decision to imprison. Men were about 12 percent more likely to be sent to prison.

- Decisions were influenced by women's nonviolent prior records (compared to men's), their minor role in the offense, childcare responsibilities, physical or mental problems, and/or a show of remorse.

- Sex had no effect on the length-of-sentence decision. Females received slightly longer sentences for less serious offenses and slightly shorter sentences for more serious offenses.

- The authors found that these same conclusions applied across levels of offense seriousness and race.[36]

Daly and Bordt conducted an extensive literature review of the chivalry question and also analyzed older data sets of court cases. They found that one-half of the studies showed sex effects favoring women, one-quarter showed mixed effects, and the remaining one-quarter showed no effects. Sex effects were evident in both recent and older data, more likely to emerge in felony offenses, urban courts, and in the decision to incarcerate as opposed to the length of a prison term.[37]

Spohn and Spears also utilize old data for their analysis (1976, 1977, and 1978). Since one hypothesis is that societal changes have possibly affected sentencing patterns and women are now receiving harsher sentences, this research can be utilized only as a comment on what occurred 20 years ago, rather than what is occurring today in this nation's courts. They found that in the processing of violent crimes, women were more likely than men to have all charges dismissed, but those that were sentenced were sentenced more harshly than males. They also found that race and sex interacted: African-American men were most likely to be incarcerated, followed by white men, African-American women, and then white women.[38]

A Selective Chivalry?

Some opponents of the chivalry hypothesis utilize sentencing data of juveniles and show that female juvenile offenders are treated to a double standard where they are more subject to control for non-criminal offenses, i.e., sexual promiscuity.[39] In more recent studies of juvenile processing, the results of chivalry studies are mixed. Bishop and Frazier studied juvenile court processing and concluded that insofar as criminal adjudications were concerned: male delinquents were more likely than female delinquents to be subject to formal intake; to be petitioned to court by prosecutors, to be detained in secure facilities until adjudication, and to receive sentences involving incarceration. Older youths, African-Americans, and males were more likely to be incarcerated. There were, however, significant interaction effects between sex and contempt charges after status offense adjudications, that is, female delinquents were more likely to be incarcerated than male delinquents in this offense category (i.e., when they were found in contempt of court after a status offense). Furthermore, female delinquents were more likely than male delinquents to be formally processed for status offenses; however, there were no findings that supported the notion that female status offenders were treated more harshly by the system, except for the contempt offense as described above and referred to by the authors as "striking and dramatic."[40] Thus, the authors conclude that the juvenile system continues to discriminate based on gender stereotypes—punishing delinquent boys more harshly than girls, but treating female status offenders more harshly than boys.

In regard to adult women, writers have hypothesized that until level of participation and actual criminal culpability is taken into account, statistical studies may be unable to accurately test whether women are treated with chivalry or simply with fairness based on lesser culpability. These writers also speculate on the possibility that women who conform to traditional roles and sex-role stereotypes (i.e., type of crime, fulfilling a role as mother and wife, and demeanor in court) may be treated differently because they are subject to informal controls (i.e., family) and, thus, do not require the formal controls of the court.[41] This is a more complicated hypothesis than a simple chivalry theory; it offers the possibility that women are treated with chivalry by courts only when they fit a certain stereotype of what is womanly in this society.

Farnworth and Teske identify three different versions of the chivalry hypothesis.[42] They test three different hypotheses. First, the *typicality* hypothesis proposes that women are treated with chivalry only when charges are consistent with female stereotypes. The *selective chivalry* hypothesis proposes that only white female offenders receive chivalry in the system. Finally, the *differential discretion* hypothesis proposes that disparity is most common in the pretrial informal decisions and least common at final sentencing. Their data analysis includes larger numbers than many of the other studies of chivalry, but addresses only two types of charges—theft and assault. However, the smallest number of cases in a single cell even when isolating gender by race/ethnicity by offense type was 363.[43] They found that African-American males, but not African-American females, were less likely than other defendants to get charge reductions. Women with no charge reduction were more likely than men with no charge reduction to receive probation instead of prison. Women with a charge reduction were more likely than men with a charge reduction to receive probation instead of jail. They found that:

> Depending on age, females without a record were 14 to 17 percent more likely than males without a record to receive probation, and 11 to 16 percent less likely to go to jail. Among those with a prior record, the greater tendency of females to be granted probation was only 3 to 4 percent and gender differences in jail sentences ranged from less than one to 4 percent.[44]

They also found that white females were about twice as likely as minority women to have assault charges at arrest changed to non-assault charges at final sentencing.[45] Thus, they conclude that there are sex effects, at least for these two crime categories, that exist apart from any influence of offense seriousness. They also found, however, that race/ethnicity is a complicating factor—it appears that African-American men are the most disadvantaged in regard to sentencing disparity, but in some respects African-American women are also less likely to receive favorable treatment, i.e., less likely than white women to see assault charges reduced. They found no evidence for the *typicality* argument since the sex effects seemed to operate in a similar pattern with both theft and assault, and the authors assume that assault is a "non-typical" crime for women.[46]

Kruttschnitt has also pursued the idea of informal versus formal control. She observed that women are subject to different control devices in this society—through economic dependence, marriage, and motherhood. Her hypothesis is that if a woman is seen as controlled by these informal elements, then the courts tend to treat her with less formal control. For instance, if she is married and her husband is the breadwinner she is more likely to receive favorable treatment from the court, i.e., probation instead of prison.[47]

Nagel provides some support for this hypothesis in her study of 2,965 (2,627 men and 338 women) cases in New York State. She included variables such as marital status, family composition, age, race, and employment status, as well as criminal career, type of offense, previous record, and other pending cases. She found that prior offenses resulted in harsher sentences only for men, although it was also noted that the methodology did not allow for taking into account the severity of prior record, therefore it was possible that women's prior arrests were less serious than men's. Interestingly, marriage only affected women's sentences, and this variable affected their sentencing in a positive direction.[48] This finding was replicated by Farrington and Morris in their study of offenses of theft in Cambridge in 1979. This study noted the difficulty of using statistical analysis when combining interval data and categorical data. They used a combination of analytical tools to arrive at the conclusion that women did receive less severe sentences than men, but that this was largely due to men's criminal histories:

> . . . the sex of the defendant did not have any direct influence on the severity of the sentence or the probability of reconviction. Women only appear to receive more lenient sentences and to have a lower likelihood of reconviction because they had committed less serious offences and were less likely to have been convicted previously.[49]

Eaton, in a qualitative study of Magistrates' courts in England, reports that court personnel viewed family circumstances differently for men and women.[50]

Visher also found differential chivalry, but in her study race, not marital status, was the complicating factor: "In these data, young, black, or hostile women receive no preferential treatment, whereas older, white women who are calm and deferential toward the police are granted leniency."[51] Young, after reviewing the chivalry literature, concluded that the findings were mixed regarding the effect of race on sentencing or sentence length. She observed that few studies examined the direct effect of race within sex categories, therefore it was difficult to say whether whites or non-whites were sentenced differentially.[52] Crew, in a study of incarcerated offenders, found that being married, having children, and being employed significantly (although weakly) affected women's sentence length, but not men's sentence length. Race, on the other hand, affected men's, but not women's sentence length.[53]

Chivalry or Justice?

Thus, several studies have found some differential processing even among women, and that this difference seems to be tied to the woman's role as mother and/or wife. Rather than paternalism toward women, the system has been described as displaying "familial paternalism."[54] Daly found no evidence of gender-based sentencing disparities among men and women without family roles; however women with dependent children received more lenient sentencing because of a concern for children.[55] Daly[56] and Daly and Bordt[57] criticized disparity studies for not taking into account all factors of sentencing. In other words, purely statistical studies could not capture the context of the crime, thus may mistakenly conclude that unequal treatment was handed out, when in fact, the result may have been perfectly just considering the circumstances of the crime:

> Women defendants or the "sex variable" have simply been inserted in the analysis without considering how gender relations shape variability in lawbreaking—the "seriousness" of the current offense and previous lawbreaking—or variability in markers of conventionality such as family, work, or community ties. Most disparity studies have adopted the "add-women-and stir" posture, endemic to social research . . .[58]

In her New Haven study, Daly looked at 189 female cases and a random sample of 208 male cases, drawing from the years 1981-1986. She used multiple regression analysis to determine whether there was disparity in sentencing, but also collected a "deep sample" of 40 male and 40 female cases matched for factors such as type of crime to explore more fully. Daly found that men were more likely to be incarcerated than women (the range was from eight to 25 percentage points), and African-Americans were more likely to be incarcerated than whites[59] (1994, 32).

Daly's statistical study would have concluded that disparity existed, but she went further with her "deep sample" and utilized narratives of the case histories. She developed a "comparative justice metric" that evaluated such things as the seriousness of the crime and the level of participation or culpability of the offender. Using the case studies and this comparative tool, she found gender differences were negligible.

IS CHIVALRY ALIVE OR DEAD?

The theorists who study whether the system treats women with chivalry have thus far been attempting to prove or disprove the existence of such differential treatment. Another application of the theory has been to accept its existence, but propose that it is declining (with increased social and economic equality between the sexes) and, thus, the observed rise in female criminality may be due to more equal processing rather than an increase in crime among women.

Daly [60] and Raeder[61] show that belief in disparity in sentencing may have fueled harsher treatment of women. Certainly so-called gender neutral approaches such as guidelines with no mitigation for family circumstances or "split the difference" approaches that average men's and women's sentences weigh more heavily on women. The difficulty of proving such a hypothesis is obtaining longitudinal data that can document changes in court treatment of women and men over time. Most analyses discussed in the preceding paragraphs have been cross-sectional, which look at court processing at one point in time.

It seems clear that women are more likely to be sent to prison than ever before. In the earlier part of the twentieth century, some states allowed for longer sentences for women given certain conditions. Because women were considered more amenable to treatment, some state's sentencing structures allowed for indeterminate sentences for women even while mandating specific ranges for men. Obviously these sentencing systems were struck down when challenged under equal protection.[62] Even with this possibility of longer sentences, the number of women imprisoned was still dramatically less than the number of men. Historically, women comprised about four to five percent of the total prisoner population. This percentage started to increase in the 1980s and the rate of incarceration for women increased dramatically, even in proportion to that of men. Table 4.5 illustrates that women are much more likely to end up in prison today for any given offense than they were 10 or 15 years ago.

Table 4.5
Percentage Sentenced to Prison by Year and Crime Category

	California		New York		Pennsylvania	
	1982	1987	1982	1987	1982	1987
Sex	Women (Men)	Women (Men)	Women (Men)	Women (Men)	Women (Men)	Women (Men)
Crime						
Homicide	71% (83.2)	73 (92.3)	52.9 (78.7)	48.1 (76.9)	53.6 (75.9)	86.7 (90)
Robbery	41.1 (64.4)	55.7 (71.3)	31.5 (60.5)	36.5 (62.3)	43.3 (74.4)	68.2 (87)
Burglary	29.5 (41.2)	39.7 (50.7)	12 (34.7)	27.6 (43.7)	34.8 (62.2)	52.4 (78.1)
Assault	17.6 (29.5)	22.6 (38.9)	16.8 (30.4)	18.1 (31.6)	23.4 (40.5)**	37.6 (67.3)
Theft	9.8 (22.3)	18.4 (32)	11.4 (23.3)*	12.1 (30.8)	18.7 (35.4)	27.2 (44.5)
Drugs	7.6 (14.6)	12.5 (23.3)	16.9 (37.6)	20.6 (38.1)	17.4 (38.3)	33.1 (46.6)

*state data lists as larceny rather than theft
**state data lists aggravated and simple separately; listed percentages are for aggravated
adapted from Simon and Landis, 1991, p. 82-84.

In 1990 the rate of women per 100,000 sent to prison was 11 (compared to 275 for men); in 1994, that figure had climbed to 45 per 100,000 (compared to 387 for men)—thus women's rate of imprisonment quadrupled compared to less than a doubling of the rate for men.[63] Thus, in 1995 there was an estimated 828,100 women on probation or parole, or in jail or prison, representing 0.8 percent of the U.S. population of women (compared to 4.9% of all men under some form of correctional supervision). About 64,000 of these women were in prison.[64] Further, there was about a 12.5 percent increase in the number of women just between 1994 and 1995 (56,891 women were in prison in 1994), and another 9.3 percent increase between 1995 and 1996 (74,730 women were in state or federal prison in 1996).[65] In fact, since 1985 the annual growth rate of female inmates has averaged 11 percent (compared to 8% for men).[66] While women still represent only 6.3 percent of all prisoners, the rate of increase shows no signs of slowing. Oklahoma (115 sentenced female inmates per 100,000) and Texas (102 per 100,000) had the highest incarceration rates of women, while Maine (at 5 per 100,000), Vermont (at 7 per 100,000), and Minnesota (at 10 per 100,000) posted the lowest incarceration rates.[67] Texas presented the largest single increase in incarceration of women with a 25.2 percent increase in one year—the number of women in Texas prisons went from 7,935 in 1994 to 9,933 in 1995.[68]

Exactly why women are more likely to be sentenced to prison for any given crime is subject to debate. Chesney-Lind points out that in the same time (1985 to 1994) that women's crime increased 36.5 percent, their rate of incarceration increased by 202 percent![69] This was also during a time when violent crimes by women showed a decline. Drug laws and the "War on Drugs" has been said to account for large numbers of women in prison— either directly through drug crimes, or indirectly, by judges sentencing women to prison for property offenses because they have a drug problem, or parole revocations because of drug use. One possibility, at least for federal prisoners, is that the United States Sentencing Guidelines do not allow for family circumstances as a mitigating factor in sentencing (18 USC §3553(a) and (b)). This means that judges are unable to take into account the needs of children or other family members even if the defendant is the sole supporter of such dependents.

The effect of race on sentencing for men or women is astounding. In 1993, for instance, the rate of imprisonment for African-American women per 100,000 was 165 compared to 23 for white women. Of course, even African-American women's rates come nowhere near white male rates (398 per 100,000), and the rate for African-American men is unbelievably high (2,920 per 100,000).[70] Nationally, about one-half of all female prisoners are African-American. For instance, in 1995 about 31,700 state and federal prisoners were white women, compared to 31,000 African-American women.[71]

Chesney-Lind and Pollock reviewed the upsurge in women's imprisonment and concluded that women have been the recipients of an "equality with a vengeance."[72] That is, both formal and informal processes of the criminal justice system have eliminated the idea of women as different—with different needs, different problems, and different propensities for criminality and recidivism. The equalization approach, however, has resulted in women being treated more like men—in the decision to incarcerate as well as the conditions under which they are incarcerated. This approach is undertaken with little or no consideration as to whether it is efficacious for society. Chesney-Lind concludes that this dramatic increase in imprisonment has occurred with barely a whisper against the wisdom of incarcerating so many women:

> Whatever the reason, there has certainly been no national outcry about the soaring rates of women's imprisonment. Instead, with little or no public discussion, the correctional establishment has gone about the business of building new women's prisons and filling them.[73]

Thus, the attention given by researchers to whether chivalry operated in the criminal courts 10 or 20 years ago seems sadly misplaced considering the dramatic increase in incarceration rates today and in recent years. It seems clear that, although chivalry may have operated in the past, there is precious little left in our current justice system.

NOTES

[1]   Adler (1975).

[2]   Simon (1975a, 2).

[3]   To use a simplified example: a base number of 10 with an increase of another 10 would be noted as a 100 percent increase, while a base number of 1,000 with an increase of 250 would only be noted as a 25 percent increase. Arguably, if these numbers represented crimes, we would be more concerned with 250 new crimes than 10 new crimes.

[4]   Steffensmeier (1980, 1981, 1983), also see Leonard (1982).

[5]   Adler (1981).

[6]   1981, 10.

[7]   1981, 11.

[8]   1981, 11.

[9]   The advantage of using the "hidden female crime" argument is that it is impossible to prove or disprove. Pollak used the argument to show that women were just as criminal as men; Adler uses the argument to attempt to explain why economic development did not create the numbers of female criminals that the emancipation theory predicted would occur.

[10]   Steffensmeier, Allen, and Streifel (1989).

[11]   Simon and Landis (1991, 3-4).

[12]   1991, 48-51.

13   Percentage increases in certain crimes categories are vulnerable to changes in other crimes categories. For instance, an increase in women's involvement in, for instance, drug crimes, would change percentages in all crime categories, such as violent crime. An increased percentage of the total in one would lead inevitably to a decreased percentage in other areas of crime—violent crime would appear to be decreasing, and it would be, but only as a percentage of the total crime of women. What that percentage decrease has to say about women's absolute activity in those categories of crime is absolutely nothing.

14   Steffensmeier (1993).

15   1993, 14.

16   1997, 100.

17   Merlo (1995).

18   1993, 17.

19   1981.

20   UCR (1995, 225).

21   Bureau of Justice Statistics (1997a, 5).

22   Bureau of Justice Statistics (1997b, 6).

23   1950, 151.

24   Nagel and Weitzman (1971).

25   Simon and Sharma (1979).

26   Moulds (1980).

27   Wilbanks (1986).

28   Fenster (1981) looked solely at male/female co-defendants to determine if sex affected decisionmaking. She studied 105 pairs of male/female co-defendants during the years 1972-1977. She found that 58 percent of the women but only 41 percent of the men received a deferred disposition, and 86 percent of the women, but only 60 percent of the men received probation as opposed to a prison sentence. On the other hand, using the police report and interview data she concluded that women played a minor role in the planning and commission of the crime in 77 percent of the cases. In only 23 percent of the cases did women play a dominant role, according to file material. However, she concluded that even controlling for such factors as prior record, females were shown to be slightly advantaged in the decision to imprison and the length of imprisonment. Gruhl et al. (1984), in their study of felony cases in Los Angeles county between 1977 and 1980, found that female defendants were treated more leniently than male defendants in the prosecutor's decision to dismiss charges and in the decision to incarcerate. They found no differential treatment in the decision to convict. This study did control for prior record, and the culpability of the defendant was operationalized to some extent by the variable of injury to victim. Interestingly, they found that African-American women received more favorable treatment than did white women; African-American women were considerably less likely than African-American men to be prosecuted or incarcerated and such paternalism was least evident among white defendants. Hispanic women were found to be prosecuted at about the same rate as Hispanic men but incarcerated much less often (1984, 464). The authors conclude that such decisionmaking was largely due to the greater likelihood of African-American women being single mothers and sole custodians of their children.

29   Nagel and Hagan (1983, 135).

30   For instance, Bridges and Beretta (1994), employing multiple regression on all independent factors and imprisonment rates in a national sample, found gender disparity. Although they conclude that levels of criminal involvement could not explain disparities in imprisonment, it is unclear how they arrived at this information using national statistics (1994, 169). In an arguably hasty assumption, they speculate that mandatory and determinate sentencing laws may result in longer sentences for men, while women might instead be hospitalized in mental hospitals. It is unclear why they assume that serious violent female offenders are more likely to be diagnosed as mentally ill than serious violent male offenders.

31   For instance, see Curran (1983) and Nagel and Hagan (1983).

32   1978.

33   Kempinen (1983), with a Pennsylvania sample covering 1970-1975, found that sentencing practices were changing with women receiving harsher sentences for certain crimes, such as robbery, during the later years of the study period.

34   Farrington and Morris (1983).

35   1981a, 1981b.

36   Steffensmeier, Kramer, and Streifel (1993, 433-435).

37   Daly and Bordt (1995).

38   Spohn and Spears (1997, 51).

39   See Chesney-Lind (1973), Smart (1976), Campbell (1981), and Figueira-McDonough (1985).

40   Bishop and Frazier (1992, 1185).

41   See Chesney-Lind (1978) and Kruttschnitt (1982a, 1982b, 1984).

42   Farnworth and Teske (1995). Unfortunately, they chose to use 10-year-old data in their analysis, which detracts from the study's current value.

43   1995, 29.

44   1995, 37.

45   1995, 38.

46   1995, 41. The authors should perhaps consider the possibility that a good portion of these assault cases take place within the context of family violence, in which case they might not necessarily represent the type of crime contrary to traditional feminine stereotypes. Assaults that are against spouses, for instance, might be treated less harshly than assaults that take place during a robbery.

47   Kruttschnitt (1982a, 1982b).

48   Nagel (1981, 1983).

49   Farrington and Morris (1983, 245). They also found that marriage or family background affected only women's sentences, not men's.

50   Eaton (1986). Originally interested in a quantitative analysis of sentencing and determining whether any differences existed in the sentencing of men and women, Eaton noticed

that a particular language in the courtroom pointed to an assumption regarding the ideal family model that affected decisionmakers and their treatment of women defendants. Her data set included 321 completed cases (210 men and 111 women defendants). She sat in the Magistrates' courts and took notes on the magistrate's reasons for the sentences and other decisions handed down. Her most general observation was that men and women were different types of offenders; most men had prior records, most women did not. Most women were responsible for the care and maintenance of children, most men were not. The majority of cases were treated in a routine manner with little explanation of decisionmaking and no indication that sex played a role (1986, 40). Eaton found that in pleas for mitigation, family circumstances was the defense used most often by both men and women. Marriage was described for both as a method of controlling the individual offender and providing an incentive for staying out of future trouble. Eaton (1986) concludes that both magistrates and probation officers endorse a typical stereotype of normal family life, i.e., with the male as head of household and the female economically and emotionally dependent, in their decisions and recommendations. These assumptions of normality disadvantage those who are single or who live in atypical living arrangements, i.e., non-marriage, or same-sex relationships. The strength of sexual stereotyping as operating to affect criminal justice decisionmaking can be illustrated by Eaton's finding that in probation officers' home visits in preparation for making a sentencing recommendation, home visits to women almost always resulted in comments in the report concerning her housekeeping, while home visits to male defendants rarely included such comments and if there were, the officer's report attributed responsibility for housekeeping to the male defendant's wife (Eaton: 1986, 67).

[51]   Visher (1983, 23).

[52]   Young (1986).

[53]   Crew (1991, 70).

[54]   Daly (1987a, 1987b).

[55]   Daly (1989b, 1989c)

[56]   1994.

[57]   1995.

[58]   Daly (1994b, 121).

[59]   1994, 32.

[60]   1994.

[61]   1993.

[62]   See Temin (1973), Schweber and Feinman (1985), and Kanowitz (1969).

[63]   Bureau of Justice Statistics (1995, 1).

[64]   Bureau of Justice Statistics (1997c).

[65]   Bureau of Justice Statistics (1997c, 108) and Bureau of Justice Statistics (1997b, 1).

[66]   Bureau of Justice Statistics (1997b, 2).

[67]   Bureau of Justice Statistics (1997b, 2).

[68]   Bureau of Justice Statistics (1997b, 2).

69   1997, 146.

70   Bureau of Justice Statistics (1995, 3).

71   Bureau of Justice Statistics (1997b, 9).

72   1995.

73   1997, 6.

Traditional Criminology: The Study of Criminal Men

5

Objectives

- Become familiar with traditional and standard theories of crime.

- Understand how the theories might explain what we know about women's criminality.

In this chapter, traditional theories of criminality are reviewed. We emphasize those theories developed by theorists in the United States, and arbitrarily draw the definition of "traditional theories" as those that developed up until about the 1960s. This is not an exhaustive review—there are dozens of criminology textbooks and more critical treatments of the theories discussed below that the reader is urged to consult.[1] Here, only the general themes of the theory are drawn to point out applications to female criminality.

THEORETICAL CONCERNS

Why do some people commit crime? Almost everyone you ask on the street, in the classroom, even in a prison, has an answer to that question. Although people's answers will vary somewhat, the elements of the answer always include some family issues (bad parents), some individual/personality issues (bad kid), some peer issues (bad crowd), and some societal issues (bad economy). Criminologists have also addressed the question—for more than 100 years, filling hundreds of books and thousands of articles that argue minutiae as well as fundamental issues in the mysteries of behavior. Their theories include (unsurprisingly) the same elements enumerated above.

If one asked, however, "Why do women commit less crime than men?" the person-on-the-street would probably answer with some version of: "Because women are taught to be 'nicer' than men" or that women are "naturally" nicer than men. The point that will be made in this chapter is that traditional criminology—the theories we discuss below—had no answer to this question because it was not even addressed.

One of the most ironic facts regarding the field of criminology was that, for the most part, one-half of the population was virtually ignored. If mention was made of women in classic texts, the implication was obvious that the problem of crime was a problem of men. The numbers of women who committed crime were too small to bother with. Why that fact alone was not enough to intrigue researchers who were supposed to be interested in the causes of crime is impossible to say. One would think that if a large percentage of a population showed disproportionately low crime rates, it would be imperative to look at factors that distinguished this group from the group that contributed a disproportionate amount of crime. The reason women were not the focus of criminologists may have to do with cultural androcentrism; that is, the paradigm that what men do is "normal" and what women do (if different from men) is abnormal. Thus, because men more often commit crime, there is a theme in traditional sociological theories that criminal behavior is, to some extent, normal; although questions concerning why certain men commit crime are asked. Since women are viewed as abnormal (compared to men's norm of criminal behavior), the question why they do or do not commit crime is irrelevant. If the question was asked, it was asked as a separate question with a different and separate answer.[2]

Why should there be different answers for why women and why men commit crime? There really is no reason why a single theory of crime should not be able to explain male and female criminal behavior. Note that this could mean a factor is identified that affected men and women differently, or a factor was identified that was differentially present among men and women. Thus, we will ask the following questions in our review of traditional theories:

- Does the theory explain the crime differential (that is, the overall lower rates of crime by women)?

- Does it explain the fact that the crime differential decreases with property crime and increases with violent crime?

- Does it explain why women's property crime has increased?

There are many different methods of categorizing and organizing theories. Classical and Positivist theories seem to be obvious discrete categories, and under Positivism, the following types of theories will be discussed: psychological theories, social process theories, and social structure theories.

CLASSICAL THEORY VERSUS POSITIVISM

Criminology classes often start with the "classical" school. The Classical School is usually described by the contributions of Cesare Beccaria (1738-1794) and Jeremy Bentham (1748-1832). Beccaria was more concerned with remaking the justice system into one that was fair and just, while Bentham could be described as more concerned with fine-tuning the system to improve the efficiency with which it could prevent crime. Both theorists used as a fundamental assumption that mankind was rational and operated with free will. Therefore, the elimination of crime could be achieved by appealing to men's rationality, and more specifically, by assuming that laws promising punishment for offenses would act as a deterrent to crime.[3] Bentham, for instance, proposed that the justice system must employ punishment in such a way that it was slightly more punitive than the perceived profit of the crime at issue (in order to deter individuals from attempting the crime).[4] Punishment should be adjusted in this way for each offense. It should be no more than necessary to deter. It should be adjusted upward in severity in relation to a decrease in certainty. Thus, the focus of these thinkers was on the legal system; the assumption was that everyone would respond to the legal system in a similar rational manner.

Siegel identified the elements of the Classical School as follows:

- People have free will and choose criminal behavior.

- Criminal solutions are attractive.

- These choices can be deterred through fear of sanctions.

- The more severe, certain, and swift the reaction, the more efficient it is in deterrence.[5]

Since women were not viewed as rational, nor did women commit a great deal of crime, other than prostitution, they were not considered in the writings of Classical School thinkers. Women in this time period were under the legal authority of their fathers and husbands, and any crimes committed by them were the responsibility of their male guardian. Obviously, the idea that all people will respond equally to a deterrent is not a viable concept, so it is not surprising that the Classical School is usually a historical preface to the theories of crime that developed after the rise of Positivism.[6]

POSITIVISM

Positivism can be described simply as: scientific method, or the search for causes using scientific method. It is typically associated with Lombroso, who is often referred to as the "Grandfather of Criminology."[7] Lombroso and the Positivist approach can be distinguished from the Classical School approach in that the focus of criminology shifts from the legal system to the offender. Individuals are not presumed to be equally rational or equal in any other way. The cause of crime, in fact, is assumed to lie in the individual. Thus, Lombroso developed his "born criminal" theory: the idea that criminals were genetically different from non-criminals, but also developed a more sophisticated typology of criminals. Later positivists in the early 1900s also looked at individual causes—both biological and psychological. The cause of crime, under the original Positivist approach, was believed to lie in the individual—criminals were different from non-criminals and criminology merely needed to understand those differences.

Since difference was a presumption under Lombroso's theory, it was consistent with the theory to distinguish women from men, and criminal women from non-criminal women. In fact, Lombroso did address the question of women's criminality.[8] Women were presumed to be biologically and psychologically different from men, which accounted for their lower crime rates. However, some women were evolutionary throwbacks, according to Lombroso, and these "primitive" women were criminal because, in his theory, all primitive women were more masculine and criminal than "modern" law-abiding women. Interestingly, however, his typology did include other types besides the purely biological criminal, and these types tapped some of the same explanations we use today, such as opportunity, influence, and passion. The Positivist tradition, with its emphasis on individual differences, can be traced through biological and psychological theories of crime.

PSYCHOLOGICAL THEORIES OF CRIME

Criminology has largely ignored psychological theories of deviance and criminality.

Andrews and Bonta argue that the rejection of psychology is due to historical events, specifically, sociologists taking on the study of crime as their role and discarding psychology as outside the realm of criminology.[9] They also criticize sociological criminology as highly theoretical as opposed to empirical. Their criticism of the sociological tradition of criminology is more than a little bitter: "The theoreticists who were so dominant in mainstream textbook criminology of the 1960s and 1970s were the fortunate ones to whom 'truth' had been revealed."[10] Perhaps their bitterness is warranted since a quick review of criminology textbooks will reveal that psychology continues to be given little attention and superficial rebuttals are usually offered to explain the absence of psychological explanations, such as the explanation that international crime rate differences "prove" social factors (such as poverty and social inequality) cause crime, or the fact that crime is so "normal" psychology cannot help much to explain origins of crime.[11]

Psychological theories can be categorized into psychodynamic theories, developmental theories, and learning theories. Of these, both developmental theories and learning theories have their correlates in sociological criminology, so to say that psychology is ignored in criminology textbooks is perhaps a misstatement of facts. Perhaps we could say that psychological theories are merely sociologized.

Psychodynamic Theories

Neither Sigmund Freud nor many of his followers had a great deal to say about crime. The psychodynamic tradition would assume, however, that crime was the result of a weak superego or ego.[12] According to psychodynamic theory, one does not develop in a normal manner when childhood trauma occurs or there is deficient parenting. Crime may occur because of unresolved feelings of guilt and a subconscious wish to be punished, or more likely because of weak superego controls over id impulses; that is, the individual cannot control impulses and pursues immediate gratification.

Sheldon and Eleanor Glueck's[13] work can be considered as an example of a psychodynamic theory.

> The major correlates of persistent and serious delinquency were antisocial attitudes, antisocial associates, a complex set of indicators of antisocial personality (restless energy, aggressiveness, impulsivity, callousness), a set of problematic family conditions (psychologically disadvantaged parents, weak affection, poor parenting, structural instability) and problematic circumstances in school and the broader community.[14]

Psychodynamic elements can also be found in several traditional and current sociological theories.[15] The difference between psychodynamic theory and sociological theory is that there is usually no mention of gender, race, or class issues as interacting with individual psychodynamic factors in human behavior in traditional examples of psychodynamic theory.[16]

The most obvious contribution of psychological theory to an understanding of criminality is the development of the concept of sociopathy or psychopathy. The psychopath has been differentiated from the sociopath in the following way: "[the psychopath is] an individual in whom the normal processes of socialization have failed to produce the mechanisms of conscience and habits of law-abidingness that normally constrain antisocial impulses" and the sociopath as "persons whose unsocialized character is due primarily to parental failures rather than to inherent peculiarities of temperament."[17] Recently, the Diagnostic Statistical Manual (DSM-IV) (used as the "bible" of mental health workers to diagnose and categorize all mental health problems) has replaced the terms psychopathy, and sociopathy, with the term antisocial personality disorder. Regardless, these definitions describe an individual who is without a conscience and unable to form sincere, affectionate bonds with others. This, of course, describes many, but not all, of those who engage in criminal behavior.

Lykken, among others, basically argues that criminal behavior develops due to poor parenting, and the increase in crime is due to an increase in the rate of illegitimacy and poor single mothers who do not discipline their children: ". . . because unsocialized people tend to become incompetent parents themselves, the number of sociopaths is growing faster than the general population, faster indeed than we can build reform schools and prisons."[18]

Application of Psychodynamic Theory to Women

Historically, psychodynamic theory explained women's behavior as operating from different motivations than men.[19] Freud had little to say directly about female criminality or deviance, but his theory of psychosexual development is used to explain why females commit crime. "Normal" development, according to Freudian theory is when the mother is seen as the first and primary sex object (for boys and girls) and the boy attempts to be like his father to gain his mother's love. This acts as the mechanism for role modeling and identification and is healthy and normal. Girls cannot model themselves after the father and feel deficient in that they do not have a penis like their father, thus they attempt to seduce their father to gain his penis. Winning a male's love (because of penis envy) is normal female development; attempting to be like a man (because of penis envy) is deviant female development, and that is the case with female criminals according to Freudian theory. Promiscuous sex is also the result of deviant psychosexual development according to this theory. Women's criminality is largely sexual, according to Freudian theory, because it derives from emotional disturbance. Other crimes by women were explained by her narcissicism.

An interesting puzzle is if it is bad parenting that causes sociopathy, why are women not equally criminal (since arguably they are equally subject to parental deficiencies)? Lykken's only comment regarding female criminal sociopaths is ambiguous. Describing a female sociopath, involved in petty crimes, with illegitimate children he says: "Like her mother before her, her involvement in crime is likely to be small-time and nonviolent, more because of lack of opportunity and *because she is a woman* and because of active avoidance on her part of such alternatives."[20] It is unclear what the phrase "*because she is a woman*," is supposed to mean. He implies that being a woman is a reason why she does not engage in more violent crimes, but why? This particular woman is further described as associating with drug dealers and she had even been shot once, so she definitely has had opportunities to choose violence. Why do most women actively avoid violence—even sociopathic women?

Psychodynamic theories are sometimes logically inconsistent and mix up sex role stereotypes with psychology. For instance, women's deviance being largely sexual is an unsupported assertion and may have more to do with the formal system's response than individual behavior. If the juvenile girl's sexual acting out is due to unresolved "Electra" complex problems, is the boy's sexual activity also derived from such unresolved "Oedipal" problems? Why is it normal for boys and abnormal for girls to be sexually active, other than the fact of societal sex-role expectations? The main problem with these psychodynamic theories is that they view male and female development as different, yet the theories that attempt to explain female development are obviously ad hoc and adaptations of the theories developed for men. Further, criminal behavior is seen as having different meanings and operating from different motivations, but no real effort has been made to document that assumption.

Developmental Theories

Theories of development address both cognitive development and social development. The general hypothesis is that all individuals progress through similar stages of understanding and maturity regarding the world around them. Those who engage in criminal behavior have, for some reason, become "stuck" at lower stages of development. They are immature—either in their response to the world, their interactions with others around them, and/or in their putting self above others.

Piaget[21] and Kohlberg[22] are most commonly identified with the cognitive development field. In the stage theory of cognitive development, it is assumed that the infant goes through qualitatively different stages of understanding. Only gradually does the child come to understand that others have needs and desires similar to self. Higher levels of maturity are necessary to understand such abstract concepts as altruism and compassion. Kohlberg carried Piaget's work into moral development, arguing that cognitive development was necessary in order to develop a moral conscience, and understandings of right and wrong varied depending on what cognitive level one had reached. For instance, very young children understand that stealing is wrong only because parents have told them so. It is much later that they come to understand more abstract reasons for why stealing is wrong.

Another version of a developmental approach is Warren's I-level theory and classification model.[23] In this developmental model, the individual is viewed as progressing through stages of increasing maturity in interpersonal relationships. Delinquents are clustered at the lower stages of the model, but it is also noted that criminality may occur at any stage, but for different reasons and motivations.

Application of Developmental Theories to Women

Developmental theorists have found that women and men do not seem to follow similar paths of development. Gilligan[24] concluded that women tended to cluster at lower stages in Kohlberg's stage sequence than did men. Although controversial, her theory was that women followed a "different" morality and were more likely to continue to utilize themes of relationships and caring, while men moved on to principles and law-based models of morality. Warren, in her use of the I-Level classification model, observed that the delinquent girls in her study tended to cluster differently, but in this stage sequence scheme, girls (at least girl delinquents) clustered in higher stages of interpersonal development. Further, under each sub-type, girls tended to cluster in the stage that emphasized relationships as opposed to group or cultural influences.[25] These differences are intriguing and consistent with the idea that women are more tuned to relationships than principles; and even delinquent girls and criminal women are more similar to other women than lawbreaking men in this regard.

Learning Theory and Behaviorism

Learning theory basically proposes that individuals act and believe the way they do because they have learned to do so. Learning takes place through modeling or reinforcement. Modeling stems from the desire to be like others, especially those whom one admires; therefore, children will act as they see their parents or peers act. The other form of learning is through reinforcement. That is, one will continue behaviors and beliefs for which one has been rewarded, and extinguish those behaviors and beliefs for which one has been punished or unrewarded. Bandura, for instance, argues that individuals are not necessarily inherently aggressive, but, rather, learn aggression. He and others also point out the learning is mediated by intelligence, and temperamental factors such as impulsivity, activity, and emotionality.[26]

Criminologists have also used social learning theory to explain drug use and other forms of deviance.[27] In fact, learning theory is reformulated in criminology as "differential association."[28]

Application of Learning Theory to Women

One of the most enduring explanations of why women commit less crime—by both laypeople and criminologists—is the idea that they learn to be law-abiding and that the social sanctions against deviance for women and girls are much stronger than what boys or men would experience. If true, learning theory is perfectly consistent with the lower crime rates observed for women. Further, it also explains why women tend to cluster in consumer crimes, since women may be more likely to learn how to fraudulently use a credit card than break into a building. Do women learn to control violence, explaining their lower rates of violent crime? Arguably, girls are taught that violence is not appropriate, while boys are rewarded (or at least not punished as severely) for using violence.

Learning theory is less able to explain rising rates of female criminality unless one argues that what is being learned is different today than in the past. This could occur in two ways; first, girls may be learning more criminal techniques and motivations for crime today than they have in the past; or, second, they are not learning to be law-abiding to the same degree they were in past years when, arguably, there was more social control over their behavior.

Finally, learning theory does not explain why cultural prescriptions are as they are; that is, why women's sex roles exclude the use of aggression and criminal activities more so than sex roles for men. Although one can avoid the question of whether women and men are *naturally* different in their inclination to violent crime by utilization of learning theory, there is still the question of why societal norms developed to control women's behavior in this way and suppress violent tendencies.

Conclusion

Psychological theories concentrate on individual factors of criminal choice. More sophisticated theories also refer to features of one's environment. So, for instance, Andrews and Bonta developed a psychological theory of crime that includes the characteristics of the immediate environment, the attitudes, values, beliefs, and rationalizations held by the person with regard to antisocial behavior, social support for antisocial behavior (perceived support from others), a history of having engaged in antisocial behavior, self-management and problem-solving skills, other stable personality characteristics conducive to antisocial conduct; and relates these to a behavioral explanation of criminality where rewards and costs of crime are mediated by individual differences.[29]

While we could wish for a more direct analysis of women's criminality in psychological theories, they do have the characteristic of accepting individual difference; therefore, differences between men and women, and differences between women, are consistent with such theories. Historically, these theories suffered from confusing societally imposed sex-role stereotypes and inherent characteristics of women (and men). Today, psychological theories assume sex-role influences, although they do not necessarily specify why such differences exist or exactly how such influences impact behavior.

We must study male criminal behavior in order to understand female criminal behavior. Many theoretical comparisons are used to explain gender differences. *Photo credit: Mark C. Ide.*

SOCIAL STRUCTURE THEORIES

If the focus of the Classical School was the legal system, and the focus of the Positivists was the individual, then the focus of early sociology was society itself. Societal factors were determined to be the causes of crime. Societal factors can include social structure (i.e., elements of society that induce criminality), and social process (i.e., the interactions within society that develop criminality). Both approaches reject the idea of the "criminal as different." In these theories, it is assumed that anyone who happens to be exposed to these factors would become criminal; thus, the approach is similar to the Classical School (which assumed sameness). However, while the Classicial School assumed all men would respond with rationality to the deterrent nature of a legal system, the sociological theories below offer more complicated assumptions. They can all be distinguished from psychological and biological theories, however, in the fundamental presumption of sameness as opposed to difference regarding human behavior, and the focus on societal elements as the cause of crime.

Social structure theories identify some aspects of society as leading to criminal choices. L.A.J. Quetelet (1796-1874) and Emile Durkheim (1858-1917) are credited as early sociologists who established the foundations of sociological criminology. Quetelet offered the information that crime occurred in reasonably predictable patterns in society, thus supporting the notion that it was something about society that caused crime rather than crime occurring at random or because of individual causes. Durkheim offered the principle that crime was normal and present in all societies. The Chicago School, however, truly began the study of societal influences on criminality when early sociologists at the University of Chicago observed that crime occurred more often in interstitial zones of the city.[30] In these zones, residential, commercial, and industrial activity could be observed; they were also characterized by low home ownership, property damage, graffiti, high rates of alcoholism, domestic violence, and mental health problems. Early sociologists discovered that these interstitial zones always had high crime rates, even though demographic groups moved in and out of them. For instance, in the latter part of the nineteenth century, Irish immigrants were the population that lived in the zones, but they eventually moved out to be replaced by Eastern and Southern Europeans, and then African-Americans moving up from the South. Thus, it seemed that there was something about the zone, rather than the people who lived within it, that generated crime. One thing that characterized such zones, of course, was lack of opportunity. Another social structure theory looked at the particular subculture that could be found in interstitial zones.

Cultural Deviance Theory

Shaw and McKay, authors of the zone theory described above, also explained that part of what was going on in the zone was the transmission of culture; more specifically, a subculture with deviant values.[31]

> Thus, the effectiveness of the neighborhood as a unit of control and as a medium for the transmission of the moral standards of society is greatly diminished. The *boy* who grows up in this area has little access to the cultural heritage's of conventional society. For the most part, the organization of *his* behavior takes place through *his* participation in the spontaneous play groups and organized gangs with which *he* had contact outside of the home . . . this area is an especially favorable habitat for the development of *boys'* gangs and organized criminal groups.[32]

Later theorists[33] expanded on the idea of a deviant subculture that existed and was responsible for the transmission of deviant values. Miller, for instance, described lower-class focal concerns of men as different from middle-class men's concerns: trouble, toughness, smartness, excitement, fate, and autonomy.[34] In these theories, the deviant is normal in his environment; that is, he has adopted the values and behavioral patterns of the culture around him. The assumption is that the deviant is similar to law-abiding folk; the only difference is the misfortune to be born in an interstitial zone.

Criticisms of the theory point out that not everyone commits crime in such zones and that it is hard to conceptualize a truly deviant subculture in the homogeneous culture in which we live. All of us are affected by the same television shows, educational programs, and societal messages. While subcultures may exist, the idea that a deviant socialization is solely responsible for criminal choices is not very likely.

Application of Cultural Deviance Theory to Women

The emphases added to Shaw's quote above reflect that these theories were almost exclusively concerned with the transmission of culture to men, by men. Women were largely ignored even though they obviously lived in the transitional zones alongside the boys and men who were being socialized to criminality. This almost complete denial of the presence of women can only be understood by considering the time period and the rapid changes that have taken place in society concerning the role of women. In the 1930s, women were relegated to "hearth and home." Although lower-class women did not have the luxury of being housewives and most likely worked outside the home, they were largely invisible insofar as "street culture" was concerned. Theorists writing in these early years were as much a product of their socialization as they described their subjects being a product of the deviant culture's socialization; and their socialization was that women were different. This sex/gender difference overrode even the differences they observed between conventional and lower-class society. Thus, women, even lower-class women, were always women and acted like women (whatever that meant)—but men were different, depending on their socialization. Cultural deviance theories are singularly unable to explain female criminality, much less any changes in female criminality, largely because it evidently was never deemed important to ask whether there were cultural differences in definitions of femininity similarly to those described for masculinity.

Social Strain Theory

Merton, the originator of the strain or anomie theory, postulated that crime occurs because of blocked access to the goals of society.[35] Arguably everyone in society feels pressure to achieve the same goal, namely monetary success. Legitimate means to achieve this goal are employment, education, family connections, and so on. Those who have no legitimate means to achieve societal goals feel strain and react with innovation, i.e., crime. Others may react with other adaptations, specifically conformity and ritualism. It is, then, part of the unique culture of the "American" society that leads to high crime: since everyone is socialized to believe they can and should achieve material success, those who do not have the means feel particular strain. In other cultures that are more static vis-à-vis class (the poor have no expectation or hope they will achieve), there is less pressure or inclination to innovate to get ahead.

Criticisms of strain theory have included the idea that the theory says little about why people adopt the particular adaptations that they do. For instance, why do some people retreat and some innovate? Also, some adaptations are not conceptually distinct, i.e., conformity and ritualism seem very similar. There is a question as to whether the goals of this society are as homogenous as the theory postulates—is it true that everyone defines success the same way? Finally, the theory cannot explain crime from those who have "made it," and it cannot explain why those who are poor do not commit crime.[36]

Cohen elaborated and expanded Merton's concepts of blocked opportunity. In his theory, he proposed that lower-class boys, blocked from legitimate avenues of success, formed delinquent groups to protect their self-respect.[37] School and legitimate employment meant failure and, thus, the delinquent boys created an upside down world of values where short-term hedonism and negative behavior were prescribed instead of delayed gratification and conformance. Anti-social activity defined the boys as tough and affirmed their masculinity. Cloward[38] and Cloward and Ohlin[39] restated the basic ideas of strain theory and Cohen's cultural strain theory in their "differential opportunity" thesis. The added dimension of the differential opportunity thesis was that some boys were blocked from legitimate and illegitimate means to financial success. Some boys have avenues with organized crime available to them that are just as productive in achieving goals, while others are blocked even from these avenues.

Criticisms of the differential opportunity thesis include those applied to the general strain theory, as well as questions regarding why all boys in the neighborhood do not belong to gangs and why there are different types of gangs. Critics point out that the idea is empirically untested, and the hypothesis that all lower-class youth reject middle-class values does not seem entirely accurate. More recent tests of strain identify it as an individual concept, rather than an inherent element of lower class youth.[40]

Application of Strain/Opportunity Theory to Women

If the strain/opportunity thesis was perfectly able to explain crime, then one would think that women should be more criminal than men because, arguably, they have fewer opportunities to achieve financial and social success, and therefore, should feel more strain. Theorists who attempt to apply the theory to female criminality must argue that women and men have different goals in this society: for instance, the common argument becomes men have the goal of financial success, women have the goal of financial success through marriage. Women's goals, it is assumed, are more often relational— to get married and to have children (traditionally). Since these goals are so easily achieved, women are not under the strain that men experience. The application would predict that only those women who are blocked from these goals would turn to crime. Thus, only those women who are blocked from achieving their own version of success (marriage) would be expected to innovate through crime or other deviant means.

Consistent with this application, Cohen proposed that when girls resorted to delinquency, their delinquency was associated with their different goal orientations (the attention of men), thus it almost always took the form of sexual promiscuity: "[male delinquency] . . . is versatile, whereas female delinquency is relatively specialized. It consists overwhelmingly of sexual delinquency."[41] Obviously Cohen mistook official reaction for actual rates of delinquency. Since the system was more concerned with girls' sexual deviance than with the boys, official reports overestimate girls' sexual delinquency. The theory is unable to explain property crime—unless one argues that the only things girls steal are the tools to "get a guy."[42]

Naffine points out that Cohen's description of societal values that the delinquent boys reject is almost purely a description of stereotypically male traits: "Autonomy, rationality, ambition and restraint with one's emotions are the attributes of the person who makes it in America, but that person is male."[43] Girls fit into Cohen's scheme only peripherally and do not evidently have a need to protect their self-image, even if employment and education opportunities are blocked to them as well. Since girls are only interested in ". . . dating, popularity with boys, pulchritude, 'charm,' clothes and dancing . . ." they do not react to blocked opportunities with an alternative culture.[44] Cohen's description of female traits runs directly counter to his description of what is normal and admirable: he identified ambition as a virtue and girls as "inactive" and "unambitious"; he portrayed altruism as inconsistent with American self-reliance and described girls as nurturing and affiliative. He described rationality as a trait associated with success and girls as emotional and sociable. He described initiative as valuable in a "get ahead" society and described girls as timid and harm avoiders. Thus, in Cohen's theory, delinquent boys are actually more "normal" than all girls, if one uses his description of normality that draws heavily from traits associated with masculinity. The delinquent boy may be "bad," but at least he is male; and there is even a "glamour and romance" associated with his antics: "[discussing male delinquency] however it may be condemned by others on moral grounds, has at least one virtue: it incontestably confirms, in the eyes of all concerned, his essential masculinity."[45]

Cloward and Ohlin, as well as the other theorists, did not see girls as part of the economic mainstream of society. It was the male, according to

Cloward and Ohlin, who "must go into the marketplace to seek employment, make a career for himself, and support a family."[46] Since females are not pressured to seek economic success, they do not pursue delinquent avenues to reach such goals. Cloward and Ohlin's only mention of girls, in fact, is to blame them for male delinquency arguing that they were the reason boys felt pressure to have money.[47]

Morris was one early theorist who applied strain theory to female delinquency: she proposed that boys will turn to delinquency when blocked from economic success goals; girls will turn to delinquency when blocked from affective (relationship) goals, since that is the measure of success for women in society. According to this theory, delinquent girls would be those who came from dysfunctional families and who "rated low in personal appearance and in grooming skills."[48] Her findings supported her theory: in a sample of delinquent boys and girls compared to a control sample of non-delinquents, she found that delinquent girls were more likely to come from broken homes, and rated their family life as unhappy. Delinquent girls evidently also displayed slightly poorer grooming habits; however, Morris not find that personal appearance overall was different between delinquent and control samples of girls.[49] Others pursued the idea that girls turned to delinquency when blocked from marriage (their legitimate means of success).[50]

Smith tested strain theory with a large sample of men and women.[51] Using self-reported delinquent and criminal acts as the dependent variable, he tested a number of alternative criminological theories. Strain was measured by agreement with statements regarding a perception of blocked opportunities and access to such things as education and employment. It was found that strain was an equally valid predictor of delinquency for both males and females, but that after controlling for strain, there was still additional male delinquency unexplained by strain.

Cernkovich and Giordano found that race complicated the strain association in their study of self-reported delinquency and perceptions of strain. Although strain was a fairly good predictor of delinquency for whites, it did not hold up as well for non-whites. It operated equally well for females as males for the white sample only.[52]

The problem with the adaptation of strain theory to women is that it assumes many things. First, that women do have different goals from men. This may be true (or it may have been true in the past), but the assumption that they turn to crime when they are blocked in their specific goal of marriage does not necessarily follow. Note that the goal of financial success is logically related to an innovative strategy of property crime or robbery (in order to achieve money); however, the goal of marriage is not logically related to an innovative strategy of crime (how does one achieve marriage through crime?). Only if one postulated that marriage was only a financial and economic goal would there be the same logical consistency between strain and crime.

The theory assumes that only women who are blocked from marriage resort to crime. Statistics do not clearly support this—many criminal women are married, and many unmarried women are not criminal. If one argues that marriage is only an avenue to financial success, the argument is supported somewhat better by statistics that indicate poor, single head-of-household women are more likely than other demographic groups to engage in consumer type of crimes. If, however, the theory assumes that marriage is the end of the rainbow for women and once achieved it is unnecessary to innovate, it denies the fact that marriage itself sometimes leads to criminal behavior, either through the influence of the man, or because the man is unable or unwilling to provide for the woman and/or children and she engages in crime as a result.

How does the theory account for increasing rates of property crime among women? One would at first assume that women have more opportunities today and should be feeling less strain (with reduced crime as a result). On the other hand, if women are less likely to marry, marry later, and/or less often able to depend on a husband to provide for them, then the theory makes sense because it would support greater rates of property crime. The basic theme of strain theory, as applied to women, is that women have been exempt from feeling the strain of economic independence and responsibility. Arguably, this has been true in the past (at least for middle- and upper-middle-class women) and not so true today; thus, it is not entirely inconsistent with current statistics. It does not explain, however, women's continued lower rates of violent crime.

Radical, Critical, or Marxist Criminology

Radical, critical, or Marxist theories of crime are placed here in a social structure section only as an organizational tool; some would argue that they should be categorized completely separately from all sociological theories because they focus on societal definitions of crime, rather than solely on factors in society that cause crime.[53] For instance, Leonard describes Marxist criminology as a different paradigm entirely from those theories discussed herein because it attacks the basic definition of crime itself.[54] Radical or critical criminology challenges the "science" of criminology and the nature of the exercise, concentrating as it does on the individual "deviant." Like labeling theory,[55] the process of defining crime is addressed in critical or radical criminology, and the nature of law as a method of social control by power holders is challenged. Under a Marxist theory of crime, crime exists in the capitalist society as "work." It is an essential element of capitalism. Criminal activity represents false consciousness; the "lumpenproletariat" do not know who their true oppressors are, thus they steal from and hurt each other. This approach expands the definition of crime to, for instance, the death of workers in unsafe conditions.

Taylor, Walton, and Young[56] and Richard Quinney[57] and others have been important figures in the development of critical criminology. Elements of critical criminology include an identification of class-based definitions of crime, a challenge to the ideology of equality, and the lack of objectivity in law. Criticisms of the theory include challenging the assumption that there are only two classes in society. Critics contend that this is an oversimplified view of society and that economic placements and power coalitions are more diverse than indicated by the theory's focus on the haves and have-nots. There is also, perhaps, a problem with the assumption that notions of law are not shared by the classes. Most in society, regardless of economic standing, agree with definitions of criminality and even rank crimes similarly. Of course, the strongest criticism of this theory (like many others) is that it does not explain the sex differential in crime rates. If women form part of the lumpenproletariat, why are they not aggressing against other members of their class in the same manner as their men?[58]

Application of Critical Criminology to Women

According to the few theorists that attempt to apply critical criminology to women's crime, sexism keeps women at home and women, therefore, suffer poverty in a way different from men.[59] While men have labor to sell and become disassociated from selves through the economic exchange of their labor, women, too, are economic commodities under capitalism—both their labor and sexuality are for sale (again prostitution is explained as the epitome of female criminality). Critical criminology does not view men and women as different, and, therefore, cannot explain the different crime rates of men and women.

SOCIAL PROCESS THEORIES

Social process theories focus on the individual's interaction with the world around him/her. Thus, relationships become important. Social process theories have more in common in this way with psychological theories, and, in fact, many could be described as social-psychological.

Differential Association

Sutherland introduced the theory of differential association in 1939 and later joined with Donald Cressey to reiterate the concepts.[60] If cultural deviance theory identifies the concept that there can be different subcultures in a society that influence the thoughts and behaviors of those exposed to such subcultures, then differential association can be described as the theory that details how that influence operates. Differential association assumes that delinquency and criminality develop because of an excess of definitions favorable to crime offered by one's close associates. That is, if family and friends are criminal, profess criminal values, and teach criminal methods, one will become criminal. This theory assumes that learning takes place most importantly within intimate personal groups and that learning includes techniques of crime, as well as motives, drives, rationalizations, and attitudes.[61]

Akers applied social learning principles to differential association.[62] He and Robert Burgess developed the differential association-reinforcement theory, which applied behaviorism and principles of learning to the sociological theory.[63] For instance, the seventh principle of differential association: "differential associations may vary in frequency, duration, priority, and intensity," changes to: "the strength of deviant behavior is a direct function of the amount, frequency, and probability of its reinforcement. The modalities of association with deviant patterns are important in so far as they affect the source, amount, and scheduling of reinforcement."[64]

Criticisms of differential association and/or Akers' formulation of it include the observation that it is not conceptually distinct from simple learning theory or behaviorism. Others argue that the theory cannot explain "irrational" crimes, such as crimes of passion. It does not explain "new criminals," that is, those criminals that develop in law-abiding families. There is a de-emphasis of personal traits (such as aggressiveness) that may be questionable, as well as the de-emphasis of choice in a more general sense. One might argue against the theory, for instance, by observing that actors choose associations to support their behavior (i.e., alcoholics who choose to develop new friendships to help them stay sober). Especially later reformulations of the theory are almost purely deterministic views of human nature, i.e., we must become criminal if we have an excess of criminal definitions, and this troubles those who perceive human nature as operating with a bit more free will.

Application of Differential Association to Women

Sutherland and Cressey maintained that the theory was general and not specific to male behavior.[65] Yet in the attempt to explain why females commit less crime, the inconsistencies appear unless one assumes that girls and boys receive different messages. Indeed, that is what is hypothesized in the application of this theory to female criminality. Girls are evidently taught from birth to conform to one model of female normality that is homogenous across social and economic categories, even though boys are exposed to a variety of different definitions of normality.[66]

Female patterns of crime pose difficulty for the differential association theory only if one assumes that sisters and brothers are exposed to the same definitions of criminality. Also, if girls are more restricted in their movements and associations, and, thus, have less opportunity to form and/or be exposed to the intimate personal groups that provide criminal definitions (gangs or delinquent peers), then they receive less criminal messages.

Applying these assumptions, one would predict, therefore, that girls that come from broken homes or homes with poor parental supervision would be more delinquent than those girls controlled in the home. Early attempts to test differential association for girls tested the idea that girls lacked social support for delinquency; unfortunately, they used different kinds of delinquent acts for boys and girls, hopelessly confusing the results. For boys, surveys identified motor vehicle thefts and assaults as delinquent acts, but for girls "heavy petting" or promiscuity were used as the operationalization of delinquency.[67] Hindelang, in a study of 1,000 schoolchildren, found strong support for the delinquent peer element of differential association for boys and to a lesser extent for girls as well.[68] Other studies also found that delinquent peer groups were highly correlated with delinquency, but more so for boys than for girls.[69]

If we accept that girls and boys learn *different* things even in the same environment and with the same exposures, then differential association theory is a valid explanation for the gender differential in crime. If we can assume that girls are no longer learning different things, and are in fact being socialized more similarly to their brothers, then it might explain the crime rate increase for property crime. In fact, if we elaborate the "definitions" of crime to include the types of crimes committed, it can explain the pattern of criminal behavior for females, i.e., consumer "shopping" crimes, such as shoplifting and credit card theft.

Control Theory

Control theory, as presented by Travis Hirschi, states that the delinquent or criminal is one who is not controlled by bonds to society, specifically attachment, commitment, involvement, and belief.[70] Attachment involves relationships; commitment involves the dedication to legitimate work and leisure activities; involvement measures actual time engaged in such activities; and belief involves the agreement and acceptance of the individual toward basic goals and rules of society. Conformity occurs because of ties to society; deviance occurs when those ties are weak or nonexistent. Conformity is associated with good school performance, strong family ties, liking for school, conventional aspirations, and respect for law. Note the difference here between control theory and differential association or cultural deviance theories; while the latter propose that individuals learn how to be criminal, in essence that they are socialized to criminality, Hirschi's formulation proposes that criminality takes place because of a lack of socialization.

In the research that supported the development of control theory, Hirschi used self-report surveys of large numbers of young people and analyzed self-reported delinquency (validated by comparison to official records) and measures of the bonds to society described above. For instance, attachment was measured by such things as supervision (Does your mother/father know where you are when you are away from home?), communication (Do you share your thoughts and feelings with your mother/father?), and affectional identification (Would you like to be the kind of person your mother/father is?).

Criticism of control theory points out that the theory does not discuss why bonds are weak or strong, nor does it include any possibility of individual action affecting such bonds. The theory also does not seem to explain corporate crime or passion crime, although it is hard to say since research in this area tends to focus solely on delinquency as opposed to adult criminality.

Application of Control Theory to Women

In a decision that was heavily criticized by the feminist critiques that emerged in the 1970s, Hirschi chose to drop girls from his sample before analysis began. Naffine, for instance, points out that Hirschi begins his exploration not with the question "why do people commit crime?" but rather with "why don't people commit crime?" yet then proceeds to ignore the largest group of non-offenders—women. Naffine notes that Hirschi does something else interesting—he transforms law-abiding behavior to become "male-like" rather than weak and passive as characterized by earlier theorists (Cohen and Sutherland).

> As Hirschi changes the field of study, from the criminal man to the conforming man, so the enriching qualities of masculinity now attach to conventionality and it is delinquency which is devalued as a symptom of emotional immaturity. Hirschi therefore alters our vision of conformity as he conceives of the conforming person as male, not female. What all this seems to indicate is a profound criminological tendency to devalue the female and value the male even when they are doing precisely the same things.[71]

Interestingly, tests of control theory idealize or devalue conformity depending on whether they are testing the theory on women or men. Hagan, Simpson, and Gillis, for instance, note that delinquency is "fun" and that females are more controlled through family associations and other forms of informal control, thus, they do not have as much opportunity for the fun of delinquency.[72] This version of control theory is not at all different from sex-role theory or the earlier applications of differential association to female conformity. Hirschi, on the other hand, conceptualized the delinquent as adrift without meaning or value or friendships; it was the law-abiding teen who was active, dynamic, and having "fun" by engaging in extracurricular and family activities.

Control theory does provide a more adequate explanation for the sex differential in crime rates than some of the other traditional theories discussed above. Jensen and Eve found partial support for the idea that females have more "bonds" to society (attachment, involvement, belief, and commitment), although they discovered that males still committed more delinquent acts even when controlling for such things as parental attachment, school grades, and attachment to teachers and school.[73] Others found that the absence of bonds was correlated with delinquency, but, again, more so for boys than for girls.[74]

Labeling Theory

Labeling theory relies on symbolic interactionism, and can be traced to the ideas of Edwin Lemert,[75] George Herbert Mead,[76] and Howard Becker.[77] The theory is unique from those discussed above in that, like radical criminology, it focuses attention on the official labeler as well as the deviant. In fact, deviance (at least secondary deviance) is believed to be caused by the actions of the labeler instead of any individual pathology on the part of the offender. The theory raises questions as to why only certain behaviors are labeled deviant, why only certain people are subject to formal sanctions, and how labels of deviance change over time. The main element of concern for understanding individual behavior, however, is the assumption that the deviant is reacting to the labeling process.

> If the deviant acts are repetitive and have a high visibility, and if there is a severe societal reaction, which, through a process of identification is incorporated as part of the "me" of the individual, the probability is greatly increased that the integration of existing roles will be disrupted and that reorganization based upon a new role or roles will occur.[78]

This theory assumes that labeling certain individuals deviant, and then acting toward them according to such a label, inevitably results in their accepting and absorbing the deviant role. While Becker assumed a great deal of volition on the part of the actor in accepting or rejecting labels, later applications of the theory presumed a more passive recipient of the labeling process.

Criticisms of labeling theory include the observation that no explanation for primary deviance is offered. Also, whether secondary deviance would not exist except for the labeling is probably untestable.[79] Schur defends labeling theory by combining it with other theories to explain primary deviance,[80] and applies labeling theory directly to women, explaining how gender roles contribute to beliefs regarding women as a deviant group.[81] However, labeling does not explain persistent criminality when offenders are not subject to labeling (hidden corporate criminality) and ignores the deterrent effect of official interventions.

Application of Labeling Theory to Women

There is very little literature by labeling theorists to help us understand female criminality.[82] For labeling theory to work for women, one must assume that women are less likely to be labeled as deviant and, therefore, do not internalize deviant labels even if they engage in primary deviance. Other corollaries are that women suffer less stigma if they are in contact with formal authorities. If true, this would explain their reduced numbers in secondary deviance. Some support for these premises are offered by research that contends that females are less likely to be stigmatized through formal criminal processing, that is, they are not given the criminal label as readily as are men.[83] Others, of course, argue that some females, especially juvenile females are more likely to be formally processed.[84] As discussed in the previous chapter, whether women are treated chivalrously by the system is difficult to determine.

In one of the few applications of labeling theory to females, Harris portrayed women as manipulated by powerful men to conform to housewifely roles and eschew criminal activity.[85] This, of course, is not labeling theory at all, but rather another version of differential association or sex-role theory. However, he went on to illustrate that the system created a criminal type (the African-American male) who was labeled as criminal because he was expendable, while women were valuable for the smooth functioning of society. Harris believed that powerful definitions of criminal and non-criminal affect individuals even before formal processing occurs; thus, women lived up to their law-abiding life script and avoided criminality.

CONCLUSION

Except for psychological theories, the theories described in this chapter assume sameness; that is, individuals are presumed to turn to criminality because of societal factors that exist apart from them and that they react to, i.e., blocked opportunity, cultural deviance influences, labels, lack of bonds, and so on. However, all these theories were developed for men, the sameness is the sameness of men, not women. If women were thought of at all, it was as different; they did not share in the deviant subculture and/or they did not feel strain. Of course, later researchers attempted to adapt the theories and test them with samples of female delinquents and women, but the adaptations seem forced, the explanations contorted. The implication is clear that women tended to complicate the theory and were better left out. Most tests conducted on these theories found that some amount of sex differential remained even after controlling for theoretical constructs. Thus, the conclusion always ended with some version of sex role theory, i.e., that women were controlled more, taught differently, and subsequently acted differently from men. In the next chapter we look at theories that more specifically attempted to explain these differences.

NOTES

[1]   Textbooks such as Akers (1997), Siegel (1989), Williams and McShane (1988, 1998), and DeKeseredy and Schwartz (1997) can be used as companion volumes, and have been used, along with other sources, for discussion.

[2]   Lombroso (1894) or Pollak (1950).

[3]   The use of the male subject is purely intentional; philosophers in this time period did not view women in the same manner as men, especially where rationality was concerned.

[4]   Bentham (1843/1970).

[5]   Siegel (1989, 96).

[6]   Although note that it has been resurrected in recent years as "Rational Choice" theory.

[7]   1894 and 1895.

[8]   1894.

[9]   Andrews and Bonta (1994).

[10] 1994, 6.

[11] Ironically, however, even though these authors lament the field of criminology ignoring psychology, in their 250-page book, women or the sex differential of crime is only mentioned nine times; and little attention is given to sex-role theory (which is social-psychological). In their book, sex or gender is mentioned in general theories of crime as a personal, individual barrier and recognized as a correlate, but nowhere in this explanation of individual differences as related to criminality is it explained *how* gender affects one's predisposition to criminality.

[12] Andrews and Bonta (1994, 130), also see Redl and Toch (1979).

[13] 1934.

[14] Andrews and Bonta (1994, 91).

[15] See, for instance, Gottfredson and Hirschi (1990).

[16] There is no reason, however, why theories must necessarily concentrate solely on individual development, or solely on the sociological elements that affect the environment and particular individual factors into which one is born.

[17] Lykken (1995, 6-7).

[18] 1995, 12. One assumes that Lykken would also blame fathers for not parenting appropriately or taking responsibility for their children. Lykken believes in requiring parental licensure to reduce the number of sociopaths (1995, 231); a solution that is as unlikely as it is unconstitutional.

[19] Mann (1984b), Pollock (1978), Gora (1982), and others review early psychological theories of female criminality.

[20] 1995, 25 (emphasis added).

[21] 1965.

[22] 1981.

23   1979.

24   1982.

25   1979.

26   1977.

27   Akers (1973).

28   See Sutherland (1939) and Akers (1994/1997). For more explanation, refer to the discussion of differential associaton later in this chapter.

29   Andrews and Bonta (1994, 111).

30   For a discussion of the Chicago School, see Siegel (1989, 162), Akers (1997, 115), or any basic criminology textbook.

31   1934/1972.

32   Shaw (1951, 15, emphasis added).

33   Sellin (1938), Miller (1958), and Cohen (1955).

34   Miller (1958).

35   1938.

36   For more discussion of these concepts, see Leonard (1982, 56-57).

37   1955.

38   1959.

39   1960.

40   Agnew et al. (1996) test strain theory by operationalizing the concept as dissatisfaction with monetary status and expectations of success. In a sample of adults in Cincinnati, they find that dissatisfaction is highest among those who are poor, and among those who desire a lot of money but have low expectations for achieving financial success. This dissatisfaction was correlated with committing income-generating crime and drug use, but the effect was stronger among those who had criminal friends. Unfortunately, sex was not used as an independent variable in this research effort.

41   Cohen (1955, 141).

42   Actually, some early theorists noted that very thought in their observation that girls tended to shoplift makeup and clothing.

43   1987, 11.

44   Cohen (1955, 147).

45   1955, 140.

46   1960, 106.

47   1960, 110.

48   1964, 83.

49   1964.

[50] Sandhu and Allen compared a group of institutionalized females to a control group of high school girls. Contrary to their theory, they found that the delinquent girls displayed markedly less commitment to marriage, yet the theorists decided that the delinquent girls were simply reacting to their recognition that they were blocked by taking on the attitude of not caring, thus their theory was "partially supported" (1969, 110). Still others compared girls and boys in a general application of strain theory by testing perceptions of blocked opportunity. Datesman et al. (1975, 107) found that there was a stronger association between perceived strain and delinquency for girls than for boys. Yet the authors then interpret these findings as if girls interpreted the "success" statements in the instrument as relating to marriage and relationship goals (even though statements specifically related to education and employment).

[51] 1979.

[52] 1979.

[53] There is also disagreement on the scope and definitional elements of these terms. Some argue that critical criminology includes feminism and post-modernism, some argue that radical and Marxist theories of crime are not the same, and so on. For our purposes, the terms will be used interchangeably and exclude feminist and post-modernist theories.

[54] Leonard (1982).

[55] Labeling theory will be discussed shortly.

[56] 1973. Also refer to their recent book (1998).

[57] 1973.

[58] For a discussion of critical or Marxist criminology, see Leonard (1982).

[59] Klein and Kress (1976).

[60] Sutherland and Cressey (1960/1966).

[61] Sutherland and Cressey (1960, 77-79).

[62] 1973.

[63] Burgess and Akers (1966).

[64] Akers (1973, 46).

[65] Unlike Cohen, who made no apologies for his purely masculine theory of delinquency.

[66] For instance: "From infancy, girls are taught that they must be nice, while boys are taught that they must be rough and tough . . . Girls are schooled in 'anti-criminal behavior patterns'" (Burgess and Akers, 1966, 142).

[67] Morris (1964).

[68] 1979, also see 1981.

[69] Smith (1979), in his analysis of a large survey sample, found that reference group deviance (his measure of differential association) explained both male and female delinquency. However, he found that when both sexes have the same exposure to delinquent friends, boys will still be more delinquent than girls.

[70] Hirschi (1969).

[71] Naffine (1987, 67).

[72]   This theory will be more fully explored in the next chapter.

[73]   1976.

[74]   Hindelang (1979) concluded that the absence of those factors identified in control theory as bonds to society were able to predict delinquency for both boys and girls. Smith (1979) also found that bonds accurately predicted delinquency for both men and women, but that controlling for bonds did not entirely eliminate the sex differential. Women with low social bonds were still more conforming than men.

[75]   1951.

[76]   1934.

[77]   1963.

[78]   Lemert (1951, 76).

[79]   Akers (1973).

[80]   Schur (1971).

[81]   Schur (1984).

[82]   Lemert's (1951) treatment of prostitutes is one exception; however, since he perceived of prostitution as a sexual deviation rather than an economic crime, it is of limited value.

[83]   Hagan, Simpson, and Gillis (1979) and Steffensmeier and Kramer (1980).

[84]   Chesney-Lind (1973 and 1997).

[85]   1977.

The Criminology of Women, Feminist Criminology, and the "New" Female Criminal

6

Objectives

- Become familiar with those theories that were developed specifically to explain female criminality.

- Contrast the explanations applied to female criminality with those applied to male criminality.

- Become familiar with the feminist critiques of the traditional theories of criminality.

- Understand the weaknesses of the argument of the "new" female criminal.

In the last chapter, traditional theories of crime were reviewed. These could be called theories of male criminality since the theorists who developed them did not attempt to explain why women committed crime, nor why women committed less crime than men. Before the early 1970s, the field of criminology was dominated by male theorists who either could not or would not recognize that one of the most interesting criminological correlates was sex. This neglect was identified and criticized by a series of female theorists who can be identified (and identified themselves) as feminists. Their critiques have been incorporated in the discussion offered in the last chapter concerning traditional theories. In this chapter, we will review their general conclusions regarding standard criminology. We will also explore the few historical theories that focused on women's criminality, as well as those that emerged in the 1970s. Not all of these theories can be called feminist, but then even the definition of feminism is subject to debate, as we shall see below. However, what all the theories discussed in this chapter have in common is a direct attempt to explain female criminality. Again, recall that any theory should be able to explain both why women commit less crime, especially less violent crime; but also, why women who do commit crime do so, and, why women are increasing their crime rates (at least in property crime areas).

EARLY BIOLOGICAL AND PSYCHOLOGICAL THEORIES

As mentioned in the last chapter, Lombroso was one early theorist who did propose to offer an explanation of female criminality. After comparing physical features of criminal women and non-criminal women, Lombroso and Ferrero concluded that criminal women were biologically inferior, in fact they were evolutionary throwbacks to a primitive state:

> . . . while the majority of female delinquents are led into crime either by the suggestion of a third person or by irresistible tempta-tion, and are not entirely deficient in the moral sense, there is yet to be found among them a small proportion whose criminal propensities are more intense and more perverse than those of their male prototypes.[1]

Women, according to Lombroso and Ferrero, were ordinarily held in check by biological traits such as passivity, but when they were criminal, they were worse than male criminals:

> . . . their moral sense is deficient . . . they are revengeful, jealous, inclined to vengeances of a refined cruelty. In ordinary cases these defects are neutralized by piety, maternity, want of passion, sexual coldness, by weakness and an undeveloped intelligence.[2]

Obviously Lombroso and Ferrero's theory of female criminality can be subject to the same criticisms as their theories regarding male criminality, as well as some gross stereotyping of gender traits. The idea that men and women were biologically different and that it was these differences that affected women's lower crime rates, however, was a theme that persisted in the theories of crime throughout the early 1900s. One thread of such research was to consider women as the "breeders" of criminality. Hahn discusses the "cacogenic" family studies of the early 1900s. These studies, fund-ed by wealthy supporters of eugenics, all found that in examples where one man had relations with a "good" woman and a "bad" woman (the illegitimate lover or prostitute), it was the "bad" woman's children who were alcoholics, vagrants, and criminals.[3] The studies, of course, ignored the social and eco-nomic implications that were involved and identified the mother's "bad seed" as the reason for generations of criminals.

Reviews of older theories pointed out how such theories identified women's biological traits as suppressing criminality.[4] For instance one early theorist argued that in the early history of humankind, women did not resort to crime because of their physical incapability (they were weaker and all crime was physical). This pattern continued even after crime did not require physical strength.[5] These early theories tended to concentrate on why the women who committed crime "went against their nature," with the assumption that it was a woman's biological and psychological destiny to be gentle, passive, and non-criminal.

Freud's 1933 assumptions about women's reproductive instinct, innate passivity, narcissism, and deceitfulness provided the foundation for the works of others such as Pollak,[6] Konopka,[7] and Vedder and Somerville.[8] One could also add Thomas,[9] the Gluecks,[10] and Cowie, Cowie, and Slater,[11] although not all emphasized similar features of the psychology of women. These early psychological theories described female delinquents and criminals as different from men in their needs, desires, and motivations for crime.

In the 1920s, W.I. Thomas postulated a biological difference in men and women that affected their psychological makeup. Women, according to Thomas, suffered from frustrations because of being left out of everything. Wishes influenced behavior, and these wishes, especially a woman's desire for response, were thought to be more intense than men's. Maternal drives, caring for the sick and helpless, and, in general being more altruistic than men were evidence of this need for affiliation. Even the prostitute exemplified this drive since Thomas perceived the crime as a desire to seek love and tenderness rather than a pure economic exchange. Women were, by nature, passive compared to men who were active. They had four desires: the desire for new experience, desire for security, desire for response, and desire for recognition. These desires largely accounted for delinquency and crime. For instance, Thomas saw shoplifting as the desire for new experience, but also for recognition and response since girls were likely to steal things that would make them "pretty."[12]

Pollak also used psychological constructs to explain why and how women committed crime, although he, unlike most of these other theorists, believed that women were just as criminal as men.[13] He discussed the devious nature of females and concluded that deviousness among women, if not biological, was aided by a woman's biology, using as examples the woman's ability to fake sexual response and conceal menstruation. His theory presumed men and women were different in their personality structure, not criminality; therefore, differences could be observed only in what crimes were committed and how they were committed. Most theorists discussed in this section concluded that men and women were different in their personality structure and emotional makeup, and that these differences reduced criminality among women.[14]

Cowie, Cowie, and Slater (1968) offered one of the most complete early analyses of the interplay between psychological and other factors in the development of delinquency. They wrote that social and psychological factors, such as poverty or broken and/or poor home environments, seemed to be better explanations for female delinquents than male delinquents. Comparing delinquent girls with delinquent boys, the girls were found to come from economically poorer homes, with more mental abnormality in the family, with poorer moral standards, worse discipline, more often a broken home, more frequent changes of home, more conflict at home, and more disturbed intrafamilial relations.

> Social factors have been found to be of very great importance in
> the causation of delinquency in boys; there is little evidence that
> they play anything like the same part in the case of girls . . . The
> effective motivational factors are connected, much more than with
> boys, with the intimate family, and with the girl's personal relations
> with her parent. (1968, 44).

They found that ". . . the girls have worse school records, and more often
have developed a hostile reaction towards schooling; they show a larger
degree of rejection of family influence; their working careers are worse."[15]
The authors proposed that delinquent girls had "defective" intelligence,
deprived childhoods, and often incestuous fathers. While they recognized
environmental factors, they believed that biological predisposition had to
play a part as well in delinquency. Further, they noted that delinquent women
tended to come from worse home environments than male delinquents,
therefore they concluded that biological factors insulated women generally
from criminality, and it was only under extreme stress that women were not
controlled by these predispositions: "The pattern of development in personality and behavior is more stable and more consistent in the female than in
the male, and can take a larger stress before being disrupted."[16] In other
words, although they recognized that women were subject to greater social
control, they were unpersuaded that social control was enough to account
for the longstanding sex differential in crime rates, so they concluded that
one had to look for "chromosomal and genetical factors."

Later feminist critiques challenged these early theorists' conclusions that
the differences between men and women were inherently biological or psychological. For instance, Chesney-Lind and Sheldon, commenting on Konopka, state:

> Konopka's more sophisticated understanding of girls' reality still
> ultimately assumed that girls and women were largely controlled by
> their biology and their sexuality. Indeed, she, like most authors of
> the early works on female delinquency, assumed that most female
> delinquency is either "sexual" or "relational" rather than "criminal"
> in nature, and was convinced that social intervention administered
> by sensitive and informed individuals could help young women
> with their problems.[17]

Review and Critique

The early biological and psychological theories of female criminality proposed that biological and psychological differences between men and
women were responsible for women's lower crime rate. Those women who
did commit crime were observed to come from markedly more dysfunctional backgrounds, therefore, it was proposed that these backgrounds overcame
"natural" and "biological" predispositions against criminality.

This prevalent view that female delinquents were more likely to come from broken homes and dysfunctional homes has been tested by numerous researchers with mixed results.[18] The research is complicated by different propositions that are conceptually distinct. First is the hypothesis that female delinquents are more likely than male delinquents to come from broken homes (because it takes a dysfunctional background to overcome "natural" or socialized predispositions against delinquency for girls, while boys need no such impetus). Second, is the hypothesis that girl delinquents are *more* affected by broken homes or family discord—this implies that boys can withstand more dysfunction in their family life than girls. These two hypotheses are distinct, but tests of them look similar—for instance, if one showed that among official delinquents, more girls than boys had dysfunctional backgrounds, does this statistic support the first hypothesis or the second?

Chesney-Lind and Sheldon review a number of studies reporting on the association between broken homes, sex, and delinquency and find mixed results. Some longitudinal studies indicate boys are more affected by divorce and other family discord than girls, some self-reports show no association between delinquency and attachment to family (even with many different measures of attachment), some show slightly more association for females, but these often use official populations, presenting the strong probability of officials reacting to home conditions differentially for girls. Chesney-Lind and Sheldon conclude that these findings are not consistent, but looking at all studies, one might conclude there is a stronger association between male delinquency and family discord, indicating males are more affected and females are more resilient.[19]

Rosenbaum also reviews a number of studies and concludes that female delinquents are more likely than male delinquents to come from dysfunctional homes. In fact, in her own study of delinquents from an early 1960s data set of the California Youth Authority, *all* the girls came from dysfunctional homes marked by abuse, divorce, alcoholism, and other elements of dysfunction.[20] Widom found that abused or neglected girls were twice as likely as a matched group of non-abused to have an adult crime record (16% compared to 7.5%); the difference among men was not as dramatic (42% compared to 33%). She also found that male victims of childhood abuse tended to commit violent crimes, while female victims tended to commit property and social order offenses.[21] Other research indicates childhood abuse and neglect is correlated with delinquency and crime.[22]

One reason studies have inconsistent findings may be too superficial measurements of dysfunction are utilized. For instance, divorce may not necessarily indicate a dysfunctional home life. It would be important to collect other measures of dysfunction, such as multiple marriages of mothers, family criminality, family violence, alcoholism, and so on. In her study of a sample of male and female offenders in New Haven, Daly concludes:

Although the men's economic and emotional circumstances growing up were not optimal, they were better than the women's for
almost all the indicators. Evidence of strained familial relations
were higher for women than men (38 versus 25 percent), and a
larger proportion of women than men (26 versus 9 percent) ran
away from home or a juvenile facility. The men's formative years
suggest less damaging and abusive family contexts than the
women's.[23]

The evidence, although mixed, seems to support the notion that female delinquents and female adult criminals are more likely than male delinquents and
criminals to come from extremely dysfunctional families. Whether this means
that girls are more resilient and there must be greater dysfunction to overcome "natural" disinclination's to commit crime, or whether girls are more
affected by dysfunctional family life is not clear, although the weight of the
evidence seems to lean toward the first hypothesis.

Sex differences between men and women—especially those that influence personality makeup—are still subject to debate, and one's position on
the matter influences assumptions and hypotheses that female delinquents
have different motivations or needs than male delinquents. One thing seems
clear—in the early 1960s and before, women's biological sex did determine
their opportunities and value system. Their delinquency was largely relational, and research was fairly consistent in the finding that they seemed to come
from more dysfunctional backgrounds than did their male counterparts.

OTHER EARLY THEORIES

While most early theories identified inherent biological and/or psychological differences between men and women, there were a few that looked at
other differences between men and women. The difference between the theories discussed above and the two theories discussed below is that the theories below do not believe gender/sex differences are inherent or immutable.

Compulsive Masculinity

Parsons, although a sociologist, presented a psychological theory identifying sex-role identification as the basis of the different crime patterns of men
and women. According to his theory, women's lack of criminality was due to
a close and nurturing female figure upon which adolescent girls could model
themselves; male children, frustrated by lack of close models, engaged in
delinquency as a reaction to the omnipresent female authority figures in their
lives.[24] Parsons noted that women were largely responsible for the socializa-

tion of the next generation, including the socialization of ethical behavior, but instead boys see the "goodness" of mothers as weak (since the dominant society disvalues her) and therefore rebel against niceness creating the "strong tendency for boyish behavior to run in antisocial . . . directions."[25]

Girls have no such sex-identity conflicts and are quite content to conform to a mother's role model, including the adoption of prosocial values and behaviors. The theory would lead to the prediction that men would be more likely to be criminal if from a mother-headed household; and women would be more inclined to criminality if from a dysfunctional household (with no good mother role-model). Further, it could be predicted that more "masculine" men would be more criminal, and more "feminine" women would be less criminal. The tests of the theory, unfortunately, have difficulty with operationalizing the constructs, largely because what theorists propose as measures of masculinity and femininity are heavily influenced by sex-role stereotypes. Also, what occurred in later theories was that the hypothesis tested became one where masculinity was correlated with delinquency for either sex. Thus, it was hypothesized that criminal women and girls would test as more masculine than non-criminal women or girls. This is not at all consistent with Parson's sex-role identity idea that boys rebel against a maternal figure.[26]

For instance, Cullen, Golden, and Cullen (1979) found partial support for the masculinity thesis in their sample of college students; masculine traits (self-identified traits such as aggression, independence, objectivity, dominance, competitiveness, and self-confidence) were positively associated with delinquent acts (self-reported) for both males and females. Yet, when controlling for "masculinity," men still committed higher rates of delinquent acts than did women.[27]

These authors defined masculinity through such measures as leadership, competitiveness, aggressiveness, successfulness, and ambition. Their findings, using a high school self-report sample, indicated that masculinity was directly related only to status offenses and not to property and violent offenses. However, this study obtained very small numbers of serious crimes (especially considering the sophisticated measures of association used). Also, one might argue with the operationalization of masculinity—why would leadership, for instance, be solely a masculinity indicator? Although sex-typed, leadership in high school can be very consistent with a definition of femininity (i.e., captain of cheerleaders, homecoming queen, etc.). The hypothesis that masculinity among both men and women would be related to delinquency is problematic—it would have been more consistent with Parsons' original thesis to test the level of femininity as a correlate of delinquency; in other words, girls should show a decrease in sex-role identity (but not necessarily revert to a masculine identity). If femininity includes prosocial values and a higher level of moral judgment (Parsons' supposition), then testing the correlation between femininity and delinquency becomes almost a tautology since girls who exhibited such values would almost certainly be less delinquent than girls who did not.

The tests of the so-called masculinity thesis are extremely problematic.[28] They suffer from poor measurement tools—what is measured as masculine ranges from high-risk activities to "expecting to pay for activities on a date." There are explicit and implicit assumptions of masculinity and femininity in these studies that are at least debatable. What does it mean to be masculine in this society (either in 1979 or 1999)? To be feminine? Have these definitions changed? One must address these questions exhaustively before attempting to apply the concepts to a study of crime. What is more fundamentally flawed is the twist of Parsons' original thesis.[29]

Sex-Role Theories

Sex-role theories point to socialization differences between men and women as the reason for women's lower participation in crime. In other words, the differences that exist between men and women are not assumed to be inherent, either biologically or psychologically, but rather learned. Sex roles are considered to be one of the most fundamental factors in identity.[30] During childhood, girls and boys recognize and absorb what is appropriate and inappropriate behavior for one's sex. During the 1960s and 1970s when sex-role theory was applied to criminology, men's and women's sex roles incorporated functions and personality characteristics that were more exaggerated than today: males were breadwinners and women were homemakers; and, males were strong, assertive, and analytical while women were passive and nurturing. The theorists below saw sex-role socialization as the single greatest explanatory factor for the crime rate differential.[31]

Hoffman-Bustamante described sex roles as the controlling factor in differential crime rates. "Females have been taught to conform to more rigid standards and rewarded for such behavior, whereas males are told to conform, yet rewarded for flouting many conventional standards."[32] She identified a number of factors that contributed to differential crime rates:

- Different role expectations and socialization patterns. Girls were expected to be nurturing and had more responsibility for home-maintenance tasks. They were also less likely to learn skills, such as handling firearms or fighting, that would be important before engaging in delinquent acts.

- Sex differences in the application of social control. Girls were more likely than their brothers to have earlier curfews, and be expected to be at home rather than allowed freedom after school.

- Differential opportunities to commit particular offenses. Since girls were more likely to be at home or at someone's house, there was less opportunity to engage in delinquent acts, such as vandalism, fighting, or other forms of delinquency.

- Sex differences in terms of access to criminal subcultures and careers. Girls were less likely to belong to gangs or to have other criminal associations.

- The classification of offenses by the legal structure in a manner that relates to sex-role differences. By this, she meant that girls were more likely to be caught up in the system for status offenses rather than delinquent offenses because their sexuality was controlled more so than boys'.[33]

Since these theories were developed 20 to 30 years ago, the models for sex-role identification for boys were cops, crooks, and cowboys, while the models for girls were almost exclusively housewives. Women were only beginning to enter non-traditional areas in the labor force and these women were viewed as anomalies. General socialization patterns were only beginning to change.[34] The real question is to what extent sex roles have changed today. Are there fundamental differences in the way girls are socialized today from 20 years ago, or are they still taught and controlled in similar ways to those described above?

Sex-role theory continues to be the most dominant theory regarding the sex differential in crime rates. *Photo credit: Mark C. Ide.*

Smart used role theory as an alternative to other theories of female criminality.[35]

> Girls are generally more closely supervised than boys, and are taught to be passive and domesticated while boys are allowed greater freedom and are encouraged to be aggressive, ambitious and outward going . . . As a result of this girls are usually expected to be non-violent and so are not allowed to learn how to fight or use weapons. Girls themselves tend to shrink from violence, and look for protection rather than seeking to learn the skills of self-defence, hence few women have the necessary technical ability or strength to engage in crimes of violence, armed robberies or gang fights.

She pointed out, however, that sex-role theory did not explain why the differences in sex roles existed. She also observed that sex roles are sometimes used by those who advance a socio-biological basis of behavior, in that what is described as behavior appropriate to one's sex role is easily translated to what is natural or "proof" of the validity of sexual differentiation. She criticized role theory in its inability to explain why certain women rejected their sex role and did engage in crime.[36]

Bottcher, in a more recent treatment of sex-role theory, attempts a qualitative study by comparing brother-sister pairs in activities and definitions of delinquency. The methodology of this study prevents any assumption of representativeness since the sample size is small (40 siblings) and identified from a juvenile facility. The sample is high-risk and the delinquency scores are from self-reports; however, the more qualitative nature of the information is, in some ways, more enlightening than some of the purely quantitative data that have been collected on sex-role theory in the past. Bottcher found, consistent with most other studies, that female siblings committed significantly less delinquency than their brothers. Even though the siblings came from the same family environment, their worlds were quite different. Girls tended to have one boyfriend and fewer friends, boys had several girlfriends and a more diffuse association pattern of peers.[37] According to Bottcher "Steady boyfriends, more exclusive friendships, pregnancies, and child care also circumscribed their activities."[38] The interviewees reflected definitions of criminality and delinquency that indicated such action was more consistent with the male sex role, as one female interviewee stated: "I'm married," she said, "and I got a baby to think of. I can't go around being crazy and wild."[39] Thus, Bottcher's research indicates that sex roles really have not changed much from the 1970s—delinquency is still considered more appropriate for boys than girls. In a conclusion, Bottcher states:

> Each source of gender definition provided potential reinforcement for male delinquency and inhibited female delinquency: internalized self-definitions that typically associated the drama and toughness of crime with masculinity; peer pressures that rewarded masculine strength and boldness, discouraged female strength and boldness, and maintained a considerable degree of exclusive male companionship; parental and organizational constraints that attempted to protect girls from delinquent activity and official delinquent sanctions, as well as from early pregnancy; physical differences, especially reproductive physiology and physical strength, that were socially defined (and emphasized) to place males at greater risk of physical harm and to hold females responsible for most family care, in addition to childbearing; and social meanings of crime that cast crime as a genuine expression of masculinity for males and a socially unacceptable expression of femininity for females.[40]

Sex-role theory continues to be the most dominant theory regarding the sex differential in crime rates, as well as other differences noted in the behavior patterns of girls and boys, and women and men. Theorists continue to examine, criticize, and test elements of the theory.[41]

Naffine, in a critique of earlier theories, points out that role theory, especially as formulated by Smart, is simply an elaboration of Sutherland's differential association theory. Naffine also criticizes those elements of Smart's theory that "psychologize" female motivation or slip into Cohen's assumptions of the passive female.[42] Naffine's preference is for a purely structural, Marxist explanation of criminality. She identifies the unanswered question in sex-role theory; specifically, why sex-role differences exist. But her answer may leave a lot to be desired if one does not happen to agree with a Marxist explanation. Of course, another answer—one that she and most other sex-role theorists would vehemently reject—is that sex roles exist because there are natural and real differences between men and women—in their biology, species function, psychological makeup, and behavioral preferences. This, of course, is exactly the premise against which feminist criminologists argue.

FEMINIST CRIMINOLOGY

In the late 1960s and early 1970s, a number of feminist analysts concisely and thoroughly pointed out the bankruptcy of traditional theories of crime that purported to explain criminality, yet ignored one-half of the population. They observed that one could not simply apply "male" theories to women; these theories used male samples, assumed male behavior was the norm, and operated under assumptions that may have applied to men, but not to women. Heidensohn was one of the first to argue that women's deviance should no longer be ignored by mainstream criminology, but women should be understood utilizing their phenomenological field—their behavior patterns, role sets, and reaction patterns.[43] Klein[44] followed with a scathing critical analysis of the major theories of crime that, at the time, largely ignored female criminality, and then Rasche,[45] Smart,[46] and Pollock[47] offered their critiques of criminology.

Smart offered one of the most detailed of such critiques, analyzing the failure of traditional criminological theories to account for female patterns of crime. She concluded that a version of role theory was the best explanation for the sex differential in crime rates. These critiques stripped traditional criminological theories of their supposed scientific objectivity and pointed out sexist views that colored the researchers' explanations and theories of criminality for women (and men). All critiques pointed out that theories for women seemed to be mired in biological or psychological causes even while theories for men had moved into sociological factors (such as opportunity, subcultural deviance, control, and so on).

Feminist analysts continue to inform and offer important observations and methods of analysis. Naffine, for instance, offers a Marxist-feminist analysis and argues that earlier critiques, especially Smart's, did not go far enough in their analysis of why role structuring exists the way it does; that is, why these differences are fostered and encouraged by society.[48] Her argument was that the economic structuring of society is the reason women are devalued and placed in a subordinate position relative to men. Naffine argues that Cohen and strain theorists glamorized male delinquents and discounted females as the "other."

> When it comes to characterizing the nature of being human, and in particular the better side of that nature, law has in common with other spheres of learning the practice of casting women outside the field of vision and involving the experiences, the expectations and the values of the male. The result, it will be argued, is that when women are finally brought into the equation, they are regarded as in some way aberrant from the human = male norm.[49]

Naffine, especially, criticizes traditional theories for seeing male criminals as exciting, active, and inventive; and if female criminals were recognized at all they were viewed as sick or dependent on male crime partners: "Female offending is trifling because nothing of public significance is demanded of women. Their criminality is seen to be narrow in scope because females have only one priority: achieving success with males."[50]

Morris also reviewed the traditional theories that ignored women.[51] For instance, she rejected those adaptations of strain/opportunity theory that proposed women had different goals from men: "Such a view is based on stereotypical beliefs rather than on evidence. Measures of men's and women's motivation to achieve show no real differences in score."[52] She also attacked Pollak's assertion of a dark figure of crime as being mostly women's crimes, and completely rejected all biological explanations for sex differences: "But neither chromosomes nor hormones shape what is defined as 'masculine' and 'feminine.'"[53]

Feminist criminologists continue to assail mainstream criminology for ignoring women and sex as a factor in criminological theory. Allen argued that each of the theories discussed in the previous chapter operated from a masculine orientation, and "universalisation" occurred by fitting women to the principles developed for men. She argued that what is needed is to start over and employ a truly sex-neutral approach to the study of crime, and quoted with favor those who point out that human bodies "create culture." By this she means that sex is a biological reality that fundamentally affects culture— the meaning that one attributes to biology is the linchpin between nature and culture's influence on behavior.[54]

Feminism: Definitions and Methodology

Feminist approaches place women in a social, economic, and political context. Feminist authors view the relationship of women with society's authority structures as part of the explanation for their deviance and conformity.[55] Heidensohn explains this thought by noting that formal and informal methods of control may help to understand all women, not only those who become involved in crime.[56] Simpson states that feminism can be understood:

> as both a world view and a social movement that encompasses assumptions and beliefs about the origins and consequences of gendered social organization as well as strategic directions and actions for social change. As such, feminism is both analytical and empirical.[57]

The contributions of these writers are not only in their critical observations regarding traditional criminology, but also their use of alternative methodology to understand crime and those who commit crime.

Yet feminism is not homogeneous. There are many schools of or approaches to feminism, and some who describe themselves as feminist would probably be vehemently rejected by other self-identified feminists.[58] Alleman offers one typology of feminism, including liberal feminism, Marxist feminism, socialist feminism, and radical feminism.[59] Another typology of feminist theory includes: liberal, Marxist, socialist, radical, and postmodernist.[60] A similar list[61] includes: *liberal feminism* (which accepts that some differences between the sexes exist, but that social, legal, and economic opportunities should be equal); *Marxist feminism* (a belief that women's oppression stems largely from economic dependency on men and that the destruction of the capitalism will also free women);[62] *socialist feminism* (which argues that both class and patriarchy conspire as dual origins of oppression);[63] *radical feminism* (which seems hard to distinguish from socialist feminism; it also rejects Marxist feminism's position that the capitalist system as the source of oppression, instead pointing to men as the oppressors of women rather than the economic system); and, finally, *post-modern feminism* (which is more a rejection of traditional science and methodology). The main point for feminism is that not all women's lives are the same, and race, ethnicity, and class shape lives in addition to gender; therefore, any "truths" are relative.

Daly and Chesney-Lind summarize some of the general points of all (or most) feminist approaches:

- Gender is not a natural fact but a complex social, historical, and cultural product; related to, but not simply derived from biological sex differences and reproductive capacities.

- Gender and gender relations order social life and social institutions in fundamental ways.

- Gender relations and constructs of masculinity and femininity are not symmetrical but are based on an organizing principle of men's superiority and social and political-economic dominance over women.

- Systems of knowledge reflect men's views of the natural and social world; [but] the production of knowledge is gendered.

- Women should be at the center of intellectual inquiry, not peripheral, invisible, or appendages to men.[64]

Arguments exist within and between feminist theorists regarding the role of natural differences and definitions of femininity and masculinity.[65] Messerschmidt offers an interesting approach, incorporating a much more complex view of masculinity within the feminist tradition.[66] In a later work, Messerschmidt continues his approach of looking at crime as structured action, in other words, criminal choices are behaviors that exist because of structural constraints and pressures stemming from one's sex, race, ethnicity, class, and place in society. He discusses girls' gangs and astutely observes that female gang members are not portraying a masculine role, as some more superficial accounts would assume, but represent a more diverse version of femininity: "[girl gangs] challenge notions of conceptualizing violence by women as simplistically 'unnatural,' 'deviant,' and 'masculine,' and points both to the importance of ongoing investigation of gender *differences* in crime and to gender *similarities* in crime."[67] His conclusion, however, that female gang members' violence is not deviant ignores the obvious—their violence is both statistically and socially deviant. Further, as he stated himself, their violence is not a version of male violence, but rather must be understood in the context of their lives, relationships, and realities.

Feminist Methodology

Feminist treatments employ qualitative as well as quantitative methods. Women are seen as making choices; they are not helpless pawns of biology or directed and pressured into crime by husbands and boyfriends. However, their choices are constrained by informal and formal social controls and such things as poverty, blocked opportunities, victimization, and sex-role stereotypes. Feminist research often makes use of case histories and women "telling their stories" in their own words.[68]

While phenomenological methods are not unique to the feminist approach; they are associated with it, and have contributed immensely to our understanding of criminal behavior. Daly discusses scholars who believe that the narrative approach is as important if not more important than the statistical method. She describes two types of reasoning—logico-scientific and narrative; each provides distinctive ways of ordering experience and constructing reality.[69] The logico-scientific looks for universal truth conditions, while the narrative looks for particular connections between events. Worral is also suspicious of empiricism as having the corner on truth. She explains that knowledge may be: dialectic (because it is contradictory and uncertain), indeterminate (because it changes with different conditions and contexts), pluralistic (because different groups ask and answer different questions), and exploratory (because it can never be assumed that one has total knowledge).[70]

The feminist approach, with its emphasis on narrative and contextual realities, has been responsible for expanding our knowledge of the female offender.[71]

Gilfus, for instance, utilizes the phenomenological method by employing a sample of only 20, but conducting in-depth interviews.[72] Her information chronicles the women's lives filled with abuse and neglect, racism, economic marginality, early motherhood, economic struggle, rape, and other victimization by men in their lives, street crimes, prostitution, forgery, and shoplifting. In her descriptions, it becomes clear that crime was a way of taking care of the people in their lives. She suggests, in fact, that childhood violence and/or neglect may "socialize women to adopt a tenacious commitment to caring for anyone who promises love, material success, and acceptance."

Chesney-Lind also used interviews and her women also describe lives filled with sexual and physical victimization, parental drinking and drug use, and "parentalization": "Like many girls in economically marginalized households, these women—as children—assumed adult responsibilities because both parents worked long hours or one parent had left the family (either temporarily or permanently). Many described having to become the 'parent' of the house, caring for their younger siblings and managing the domestic chores of the house." In Chesney-Lind's interviews, girls reported being beaten for drinking or smoking or staying out; things their brothers did with impunity. Some, however, started their drug use through initiation by their parents. Many started their own family to escape their parents' control; paradoxically, their family often became their sole source of support caring for their children and providing them a home when drug use eliminated all other options.[73]

Worral offers yet another phenomenological study in her study of 11 offending women. She concludes that there are fundamental elements of differences between women's experiences and men's experiences regarding criminal actions. She notes the following:

- There is a particular and unique social disgrace in being a criminal woman.

- There is a sense of guilt and low self-esteem that many women have about themselves as women.

- Women seem to have apparent difficulty in communicating what they want to say.

- Women who break the law must compensate for their "unfeminine" criminal behavior by presenting themselves as domesticated, sexually passive, and constitutionally fragile. (She refers to this as the "gender contract.")[74]

Carlen reminds us that women cannot be described simply by statistics or profiles.[75] First, she reminds us that statistics that show women in prison are more likely to be single, come from abusive backgrounds, and have histories of addiction should not be taken to represent all female criminals, since other data indicate that courts are less likely to sentence to prison those women who are in stable marriages and who have relatively "normal" lifestyles. She also gathered together autobiographical accounts of women and let the women speak for themselves for large portions of the book. She writes:

> The essential criminal woman does not exist. Women who break the law come from all kinds of backgrounds, though, as with male lawbreakers, those women who land up in prison are much more likely to have come from the lower socio-economic groups than from the higher ones.[76]

Carlen sees women as turning to crime for "fun, independence and success" lifting them out of the social disabilities imposed upon women:

> [a female criminal discussing her life] I loved the excitement of villainy, the highs, the buzz; the absolute thrill of avoiding the cloying norm that, to me, boded some kind of death knell. I was only alive when taking chances along with the others who lived that way as well.[77]

The narrative approach has its own drawbacks of course. Numbers are typically quite small and, therefore, one questions whether interviewees are "typical." Carlen's point that prison samples are not representative of all criminal women is correct, but then again, her own small sample cannot necessarily be representative of all female criminals either.

One difference between phenomenologists and empiricists is accepting the interaction between the offender and system. Empirical approaches fail to capture the dynamic of "doing justice." The system operates on the offender and influences future acts (association in prison, loss of family ties, children, stress of imprisonment and/or release leading to drug use, and so on.) Worral reminds us that the actions of system come from meanings ascribed to actions of offenders, but the stigma and disruption that follows entry into the system become causal influences themselves, creating new relationships and different problems that occur as life continues.

Review and Critique

The application of feminist scholarship to the understanding of crime and other phenomena should not be understated. Feminist scrutiny questions the basic underpinnings of knowledge sets. For instance, Smart questions the approach of teaching women's courses, having books titled "Women and . . .

(the law, etc.)," because it sets women apart as "the other" and assumes the male experience as the norm. Many examples exist in research in law, medicine, and the social sciences that show women are afterthoughts and footnotes to the collection and analysis of "truth."[78] Many writers in feminist jurisprudence, for instance, have discussed the idea of how the law is profoundly gendered—from its analysis of the "reasonable man" concept, to its regulation of women's bodies, through definitions of criminality.[79] Smart argues that empiricism never is removed from cultural influences, and that the question of creating knowledge about women will always be contaminated by the male opposite end of the spectrum.[80]

Feminists correctly point out that researchers are influenced by their socialization, but might also be criticized for wearing their own unique blinders when analyzing others' research. Morris, for instance criticizes early applications of strain/opportunity theory to women; questioning the assumption that girls had different career goals than boys and arguing that there was little support for that assumption.[81] However, Morris might be faulted for applying a 1980s cultural bias to 1960s research. First, it is not unreasonable at all to assume that girls in the 1960s had different career goals from girls in the late 1980s and 1990s. Also, career goals are not as important an indicator of strain/opportunity as, perhaps, career goals relative to family goals. More girls today will express career goals; however, there may still be differences between girls and boys in the emphasis placed on career goals versus family goals, and if there is, this difference might be important for entry into delinquency.

Smart criticizes Konopka for attempting to collect facts without "apriori theorizing" because, she says, the collection of facts is biased by implicit, unstated cultural assumptions. She also criticizes Konopka's premise that delinquent girls exhibited a need for support more so than did delinquent boys and that this was instrumental in their delinquency: "My criticism of Konopka's assumptions about the special needs of adolescent girls hinges on the meaning of the concept 'need.' Because of her psychological orientation it becomes apparent that she means inherent needs rather than culturally determinate needs."[82] But it is because of Smart's sociological and feminist orientation that she views such needs as purely culturally determined and not inherent. She argues herself that one has to be suspicious of theory and facts (because theorizing and fact collection is based on cultural influences), thus feminist theory, which postulates that differences between the sexes are due to socialization and these learned sex roles are due to the gendered nature of power in society, also must be looked upon with suspicion. In other words, under post-modernism, if there is no objective truth, why would we assume that feminist theory is any less biased and culturally grounded than the "truths" it rejects? Smart recognizes this very problem, applying it to feminist jurisprudence: "The search for feminist jurisprudence seems to be vulnerable to this tendency to want to claim that its truth is better than other truths."[83]

To review: feminist criminology has helped to uncover the sexism that influenced all earlier traditional theories of crime. Fundamental points emerge from feminist criminology:

- There is a need to study women, but to do so without comparing them to men. Scientific queries should reject the approach of using men as the norm and women as the other. There is no question that this is the most important message of the above review; the problem goes far beyond criminology and touches every aspect of knowledge collection, whether one looks at medicine, law, or other forms of social science.

- There is a need to consider women as heterogenous rather than homogenous. Factors such as class, race, and ethnicity also affect women's lives. Again, an important contribution of feminist analysis has been to "deconstruct" knowledge—not only as it exists regarding "truths" about men and women, but also about "women" themselves; specifically, identifying the point that women's lives are different.

- Definitions of crime are largely based on class structure. This Marxist/radical emphasis runs through many, but not all feminist analyses. The emphasis is helpful to an understanding of why some corporate and economic crimes are not punished, but ultimately fails to resolve other issues. The idea that the capitalist structure "causes" crime is not too different from economic theories of crime, and, like economic theories of crime, does not explain the gender/sex crime differential.

- Post-modernism questions whether we can ever "know" something objectively; so-called neutral science is considered a sham and criminology's search for causes is bankrupt because even the question is framed by androcentric, sexist, classist, and racist definitions of crime, criminals, and cause. This criticism of established "truths" must cut both ways; if no one is neutral, then that includes feminists themselves, and their version of "truth" is still only a single version to be compared to others.

THE "NEW-NEWER-NEWEST" FEMALE CRIMINAL: WOMEN'S LIBERATION AND CRIMINALITY

Every decade or so, one or more theorists assume that progress in social equality between men and women has led to increased criminality among women. Interestingly, regardless of the decade, the idea is that "recent" progress has led to a "new" female criminal.

In 1923:

> The modern age of girls and young men is intensely immoral and
> immoral seemingly without the pressure of circumstances. . . . [i]s
> it the result of what we call "the emancipation of woman," with its
> concomitant freedom from chaperonage, increased intimacy
> between the sexes in adolescence, and a more tolerant viewpoint
> towards all things unclear in life?[84]

In 1931:

> In the fight for Emancipation women have won most of their objec-
> tives and they have good reason to be jubilant at their success. Yet
> could they have foreseen the future twenty years ago, they would
> probably have relinquished the struggle, afraid of the consequences
> of their coming triumphs. . . . Speaking broadly, it is my belief that
> many more women have become criminally minded during the past
> few years than ever before . . . they have shown greater imagination
> and, in some cases, greater initiative than men.[85]

In 1950:

> Woman with all her success in getting access to new fields and new
> social roles has not been able to get rid of her more traditional func-
> tions. She still is the homemaker, the rearer of children, and the
> shopper. Man—albeit grudgingly—has accepted her as a competi-
> tor, but he has as yet refused to become her substitute in the social
> sphere. Thus, with her burden of social functions increased, it
> seems probable that her opportunities for crime have not just
> changed but increased correspondingly.[86]

In 1975:

> Like her legitimate-based sister, the female criminal knows too much
> to pretend or return to her former role as a second rate criminal con-
> fined to "feminine" crimes such as shoplifting and prostitution. She
> has had a taste of financial victory. In some cases she has had a taste
> of blood. Her appetite, however, appears to be only whetted.[87]

And, in 1990:

> We needn't look to the dramatic example of battle for proof that
> violence is no longer a male domain. Women are now being arrest-
> ed for violent crimes—such as robbery and aggravated assault—at
> a higher rate than ever before recorded in the U.S.[88]

The last quote comes from Crittenden's popular article titled "You've Come a Long Way, Moll", and it is in the popular media that the idea of a new violent female criminal generates attention. It is unclear what to make of such cyclical observations; in fact, women's crimes have fluctuated, but mostly increased since statistics have been collected, as have men's. While women's crime increases always seem to be explained by increased social freedoms, men's increases are not. The theme of such observations is that, given the chance, women will act "just like men."[89] The recurring appearance of the "new" violent criminal would be amusing if one did not suspect that the concept is partially responsible for the increased imprisonment rate of women discussed in Chapter 3.

The idea that women's criminal activities will increase as they become more liberated assumes that social role is almost entirely responsible for their historic lack of involvement in crime. In essence, women and men are considered the same in criminal inclination and it is only opportunities and socialization that have kept women from parity with men in crime rates. The most recent theories base their propositions on the idea that a "women's movement" changed the social roles appropriate for women, and, in turn, increased their commission of crime. Actually, there have been several "women's movements" in this country.[90] The exact history and parameters of this movement are hard to pin down, much less identify what impact they have had on societal norms and sex roles. Even today, many women prefer not to be labeled as feminist, even while enjoying the benefits of equal employment that have come largely because of the efforts of those who coined the term. Further, the idea that a woman's movement has led to some type of social and economic emancipation for women is subject to scrutiny. While women represent equal numbers in the labor force, their familial roles have changed less readily.[91]

Adler's Masculinization Theory

Freda Adler proposed simply a slightly different version of the masculinity theory discussed in the beginning section of this chapter. She associated criminality with masculinity, as the earlier theories did, and then proposed that the so-called liberation of women in the 1960s and 1970s caused women to take on more stereotypically "masculine" traits such as competitiveness and aggressiveness. Her descriptions of the new female criminal indicated that criminality was exciting, glamorous, and fun. In essence, she endorsed Cohen's early fascination and attraction to deviance and celebrates women getting their chance at the fun.[92]

As discussed in the first chapter, the percentage increase figures that Adler offered in support of the new female criminal were an extremely poor choice of statistics because they are subject to the problem of small base numbers. Even more fundamental flaws in her thesis, however, are the assumptions that crime is masculine, and females will adopt masculine traits when they achieve some modest levels of social and economic equality. As stated above, those researchers who attempted to identify an association between masculine traits and criminality among women have been largely unsuccessful.[93]

Later tests of the liberation theory employ cross-cultural comparisons. The assumption is that those societies in which women have achieved some level of economic and social equality will also show higher levels of female criminality.[94] Results have only partially supported such a thesis. For instance, Marshall found that in a sample of Western nations, women's employment figures were positively correlated with increased levels of theft and fraud, although they did not show higher levels of robbery or burglary.[95]

In this study, it was found that the two countries with the highest proportionate female crime (New Zealand and Portugal) have relatively low rankings on economic participation; while three countries with low female criminality (Denmark, Finland, and Japan) had relatively high levels of economic participation of women.[96] Obviously, the relationship between economic participation and criminality is more complicated than the liberation theory postulates. Relationships between specific crimes and the economic variables used, or between specific economic variables and crime showed inconsistent and sometimes unexplainable patterns; therefore, conclusions drawn from this research should be extremely tentative and general.

Steffensmeier, Allen, and Streifel also conducted a cross-national test of the liberation theory using data from 69 countries to test four explanations between development and female percentage of arrests.[97] The theories they tested were the gender equality theory (liberation theory), economic marginalization theory, opportunity for female-based consumer crimes, and social control theory. They concluded that rather than economic and social liberation, other theories better fit the data. There was evidence that the countries that showed higher levels of female criminality could be explained by a general opportunity theory, i.e., that economic development led to greater amounts of small consumer-items in the marketplace and these items were easier and more tempting to steal. This factor corresponded with the entry of women into the workplace, and was probably more explanatory than any economic liberation of women that came with their labor force participation. They also found the formal patterns of social control changed so that countries with higher levels of development utilized more formal processes of arrest and prosecution—this would increase the apparent numbers of women's crimes.

Simon's Opportunity Theory

Rita Simon's version of "opportunity theory" indicated that women's employment opportunities would create criminal opportunities and women would then take advantage of such opportunities and commit those crimes.

Simon's thesis proposed in 1975, and then reiterated in 1991, explains that women's increased professional opportunities led to employment-related crime.[98] Using labor market statistics, she explained that women's participation increased dramatically between the 1950s and 1970s. Women's opportunities in education and entry into the professions also increased.[99]

Before one makes too much of the economic equality seemingly occurring for women, it should be pointed out that more recent statistics are less encouraging. Also, among African-Americans, women's and men's incomes converged, but among whites, the gap increased.[100] Even in professional, technical, and managerial positions, women continued to earn about two-thirds of men's salaries, and more recently, the gap has started to widen again.[101]

Table 6.1
Ratios of Median Annual Income of White and African-American Women and Men

Year	African-American Females/ African-American Males	White Females/ White Males	African-American Females/ White Females
1955	.34*	.65	.51
1965	.39	.58	.68
1975	.57	.58	.98
1985	.83	.67	.90
1995	.86	.73	.86

*Read as African-American females earned 34 cents for every dollar earned by African-American males; white females earned 65 cents for every dollar earned by white males; and African-American females earned 51 cents for every dollar earned by white females in 1955.

Adapted from Simon and Landis, 1991, p. 37. Year 1995 calculated from U.S. Bureau of Census, Statistical Abstracts of the United States 1996, p. 426.

Simon notes, also, that physical opportunities for women will never be equal, thus such crimes as robbery would probably always be less common for women "robbery probably best illustrates the greater natural advantages that men have over women."[102] It is unclear, however, why this would necessarily pose an obstacle to potential female robbers since a gun would seem to more than equalize any "natural advantages" and one could always choose a weaker victim. In fact, in many cases of female-perpetrated robberies, the victim is elderly and frail; therefore, it is unclear why women, if they were equal to men in their inclinations, would not be equal in their participation rates.

The critics of Simon's theory argued that there are four weaknesses in the opportunity theory structure as exemplified by these contrary findings:

- Women and men do not act similarly even given similar circumstances.

- Women's gains in employment do not consist of positions of power and access to money as Simon predicted.

- Women criminals are not "liberated" and in fact, espouse more traditional views than non-criminal samples.

- Women's increase in larceny/theft crimes are not the types of crimes that Simon predicted would increase.

The first criticism of the opportunity theory proposes that men and women do not act similarly even given similar circumstances. For instance, women in poverty should have responded to it with crime to the same degree as men; yet they do not.[103] Arguably, men and women could never be similar living as they do in different realities shaped by sex, society, and social roles.

Another set of criticisms targets Simon's assumption that women have indeed made progress in labor opportunities. Although women's participation in the labor market has increased dramatically since the 1950s, one might argue that their participation in employment has been largely constrained to low-level clerical and retail forms of employment that do not offer the embezzlement opportunities predicted.[104]

The third criticism questions whether the woman's movement has impacted the female criminal at all:

> The women's movement has neither involved nor benefited the majority of women in the U.S. It has not even brought true equal opportunities for the minority of white middle and upper class women who have been most directly involved with the movement. Therefore, any discussion of the link between women's criminality and the women's movement is unrealistic.[105]

In studies of female offenders, it has been found repeatedly that female criminals espouse essentially traditional sex stereotypes and reject the feminist agenda.[106]

Finally, the last criticism of Simon's opportunity theory is that while the trend of female offending may seem to support Simon's notion that women are taking advantage of employment opportunities to increase their rates of embezzling and other employment-related crime, there is evidence that the larceny/theft increases that have occurred are in the consumer crime areas historically associated with women. In other words, women's increases in crime continue to be in check forging, shoplifting, and credit card fraud—not high-level embezzling.[107]

Tests of Simon's and Adler's theory do not show that crimes by women have changed in the manner predicted, although Simon's theory has generated a little more support than Adler's.[108]

CRIME, POWER, AND SEX ROLES

While the emancipation theories proposed that women have gained opportunities and these opportunities have led them to crime, the theories discussed below argue either that opportunities and freedoms have not changed much, or that they do not relate to power, which is the true correlate of crime.

Economic Marginalization

The "economic marginialization" theory explains that women's participation in larceny/theft crimes is rising not because of recent employment opportunities for women, but rather recent negative progress in women's economic stability. Arguably, women are in a worse financial position than they were 30 years ago because of no-fault divorce, increasing numbers of single head of household families, and the low rate of child support payments. Although women have entered the workforce in large numbers, in fact they now exceed men in the labor force, their jobs tend to be low level and low paying.[109]

Between 1970 and 1986 there was a threefold increase in the number of people who had been divorced. Increases in divorce were greater for African-American women than for white women; and greater for all women than for men.[110]

Table 6.2
Divorce 1970-1986

all races	1970		1980		1986	
	women	(men)	women	(men)	women	(men)
percent divorced	5.2	(3.3)	11.0	(8.2)	13.9	(10.7)
percent divorced (white)	5.0	(3.1)	10.5	(7.9)	13.4	(10.7)
percent divorced (African-American)	7.7	(5.5)	16.5	(12.6)	20.7	(13.2)

Adapted from Simon and Landis, 1991, p. 27.

In 1980, 10.5 percent of family households were headed by women (46.6% divorced; 16.7% never married), and 58 percent of those households contained children.[111] In an average city 80 percent of all African-American families living below the poverty line are headed by women.[112] In a recent economic survey it was found that African-American women who were head of their household earned the least of all groups—while they earned an average of only $239 per week; white women earned $290, African-American men earned $302, white men earned $410, African-American married couples earned $457, and white married couples earned $567.[113] Female crime, according to the economic marginalization theory, has increased because more women are single, head-of-household, and have no means of economically providing for their families. Theorists point out that most crimes committed by women are largely petty, economic crimes.[114]

Simon and Landis question why women's participation in larceny/theft crimes has continued to rise even while their participation in professional and managerial positions has also increased. They argue that there should be a negative correlation between these two factors, according to the economic marginalization theory.[115] However, one might argue that increased participation in economically rewarding jobs would be negatively associated with participation in crime rates *only if* they were the same women who had been trapped in "pink ghetto" jobs or were unemployed, that were allowed to achieve economic stability through better job opportunities. There is no reason to believe that this is the case. One might just as easily presume that those few women who are obtaining professional and managerial level jobs are those women who 30 years ago would have been comfortably ensconced in suburbia with a station wagon. Women in poverty or on the edge of poverty are not becoming bank vice presidents—30 years ago or today. Simon and Landis go on to recognize this very possibility:

> Increasing numbers of upwardly mobile women may be committing white-collar crimes in the same proportions as similarly situated men at the same time that increasing numbers of their downwardly mobile sisters are committing the petty thievery, shoplifting, forgeries, and frauds that are available to them in their social positions.[116]

Economic marginalization would seem to predict even greater percentage increases of crime than what has occurred. Further, there are no good studies to explicate exactly what kinds of crimes women are committing in the larceny/theft category, so it remains mere speculation as to whether increased employment opportunities have led to higher-level economic crimes or whether women's crimes remain the same type of petty larceny as before.

Socialist/Marxist Explanations

Related to the theory of economic marginalization is Messerschmidt's explanation that economic arrangements, specifically, capitalism and patriarchy, are fundamental influences on crime.[117] He defines patriarchy as a "set of social relations of power in which the male gender appropriates the labor power of women and controls their sexuality."[118] According to this theory, gender and class shape one's possibilities. There are definite gender-appropriate and class-appropriate forms of conforming and non-conforming behavior: "low female criminality is related to primarily women's subordinate position in patriarchal capitalism. Female subordination in the family means young women are more closely supervised—mainly by their mothers—than their brothers . . ."[119] Messerschmidt goes on to say: "The fact that females are subordinate and therefore less powerful in economic, religious, political, and military institutions worldwide means that females have less opportunity to engage in serious criminality."[120] He argues that when women do engage in criminality, it reflects their subordinate position in the gender/class hierarchy.

This sounds very much like the old sex-role theory discussed in the first section of this chapter. The theory merely places sex roles in context; that is, the power relations exist in the way they do between men and women through economic power structures, i.e., men controlling all economic power. Why this is so is answered by socialist feminism with the original biological differences between men and women, i.e., that men controlled food sources while women took care of children, and this differentiation of labor set the stage for men to seize all economic power in subsequent development. The theory itself does not explain increased crime rates among women, although it might be consistent with either the liberation theories (women are gaining economic power), or the economic marginalization theory (women are losing economic security and their crimes stem from their powerlessness).

Hagan's Power Control Theory

Hagan calls his approach "structural criminology," and proposes a power-control theory of crime causation.[121] In this theory, family class structure consists of the configurations of power between spouses that derive from the positions these spouses occupy in their work inside and outside the home.[122] Gender relations refer to the activities, institutions, and relationships that are involved in the maintenance and renewal of gender roles, in the family and elsewhere. These activities include the parenting involved in caring for, protecting, and socializing children for the roles they will occupy as adults. According to power-control theory, family class structure shapes gender relations, and in turn delinquency. There are three levels of the theory: social-psychological processes, social positions (gender and delinquency roles), and class structures by which families are socially organized.[123]

According to this theory, girls and boys are controlled differently by parents, which leads to risk preferences (boys prefer more risks than girls because they receive less parental control). Risk preferences then lead to delinquency. Gender also influences delinquency directly by official designations (i.e., girls are more likely to be targeted for sexual misbehaviors).[124] This theory revives once again the traditional view that delinquency is fun, exciting, and dynamic, and girls are boring and passive because they do not engage in delinquency to the same degree as boys do. For instance:

> . . . our assumption is that delinquency frequently is fun—and even more importantly, a kind of fun infrequently allowed to females. Said differently, delinquency may involve a spirit of liberation, the opportunity to take risks, and a chance to pursue publicly some of the pleasures that are symbolic of adult male status outside the family.[125]

Thus, daughters are disproportionally controlled and not allowed "the fun of delinquency," and this parental control "diminish[es] the preferences of daughters to take risks."[126] It is not clear why parental control would create risk-averse girls, one might argue it seems just the opposite, that parental control would push girls into taking risky behavior as rebellion against such control. To continue, the theory argues that as women enter the workforce, the informal controls of the family decrease, and formal controls of state increase; the theory presumes that egalitarian families would have more delinquent daughters.[127]

Tests of the theory use outside employment as a measure of egalitarianism in a marriage.[128] As expected, findings showed maternal controls of daughters strongest in patriarchal families and equal to controls for boys in egalitarian and female-headed households.[129] However, findings did not conform to the theory's predictions in other ways. Results indicated that controls on sons were highest in female-headed households, which, according to the theory, should mean that boys in such households had the least risk preference and the least delinquency, but the findings indicated delinquency was highest for boys in female-headed households, and lowest in patriarchal households.[130] Risk preference was highest for boys in female-headed households, even though control was highest in such households—why would strong parental control not create risk avoidance in boys as well as girls? Unfortunately, the author does not explain these results in the discussion. Interestingly, although the levels of delinquency for girls is higher in egalitarian and female-headed households, even in these samples, it is still only one-half that of boys.[131]

Morash and Chesney-Lind offer the following critique of the power control theory:

- Gender differences in youth crime appear in families regardless of whether they are patriarchal or egalitarian.

- The quality of the relationship with the mother is very important in explaining low levels of youth crime, particularly for boys.

- The experience of negative sanctions from the father explains youth crime for both genders.

- Social class rather than risk-taking socialization is a much better predictor of youth crime for both boys and girls.[132]

Chesney-Lind and Sheldon add to the critique of Hagan's theory by offering the following observations:

- The authors of the theory assume most adolescents live in two-parent families and argue that female-headed households are equivalent to upper-status egalitarian families with both parents working (this is probably extremely inaccurate since female-headed households are likely to be economically marginal and suffer from a host of other factors that derive from poverty).

- The authors merge direct control and indirect control through attachment (in other words, curfews and direct control over children are different forms of control than the control that comes through "attachment," meaning the children care about what parents think and therefore control their own behavior whether parents are there or not; this theory utilizes only direct control measures).

- While the theory assumes that women's entry into the labor force has had a direct effect on female delinquency, there is no evidence to support this.

- The theory pays no attention to class; it assumes lives are similar for girls in upper-class families where mothers work and lower-class families where mothers work.[133]

Tittle's "control balance" theory utilizes constructs of power to explain delinquent choices. The theory is a psychological one that proposes an individual will react in different ways to control, and presents a complicated scenario of different alternatives of conformity, submission, and deviance. Tittle also discusses the application of the theory to female offenders.[134] Tittle's theory proposes that higher levels of control lead to acts of rebellion. Since females are under greater controls, they should be exhibiting greater acts of rebellion, but his speculation to support this prediction included rebellious behaviors such as "pouting" and not performing their maternal functions to the degree they should.[135] In a critique of Tittle's theory, as it relates to female delinquency, Jensen and Westphal argue that control balance theory inaccurately depicts female behavior as passive and male behavior as more conforming.[136] Tittle disputes their interpretation, arguing that they have misinterpreted his application of the theory to female delinquency, but the controversy points out the problems that occur when a theory developed to explain male delinquency or criminality is applied to women.

Both Hagan's power-control theory and Tittle's control-balance theory illustrate the problems in trying to operationalize and test complicated constructs. Neither theory offers substantially more enlightenment concerning female criminality than the old sex-role theory, simply that girls learn to be less delinquent because to be "nice" is part of their sex-role identity.

A few sex-role theories come to grips with other issues that impact upon female and male criminality, i.e., such things as race, class, and ethnicity. Simpson[137] and Simpson and Elis[138] present examples of research that attempt to explain the relative influences of race and gender on delinquency and crime. Simpson explores the "uniquely situated population of 'underclass'" African-American females and reviews evidence concerning the differential crime patterns of African-American women (specifically that they commit more "street crime" than white women), and evaluates the theories available to explain the differential—neo-Marxian, power control, and socialist-feminist. She concludes that class, gender, and race are best understood as intersecting systems of power and control. While evidence is fairly clear and consistent concerning the relative power of these groups in the workplace (white men have the most power, African-American men have the least), power/control relationships within the family structure are more complicated. For example, which family structure is more egalitarian—white, middle-class; or lower-class, female, African-American single, head-of-household? It is not at all clear whether one assumes that egalitarian relations include more constructs than simply economic factors. Some of Simpson's conclusions are unclear; for instance, she states: ". . . family structure among impoverished whites is more likely either to be nuclear or isolated, single-parent units. These structures are less conducive of breakdowns in patriarchal control, and violent crime opportunities are fewer than in the extended and integrative domestic networks of underclass blacks."[139] It is not clear whether she means that criminal opportunities are related to the integrated nature of underclass African-American families, and if so, why? Other conclusions are clear and persuasive:

> Black females, given their dedication to keeping home and community together . . . are more apt than black males to delegitimate violence. However, given their racial oppression and differential experience of patriarchy in the family, black females are perhaps less apt to delegitimate violence than their white counterparts.[140]

Simpson and Elis provide one of the few attempts to combine factors of gender and race/ethnicity to understand delinquency and crime. They propose that "hegemonic" masculinities and femininities are defined within social institutions such as work, family, peer groups, and school, but that "gender" is modified by race. A review of numerous studies of delinquency and crime show that variables seem to present different patterns depending on race/ethnicity. They use self-report data from the National Longitudinal Survey of Youth to explore these associations. For instance, they find that previous research would have predicted that parental influences should operate more strongly for whites than for African-Americans, yet they found that just the opposite was true.[141] Peer influences seem to be more influential for whites than for African-Americans, but in an example of how race and gender/sex interact, they find that peer influences are also stronger for boys than for girls.[142] The statistical associations uncovered in this research point to exceedingly complicated interactions between gender, class, and race/ethnicity that researchers are only beginning to grasp.

CONCLUSION

Feminist critiques of criminology displayed the weakness of traditional theories to account for the lower rate of crime by women. Theories specific to women historically concentrated on biological or psychological differences between men and women, but these were roundly rejected by later theorists in favor of sex-role differences, that is women are socialized and controlled in such a way that reduces the inclination or opportunity for crime. The underlying assumption is that women and men are similar in their criminal inclinations, but are subjected to different societal influences. Yet, sex-role theory does not answer for us the most obvious question—why have sex roles developed in the way they have; why are women socialized to be more prosocial, affiliative, and less aggressive (or as some would say, passive, risk-aversive, and submissive)? Some theorists assume that sex roles are entirely malleable and differ in a multitude of ways across different cultures, but the evidence does not support this assertion. In almost all societies women have been the nurturers, caregivers, and child minders, while men have held economic and social power. Socialist feminism is one of the few approaches in this chapter that at least answers the question by pointing to original (anthropological) differentiation of labor as the beginning of sex-role differences and distribution of power.

Before sex-role theory can ultimately answer the question of criminal behavior differences, it should be more fully explicated as to what sex roles are—both historically and today. Research presents muddled findings because some researchers today use old data sets from 20 or 30 years ago, and there are continuing and unresolved questions concerning just which personality features are consistent with the masculine sex role and what ones are consistent with the female sex role. Further, and perhaps more importantly, there is little attention to the question of the origins and societal functions of sex roles. This is important because of the proposition that sex roles are changing and leading to more criminal behavior by women. If there is no underlying societal or socio-biological reason for sex roles—if indeed women and men are equal in their criminal propensities—then the liberation theorists would be correct that social and economic freedoms should lead to greater criminality. If, however, there are underlying differences between men and women, then increased social and economic opportunities would not necessarily lead to similar violent criminal behavior between men and women. The statistical evidence, such as it is, does not support the view that men and women are becoming more similar in their criminal behavior patterns, even in the past decade when they have become more "equal" in other spheres of life. Whether this means that there are underlying differences in men's and women's criminal propensities is a complicated question—what lies at the center of the controversy is the age-old question: how are men and women different? Before we tackle that question, however, we will revisit mainstream criminology and see if the feminist critiques of the 1970s have led to more enlightened and comprehensive attempts by criminologists to explain criminal causation.

NOTES

[1]   Lombroso and Ferrero (1958/1894, 147). Female criminals had fewer atavistic character-istics (physical deformities that indicated evolutionary retardation) than male criminals, even by Lombroso's standards, forcing him to revise the theory developed for male crim-inals. He concluded that *all* women have evolved less than men; therefore women crim-inals (the least evolved of all) do not display atavistic qualities. Another part of the expla-nation included the idea that since atavistic qualities are unattractive and ugly women do not attract mates, these atavistic qualities are screened out of the gene pool, even while criminality remained.

[2]   1958, 151.

[3]   1980, 1998.

[4]   See, for instance, Gora (1982), Leonard (1982), and Pollock (1978).

[5]   Pike (1876).

[6]   1950.

[7]   1966.

[8]   1970.

[9]   1923.

[10]   1938.

[11]   1968.

[12]   Thomas (1923).

[13]   1950.

[14]   For instance, Konopka was a clinician who observed that female delinquents tended to come from extremely poor home environments. She noted, for instance, that loneliness; problems with communication, and identification with a delinquent mother character-ized the lives of delinquent girls. She concluded that delinquent girls may have greater needs of dependence, but come from families that do not give them care and nurturance. Their delinquency stems from their need for support. She argued that official interven-tion should be to restore, instead of tear down, the girls self-esteem and proposed a more caring approach to female delinquents than she observed in official reactions (1966, 40).

[15]   1968, 166.

[16]   1968, 176.

[17]   1992, 61.

[18]   For instance, Datesman and Scarpetti (1980b) found that the assocation between broken homes and delinquency was mixed. For whites; girls were more likely than boys to come from broken homes only for personal crimes (i.e., incorrigibility and running away), but for property crimes there was no difference. For African-Americans, however, boys were more likely than girls to come from broken homes. Gora (1982) reviewed the studies concerning broken homes, but does not reach a conclusion regarding the association. Dembo et al. (1995, 21) reporting on male and female delinquents, found that girls' behavior was more often related to an abusive home life, while boys' involvement seemed to stem more often from delinquent peers.

[19]   1992, 72-73.

[20]   1989, 1993.

[21]   1988a and 1988b; also see Widom (1995 and 1991).

[22]   For instance, Pollock (1998, 66-67) reviews a number of prison sample survey findings that indicate one-third or more of women in prison have been victims of sexual or physical abuse as children. Further, that they may be as much as three times as likely as men in prison to suffer such abuse and six to 10 times as likely as a general population of women to suffer such abuse.

[23]   Daly (1994a, 63).

[24]   1949/1954.

[25]   1954, 306.

[26]   For instance, Silverman and Dinitz (1974) found that in an institutionalized sample, those boys coming from a household headed by a single mother were self-identified and identified by houseparents as "hypermasculine," meaning that they were more likely to engage in excitement-oriented, high-risk activities. This was a clear test of Parson's original thesis; later applications used both male and female samples and tested the correlation of hypermasculinity and masculinity with delinquency/crime for both men and women.

[27]   1979. One must view these findings with some suspicion since the types of delinquent acts were not very serious.

[28]   Widom (1979, 1981), at least, provided tests of both masculinity and femininity using the Bem Sex-Role Inventory, but unfortunately used a sample of only 73 women in custody and a control group of 20 women. Her findings provided no clear support or rebuttal to the masculinity thesis. Offenders were no more "masculine" than non-offenders, but high recidivists were less "feminine." The latter finding, depending on the operationalization of "feminine," may provide support for Parsons' original thesis. Bunch, Foley, and Urbina (1983) also used a prison sample of only violent offenders (they experienced a high refusal rate and so their sample could not even be considered representative of the violent offenders in this prison). They found that these violent women criminals did not exhibit high scores on a masculinity/femininity scale. In fact, female scientists and varsity athletes had higher androgyny scores than did female criminals. They conclude: "female prison inmates do seem to be more conventional in their personality characteristics, and perhaps closer to the general female population, than women who have chosen atypical careers" (1983, 75). They also found that violent female criminals in prison expressed less favorable attitudes in support of the women's movement than did female college or high school students (1983, 76).

[29]   Note how this problem arises because of the androcentric construction of the problem; researchers test masculinity as the correlate to crime, and assume that the absence of masculinity is femininity. The possibility that femininity does not exist solely as the opposite of masculinity is evidently an impossible concept for many to grasp.

[30]   Naffine (1981, 83).

[31]   Bertrand offers an early sex-role explanation for women's low crime rate: "While our culture condones and even expects a certain amount of acting out and aggressive behavior in young boys, it is less tolerant of the foibles of young girls . . . Hence, to a certain degree, it would be fair to say that the normal, conforming male is permitted, and will be prone to engage in a certain amount of antisocial and illegal behavior. The opposite is true of females: the more conforming and the more 'normal,' the less delinquent and misbehaving" (1969, 74).

[32]   1973, 120.

[33]   1973, 117.

[34]   One example of an early study that concluded sex-role theory was the best explanation for sex differences in crime rates was Jensen and Eve's (1976). They argued against biological bases for such a differential because, they point out, the differential was decreasing and showed variability across countries—those countries where women were least emancipated showed the greatest differential in crime. They quote Sutherland and Cressey's (1960/1966) notion that the crime differential between the sexes varied depending on such things as the size of the community, with age, with time, and with degree of integration in the family, among other things. Therefore, these differences "proved" that biological sex differences were not as robust an answer as sex roles and socialization patterns, although Jensen and Eve cautiously pointed out that even though the differential decreased in certain settings it never disappeared—girls and women always, everywhere, committed less crime than boys and men. They go on to test various sociological explanations for delinquency on the sample of girls from the Richmond Youth Study that Hirschi dropped before analyzing the results to develop control theory. Their findings indicate that boys were more likely to be delinquent even when controlling for parental attachment and supervision patterns, although they did influence the delinquency of girls and boys in predicted directions. In fact, in their analysis, no factor or factors completely explained a lingering unexplained sex differential causing them to at least consider a biological basis for such a differential. In the end, they concluded that sex role/sociological explanations were more persuasive, but they did not close the door to biological predispositions as well (1976, 446).

[35]   1976, 66; also see 1979.

[36]   1976, 69.

[37]   Bottcher (1995).

[38]   1995, 43.

[39]   1995, 45.

[40]   1995, 52.

[41]   For instance, Rosenbaum (1980) applied sex-role theory to prostitution. According to Rosenbaum, the prostitute and especially the "call girl" is only an extreme of accepted sex-role characteristics in society. Thorne (1993), although not a criminologist, provides an interesting recent study of sex roles by looking at gender play among children. She attrib-

utes differences in play to socialization (even though her observational study clearly showed that elementary children separate themselves by gender in play even when teachers attempt to integrate them). Even in pre-school and early elementary school, sex roles have been formed and girls are considered "nicer" than boys. Thorne assumes that these assumptions force girls to display themselves as "good" and "nice," but then girls may displace anger and conflict onto boys, defining them as "naughty." Boys, in turn, may project forbidden feelings of vulnerability and dependence when they taunt girls as "crybabies" and "tattletales."

Interestingly, this ethnographic study observed early sex-segregation and gender differences in play activities even in those situations where adults attempted to provide a gender-neutral environment. Thorne, like most sex-role theorists, presumes that all differences observed were because of socialization even though her study provided no evidence the rougher play of boys and the relational play of girls was purely a product of socialization. Evolutionary psychologists and biosocial theorists would utilize Thorne's observations of proof of their theory of "natural" differences, and point out that it benefits the species for pre-pubescent children to prefer to play apart so children do not become interested in sex too soon, and rougher play among males is merely evidence of "natural" sex differences in functions for the species.

[42] 1987, 49.

[43] 1968.

[44] 1973.

[45] 1974.

[46] 1976.

[47] 1978.

[48] 1981, 1987.

[49] 1987, 4.

[50] 1987, 25. It should be pointed out that Naffine is not the only writer who notes this tendency to view delinquency, when committed by males, as exciting and fun. Jensen (1988) also makes almost the same observations in his analysis of how delinquency was viewed by early researchers.

[51] 1987.

[52] 1987, 6.

[53] 1987, 42.

[54] 1989; also see Howe (1994).

[55] 1986, 8.

[56] 1985, 199.

[57] 1989, 606; also see Simpson and Elis (1995).

[58] This author, for instance, suspects that she would be so defined. Morris (1987, 15) discusses the difficulty of identifying feminist criminologists—reviewing Heidensohn, Carlen, and Smart, among others, in terms of their "fit" with feminist ideology.

[59] Alleman (1993).

60   Belknap (1996).

61   Akers (1997); although his descriptions derive from Tong (1984).

62   Vold, Bernard, and Snipes (1998) argue that the Marxist view believes crimes are defined as such because they threaten the economic power structure, or the actions threaten men's control over women's bodies.

63   While Marxist feminists concentrate almost exclusively on capitalism as the culprit in the oppression of women, socialist feminists argue that power is not only economic and that women were oppressed before the development of capitalism. Vold, Bernard, and Snipes (1998, 279) explain that socialist feminists emphasize natural reproductive differences as the origin of the power differential between men and women: "Therefore, the key to an egalitarian society lay not in women taking ownerhsip of the means of economic production, but in women taking control of their own bodies and their own reproductive functions." Alleman, in his description of socialist feminism quotes Firestone (1970), and offers the following as principles:

1.   Women were at the continual mercy of their biology (i.e., childbirth, wetnursing). This made them dependent on males.

2.   Human infants take a long time to become independent.

3.   Basic mother/child interdependency existed at all times, in all cultures.

4.   Natural reproductive differences between sexes led directly to first division of labor based on sex, this division was the origin of all other divisions of labor and power.

5.   Female oppression is due to ownership of women's bodies; their dependency is due to their biology.

64   1988, 504.

65   Phillips (1987), among others, discusses the arguments among feminists. For instance, some approaches accept natural differences, most do not. Some point to biological differences as the source of oppression, some point to economic features of society. All, however, argue that traditional theorists were sexist—both in largely ignoring women's criminality, but also in their easy acceptance of sex-role stereotypes to explain differences in the behavior patterns of men and women. Messerschmidt (1993) also reviews traditional criminological theories, but also critiques "cultural feminists" because of their simplistic view of "women as good, men are bad." He argues that structural constraints for both men and women need to be explored to explain why men commit the crimes they do and presents a discussion of definitions of masculinity. He brings out the important point that maleness is not homogenous, no more so than femaleness is; and that men are just as influenced by structural constraints such as race and sex as are women: "The radical and cultural feminist focus on alleged differences between men and women acted to obscure differences among men" (1993, 45).

66   1993, 113. His arguments, however, can be criticized as well. For instance, he analyzes the Central Park jogger rape case (where a young, female, white stockbroker was attacked while running in Central Park, beaten, and raped by a group of African-American young men who were on a "wilding" spree). Messerschmidt argues that these young men had no other access to definitions of masculinity; therefore, they used aggression against woman to prove their masculinity (this argument could also apply to robbery or other violent crimes and sounds very similar to Katz' argument regarding the "seductions" of crime).

However the idea that rape is a desperate alternative to define oneself as masculine by those who are barred from other definitions of masculinity does not seem to be the answer that would explain acquaintance rape, fraternity and sports team rapes, rapes during war, and so on. Radical feminists would argue, alternatively, that men do not use rape against women as a last resort to define themselves as masculine; that aggressive sex is as much a part of masculinity as is football (or any other culturally emphasized sport).

[67] 1997, 117.

[68] See, for instance McLeod (1982), Carlen (1983), and Carlen (1985).

[69] 1994b, 126. Daly's particular application of narrative is in sentencing, but the approach can be used to understand criminal causation as well.

[70] 1990, 6.

[71] For instance, studies have explored female offenders' experience of childhood abuse, motivations for drug use, and their relationships with their children.

[72] 1992.

[73] 1997, 127.

[74] 1990, 140.

[75] 1985.

[76] 1985, 10.

[77] 1985, 29.

[78] In medicine, fundamental "truths" regarding heart disease and cancer risks were found using only male samples, calling into question their relevance to women. Even in language, maleness is the norm and only small steps have been taken to neutralize our heavily gendered language.

[79] See, for instance, MacKinnon (1983), Heidensohn (1986), and Lahey (1985).

[80] 1995.

[81] 1987.

[82] Smart (1976, 65).

[83] 1989, 71.

[84] Thomas (1969/1923, 84-85).

[85] Bishop (1931, 3-4).

[86] Pollak (1950, 75).

[87] Adler (1975, 15)

[88] Crittendon (1990, A14).

[89] This assumption that women would act like men is a perfect example of an androcentric approach—women must act like men given social conditions more similar to men, because after all, men are normal and women are not.

90   The first may be identified as occurring contemporaneously with the emancipation efforts during and after the Civil War; this movement unsuccessfully fought for suffrage and, more successfully, argued for increased legal rights for women, i.e., the right to contract. There was a quiescence in women's issues until the second World War at which time women entered the labor force, politics, and other spheres of the public domain in numbers unmatched in past years, obtaining such things as state-paid child care for working women. Yet after WWII ended and women vacated their jobs for returning soldiers, so too did the activity of women's rights end, not to be revived again for another 30 years. In the first women's movement, freedoms for women were compared and associated with those of African-Americans; the most recent women's movement also came on the heels of a civil rights activity for African-Americans and other minorities. Gora (1982) places the upswing of the so-called women's movement in 1963 when there was a presidential commission on the status of women in society; and also, in that year Betty Freidan's, *The Feminine Mystique,* was published. Also, there was the addition of sex to Title VII of the Civil Rights Act of 1964, which eventually led to women entering all non-traditional fields of employment. Women were involved in the anti-war movement and in civil rights organizations, but eventually came to realize that in the fight for social opportunities for minorities, their role was to make the coffee. Simon and Landis (1991, 17-19) note that various factions broke off and became either more or less militant. The National American Woman's Suffrage Association (NAWSA) became the League of Women Voters and this organization is considered the most middle class and most conservative of all women's organizations. The National Organization for Women (NOW), founded by Betty Freidan in 1966 concentrated also on legal and economic problems, but did so less firmly entrenched in the existing political structure. The membership again, was largely white, well educated, professional women. Other groups were less long lasting; and some were quite radical.

91   Even the much-maligned Pollak noted that men were unlikely to take over domestic roles, in 1950, or if current evidence is accepted, in 1998. Although there have been slight percentage changes in the number of hours men work at household chores, the differential is still very wide, even though women have had dramatic changes in participation in the workplace. Therefore, it is questionable whether women have gained "freedom" or "responsibility." Especially when one considers that no-fault divorce has also accompanied women's entry into the workplace and the end result has been divorced women's average income going down and divorced men's average income going up. Today, large numbers of single female head of households exist below the poverty line, hardly consistent with the themes of the "liberation" hypothesis (Faludi, 1991).

92   See Note 50 in this chapter for a related discussion of this concept.

93   For a review, see Crites (1976), Leonard (1982), Smart (1976), Steffensmeier (1978), and Norland and Shover (1977).

94   Adler (1981).

95   Marshall (1982). Macro-level analyses are extremely problematic, however. For instance, measurement differences exist in how crimes are defined, as well as formal processing differences, i.e., the likelihood of getting arrested. Other measures also are crude, i.e., employment rates as a measure of social and economic emancipation. Marshall discusses the validity of Interpol data as well as the measures she employed—labor force participation rate, index of femaleness of economic activity, index of femaleness for administrative and managerial work, index of femaleness for clerical work, index of segregation of economic activity by occupation, and index of segregation of economic activity by industry (1982, 26).

[96]   Marshall (1982, 29).

[97]   1989.

[98]   1975, Simon and Landis (1991).

[99]   Between 1950 and 1985, the percentage of women earning bachelors degress increased from 23.9 perent of all degrees to 49.4 percent of all degrees. Even in the professional areas, women have made advances, especially in medicine and law. In 1960, women earned only 5.5 percent of all medical degrees, but in 1986 they earned 30.8 percent of all medical degrees. In law, the parallel percentages were 2.55 in 1960 and 39 percent in 1986; dentistry 0.8 percent to 22.6 percent, and in engineering 0.4 percent to 12.5 percent. Simon and Landis (1991, 32-35).

[100]   Simon and Landis (1991, 35-36).

[101]   Simon and Landis (1991, 37).

[102]   Simon and Landis (1991, 4).

[103]   Daly and Chesney-Lind (1988) and Leonard (1982).

[104]   Crites (1976), Steffensmeier (1980), and Chapman (1980).

[105]   Feinman (1980/1986, 28).

[106]   Giordano and Cernkovich (1979) and Widom (1979).

[107]   Steffensmeier (1978, 1980, 1981, 1993) and Steffensmeier and Streifel (1992).

[108]   Gora (1982) looked at arrest trends in one city instead of utilizing UCR data to test Adler and Simon's theory. She reviewed arrests from 1939 to 1976 and found dramatic increases between 1959 and 1969, but then these increases leveled off after that so the women's movement did not precede the most dramatic rise. In fact, increases came and were supportive of sex-role theory in 1969 but by 1976 had retreated to patterns more similar to 1959 in seriousness and ratio to male arrests. Simon and Baxter (1989) looked at 31 countries' male and female arrest figures (but evidently did not use population numbers to compute rates). The authors looked at educational attainment, gross national product, level of industrialization, and percentage of females in labor force over a 19-year-period. They found that:

> "over the 19-year time span there were comparable levels of increase among crime, arrest, and female arrest rates from 1962 through 1980. . . . For homicide and major larceny, the percentage of female offenders actually decreased slightly. Women continued to play relatively minor roles in those societies' violent criminal activities" (1989, 194).

[109]   Klein and Kress (1976), Smart (1976), Chapman (1980a, 1980b), Datesman and Scarpetti (1980a, 1980b), Box and Hale (1983), Chesney-Lind (1986), Feinman (1986), Miller (1985), and Messerschmidt (1986).

[110]   Simon and Landis (1991, 26-27).

[111]   Simon and Landis (1991, 27).

[112]   Taylor (1993, 192).

[113]   McLeod (1995).

[114]   Box and Hale (1983), for instance, found, in their study of crime in Britain, that financial insecurity was the most important variable in predicting female criminality.

[115] 1991, 11.

[116] 1991, 15.

[117] 1986.

[118] 1986, x.

[119] 1986, 44.

[120] 1986, 44.

[121] 1989.

[122] 1989, 145. Also see, Hagan, Simpson, and Gillis (1987 and 1988) and Hagan, Gillis, and Simpson (1985).

[123] 1989, 151.

[124] 1989, 145.

[125] 1989, 152.

[126] 1989, 154.

[127] Note that this portion of the theory observes that economic liberation for women will result in greater crime, but for different reasons than Adler's or Simon's "liberation" theory.

[128] 1989, 170. Many would disagree that outside employment necessarily leads to egalitarianism in a marriage; the concept (which is interpersonal) is more complicated than who is bringing home a paycheck, and the simple fact of outside employment does not even indicate salary differential, although there was an attempt to measure work status by designations of work as "command" and "obey" classes of employment.

[129] 1989, 180.

[130] 1989, 183.

[131] 1989, 185.

[132] 1991.

[133] Chesney-Lind and Sheldon (1992, 92-97).

[134] 1995.

[135] 1995, 232.

[136] Jensen and Westphal (1998).

[137] 1991.

[138] Simpson (1991).

[139] 1995, 27 (notes omitted).

[140] 1995, 129.

[141] Simpson and Elis (1995, 62).

[142] 1965, 63.

Current Theories: Here We Go Again?

7

In this chapter we will look at the theories of crime developed in the last 30 years or so. The "great debate" between life-course/development theories utilizing longitudinal research and "the general theory of crime" will be discussed, as well as rational choice and social support theories. Despite the scathing criticism of feminist researchers in the 1970s of traditional theories, these current theories persist in virtually ignoring sex as a variable in crime causation. Although most writers throw in a paragraph or two noting the sex differential and conclude the sex difference in crime rates has something to do with parental supervision or socialization, they have yet to integrate sex into theoretical treatments, or change the androcentric orientation of criminology. It is truly amazing to consider that much of the research that purports to "test" these theories or compare the theories against each other exclude women completely and use samples composed entirely of boys and/or men. As indicated in the title of this chapter, current theorists either did not read or did not accept the feminist critiques of traditional theories because . . . here we go again!

LIFE-COURSE/DEVELOPMENT THEORIES

Longitudinal studies identify a cohort (a selected group of individuals), and then follow this group for a long period of time, collecting the same types of information at various points in the individuals' lives. Typically the follow-up period extends throughout childhood and into adulthood.[1] A different approach is to use cross-sectional research. This approach utilizes a large sample and collects a great deal of information relevant to the dependent variable (delinquency or crime) and to the independent variables (whatever is hypothesized as causal). Then statistical tests are conducted to determine the association between the independent variables and the presence of the dependent variable (delinquency). Proponents of longitudinal research argue that cross-sectional research cannot discover how factors work at various times in one's life; proponents of cross-sectional research argue that one can capture that information by utilizing age as an independent variable; and some argue that factors influence individuals similarly at various times in life, therefore no new information is learned by collecting information from cohorts.[2]

The longitudinal approach has been used by those who have developed life-course or developmental theories. A related approach is the "career criminal" approach that incorporates the notion that certain offenders develop a professional orientation to crime while most commit only occasional crimes.[3]

Longitudinal research identifies those correlates of delinquency that emerge during the lifetime of the cohort members. For instance, Farrington, Ohlin, and Wilson identified the following as correlates of delinquency and criminology:

> We know that the typical high rate offender is a young male who began his aggressive or larcenous activities at an early age, well before the typical boy gets into serious trouble. We know that he comes from a troubled, discordant, low-income family in which one or both parents are likely to have criminal records themselves. We know that the boy has had trouble in school—he created problems for his teachers and does not do well in his studies. On leaving school, often by dropping out, he works at regular jobs only intermittently. Most employers regard him as a poor risk. He experiments with a variety of drugs—alcohol, marijuana, speed, heroin— and becomes a frequent user of whatever drug is most readily available, often switching back and forth among different ones. . . .[4]

Thus, individual differences, family influences, school influences, and peer influences were all identified as potential influences on the onset of, continuation in, and desistance from crime. The longitudinal study conducted by the Harvard Program on Human Development and Criminal Behavior collected data relevant to all these factors.[5]

A wide range of hypotheses concerning the development and persistence of delinquency is tested in longitudinal research. The following are presented by one group of researchers.

- Genotype differences among individuals are the primary determinant of a latent trait for antisocial behavior. Latent traits are more "frequently and more completely expressed" in males than in females.

- The sensitivity and consistency of primary caregivers to the emotional needs of infants determine the parent-child relationship.

- Inconsistent and insensitive discipline practices eventually result in the development of conduct disorder and delinquency.

- Genotype differences determine a latent trait that is more fully expressed in adverse social environments than in supportive environments.

- Low verbal intelligence contributes to early risk for conduct disorder and delinquency by delaying the acquisition of social skills.

- The prevalence of latent traits for conduct disorder and delinquency and for low verbal intelligence can be reduced by good health practices, early intellectual, and social skills development and competent caretaking and discipline practices.

- Delinquent and criminal behavior will increase as social control decreases (attachment to school, work, marriage, and family life).

- Rejection by prosocial children during pre-adolescent years promotes solidification of delinquent peer networks.

- Once individuals become delinquent, peer networks predict their persistence in and desistance from delinquent activity.

- Community structure has contextual effects on criminal behavior that are independent of individual characteristics and peer networks.

- Individual characteristics, family process, and life-course transitions interact with community characteristics to explain patterns of criminal behavior.[6]

Further, the processes involved in delinquency are predicted to be different depending on the age of onset. That is, life-course and development theorists perceive that the early onset delinquent is different from that one who begins in adolescence.[7] Younger age of onset is hypothesized to be correlated with: low intelligence, high impulsiveness, child abuse, harsh and erratic parental discipline, cold and rejecting parents, poor parental supervision, parental disharmony, separation, and divorce, one-parent female headed households, convicted parents or siblings, alcoholic or drug-using parents or siblings, non-white race membership, low occupational prestige of parents, low educational level of parents, low family income, large family size, poor housing, low educational attainment of the child, attendance at a high delinquency school, delinquent friends, and high crime area of residence.[8]

A Cambridge longitudinal study tracked British men from age eight to age 32. Especially important was the finding that there were different groups with different "trajectories" of offending; that is, some groups had an early onset of offending and were chronic, others started offending in adolescence and were more likely to decrease their criminal activity as they matured than the first group.[9] Farrington describes the results of the Cambridge longitudinal study:

> [we] found that the typical offender—a male property offender—tends to be born in a low-income, large-sized family and to have criminal parents. When he is young, his parents supervise him rather poorly, use harsh or erratic child-rearing techniques, and are likely to be in conflict and to separate. At school, he tends to have low intelligence and attainment, is troublesome, hyperactive, and impulsive, and often truants. He tends to associate with friends who are also delinquents.[10]

Farrington goes on to describe the young adulthood of the above offender as characterized by frequent unemployment, versatile deviance, violence, vandalism, drug use, drinking, reckless driving, and sexual promiscuity. Criminality declines in the late twenties when these men get married and have children. Their thirties are described as marked by divorce, periodic unemployment or low-paying jobs, frequent moves, heavy drinking, more violence, and more drug taking.[11]

In this Cambridge study, one-third of the men admitted delinquency but five percent were responsible for 50 percent of all delinquent acts. This illustrates how incidence figures tell us something more than merely prevalence figures. There was an absolute decline of antisocial acts among all in the cohort between 18 and 32, but the worst offenders at 18 were also the worst at 32.[12] This study concluded that risk factors associated with a persistence of criminality after age 21 included lack of leisure time with father during childhood, low intelligence, employment instability, and heavy drinking. Desistance was associated with the increasing costs of crime (long prison sentences), the importance of intimate relationships with women, increasing satisfaction with jobs, and becoming more mature, responsible, and settled with age.[13]

Cohort samples for longitudinal studies often exclude women.[14] Farrington explains why women were ignored in his longitudinal research:

> Because of the difficulty of establishing causal effects of factors that vary only between individuals (e.g., gender and ethnicity), and because such factors have no practical implications for prevention (e.g., it is not practicable to change males into females), unchanging variables will not be reviewed in this chapter. In any case, their effects on offending are usually explained by reference to other, changeable, factors. . . For example, gender differences in offending have been explained on the basis of different socialization methods used by parents with boys and girls, or different opportunities of males and females for offending.

This is an interesting comment and deserves some attention. At first, he seems to say that because sex is an unchangeable factor it is not worth studying; this begs the question, of course, as to what it is about sex that affects the choice of crime. Then he changes the explanation so that it is not sex that explains crime but some other factors such as socialization or opportunities, that, arguably, are subject to change. If socialization patterns influenced the inclination to make criminal choices, it seems one would want to study socialization differences. However, if one utilizes a sample composed entirely of boys, it would be impossible to examine how such a factor worked differently on girls and boys to account for their different crime rates.

He goes on to talk about mother-only households, Attention Deficit Disorder (ADD) and hyperactivity (conduct disorders that are much more prevalent among boys), sensation seeking, and low physiological arousal, intelligence, poor supervision and erratic discipline, neglectful parenting, broken homes, criminal parents, large families, socio-economic status, poor housing or public housing, socially disorganized neighborhoods, and peers as causal elements in the development of delinquency.[15] However, by excluding women from the cohort sample, this study is unable to determine the relative effects of these factors on male and female delinquency and criminality.

Farrington argues a model that includes different stages of developing delinquent/criminal behavior patterns. At first, *energizing factors* (desires for material goods, status among intimates, excitement, boredom, frustration, anger, and alcohol consumption) tempt individuals to commit delinquent acts. Then, in the *directing stages,* socially disapproved methods of satisfying motivations are either habitually chosen or not.[16] The *inhibiting stage* is the process by which antisocial tendencies can be reduced by internalized beliefs and attitudes that are built through social learning process, a history of rewards and punishments, a strong conscience (which he believes comes from love and close supervision), and empathy (which comes from parental warmth and loving relationships). Those with high impulsivity and low intelligence are less able to build up internal inhibitions against offending. In the *decision-making stage* the actual choice of criminal action or not depends on opportunity costs and benefits and subjective probabilities of different outcomes for each situation.[17]

As with most longitudinal research, Farrington and his colleagues place a great deal of importance on the family. Early prenatal and postnatal influences affect intelligence scores and behavior problems of children and, in other ways, the family is seen as the transmitter of delinquency.[18]

Farrington's discussion is broad and comprehensive—the factors identified are exhaustive and the model by which he proposes they operate is logical. The only problem with his explanation is the superficial and easy dismissal of sex as a variable. Until developmental models such as Farrington's are able to explicate exactly how sex affects criminal choices, the theories cannot explain the sex differential in crime rates.

Wolfgang, Thornberry, and Figlio report their findings from a longitudinal study that started in 1945.[19] The findings of this longitudinal study were very similar to those above. Basically all cohort studies indicate that individuals have varying levels of delinquency, and those serious delinquents with early onset delinquency tend to come from more dysfunctional homes.

A longitudinal study conducted in New Zealand indicates that there are differential rates of offending by individuals in the cohort.[20] Separate latent factors seemed to underlie childhood and adolescent onset of antisocial behavior. Childhood antisocial behavior was related to low verbal ability, hyperactivity, and negative/impulsive personality; but adolescent onset of antisocial behavior was related more strongly to peer delinquency. Furthermore, adolescent onset antisocial behavior was more likely to be property crime, while childhood onset antisocial behavior was more likely to result in violent crime.

Sampson and Laub, after coding and analyzing the 18-year-old data of Sheldon and Eleanor Glueck, confirmed that childhood behaviors were highly correlated with later delinquency and criminality. They explain the findings of their study as follows:

- Social structural factors combined with informal family and school social controls explain delinquency in childhood and adolescence.

- There is continuity in antisocial behavior from childhood through adulthood.

- Informal social bonds in adulthood to family and employment explain desistance in criminality over the life span despite early childhood propensities.[21]

As with all life-course theories, this one proposes that later adult factors affect the persistance or desistance from criminal behavior, although the theory is also sociogenic in that they see some levels of stability in criminal careers over the life-course. They argue against Gottfredson and Hirschi's[22] premise that there is consistency in criminal propensities over the life-course, finding that marriage, moving, and entry into the armed forces is correlated with a reduction of antisocial behaviors while unemployment is associated with persistence.[23] These authors argue that types of social control vary by age. When one is young, social control is provided by the family, school, peer groups, and the juvenile justice system. During young adulthood one may be controlled through higher education, vocational training, work, marriage, and the adult criminal justice system. Middle adulthood contains controls from work, marriage, parenthood, investment in the community, and the criminal justice system. They see informal social controls as emerging from the "role reciprocities" and interpersonal bonds linking members of society to one another and to wider social institutions such as work, family, and school.[24]

Because the Gluecks' data included biological, sociological, and psychological variables, these authors were able to consider many influences that they then placed into a model of delinquency/criminality. Most importance was placed on family discipline practices, supervision, and child-parent attachment.[25]

Table 7.1
Sampson and Laub's Development Theory

A set of predisposing factors:
- structural and background factors
- low family SES
- family size
- family disruption
- residential mobility
- parent's deviance
- household crowding
- foreign born
- mother's employment

Combined with individual constructs:
- difficult temperament
- persistent tantrums
- early conduct disorder

Which interact with social control processes:
- family
- lack of supervision
- threatening/erratic harsh discipline
- parental rejection
- school
- weak attachment
- poor performance
- delinquent influence
- peer delinquent attachment
- sibling delinquent attachment

That then leads to:
- delinquency
- length of incarceration

Which, in turn, influences:
- social bonds
- weak labor force attachment
- weak marital attachment

And, ultimately, creates the continuation of:
- crime and deviance.

Adapted from Sampson and Laub, 1993, p. 244.

Unfortunately, the Gluecks' data that Sampson and Laub's study utilized are now quite old. One wonders whether such an old data set has any applicability in today's world. Further, the sample is composed solely of white males. Therefore, the applicability and usefulness of such findings is at least debatable. On the other hand, their model and the conclusions drawn from the analysis are not all that much different from other life-course/development theories. The most unfortunate drawback of their model for the purposes of this book is that the sample precluded their consideration of sex and gender; therefore sex is not even considered as a predisposing or structural variable.

THE GENERAL THEORY OF CRIME

Hirschi's (1969) "control theory" generated a wealth of theoretical and analytical response in criminology in the 1970s, and Gottfredson and Hirschi's (1990) "general theory of crime" has done the same in the 1990s. Actually, the two are not all that different. While control theory postulates that various bonds to society (attachment, commitment, belief, and involvement) control the individual and prevent delinquency, the general theory of crime proposes, simply, that individuals are born with and/or are raised to have different levels of self-control. Gottfredson and Hirschi propose that "crime is a natural consequence of unrestrained human tendencies to seek pleasure and avoid pain."[26] Crime is composed of "acts of force or fraud undertaken in pursuit of self-interest."[27] The authors agree with rational choice and routine activities theory that argue for crime to occur there must be offender motivation, but also there must be lack of guardianship and a suitable target. Gottfredson and Hirschi argue that most criminal theories only concentrate on the first (criminal motivation).[28]

In their definition of crime, they argue that there are no real differences between serious and non-serious crimes: "Murder may be among the least motivated, least deliberate, and least consequential (for the offender) crime."[29] Therefore, one can look for a similar cause for both serious and non-serious crime. In other words, they reject the idea of specialization or the assumption that at least some criminals may be "career criminals" and adopt a career orientation, committing many crimes of a specialized nature and developing skills in that area in the same way that any professional would. Gottfredson and Hirshi argue that most research shows that criminals are generalists, citing research that shows most criminals commit a wide range of different types of crimes.[30] Their conclusion that crime is a unitary construct is contrary to the point made in the first chapter of this book that crime is composed of a multitude of very different behaviors—from minor income tax fraud to hired murder. Although, arguably, some behaviors are so different (in seriousness, predisposition, and motivation) as to prevent a single unitary theory from explaining all criminal behavior, Gottfredson and Hirschi do not agree and propose that one variable explains all criminal offending—self-control.

In their work, they first explore other potential explanations of crime. In a somewhat superficial analysis of biological and biosocial approaches, they conclude that:

> We would not be surprised to learn that the true genetic effect on the likelihood of criminal behavior is somewhere between zero and the results finally reported by Mednick, Gabrielli, and Hutchings. That is, we suspect that the magnitude of this effect is minimal.[31]

In an interesting argument disputing any role of biology in the construct of aggression, they argue that because criminals are aggressive in some circumstances and not in others, the personality characteristic cannot be said to be "caused" by a biological construct. However, one might make the same argument to their general theory of crime. If lack of self control is said to be the "cause" of all crime; why do criminals have self-control in some situations and not others? Why do they not steal every time they have an opportunity; and why do they not commit many more crimes? Basically, why can they control themselves in some situations and not others? Probably because their *predisposition* to impulsiveness is moderated by varying levels of rationality, attachment, and other variables yet to be determined, just as aggressive individuals have a predisposition to aggression that can be moderated by variables such as rationality, training, and affection.

Interestingly, the construct that they base their theory upon—self-control—is merely the reverse of impulsiveness, a construct that is fairly well established as a personality trait and one that is most probably genetic (inheritable). Gottfredson and Hirschi evidently reject the biological research that shows impulsivity is, to some extent, a personality trait with which one is born, and favor, instead, a sociological explanation of parental discipline as creating the individual's ability to control impulses. They also cite with approval the Gluecks and others who have established a correlation between intelligence and delinquency, and intelligence is almost certainly a biological construct, although one greatly moderated by environment, so it is hard to understand why they discount biological explanations so completely. Finally, they make very little mention of sex as an independent variable highly correlated with delinquency/criminality. One assumes they would, at least, agree that sex was a biological construct; however, they evidently attribute the sex differential to socialization.

Gottfredson and Hirschi propose that people with low self-control commit criminal acts and a host of other dangerous and impulsive behaviors; people with more self-control do not. Criminal acts provide immediate gratification, are relatively easy, exciting, risky, and/or thrilling. These characteristics appeal to low self-control types who lack diligence; are adventuresome, active, and physical; and cannot delay gratification. Crime provides meager long-term benefits, but low self-control types do no think ahead, and are not good at planning. Crimes often result in pain or discomfort for the victim, but low self-control types tend to be self-centered, indifferent, or insensitive to the suffering and needs of others. Further low self-control types also are engaged in other activities indicative of low self-control, such as smoking, drinking, using drugs, gambling, having illegitimate children, and engaging in illicit sex.

> In sum, people who lack self-control will tend to be impulsive, insensitive, physical (as opposed to mental), risk-taking, short-sighted, and nonverbal, and they will tend therefore to engage in criminal and analogous acts.[32]

They anticipate their critics by arguing that low self-control can explain white-collar crime as easily as it can explain "garden variety" opportunistic crime: "[discussing white-collar criminals] They too are people with low self-control, people inclined to follow momentary impulse without consideration of the long-term costs of such behavior."[33] According to these authors, those who embezzle have less self-control than those who do not embezzle (but evidently have more self-control than those who did not go to school for years, graduate, get hired by a business, and maintain a decent reputation long enough to rise to some level of trust).[34] They also anticipate critics who might point to organizational crime (Mafia and gangs) since descriptions of such criminal enterprises involve what is apparently a good deal of control—both external and self control—in the operation and continuation of such criminal activity. Gottfredson and Hirschi, in response to the example of organized crime, simply disbelieve the existence of Cosa Nostra, and in response to gangs, propose that gang members do not trust or like each other and are largely unorganized.[35]

According to Gottfredson and Hirschi, the reason some individuals have low self-control and others have more self-control is parental discipline practices: "The major 'cause' of low self-control thus appears to be ineffective child rearing."[36] Further: "The minimum conditions seem to be these: in order to teach the child self-control, someone must (1) monitor the child's behavior; (2) recognize deviant behavior when it occurs; and (3) punish such behavior." To support the notion that parental discipline practices are correlated and causal in the development of delinquency, they point to Sampson's finding[37] that the percentage of the population divorced, percentage of households headed by women, and percentage of unattached individuals in community are powerful predictors of crime, as well as that research that finds a correlation between broken homes and delinquency.[38]

Gottfredson and Hirschi propose that people with low self-control commit criminal acts, and people with more self-control do not. This woman is being arraigned on heroin charges. *Photo credit: Mark C. Ide.*

In a later work reviewing and elaborating upon the general theory of crime, Hirschi argues that the family may reduce the likelihood of criminal behavior by socializing its children, more specifically, by teaching them self-control. Further the family may reduce the likelihood of delinquency by restricting its children's activity, and maintaining actual physical surveillance of them. It may reduce the likelihood of delinquency by commanding the love, respect, or dependence of its members (although it does not fully explain how this might lead to less delinquency). The family may also reduce crime by guarding the home, thereby protecting it from potential thieves, vandals, and burglars (although it is not clear why a burglar alarm system would not do the same thing). He argues also that the family may reduce delinquency by protecting its members, by deterring potential fornicators, assaulters, molesters, and rapists (although he does not explain how this proposal might reconcile with research that indicates youngsters are likely to be raped, abused, molested, and assaulted by family members). Finally, according to Hirschi, the family may reduce delinquency by acting as an advocate for the child to probation or parole and be willing to guarantee the good conduct of its members.[39]

The argument then goes that if one comes from a single-parent family, or alternatively, one comes from such a large family that parents are unable to parent effectively, then the advantages above are eliminated. For example, he proposes that single-parent families cannot protect children, supervise them, or protect the household. However, after reviewing the evidence he concludes that the effects of single-parent families on delinquency were small and not significant. However, the number of siblings did have an effect:

> Whatever one may think of these assertions, the fact is that children from large families score lower on intelligence tests (especially those tests that emphasize vocabulary or verbal ability), get poorer grades in school, expect to obtain less education, and actually complete fewer years of schooling than children from small families . . .[40]

Instead of considering intervening variables, such as income, religion, or culture, Hirschi concludes that large family size and the children's delinquency are both caused by the same variable—low self-control of the parents: "So, our theory suggests that size of family predicts deviant behavior in the children because it is itself an indicator of parental self-control."[41] The problem with this conclusion is that it ignores the multitude of reasons some families have children—Catholics are prevented from using birth control, some cultures value large numbers of children, some people simply like babies (even if they do not quite know what to do with them when they grow up a little).

Although Hirschi identifies large family size as a correlate of delinquency, he concludes there is less empirical support for the notion that single-parent households are associated with delinquency. He points out the difficulty of ascribing causality to single-parent households when crime has been decreasing in the same time period as single-parent households have been increasing.[42]

Gottfredson and Hirschi argue that the age effect (the graduate desistance of crime in the late twenties and early thirties) can be explained by the continued socialization of the individual over the lifecourse.[43] They reject evidence of other personality differences between delinquents and non-delinquents, describing such research as "unimpressive."[44] Arguing against the idea proposed in life-course theories (and Hirschi's own control theory) that certain factors provide informal controls and influence the desistance of delinquency/criminality, they argue that such an approach denies the participation of the actor. In essence, they argue that if a correlation can be shown between marriage and reduction or elimination of delinquency, it is because low self-control types do not get married, only those with more self-control do: "Apparently, girlfriends, like jobs, do not simply attach themselves to boys. Instead, there is some sort of self selection to the treatment condition."[45]

Their treatment of sex and gender is, to say the least, brief: "It is beyond the scope of this work (and beyond the reach of any available set of empirical data) to attempt to identify all of the elements responsible for gender differences in crime."[46] One might question, then, why they feel justified in calling it a "general" theory of crime. Interestingly, in an oblique reference to potential explanations of the sex/gender difference, they seem to point to biological differences: "It seems to us to follow that the impact of gender on crime is largely a result of crime differences and differences in self-control that are not produced by direct external control."[47] If the "direct external control" can be assumed to be the parenting practices that they described as causal to low self-control, it is unclear what other "differences in self-control" might exist other than biological. If so, their reference to gender is disingenuous since what they meant to say was sex differences, not gender differences, account for the crime differential. However, it is hard to know what they meant by the statement.

In a later work, Gottfredson and Hirschi restate their general theory of crime and answer their critics.

> Criminal acts are a subset of acts in which the actor ignores the long-term negative consequences that flow from the act itself (e.g., the health consequences of drug use), from the social or familial environment (e.g., a spouse's reaction to infidelity), or from the state (e.g., the criminal justice response to robbery). All acts that share this feature, including criminal acts, are therefore likely to be engaged in by individuals unusually sensitive to immediate pleasure and insensitive to long-term consequences. . . . The evidence suggests to us that variation in self-control is established early in life, and that differences between individuals remain reasonably constant over the life-course.[48]

They argue that their theory is consistent with research that identified the importance of family,[49] opportunity theory,[50] and a maturation effect;[51] but that the theory is inconsistent with the career criminal theory, the existence of organized crime, the idea that adolescent delinquency is different from adult criminality, or that white-collar crime is different from street crime, and the idea that crime is learned. They namely describe and address criticisms that attacked the legitimacy of their theory, some of which are briefly summarized below.

- The theory is too general, lumping crime into the same category as accidents and bad habits. They argue that the criticism could also be applied to the medical theory that whooping cough and diphtheria are caused by germs. In other words, perhaps the best theory is the one that is the most general. On the other hand, one assumes the authors know that whooping cough and diphtheria are not caused by the same germ.

- The theory is tautological, meaning that they explain crime by saying criminals have low self-control, and then prove it by arguing that people with low self-control commit crime. They argue that being called tautological is a compliment because it implies internal consistency. Other theories, they argue, do not "explicitly show the logical connections between . . . the actor and the act." It seems, however, that the argument regarding whether the theory is tautological misses the essential point. A good theory should be able to independently predict the result (delinquency or crime) without having to wait for it to occur. Whether one can predict crime from other evidence of low self-control is the issue; not whether such measures are correlated with crime and vice versa. Thus, although they argue that they have independent (of crime) measures of low self-control: "we would propose such items as whining, pushing, and shoving (as a child); smoking and drinking and excessive television watching and accident frequency (as a teenager); difficulties in interpersonal relations, employment instability, automobile accidents, drinking, and smoking (as an adult) . . ." do these measures predict crime? One might argue that while criminals exhibit such behaviors, many who also exhibit the behaviors do not engage in serious criminality.

- The theory is based on erroneous conceptions of the relation between age and various behaviors. Critics argue that the causes for the onset of crime may differ from causes of persistence in and desistence from crime.

- The theory ignores important distinctions between the incidence and prevalence of criminal or deviant behavior.

- The theory fails to distinguish among classes of offenders who differ markedly in level and variety of their deviant behaviors.

In answer to the last three criticisms above, they argue that studies do not show any differences between incidence (participation rates) and frequency rates and incidence rates do not add anything to our understanding of criminality. This debate regarding the relative importance of longitudinal versus cross-sectional research continues.[52]

They also describe and respond to such criticisms as: the theory fails to anticipate important differences among offenders in sensitivity to institutional experiences or sanctions; overstates the importance of self-control, regarding it as sole cause of crime; and ignores the fact that self-control is not the stable, general trait the theory claims it to be.[53]

Tests of the General Theory

Gibbs and Giever provide the best review of the multitude of tests that have attempted to determine the extent of association between measures of low self-control and delinquency or criminality.[54] Not all of these studies will be reviewed here, rather we will address a few as representative samples, and discuss those that tested the theory against any interactive effect with gender/sex.

Zager is one of the few that apply the general theory of crime to the sex/gender crime differential. First, she points out that the sex differential is quite large, it is larger for developed countries than undeveloped, it is growing smaller in the United States in recent years, it is different for different crimes, and shrinks to nothing for such activities as running away, smoking, and shoplifting. She then examines the relationships between gender, self-control, and crime/delinquency using the Richmond Youth Data from the 1960s. She operationalizes lack of self-control by alcohol use, marijuana use, obscene phone calls, avoiding payment, strong-arming students, and joyriding, and attitudinal measures such as honesty (negative measure), short-sightedness, and concern for victims (negative measure).[55] Zager found what she expected to find—that gender was more highly correlated with crimes with high male/female ratios and self-control measures more correlated with crimes with low sex ratios. She concludes that gender should be seen as an opportunity factor, since if it was a self-control factor, it would vary equally across types of crimes.[56]

Longshore, Turner, and Stein tested the construct validity of one self control scale among drug-using criminal offenders. They found that factor analyses identified five subscales, most of which were consistent with the general theory of crime. They also found that crimes of force and fraud were more frequent among people scoring lower on self-control as measured by this scale. One interesting finding from this study was that risk-seeking and impulsiveness/self-centeredness were as valuable as the overall self-control scale in predicting crimes of fraud, while risk-seeking and temper were as valuable in predicting crimes of force.[57] The authors propose that perhaps self-control adds no new explanatory power to the question of criminal choices and that risk-taking or impulsiveness may be related to other sociological theories or neurological theories better than self-control. They also found that the five factors composing the scale of self-control were not as correlated with women's criminality as other correlates mentioned in the literature.

Evans et al. review many other tests of the general theory of crime and conclude that most empirical tests have provided impressive support for the correlation between the construct of low self-control and delinquency/crime. They then offer their own test of the general theory of crime by using two distinct measures of self-control, an attitudinal measure and an analogous/behavior scale. They test whether these measures of low self-control are correlated with delinquency/crime and also whether they are correlated with life chances, life quality, and other social consequences.[58] Although both men and women formed part of the sample, sex/gender was not disaggregated, except that they controlled these factors when testing for the influence of self-control, so it is impossible to tell from the findings whether the theory holds equally true for both sexes. They find that both behavioral and attitudinal measures of self control are correlated with delinquency/crime. They also found, however, that some effects of criminal associates and internal criminal values remain significant when entered into the equation, thus presenting the possibility that social learning theory and self-control may both help to explain criminal choice.

Critique and Review

The general theory of crime has spawned the current generation of criminological theses, dissertations, and journal articles. The authors argue articulately and persuasively for their single construct theory, attacking competing theories and buttressing their arguments by selected research findings. Yet, ultimately, it must fail as the "general" theory of crime because it is not general—it does not explain the sex/gender differential. Only when they are able to explain how the same families can raise boys with low self-control and girls (evidently) with higher levels of self-control would the theory make sense as a simple explanation of criminality.

Miller and Burack discuss this weakness of the general theory of crime.[59] They argue that the theory presents a false gender neutrality, that the authors ignore gender, race, and class in their explanation of criminal choice. They also criticize the theory for mischaracterizing male violence committed against women and ignoring feminist scholarship concerning gender division of labor, as well as scapegoating the mother as the source of ineffective child-rearing. These authors dispute Gottfredson and Hirschi's typology of rape as well as their statistics regarding prevalence.[60] Further, they argue that the general theory of crime misdefines rape solely as an action resulting from sexual impulse rather than include the power elements of rape, as have been well accepted in the relevant literature; the same mischaracterization is made regarding domestic violence. And while Gottfredson and Hirschi describe battering as simply the result of irritation and low self-control, these authors argue that they ignore the patriarchal supports that allow and, to some extent, provide justification, for such action. The authors are also unpersuaded by the tacit gender neutrality Gottfredson and Hirschi exhibit when discussing parenting. They argue that the theory is implicitly "mother-blaming" because most socialization tasks fall to the mother, and the single-parent households targeted as lacking in socialization to develop self-control are almost always headed by women. Rather than admit this and deal with the social reality that socialization to a large extent equates to mothering, the general theory of crime pretends there is gender neutrality in this part of the theory. In fact, Miller and Burack argue that the theory can be read to condemn advances made by women in social and economic opportunities:

> It is, indeed, easy to conclude from the general theory that were women to stay home with children, monitoring and rearing them using native parental wisdom (the psychological theory specified by the theory is sparse and intuitive), the problem of criminality would be largely solved within a generation.[61]

Another criticism is that the theory does not include any concept of the meaning of actions and how personal meaning interacts with and influences self-control. Values, motivations, and meanings interact with individual self-control, explaining why some people show a great deal of self-control in some areas and none in others.[62] Further, there is a difference in the acts labeled criminal and those merely injurious to one's health, because, by the author's own definition of crime, it is those acts that "through force or fraud" result in self benefit by hurting someone else. Many people drink and smoke—relatively few of us commit acts of force or fraud. It seems that some type of moral sense or empathy is the missing element in Hirschi and Gottfredson's theory. By adding this construct, one can remove the examples of those of us who have little self-control in those areas of our lives that harm no one but ourselves. In other words, there are many more "weak" people than there are "criminal" people.

Reconciling the Life-Course Theories and General Theory of Crime

Several authors review the "bitter" dispute between the relative merits of cross-sectional research versus longitudinal research, as well as the relative worth of life-course theories versus the general theory of crime.[63] The authors identify the major points of dispute, including the idea that self-control can (or cannot) change over the life-course. Sampson and Laub propose that those who marry develop self-control, while Hirschi and Gottfredson believe that people with low self-control are unlikely to marry. This is clearly an illustration of the problem of correlation not explaining causality—only longitudinal data would indicate whether those who were actively impulsive/criminal in youth desisted upon marriage, yet confronted with such research Gottfredson and Hirschi would probably simply say that the people who married had at least more self-control than those who did not marry.[64]

Cohen and Villa resolve the dispute by proposing that Gottfredson and Hirschi's model describes sociopaths, which comprise a small, distinct group of those who deviate. Most delinquents and criminals, however, can be described by Sampson and Laub's model.[65] Neither model is criticized for ignoring the sex/gender differential.[66]

Paternoster and Brame also propose that neither the developmental model nor the static criminal propensity model of the general theory of crime provides the best answer to criminal causation.[67] Rather, they argue a middle ground, stating that there are multiple pathways to delinquency, that these pathways are more similar than different, and that past offending and life experiences affect future criminality. These authors present an excellent review of the two theoretical approaches, provide a comprehensive review of evidence, and offer a cogent, logical integration of the two. However, nowhere in their 30 or so pages of discussion do they mention gender or how neither of the two approaches comes to terms with the sex/gender differential. It is almost as if women do not exist in the current debate taking place in the literature over the relative merits of the two approaches or how they can be integrated.[68]

RATIONAL CHOICE THEORY

Recall that the Classical School assumed that men were rational and could be deterred from crime by making the punishment swift, sure, and proportional to the perceived profit of the crime. The Classical School assumptions disappeared with the rise of positivism and then the sociological dominance of criminology presented almost entirely sociologically deterministic theories for many decades. In the last decade or so, however, the Classical School has been revived with rational choice theory. This modern-day theory presumes that criminals rationally choose criminal action because the immediate rewards are more persuasive than uncertain punishments.

Cornish and Clarke developed and applied the rational choice theory to residential burglary.[69] They indicated, by their research, that burglars were influenced by such factors as the affluence of the neighborhood, the presence of bushes, nosy neighbors, alarms, dogs, placement on the street (i.e., corner), access to major arterial, and so on. The conclusion is that burglars do not pick a house at random, they identify and target those houses that they have the best chance of burglarizing without getting caught. Although the theory makes sense with burglars, it has been applied (some would say to less success) to all other crimes as well.

Piquero and Tibbetts argue that rational choice theory should be combined and tested along with self-control theory to form a more comprehensive approach to the explanation of crime.[70] In other words, a theory that includes both situational factors (opportunity and risk factors) and personal self-control (low or high), will explain more than simply looking at one or the other of the factors. They test their integrated theory with a sample of college students. Although they included both men and women in their sample, they did not disaggregate by sex so it is impossible to tell if their theory works equally well for both sexes.

Cohen and Felson present a slightly different theory—the so-called routine activities approach.[71] They argue that predatory crime rates are influenced by routine activities that satisfy basic needs such as food and shelter. For a crime to happen, there must be a motivated offender, suitable targets of criminal victimization, and the absence of guardians of persons or property: "convergence in space and time of the three minimal elements of direct-contact predatory violations."[72] Any changes in routine activities lead to changing opportunities for crime. For instance, the increase in the number of working women after WWII meant that more homes were left unattended during day and this created the opportunity for burglaries to occur. Most sociological theories look at the motivation of the offender, and these authors argue it is also fruitful to look at changes in opportunities or guardianship. Tests of this theory focus on demographic, macro-level changes in society.[73]

Anderson and Bennett review the multitude of studies that have tested the routine activities theory and then offer their own approach.[74] They test the theory with cross-national time series analyses and are able to test it against the factors of economic development and gender. They conclude that the theory's principles work best to explain minor theft arrests for men in developed nations. The theory does not seem to fit data from undeveloped countries, nor does it explain completely women's theft rates (although motivation and guardianship did show some correlation with minor theft rates for women).

Note that the general theory of crime might be consistent with the routine activities approach because it identifies the correlation of crime with an increase of opportunity and/or a decrease of guardianship; with the related assumption that those with low self-control will take advantage of these opportunities when presented to them. The rational choice theory, however, is not so consistent since it presumes that the criminal rationally chooses his or her actions and does not operate simply from low self-control. It is neither consistent nor inconsistent with the life-course theory; one could argue that it proposes a career criminal orientation that would not be affected by life changes, but one could also argue that there is no reason that the theory could not make room for different variables operating in the risk weighing thought processes of the offender.

SOCIAL SUPPORT THEORIES

One final category of new theories might be called the social support or social disorganization theories. If the rational choice theory resuscitates the Classical School, then the social support/social disorganization theories of today revive the old Shaw and McKay (Chicago School) ideas of the community as a prime factor in crime causation. Reiss and Tonry, as well as other theorists, look at lifestyle, social disorganization, and other elements of the community as affecting victimization rates and/or offending rates.[75] These theories tend to look solely at macro-level factors that are correlated with crime causation. For instance Sampson looks at marital rates.[76] He finds that divorce is associated with high rates of African-American and white adult offending and the presence of married couples had negative effects on African-American and white juvenile offending rates. Higher racial income inequality, poverty, and low occupational status were associated with significantly higher rates of robbery and homicide. He also found that a high risk of jail incarceration produced low robbery rates. Sampson reviews the effects of both the formal methods of control and more informal methods, such as the family.[77] Macro-level research, by its nature, however cannot identify more specifically how these factors affect crime. The statistics gathered, for instance, typically cannot isolate incidence or prevalence patterns, that is, whether it is a few people in the community committing much crime, or whether it is a lot of people committing some crime; therefore, any statistical associations identified would have to be further researched. Still, the idea that the community influences criminal choices is a fairly well established and accepted proposition in criminology.

Bursik and Grasmick also pay homage to Shaw and McKay's early work on Chicago:

> Overall, the studies that have been conducted suggest that the neighborhood does have a significant effect on the probability of criminal behavior that is independent of the effects that can be attributed to the personal attributes of the residents of the community.[78]

Frank Cullen identified social support as an "organizing concept" in his 1994 Presidential Address to the Academy of Criminal Justice Sciences. He first identified social support as that support (actual or perceived instrumental and/or expressive provisions) to the individual delivered through government social programs, communities, social networks, families, interpersonal relations, and agents of the criminal justice system. The theory states that the more social support exists for the individual, the less criminal choices will be made. He presents the following propositions.

1. America has higher rates of serious crime than other industrialized nations because it is a less supportive society.

2. The less social support there is in a community, the higher the crime rate will be.

3. The more support a family provides, the less likely it is that a person will engage in crime.

4. The more social support in a person's social network, the less crime will occur.

5. Social support lessens the effects of exposure to criminogenic strains.

6. Across the life cycle, social support increases the likelihood that offenders will turn away from a criminal pathway.

7. Anticipation of a lack of social support increases criminal involvement.

8. Giving social support lessens involvement in crime.

9. Crime is less likely when social support for conformity exceeds social support for crime.

10. Social support often is a precondition for effective social control.

11. A supportive correctional system lessens crime.

12. Social support leads to more effective policing.

13. Social support lessens criminal victimization.

14. Social support lessens the pains of criminal victimization.[79]

This theory encompasses not only criminology, but also law enforcement, victimology, and corrections. It is theoretically consistent with a number of trends occurring today in criminal justice such as community policing and restorative justice. No direct application of social support theory has been conducted, however, to the sex differential in crime rates.

CONCLUSION

We have reviewed most of the current criminology theories today; none of them specifically and directly addresses the sex differential; therefore, it is not surprising that none explain the sex differential very well. None, in fact, give more than a passing reference to sex or gender in their explanation for criminal causation. It seems that the group of researchers who explore female criminality continue to operate out of sight and out of mind in a territory foreign to the sovereign entity of criminology. Male researchers seem almost to not know what to do with women, so they ignore them. Although their language is a little more politically correct than Cohen's, it is clear that theorists today have just as little regard for the problem of female criminality as did Cohen and others in his time period.

Life-course/development theories routinely employ male-only samples and, thus, can hardly be said to be general explanations of criminal development. The authors of the general theory of crime stated that it was "beyond the scope" of their work to explain the sex differential, although they still proposed to present a theory of crime that explained all crime (presumably for everyone). Rational choice theory does not even address the sex differential, although presumably it would apply in such a way that women would have more to lose, and therefore rationally choose not to commit crime that a man might commit. Social support/social disorganization theories are macro-level theories that help to understand general levels of crime in a neighborhood or society, but do not explain individual motivation to commit crime, therefore, again, do not address the sex differential. If the theorists above do mention the sex/gender differential, they propose that socialization and supervision differences probably account for different crime rates. It is not clear why the differential continues to exist despite the massive social changes that have occurred in this society over the last 30 years, or indeed, why the sex differential has continued to exist in criminal statistics for as long as crime records have been kept. In order to develop a truly "general" theory of crime, it is essential to come to terms with the sex differential. In the next chapter, biological theories are considered—because sex is a biological fact, it is logical to look at biological theories to help us understand how sex may affect crime choices.

NOTES

[1]   The model for such studies can be found in medicine. In medicine, longitudinal studies have helped to identify the correlates of heart disease and tracked the benefits of exercise; while in criminology, longitudinal studies help to identify correlates of delinquency and track the effects of childhood abuse or neglect, low IQ, and a number of other independent variables.

[2]   The debate seems to be somewhat irrelevant since both types of research have something unique to offer, and there is no need to select one as the exclusive approach to studying crime.

[3]   Farrington (1996, 72) describes the criminal career approach as one that is interested in "the development of human behavior." It is proposed that childhood behavior patterns are associated with adult behavior patterns. This research is interested in *incidence* not necessarily *prevalence* of crime; with incidence referring to the frequency of individual criminal acts or antisocial conduct by an individual and prevalence referring to the number of criminal acts by everyone. Arguably, cross-sectional research may provide prevalence figures, but it could never identify the incidence of criminal behavior for each individual over a life span or portion of a life span—only longitudinal research can do that.

[4]   1986, 2.

5   Tonry, Ohlin, and Farrington (1991, 11).

6   Tonry, Ohlin, and Farrington (1991, 23).

7   Tonry, Ohlin, and Farrington (1991, 142).

8   Tonry, Ohlin, and Farrington (1991, 142).

9   Nagin, Farrington, and Moffitt (1995).

10   1996, 69.

11   1996, 69.

12   1996, 76.

13   1996, 81.

14   For instance, in the Harvard longitudinal study, prenatal cohorts included both boys and girls, but other cohorts contained only boys because:

> The major focus on males follows from a concern with having a sufficient number of predatory and violent offenders in the study population and our belief that 500 males in each age group would be the minimum required.
>
> . . . In our research plan, females hold prominent roles in the birth cohort, which will be followed into childhood and possibly longer, and in a sibling cohort, which will straddle adolescence and the transitions to parenting and other adult family roles. We are at present undecided whether more or less attention than is now contemplated should be devoted to female subjects and to gender differences in development (1991, 11, 14).

Blumstein, Cohen, Roth, and Visher (1986) also present their findings from a longitudinal study and are cited as supporting the "career criminals approach" since their research identifed a segment of the cohort that was disproportionately responsible for crime. Again, however, in this two-volume set, there are no entries for sex, gender, or females in either index. Evidently female career criminals are not worthy of study.

15   Farrington (1996, 104).

16   The choice may be linked to age and social status. For instance, those with other opportunities may satisfy excitement by different means than grafitti or other delinquencies.

17   Farrington (1996, 104).

18   Rowe and Farrington (1997) found that criminal convictions of parents were highly correlated with criminal convictions of the child(ren). There was also a correlation between siblings (when one sibling had a conviction, it was likely that the other would too), however this correlation was stronger for same-sex siblings than opposite sex siblings. They concluded that the effect of parental convictions was direct, that is, it could not be explained by other dysfunctional variables of the family environment, however the methodology employed did not allow a determination of whether the transmission could be considered genetic or through socialization.

19   Wolfgang, Thornberry, and Figlio (1987). This birth cohort study was published originally as "Delinquency in a Birth Cohort" in 1972 when the cohort were in their twenties.

20   Moffitt (1993) and Bartusch et al. (1997).

21   Sampson and Laub (1993, 7).

22 See Gottfredson and Hirschi (1990). This theory will be explained shortly.

23 1993, 12.

24 1993, 17.

25 1993, 244.

26 Gottfredson and Hirschi (1990, xiv).

27 1990, 25.

28 1990, 24.

29 1990, 43.

30 In fact, they argue that those who support "career criminal" research have ulterior motives: "Other reasons for survival of such ideas may be found in the interest of politicians and members of the law enforcement community who see policy potential in criminal careers or 'career criminals'" (1990, 91).

31 1990, 58. Cites omitted. The authors set up "straw dog" arguments (exaggerated positions said to represent the opponent's point of view that are easily destroyed), such as the following phrase that purports to summarize the biological perspective: "Human behavior, like any animal trait, must therefore be governed by the laws of nature rather than by free will and choice" (1990, 57). Obviously biosocial or biological theorists today no more reject free will than do sociological theorists. Each proposes that the determining factor (biological factors or sociological factors) predispose one to criminal choices. Actually, most biological theorists recognize that biological factors interact with sociological factors to create the predisposition to delinquency; the same cannot, however, be said about sociological theorists since most reject any influence of biological factors absolutely and dispute their influence as do Gottfredson and Hirschi. The authors criticize adoption studies on methodological points, but ignore the published literature on twin studies, testosterone studies, brain lateralization, and all other forms of biological positivism.

32 1990, 90.

33 1990, 191.

34 Reed and Yeager (1996) critique the general theory of crime especially as it relates to organizational offending. They argue that Gottfredson and Hirschi propose that their theory can explain all crime, including white-collar crime, but their examples were white-collar crimes that most resembled street crime (i.e., embezzling). They disagree with Gottfredson and Hirschi's assumption that white-collar crime is relatively rare because the business world screens out people who are impulsive and lacking in self-control. On the contrary, they argue that there are widespread illegal and unethical business practices that are standard in the business world. This flies in the face of the general theory of crime's proposition that there are only a few white-collar criminals who are undersocialized and lacking in self-control. They discuss the complex nature of structural supports for such activity and the importance of motivation. Explaining how some managers use protection of the company as the rationale for lawbreaking, they discuss how offenders distance themselves from the immorality of the actions. The discussion persuasively argues against the application of the general theory of crime to organizational offending.

35 1990, 208. Their cites to gang research, however, date back to the 1960s and they do not consider more recent findings.

36 1990, 97.

[37]   Sampson (1987).

[38]   1990, 103.

[39]   Hirschi (1994, 53-58).

[40]   1994, 64.

[41]   1994, 66. What is being argued, evidently, is that people with self-control would use birth control—or perhaps not have sex in the first place. One assumes he includes the father's lack of self-control as well as the mother's.

[42]   Strangely, he does not point out that this fact is not necessarily inconsistent with a correlation between poor, single-parent households and delinquency. There has been an increase of single-parent households across all income levels—it is not farfetched to hypothesize that it is only in poor, single-parent households that one would find a correlation because of the lack of supervision, and parenting that he described.

[43]   1990, 109.

[44]   They argue that because measurements of traits include behaviors that could be defined as criminal so, in effect, the research is measuring the same thing when it proposes that a correlation exists. For instance, such personality constructs as aggression would measure certain acts that would also be defined as delinquent or criminal; antisocial personalty disorder utilizes a variety of behaviors that would be also be defined as delinquent and criminal, and so on. Arguably, one could say the same about their own research; they propose that low self-control is correlated with delinquency and then measure it by a variety of acts, many of which can be defined as delinquent. They defend their approach by arguing that other acts of low self-control are distinct from delinquency/criminality, yet one notices that such acts are at least delinquent, i.e., drinking and smoking.

[45]   1990, 139. The authors do not seem fully convinced that girlfriends are not simply leeches, but more to the point, their rejection of the notion that attachments and jobs can act as informal controls on the individual's behavior, is less empirically supportable than the reverse. The possibility that only individuals with self-control get married is not supported by any findings.

[46]   1990, 149.

[47]   1990, 149.

[48]   1994, 1; they are responding especially to Akers (1991).

[49]   Gluecks (1934).

[50]   Cohen and Felson (1979).

[51]   Hirschi and Gottfredson (1983).

[52]   See Gottfredson and Hirschi (1986 and 1987) and Blumstein, Cohen, and Farrington (1988a, 1988b).

[53]   1994, 6-10.

[54]   Gibbs and Giever (1995).

[55]   Zager (1994).

[56]   Zager's findings are interesting, but they can be subject to criticism. First, the relevance of 30-year-old data is somewhat questionable, especially when one is studying something like gender, because gender roles have changed a great deal in the last several decades.

Second, the operationalization of self-control is somewhat problematic—the activities used are pure delinquency measures (recall the tautology argument raised above), and the attitudinal measures (such as concern for the victim or honesty) arguably are constructs other than self-control. Finally, it is not clear why sex is considered an opportunity measure because it explains more of the variance for crimes with a high sex ratio. The problem with the general theory of crime and the construct of self control as the only explanation for crime is that the theory does not consider the meaning of acts. Self-control might operate differently with men and women and result in different rates of offending based on meaning of actions. Girls and boys might commit the same activities, but do so for different reasons.

[57] 1996, 222.

[58] Evans et al. (1997). This study illustrates, unintentionally perhaps, some of the problems involved when attempting to operationalize a construct such as self-control. The authors use an item indicating "nights out" as a measure of low self-control. They argue that this is consistent with the proposition that those with low self-control do not like disciplined schedules, work or school, and so on. Arguably, however, one can enjoy "nights out" and still be highly disciplined. Nights out, in fact, is probably highly correlated with certain age groups (late teens and early twenties) and thus, will almost surely be positively correlated with delinquency since age is also strongly correlated. Does this mean, however, that these individuals have low self-control or a greater desire for excitement? Are those substantially similar constructs? Probably not, yet they may be statistically related. The study loses some representativeness because it restricted the sample to whites.

[59] 1994.

[60] 1994, 121.

[61] 1994, 129.

[62] This author, for instance, would like to think she has great self-control for study, work, household maintenance, and other areas of life, but admits she has little to none for maintaining an exercise program or avoiding chocolate chip cookies. Alternatively, there are a lot of impressive body builders in prison—these men will force themselves to go out to the yard and "pump iron" for hours a day in extreme heat or cold, yet they are in prison for committing crimes. To say that they have more self-control than those fellow prisoners who are in the corner using drugs, but less than us who do not commit crime, is a weak response to this argument.

[63] See, for instance, Cohen and Villa (1996) and Loeber and LeBlanc (1990).

[64] Cohen and Villa (1996, 133).

[65] 1996, 146.

[66] In fact, in Cohen and Villa's explanation of gender, it is difficult to figure out what exactly they are saying:

> Like age, gender differences in crime also are invariant over both place and time, with all sources of data agreeing that males are everywhere more likely than females to engage in crime (even when opportunity and supervision are held constant). Research indicates that male and female differences in the use of force and fraud begin very early in life (even before differences in opportunity are possible) and persist throughout adulthood. Females are, in general, more closely supervised by parents than are males. Supervision and socialization are not synonymous concepts. Research indicates that they each may have independent effects on the propensity for

crime. Effective child-rearing techniques (such as those described above) may foster the same anti-criminal attitude and behavior in both males and females, even when they are supervised differently (1996, 146).

It is hard to know what to make of this statement. If the sex/gender differential is so invariant across time and place, why assume it is socialization or supervision? Why the assumption that socialization would foster similar behavior if girls and boys were supervised differently? Even if one agrees that socialization patterns may help to control criminal tendencies in boys, would not the supervision differences mentioned above, also be helpful?

[67]   Paternoster and Brame (1997).

[68]   One other discussion seeking to explicate the value of the two theories is offered by Vold, Bernard, and Snipes (1998). They refer to the criminal career school versus the general theory of crime as "The Great Debate." Again, the main point of contention is whether frequency of offending is an important issue relative to age, or as Gottfredson and Hirschi argue age affects everyone equally, so it is not necessary to do longitudinal research. In other words, one can believe that there is a stable criminal propensity throughout life, or one can believe that criminal career individuals exist (and different factors affect age of onset, duration, and frequency; thus, it is necessary to build separate models for different life stages to explain criminal behavior) (1998, 289). These authors view the developmental theories of LeBlanc, Thornberry, and Sampson and Laub as resolutions of the criminal career debate, since they argue different groups exist.

[69]   1986.

[70]   1996.

[71]   1979.

[72]   1979, 589.

[73]   Jensen and Brownfield (1986) apply the routine activities approach to victimization using a high school sample. They conclude that one of the drawbacks of most analyses using the routine activities approach is neglecting the fact that one of the strongest "activities" associated with victimization is delinquency. They examine this relationship among other factors associated with victimization. One finding they present is that delinquent activity is more explanatory than sex/gender to explain the lower rate of victimization for women. The types of victimization that could be largely explained by activities were interpersonal violence without weapons. With other types of victimization, however, the sex/gender differential remained even after controlling for activities, although using multiple regression, they were able to explain a good portion of the variance by activities. They speculate that the victimization of interpersonal violence without weapons may tap into some type of activity, such as date rape, that is present more often than other types of victimization for women.

[74]   1996.

[75]   Reiss and Tonry (1986).

[76]   Sampson (1986), also see Byrne and Sampson (1986).

[77]   1986.

[78]   1993, 29.

[79]   1994, 532-559.

Biological and Biosocial Explanations of Crime

8

Objectives

- Understand the differences among biological theories of crime, specifically between biological and biosocial theories.

- Become familiar with the criticism directed to such theories and the empirical support for them.

Criminology textbooks, when discussing biological theories, typically start with Lombroso's theory,[1] briefly discuss other early biological theories such as the body-type theory (that mesomorphs are more likely to be criminal), XYY theory (that those with an extra Y chromosome are more likely to be violent and criminal), and testosterone (that those with greater levels of testosterone are more likely to be aggressive). The textbook usually explains that biological theorists are looking for some inherited "criminality." Then twin studies and adoption studies are reviewed, and finally, most criminology textbook authors conclude that there is only weak and ambiguous evidence that supports a biological link with crime, and that sociological explanations (that fill the other 80-90% of the book) are better able to explain criminal choices.

Criminologists obviously recognize that three of the strongest, longest-standing, and most cross-cultural predictors of crime (age, sex, and race) are biological constructs. Of the three, only race shows strongly different patterns cross-culturally.[2] Furthermore, race, as a biological construct, is mediated by interracial mixing so that most people do not represent pure racial phenotypes. Contrary to the complications race presents, the other two strongest correlates are age and sex and they are, for the most part, categorical.[3] Why, then, is it even argued that biology is relevant to crime causation if it is clearly predictable that young males are the most crime prone group and elderly females are the least criminal, in all countries, in all cultures, for as long as records have been kept?

Part of the reason that biological approaches in criminology have been so completely rejected and ignored is that there are serious policy implications for such theories. It is argued that such theories lead to eugenics, or other methods of control that are repugnant to our democratic ideals.[4] Feminists disparage biological theories because, they argue, the theories hark back to the days when women were told their "natural" or "God-given" role was sole-ly that of "mother of the species," and, thus, women should stay in the home and not involve themselves in the economic or political world. Biological research has been, therefore, unfunded, and those researchers who attempt such studies often find themselves professionally attacked for doing so.[5] The fact that biological research could be misused is a serious argument that deserves attention; to carefully review the biological research that has been conducted and decide that it is unpersuasive is certainly an option; but to arbitrarily decide that such research should not even be done seems to be to ignore the "elephant in the living room."

This chapter is not a complete primer on biological theories in criminolo-gy. The different threads that are present in biological approaches are touched on, but the interest here is how this research can help us understand the sex differential in crime rates. The key point of this chapter is that the sex differ-ential exists—there are long-standing, cross-cultural, and consistent differences in men's and women's propensity to commit crime, especially violent or victim-harming crime. The question is why? Sociological approaches, as discussed in previous chapters, come to the conclusion that the sex/gender differential exists because of socialization and/or supervision differences that occur in the family and in larger society. In other words, men and women are the same in their criminal propensities, it is just the way they are treated that causes differ-ent behavior patterns. A biological approach proposes that socialization and supervision differences exist and are influential, but that there are also funda-mental differences between men and women beyond simply who gives birth; and that these differences interact with socialization to create the sex/gender differential. A biosocial approach would add that socialization differences do not develop arbitrarily, that there are anthropological and species-survival dri-ven reasons why human behavioral patterns form in the way they do.

Biological approaches of crime can be categorized as an organizational tool. The first division is to separate biological from biosocial approaches. As mentioned above, biological approaches look at biological differences that influence behavior (e.g., testosterone level or personality characteristics such as impulsivity); while biosocial approaches take a broader view and explain how these differences, and their related behavior patterns, may relate to sur-vival of the species. These two approaches form the two major divisions of the chapter. Biological approaches can be further broken into inherited trait theories (genetic) and organic postnatal theories. The first would look for traits, or other biological differences that appear to be inherited. Research studies of inheritance look at the level of "concordance" between biological parents and children, or siblings, or twins. The assumption is not that crimi-nality itself is inherited; rather, there is some biological trait (such as impul-sivity, aggression, intelligence, or some other yet to be identified trait) that creates a predisposition to criminality. Organic, postnatal theories identify some biological characteristics that seem to be highly correlated with criminality. For instance, a brain tumor that puts pressure on the violence center of the brain may result in irrational, uncontrolled violence or other brain dysfunctions may also cause aggressive behavior. Even extreme food allergies may have behavioral implications (irritability, "foggy" thinking). These effects are biological, but not necessarily inherited. A factor may be both inherited and have direct effects; for instance, testosterone is identified as influencing the level of aggressiveness in an individual and it may be that an individual's level of testosterone is inherited. Drug use is obviously not inherited, but recent research indicates that one's propensity to become addicted to drugs may be inherited, and then drugs in some cases, in turn, affect brain chemistry.

Andrews and Bonta review genetic theories of crime and point out that the methodological problem has always been separating out genetic effects from socialization effects.[6] One way to do this is twin studies—these studies identify and track twins (both monozygotic and dizygotic) and look to see concordance or discordance in such things as intelligence, delinquency, alcoholism, and other behavioral indices. Higher rates of concordance among monozygotic twins than dizygotic twins lend support to biological explanations of crimes because monozygotic twins share the exact same genetic make-up. Several studies have supported this, but they typically utilize small samples and there were methodological problems with earlier studies. Even more recent studies, however, continue to find differences, i.e., one study reported that monozygotic pairs showed 55 percent concordance compared with 13 percent of dizygotic pairs. An alternative argument offered against a genetic explanation is that identical twins are treated more alike than fraternal twins and that might account for the concordance; therefore, both monozygotic twins and dizygotic twins separated at birth are studied (although these studies usually have very small sample sizes). There seems to be mild support for a genetic link. Other studies look at the concordance between the criminality of children and their adoptive parents and biological parents.[7] Our concern is solely with sex differences and how they might explain differences in the propensity to commit crime, thus the controversy concerning the studies of inheritance are less relevant to us than those studies that identify sex differences and link these differences to delinquency/criminality.[8]

BIOLOGICAL DIFFERENCES

PMS/XYY

These two somewhat-related theories are typically used to debunk the idea that biology predisposes one to criminal behavior. The first identifies premenstrual syndrome (PMS) as causing women to become exceedingly violent and/or criminal. The second identifies an extra Y chromosome as causing those men who have it to be criminally violent. Both theories have suffered from weak methodology resulting in ambiguous and/or suspicious findings. A more general argument, however, is that neither—even if true—explains much crime.

Few women suffer from PMS—at least to the extent necessary to create extreme behavioral changes.[9] Walsh reviews studies that show that 62 percent of women's violent crime comes during four days before and four days into the menstrual cycle; more rigorous studies still show 44 percent of women's violent crime occurs during the menstrual cycle, which is statistically significantly higher than the 33 percent one would expect.[10] He suspects that PMS is probably only a trigger or disposition factor. Criticism of these studies include the fact that they are typically of incarcerated populations, that women have different lengths of menstrual cycles so that expectation of 33 percent would only be true for a cycle lasting approximately 24 days, and that the studies do not measure to what extent women experience PMS symptoms. Other reviews have also cited the difficulties present in studies that purport to measure the influence of PMS on women's criminality.[11]

Again, however, the strongest criticism of such theories is that the true syndrome of PMS affects very few people. Another "biological" explanation, the idea of "lactational insanity," also affects a very small number of women—those who suffer from extreme post-partum depression.[12] More importantly, such theories do not address the obvious fact of women's general *lack* of criminality. It is interesting to point out that both the PMS and the XYY theories are related to a surfeit of "maleness"—those women who suffer from PMS experience an extreme decrease of female sex hormones (progesterone and estradiol), but testosterone remains high during the time period in question, and XYY men have the extra male chromosome that assumedly does something to their biology, although exactly what is unclear.

Testosterone Studies

There has developed a fairly impressive body of knowledge regarding the correlation between testosterone and aggression, although such research has also been subject to heavy criticism. Although both men and women have testosterone in the body, men have about 10 to 15 times more testosterone than women. Therefore, the idea is that when we observe male aggression, we are observing the effects of testosterone. Basic problems with such research include accurate measurements of testosterone; a valid definition and operationalization of the construct of aggression; and understanding the interactive effect of testosterone production, aggressive behavior, and environmental cues.

Maccoby and Jacklin, in a comprehensive review and analysis of sex/gender differences, concluded that most differences observed between men and women could be attributed to socialization. However, they also concluded that the differential level of aggressiveness observed among men was a sex difference rather than a gender difference (although, of course, aggressive impulses can be moderated by culture). They supported their conclusion by the following observations:

- Males are more aggressive than females in all human societies for which evidence is available.

- The sex differences are found too early in life, at a time when there is no evidence that differential socialization pressures have been brought to bear by adults to "shape" aggression differentially in the two sexes . . .

- Similar sex differences are found in man and subhuman primates.

- Aggression is related to levels of sex hormones that can be changed by experimental administration of these hormones.[13]

Research in this area utilizes non-human subjects such as other primates, and usually finds a correlation between high levels of testosterone and high levels of aggressive behavior. Testosterone production, however, is variable, and some measurements are less accurate than others. Further, testosterone production seems to be moderated by environmental factors, and obviously the translation of aggressiveness to behavior is subject to social control, meanings ascribed to behavior, and learning, which may account for the ambiguous findings.

Tedeschi and Felson refer to testosterone as having a "permissive effect" on aggression: ". . . the presence of testosterone permits aggressive behavior to occur, whereas its absence disallows such behavior. This permissiveness effect is importantly modified by the previous learning experience of the organism."[14]

Studies indicate some link between testosterone and aggression, although such a relationship seems to be socially mediated.[15] For instance, alpha monkeys (group leaders) will experience a rise in testosterone but lower status male monkeys will decrease their testosterone production. This indicates there is an interaction between testosterone secretion and environmental cues. It is not clear, however, whether this finding has any application to human testosterone production.

Thus, the findings regarding testosterone levels and aggression are mixed. Several studies reviewed show no relationship between testosterone and aggression; however, it was unclear in these studies how aggression was defined, and samples were college students, not violent criminals. Those studies that used violent criminals were more likely to find elevated levels of testosterone.[16] Walsh concludes that there must be environmental influences on testosterone production, therefore, the connection between testosterone and aggression is more complicated than a simple direct association.[17] Only one study of 18 found a strong positive relationship between testosterone and aggressive behavior; five found a weak positive relationship, six showed a moderate positive relationship, and six found no relationship.[18] Walsh explains that most studies that found correlations focused on behavior, those that found no relationship utilized psychological tests to measure aggression. He mentions that in a European study of 2,055 offenders, it was found that only 7.4 percent castrated rapists recidivated with any sex crime in a 25-year follow-up, while 40 percent of non-castrated rapists recidivated in the same time period (1995: 86), indicating that testosterone may at least have some connection to violent sex crimes.[19]

The studies above all explore testosterone levels among men. A more obvious comparison, of course, is the level of testosterone present in men as compared to women. Most researchers do not argue the point that aggressive impulses and testosterone levels are lower in women. Although there are some who argue that women are as aggressive as men and simply display their aggression differently or suppress it because of socialization and social control; those who hold this view must explain the large body of research that finds otherwise.

Brain Differences

There is increasing evidence that the brains of men and women are different—in size, the complexity of neural networks, and the development of neural pathways in the right and left hemispheres, as well as the neural pathways that connect them.[20] Studies of biological factors such as autonomic nervous system factors, brain wave patterns, cerebral dysfunctions and cerebral hemisphere functions, endocrinology, neurochemistry, testosterone, and metabolic dysfunctions tend to support the idea that men and women are biologically different in ways that far exceed simple reproductive capacities.

Brain Lateralization, MAO, and Other Brain Chemistry Research

There is some evidence to indicate that men's and women's brains develop differently; specifically, women's brains are likely to have more neural pathways in the left hemisphere while men's right hemisphere is more developed. Women also show more connections between the two hemispheres. Brain lateralization means that brain functions are more likely to occur in one hemisphere: "Individuals who are more lateralized tend to show greater hemispheric specialization in processing information relative to less lateralized individuals."[21] Certain behaviors are evidence of lateralization, such as left handedness (right hemisphere lateralization). Males are more likely to be left-handed, and also have higher rates of learning disorders. Research indicates that left-handers are more likely to be "less analytic, more emotional [and exhibit] more impulsive response modes."[22]

Walsh presents evidence to indicate that women are less specialized (or "lateralized") than men: "The dominant (usually left) hemisphere organization of the female brain is superior to that of the male, while the usually non-dominant right hemisphere organization of the male brain is superior to that of the female. The female brain is less specialized or 'lateralized' than the male brain . . ."[23] One piece of evidence of this is that "the cortical rind of the right hemisphere is thicker in males, and that the cortical rind of the left hemisphere is thicker in females."[24] The right hemisphere, according to Walsh, is associated with negative emotions, anger, and aggression, while the left is associated with positive emotions, altruism, and feelings: "brain lateralized male[s] tend to be more 'self-oriented,' while the more integrated female brain tends to be more 'other' and 'us oriented.'"[25]

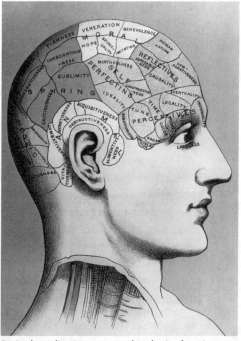

Brain lateralization means that brain functions are more likely to occur in one hemisphere. There is some evidence to indicate that the left hemisphere of the brain is more developed in women, and the right hemisphere is more developed in men. *Illustration credit: CORBIS-BETTMANN.*

These findings are not necessarily clear, however, nor are they consistent.[26] Further, the lateralization information seems to fly in the face of other perceived differences between men and women, e.g., that men are more "left brain" because they are analytical and spatially oriented, and women are "right brain" thinkers because they are more emotional and intuitive.

Low levels of monoamine oxidase (MAO), a chemical found in the brain, is linked to psychopathy, alcoholism, sensation seeking, impulsivity, extraversion, schizophrenia, and criminal behavior.[27] Men, on average, have about 20 percent less MAO than women, and this difference exists at all ages.[28] Studies report findings showing that MAO levels are linked to delinquency:

> . . . when some Swedish physicians measured the amount of MAO in the blood of over one thousand eighteen-year-old boys, those with low levels of MAO were more impulsive and more interested in seeking out excitement than were high-MAO boys. The low-MAO boys who also had lower than average intelligence were the most at risk; they were more likely than any other group to abuse alcohol and drugs and to reveal various psychological problems.[29]

Associations are consistently found between low MAO activity and various correlates of criminal behavior, such as impulsiveness, childhood hyperactivity, learning disabilities, sensation seeking, substance abuse, and extraversion. Age, sex, and race are all evidently corrrelated with MAO activity.[30] Testosterone evidently depresses MAO levels. In fact, testosterone levels are at their highest and MAO levels at their lowest during the second decade of life (10-20), roughly corresponding with the crime-prone age years. Walsh explains that there is a two- to three-fold increase of MAO and a 10-fold decrease of testosterone between ages 30 and 80. Women have only about five percent of the testosterone that men have and 15 to 20 percent more MAO. Walsh also states that African-American men have five-10 percent more testosterone and about 10-15 percent less MAO than white males.[31] The exact function of MAO and why or how it might be related to delinquency as well as the other dysfunctional patterns mentioned above is more complicated, although it may have something to do with the reaction to stress:

> Among males, the experiencing of stressful events has the effect of increasing norepinephrine (the "action hormone") secretion and increasing right hemisphere (the "action hemisphere") brain activity. The opposite effect is usually seen in females for whom stressful events tend to lead to a decrease in norepinephrine secretion and a decrease in right hemisphere activity. For females, stressful events tend to be experienced in the left hemisphere, leaving them more prone to depression as they verbally mull over the event. Low MAO among males would have the effect of allowing for the prolonged stress, and hence an increased probability of violence.[32]

However, the measurement of MAO levels is somewhat problematic; for instance, there may be too strong an assumption that the level of MAO and serotonin in the brain is related to their levels in the bloodstream where they are measured.

ADD and Hyperactivity

There is consistent evidence that hyperactivity and Attention Deficit Disorder (ADD) are correlated with delinquency. It has been reported that those diagnosed with hyperactivity as children were 25 times more likely to exhibit later delinquency.[33] ADD and hyperactivity tend to be more common for boys than girls; it has been reported that hyperactivity is four to six times more common in males.[34] Denno also reports that delinquency is linked to ADD, hyperactivity, overactivity, perceptual-motor impairments, impulsivity, emotional lability, attention deficits, minor disturbances of speech, intellectual defects (learning disabilities), clumsiness, neurodevelopmental lag, psychogenic factors, minor physical anomalies; and that these features may be the result of genetic transmission, poor living environment, prenatal or birth trauma, or a combination of the above.[35] Evidence indicates that many children outgrow predisposing factors, but those who do not are more likely to be delinquent.[36]

Denno reports that men have experienced a higher incidence of prenatal and perinatal mortality and complications, reading and learning disorders, and mental retardation, as well as left hemisphere deficits.[37] In general, men are more prone to learning dysfunctions due to brain differences.

> Unfortunately when men are born they are on average much less amenable to socialization than women. Compared to their sisters, men are born neurologically less advanced: they are four to six weeks less well developed and thus, correspondingly, more in need of care. They are more likely to be hyperactive, autistic, color-blind, left-handed, and prone to learning disorders.[38]

Intelligence Studies

There are numerous, hotly debated, issues involved in the research concerning intelligence. The first is whether intelligence can even be defined and/or measured. What exactly is intelligence? Most commonly agreed upon definitions divide intelligence into verbal/language abilities and spatial/mathematical abilities. The IQ test is widely accepted by educational and psychological researchers, but criticized heavily by sociological researchers who argue that it is racially and culturally biased. The next point of controversy, assuming one can agree upon some definition of intelligence, is whether intelligence is inherited. Again, while some researchers maintain the evidence is clear and convincing, others argue that the correlation in IQ scores between parents and children or between twins or between siblings is simply the product of family environment or other social factors (such as poverty) rather than a product of inheritance. Finally, there is the issue of the relationship between intelligence and delinquency/criminality. Most researchers accept that there is a correlation between intelligence scores and delinquency/criminality, but while some argue the relationship is purely spurious (that both are affected by some other factors, i.e., poverty, family dysfunction, school performance), others believe that the relationship exists even after controlling for all other factors.[39]

Eysenck and Gudjonsson review many studies on intelligence—they present findings that indicate that intelligence is correlated with personality, delinquency (even when controlling for SES or race), and race.[40] The correlation with race is obviously an extremely sensitive and problematic finding in this research. Note, however, that because intelligence may be moderated by environmental factors, there is no reason why intelligence cannot be generally subject to inheritance, but also be influenced by social factors that result in apparent other correlations, such as race.

Andrews and Bonta also review the findings on intelligence and delinquency and conclude that most studies find there is a correlation between delinquency and intelligence, and this relationship exists independent of class or race.[41] Raine finds that it is in the verbal/language area that delinquents have especially low scores.[42]

Denno, after reviewing studies on intelligence, suggests that the relationship may be one where intelligence affects school performance, which in turn affects delinquency.[43] One interesting finding she presents has to do with the connection between intelligence and moral development.[44] First, it is noted that delinquents tend to have lower verbal/language scores than nondelinquents.[45] Then, it is noted that verbal/language development is related to cognitive stages of moral development.[46] Thus, there may be some relationship between not simply intelligence *per se* but, rather, the particular aspect of intelligence that has to do with cognitive levels of understanding abstract principles such as altruism and utilitarianism.

It appears that female delinquents, just like male delinquents, exhibit lower scores on intelligence tests. In fact, it was found that the correlation between delinquency and lower scores was even stronger for women than it was for men:

> Great disparities were found in percentile differences at adolescence for violent and nonindex female offenders on nearly all achievement tests, including mathematics . . . highly significant differences appeared for tests of a number of skills, including language, reading, and mathematics . . . percentile differences between violent female offenders and non-offenders were considerably greater than those for males, and they incorporated more tests, such as mathematics. Thus, female offenders appear to deviate more on tests of intellectual abilities.[47]

Denno's research did not support a direct link between intelligence and delinquency. Rather, she argued that the mediating variable was school performance. Also, intelligence seemed to be related to family and environmental variables.

> Concerning repeat offense behavior among females, . . . significant differences exist mostly for family-related variables. Significantly more female repeat offenders come from families where the father is absent, where there is a foster or adoptive parent or institution, and where there is marital instability, lower income, and lower education of the household head.[48]

> In the present study, intelligence scores demonstrated no direct effect on delinquency for either sex; however, intelligence had indirect effects on delinquency through school achievement . . . Moreover, violent and chronic delinquents evidenced generally lower scores on some tests of intellectual ability at early ages . . .[49]

Personality Trait Differences

Personality traits have long been associated with delinquency/criminality. Such traits as impulsiveness, aggressiveness, extroversion, and other traits have played a role in very early studies as well as more recent ones. For instance, Gottfredson and Hirschi's "General Theory" isolates a personality trait—low self-control—as the causal element in all criminal choice. Their only dispute with biological theorists (who would use the trait of impulsiveness rather than low self-control) evidently is that while the general theory of crime explains that the trait occurs through ineffective parenting practices, biological theorists would argue that the trait is inherited although it may be moderated by good parenting or exacerbated by bad parenting.

There is a great deal of evidence to indicate that delinquents are more likely than non-delinquents to have certain personality traits. These traits include: extraversion,[50] impulsivity, aggressiveness, and sensation-seeking, among others.[51] A cross-national study (using samples from New Zealand and the U.S.) attempted to respond to all previous criticisms of research exploring the association between personality traits and crime. Study findings indicated that delinquents scored significantly higher on a personality trait called "Negative Emotionality" and one titled "Weak Constraint." In other words, when the personality of the individual is predisposed to experience aversive emotional states, and have low impulse control, they are more likely to be delinquent.[52]

Longitudinal studies that support life course/development theories also identify a constellation of personality traits as highly correlated with delinquency/criminality. Farrington and West found that offenders and non-offending siblings or peers might share such characteristics as low family income, large family size, likelihood of convicted parent, low nonverbal IQ scores, and poor parental practices, but offenders were more likely to be active and social while non-offenders with the above characteristics were likely to be loners, unambitious, in conflict with families, in debt, and possess low social status.[53] Thus, it is a persuasive argument that social/environmental factors combined with internal personality constructs better explain delinquent choices than either one or the other.

Another issue, of course, is whether these personality traits are biological or developmental; further are personality traits differentiated by sex? Caspi et al. discuss the potential for biological causation in the personality traits linked to delinquency. They propose that research findings that indicate lower serotonin levels in the brain of violent criminals may provide an explanation since low levels of serotonin might account for both negative emotionality and impulsivity.[54] Raine reviews studies that show reduced serotonin and norepinephrine levels in antisocial individuals and argues that this fact can be combined with theories of underactive behaviorial inhibition systems in antisocials (meaning that their bodies do not learn from punishment).[55] Although Raine admits that there are problems with measurement (e.g., whether to take samples from blood or urine; and how to measure antisocia-bility), he concludes that there is evidence that supports the idea that antiso-cials have poor conditionability, and some studies show that criminals from higher socio-economic status classes have even lower conditionability than those from lower classes (which would support interaction effect of social class on delinquency). He cites with approval Eysenck's idea of condition-ability (that extraverts have poor conditionability and this leads to delin-quency because they do not develop a conscience).[56] He argues that a "lower resting heart rate has been consistently found to characterize non-institution-alized, young antisocial groups and probably represents the best replicated biological correlate of antisocial behavior, probably reflecting fearlessness and underarousal."[57]

There is also some evidence to indicate sex differences in personality traits. Men are predisposed to have personality traits of impulsivity and sensa-tion seeking, probably because of brain chemistry. Several authors point out that men have lower conditionability, in essence their brains do not absorb messages as quickly as do women's brains. Low conditionability, in general, leads to sensation seeking since it takes more stimulation to satisfy. After reviewing a wide range of studies concerning sex differences in the brain,

> What is suggested by these facts is that criminal and antisocial behaviors, forming the opposite end to altruism on a continuous scale ranging from one extreme to the other, are in part the prod-uct of genetic features of the organism related to the masculiniza-tion of the brain and the degree to which androgens are present in the individual. These androgens influence behavior through their effect on the arousal system, primarily, but also in other ways, for example, through producing a right hemispheric shift, masculine physique, and other characteristics discussed. Low arousal, thus related to androgen secretion, affects conditioning, brain sensitivi-ty, and other variables that are expressed in human conduct, in par-ticular the intensity of temptation, the absence of a "conscience," a failure to be deterred by painful punishments, and so on.[58]

Other research makes the connection between these findings and the fact that men, more than women, are likely to display these characteristics. Walsh looks at the research concerning "cytogenetic anomalies" (those individuals who have sex organs of the other sex or in other ways are statistically abnor-mal in their sexual biology).[59] He presents sex as a continuum instead of a dichotomous variable; the continuum is based on neurohormonal criteria from extreme "femaleness" to extreme "maleness." There is obviously a great deal of male/female overlap in brain chemistry; and even though certain brain differences between men and women have been isolated, there is obviously a great deal of variability within a sex as well. External genitalia is the best obvious indicator of the masculinization or feminization of the brain; and there are small numbers of individuals who exhibit intersex anomalies. Turn-er's Syndrome females are excessively "female" since they lack a second sex hormone; they exhibit deficits in right hemisphere brain functioning and suffer "space-form blindness" due to extremely poor visual/spatial skills. Their mean verbal IQ is significantly greater than their mean performance IQ; in essence their brain has not been "masculinized" at all, not even to the extent of statistically normal women. XYY males, on the other hand, are excessively masculine because of the extra Y chromosome; research indicates that they display hypermasculinity, including aggression and low verbal IQ. Walsh also discusses other groups falling on other locations of the continuum. In general, findings indicate that all groups display personality characteristics consistent to their placement on the continuum from hyperfeminine to hypermasculine; thus sex (and the neurohormonal reality of sex) affects personality traits in fundamental ways.[60]

Eysenck and Gudjonsson argue that three elements of personality—emotional stability (N), emotional independence (P) and introversion-extraversion (E)—are correlated with the propensity to make criminal choices.[61] The individuals who possess high P scores are described as aggressive, cold, egocentric, impersonal, impulsive, antisocial, unempathetic, creative, and tough-minded. Those who have high E scores are sociable, lively, active, assertive, sensation-seeking, carefree, dominant, and adventuresome. Those with high N scores are anxious, depressed, high guilt feelings, low self-esteem, tense, irrational, shy, moody, and emotional.

The most well-known element of this theory posits that biologically determined low degrees of arousal and arousability in extraverts (and possibly in persons high on the psychoticism scale) lead to behaviors (risk-taking and sensation-seeking) that increase the cortical level of arousal to a more acceptable level. Behaviors of this type are not *necessarily* antisocial (they could be sport-related activities or daredevil stunts), but they *might* be antisocial because these behaviors are exciting and produce the level of cortical arousal that extraverts require (aggressive interactions, driving fast, shoplifting).[62] Further, according to this theory, extraverts do not learn as easily as introverts because they need higher stimulation. Therefore, they may not absorb societal lessons that lead to law-abiding behavior: "As introverts form conditioned responses . . . more readily than extraverts, they are more easily socialized through Pavlovian conditioning and hence are less likely to indulge in antisocial activities."[63]

Wood et al. present a model that incorporates physiological processes and learning theory.[64] They first review the studies that identify personality traits common among delinquents/criminals, such as impulsivity, hyperactivity, sensation-seeking, risk-taking, and low self-control. They then link these personality traits to neurophysiological mechanisms, specifically that risky activities may release more endorphins in certain individuals than others because of brain chemistry. The differential experience of endorphins means such behaviors become more internally rewarded for some than others, with the corollary prediction that they will continue to engage in such behavior.[65]

Sex differences exist in cortical arousal levels, and men, in general, are more likely to be extraverts (have low cortical arousal).[66] Behaviors that are evidently androgen-influenced and can be influenced by artificially introducing androgens into the system include: assertive erotic sexual behavior, status-related aggressive behavior, spatial reasoning, spacing behavior (including territoriality), pain tolerance, retarded acquisition of aversive conditioning, diminished fearful emotional responses to threats, task control-oriented tenacity, transient bonding tendencies, peripherealization, sensation-seeking, and predatory behavior.[67]

Even mainstream criminologists are beginning to accept the importance of personality traits and recognize that these may have a genetic influence.

> Among the individual charactertistics that are associated with the use of physical coercion and have a heritability component are intelligence, extraversion-introversion, impulsiveness, emotionality, conditionability, fearfulness, activity level, arousal level, tolerance of pain, size, strength, and sexual drive. Some of these characteristics may help explain gender and age differences in violence.[68]

And theorists that support the idea of biological predisposition argue that personality differences do not inevitably lead to delinquency, no more than social factors inevitably lead to delinquency: ". . .to find that certain traits of personality—such as impulsivity, anxiety, sociability, or whatever—are correlated with antisocial behavior is not to say that they *inevitably* produce such behavior."[69]

Integrated Theories

The findings above all point to the idea that sex differences have some link to criminal choices. The few studies that will be reviewed in this section are noteworthy because of the comprehensive nature of their approach—both in terms of looking at a broad range of biological factors, as well as drawing in social and environmental factors. Theorists integrate "predisposing factors" that are biological, with the environment one happens to be born into in an explanation of the likelihood of criminal offending. Longitudinal studies, by their nature, are more likely to identify biological factors that are correlated to crime; although not all those who conduct longitudinal research agree that biological factors are causal in criminal choices.

Denno incorporates both biological and sociological factors to form an integrated explanation of criminality and delinquency.[70] Denno looks at predisposing factors (that increase the likelihood of criminality), facilitating variables (that in combination with predisposing, increase the likelihood of delinquency), and inhibiting variables (that counteract predisposing factors and decrease the probability of delinquency).

Table 8.1
Denno's Developmental Model

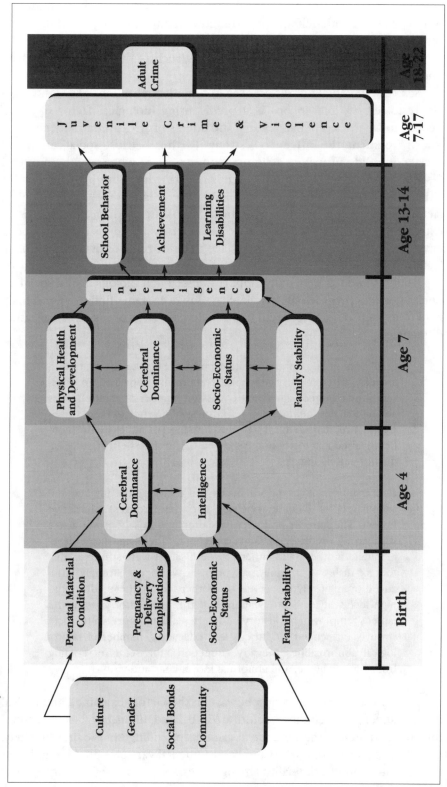

From Denno, 1990, p. 26.

The longitudinal data indicated that both social and biological factors were correlated with delinquency. Denno's findings were reported in earlier sections regarding brain lateralization, ADD, and intelligence factors. She also found evidence of other predisposing factors, such as low birth weight,[71] lead poisoning,[72] and head injuries.[73]

Sex (as the vehicle of differences in brain lateralization, ADD, MAO levels, testosterone, and so on) is a predisposing biological factor of delinquency in Denno's schema.[74] While the effects of sex can be moderated by the environment, the influence is strong. Further, because socialization and social control do influence delinquency/criminality; women who do offend (especially those who commit violent offenses), are more likely to exhibit either significantly higher correlations between delinquency and biological factors such as low intelligence (because biological factors have to be extreme to overcome socialization), or extreme dysfunctions in family/social environments (because they would have to be extreme to overcome biological predispositions).[75]

Denno's findings generally support the idea that biological and socialization factors suppress female criminality. However, some findings are frankly hard to explain and do not seem to offer clear patterns of sex or socialization differences.

> Predictors of adult and juvenile crime were similar for males and females, although clear gender differences also appeared. Four factors showed direct significant effects on number of adult offenses among females: number and seriousness of juvenile offenses, disciplinary problems at age 13-14, and low level of father's education. Being raised in a foster home showed the strongest effect on delinquency among females.[76]

> Concerning adult crime for males and females, the number and seriousness of juvenile offenses had the strongest predictive impact. The number of disciplinary problems in school was also a very strong predictor for females, whereas low language achievement and mother's and father's low education were strong predictors for males. . . . Adult male offenses were most strongly influenced by relatively low levels of mother's and father's education, high levels of lead intoxication, and the number of gaps in the father's employment history. Adult female offenses were most strongly influenced by father's low education, number of neurological abnormalities (negative direction), the status of coming from a foster home, and abnormal movements and vision.[77]

Denno's study, while comprehensive in the factors examined and logical in the manner in which these factors are integrated, ultimately fails to account for a large amount of the variance in criminal offending: "In the present study, complete models of biological and environmental variables predicted 25 percent of future adult criminality among males and 19 percent of future adult criminality among females. Although these percentages are statistically significant, 75 to 81 percent of behavior is left unexplained."[78]

Widom also presents an integrated theory of criminal behavior and psychopathology.[79] Physiological and genetic predispositions (including sex) interact with socialization experiences to produce personality, which then affects situational factors that lead to behavior. Behavior, in turn, leads to society's response that then affects individual attitudes, norms, and expectations about behavior. Many of those who conduct longitudinal research have identified prenatal or perinatal differences that distinguish children who eventually become delinquent. These researchers cautiously include biological factors into their developmental schemas as predisposing factors.[80]

Walsh might also be considered an integrated theorist because he considers parenting practices as well as inheritable traits in the development of delinquency/crime.[81] For instance, while he points out differences in brain lateralization between men and women, he also explains that parenting may affect the development of neural functioning.

> With regard to brain laterality and environmental experience, there is a fair amount of evidence that early experience (handling and stroking) positively influences hemispheric integration, at least in animals. Parental rejection, by definition, means less tactile stimulation, interaction, and communication between parents and child, leading to deficits in left hemisphere development that are reflected in the child's poor verbal abilities.[82]

Thus, he explains the finding that female delinquents tend to come from more dysfunctional homes than male delinquents because their sex predisposes them to hemispheric integration but their environment sabotages brain development by lack of nurturance.

Walsh argues that parenting practices are incredibly powerful influences in brain development and subsequent behavior.[83] Research on mother-child bonding and affectional deprivation indicate that these early life experiences affect life-long mental health, self-esteem, coping abilities, and violent behavior. Walsh argues that "love" is not just nice, it is absolutely necessary for normal development: "I wish to locate love in a fully corporeal way in the neuronal lattices of the brain as part of our emotional programming."[84] He discusses the fact that human infants have undeveloped brains.[85] The effect of the undeveloped brain is that the human is more "plastic" than other mammals; there is less "hardwiring" (meaning instinct driven behavior). Humans benefit because they gained the qualities of rationality and are flexible learners, but the negative effect of plasticity is that we are very vulnerable to environmental effects in the first two years of life while the brain develops.

The exact nature of learning "love" is somewhat . . . shall we say, technical.

> Interneuronal communication becomes habitual the more often the electrochemical synapses governing a particular response are activated, meaning that the "competition" is biased in favor of the

[neuron] populations that receive the greatest amount of stimulation during early development. The process of forming and maintaining new synapses is rather like the establishment of a trail in the
wilderness. The more often the trail is trodden, the more distinct it
becomes from its surroundings and the more functional it
becomes.[86]

Research indicates that talking to, holding, stroking, and cuddling babies not
only soothes them but actually aids their brain development. Contrarily, lack
of such stimuli retards brain development. Rhesus monkeys that were
deprived of "love" showed reductions in cortical branching, there was altered
electrophysiology in cerebellar and limbic regions, a reduction in norepinephrine concentrations, and they exhibited neurobiological and behavioral
supersensitivity when exposed to pharmacological agents or novel stimuli.
Walsh explains that stimulation is related to brain growth, branching of cortical connections, and myelin formation:

> It is a basic neurophysiological principle that the more frequently
> the nerve fibers of the brain are used, the more rapidly they
> become myelinated. The increased myelination results in greater
> ability to function in the environment, as determined by greater
> curiosity, problem-solving ability, dominance, and general liveliness
> among petted animals.[87]

Walsh cautions that there may be problems in applying these findings to
humans, but it does indicate that early deprivation may lead to brain development deficits and a reduced ability to cope with stress.[88] The ability to
learn is obviously related to brain development. For an individual to develop
a conscience, the person must absorb "lessons" regarding what is bad behavior. Bad behavior must be associated with fear and/or guilt in order for a conscience to develop. If the individual has an autonomic nervous system that is
relatively unresponsive to fear, then the person is less likely to control aggressive actions because the contemplated aggression does not evoke fear and
anxiety.[89]

Walsh argues that deprived and neglected children are repeatedly
exposed to stress and that such a constant barrage of stress eventually "shuts
down" the body's normal responses to stress (because it becomes "normal"
and the body stops initiating the fight-or-flight syndrome).[90] Evidence indicates, for instance, that many abused children have been shown to possess
autonomic nervous system's unreactive to fear and anxiety. The possible
effect of such autonomic nervous system development is that these individuals will become relatively immune to normal stress—they may engage in "fear-
less" behaviors, or engage in antisocial behavior themselves because their
autonomic nervous system does not give them the cues that such behavior is
stressful. He also points out that some research indicates that those subjected to chronic stress in childhood may react with hyporeactivity to mild stressors (not respond) but hyperreactivity to severe stressors (overreact).[91]

Walsh also discusses endocrine functioning and criminality. He explains that sex hormones are the most powerful hormones secreted by the body.[92] Androgens (male hormones such as testosterone) are responsible for the development of muscle, and associated with many other physiological and psychological characteristics. Female sex hormones (estrogens such as estradiol, and progestins such as progesterone) are related to the formation of fat and prepare the body for childbirth. The effect of sex hormones on behavior is influenced by their absolute levels, but also important are their ratios, the number of receptor sites available, and when they are released (i.e., in utero, during puberty, or later).[93] The "human brain, like the human body, is intrinsically female. . . ."[94] It is only when it is exposed to testicular androgens between the sixth and the eighth week of gestation (the "androgen bath"), that male characteristics start to develop.

> Once the brain is "sexed," the hypothalamus organizes hormone-secretion patterns in different ways; that is, sex hormones interact differently in male and female brains in areas sensitized in utero to be receptive to them. Both the estrogens and androgens act on the limbic system, the brain's emotional center, in areas that are structurally different in males and females . . . Estradiol promotes nurturing behavior in females by lowering the threshold for firing the nerve fibers in the media preoptic hypothalamic area . . . testosterone, on the other hand, lowers the firing threshold of the amygdala, the area of the brain most associated with violence and aggression. . . .[95]

Walsh firmly believes that sex hormones are responsible for emotional and behavioral differences between men and women. He proposes that numerous studies find that older females are altruistic, nurturant, and empathetic, while younger males are dominant and aggressive.[96] He discusses critics who dispute biological differences between the sexes in favor of socialization.[97]

Walsh argues that men and women are "ruled" by both biology and socialization and it is ridiculous to ignore either. Biological sex differences act to reduce violent criminality among women and increase its likelihood among men. Women's brains are "pre-wired" for altruism and "otherness." They have greater sensitivities to human emotions, and they are less impulsive. They also have greater verbal skills, which reduce frustration that leads to aggression.

The most controversial portion of Walsh's theory is his explanation that the association between race and criminality is biological. According to Walsh, the association can be explained largely through the intervening variables of IQ differences, the r/K theory of sex selection,[98] and testosterone levels (which are higher in African-Americans). Obviously any theory that proposes biological racial differences should be subject to extreme scrutiny. It is beyond the scope of this work to do so, however, and that task will no doubt be taken up by many others.[99]

Although Walsh is perhaps one of the strongest proponents of biological explanations of crime today, he recognizes and incorporates the effects of socialization into his explanation of criminal choices. One may certainly question his results, especially as concerning racial differences, however the arguments concerning sex differences are persuasive.

Critique and Review

Critics of biological theories argue that biology cannot explain criminal choice because crime rates vary across cultures and show patterns related to social factors such as urbanization; thus how can a constant (inherent nature) explain a variable (crime rates).[100] Others argue that gender is more powerful than sex and that all observed sex differences are really the product of socialization.[101] Feminists, especially, scorn biological theories and view them as evidence of patriarchy.[102] Other critics argue that the methodology used to support biological theories is weak.[103] Other problems with biological research concern the practice of comparing prison samples to controls and assuming prison samples are representative of criminals; using formal and official reports as accurate measurements of criminal behavior, and such studies typically do not differentiate between occasional criminals and chronic criminals.

However, it appears that many criminologists are now beginning to accept that criminal choices are at least partially influenced by predisposing biological factors. Earlier, a few integrated theories were presented that include both biological factors as well as social structural factors as predisposing the individual to delinquency/criminality. Vold, Bernard, and Snipes, in their review of current theories, observe that even strongly sociological treatments of criminology are now recognizing the influence of biology (mediated by environmental, and structural concerns).

> Biological theories are necessarily part of a "multiple factor" approach to criminal behavior—that is, the presence of certain biological factors may increase the likelihood but not determine absolutely that an individual will engage in criminal behaviors. These factors generate criminal behaviors when they interact with psychological or social factors.[104]

In fact, for most, the matter of biological versus sociological influences are simply a matter of emphasis; while biological researchers say biological predispositions (including sex differences) are mediated by environmental factors, sociological researchers argue that social structural and environmental factors interact with biological factors (including sex differences). No one argues determinism, and no one is very clear on how exactly to isolate the exact variance that can be explained by one or the other factors.

Generally, it appears that genetic and psychophysiological contributions to criminal conduct will be greatest when the social milieu is least supportive of crime. Thus, for example, the genetic effect is greater when the more serious, rather than less serious, crimes are sampled [notes omitted], and greater among women than among men. Under conditions in which crime is relatively infrequent and/or is subject to the highest levels of control, the biopsychological factors emerge most strongly.[105]

More importantly, as we will discuss in the next chapter, prevention efforts take pretty much the same form, whichever emphasis one prefers.

BIOSOCIAL THEORIES

The definition that we will use for a biosocial theory is one that explains sex differences and other biological traits through some evolutionary explanation. For instance, Daly and Wilson present a theory of homicide that utilizes a biosocial approach. They argue that homicide is adaptive and part of natural selection. Reviewing statistics of homicide, they point out that it is rare for offenders to kill blood relatives (only 6% of their sample were blood relatives) consistent with an evolutionary explanation of survival.[106] They explain infanticide as naturally adaptive in cultures with few resources as a way of ensuring survival of other offspring.[107]

The authors go on to apply sociobiological explanations to other forms of homicide. For instance, they argue that it is no coincidence that men kill women who they perceive as unfaithful; even common law recognized the "natural" right of man to protect his progeny. Sexual jealousy is an evolutionary predisposition, argue the authors, because every species has an instinct to propagate itself and eliminate rivals. The authors review numbers of studies that show sexual proprietariness, jealousy, or fear of losing women as the most common reason for male spousal homicide while female motivation is more often self-defense.[108]

Further, they point out that stepfathers are much more likely to kill than natural fathers. This is compared to other male mammals who kill offspring of their mates belonging to other males. So many killings are related to honor and status, according to the authors, because of the "selection advantage,"—in almost all species, men "show off" to attract women. It is a natural evolutionary pattern that ensures species survival—the strongest male will prevail and pass down his genetic legacy.

Women are selectively adapted to parental investment, not sexual proliferation. The authors point out that women's tendency to participate less in violent actions extends through all cultures and throughout time. Female choice theory[109] assumes that females select those males who they believe will stay with them and provide for them over a long period of time, and do not select those males who they believe will be promiscuous and leave. Males are biologically disposed to try to impregnant as many women possible, therefore they will "perform" those behaviors that will get them selected; however, their biological inclinations are different, therefore once a woman has selected the male, he has less incentive for acting the way he did during courtship (a sort of sociobiological rationale for infidelity!).

Walsh argues that sex-specific survival tasks account for a range of biological and psychological differences between men and women:

> Females were more diverse in the tasks they had to perform in the hunting and gathering societies that have characterized the life of the species for 99.9 percent of its history. Females were thus subjected to a different and less specialized selection process that was perhaps responsible for their lesser degree of brain laterality. Woman's role as nurturer, caregiver, comforter, and peacekeeper exerted pressure for the selection of social skills such as language and greater emotional sensitivity.[110]

He further argues that the lesser laterality of women is more emotionally healthy; it allows them to be more flexible and less "self-oriented." Sex differences are the result of evolutionary needs—males hunted and fought for power, women had children; males have higher aggression, dominance, visual-spatial skills, women needed to be more nurturing and communicative.

As mentioned previously, the r/K theory explains that two patterns of reproduction exist. The first occurs when men look to propagate and invest little in childcare (they spread their seed, but do not watch them grow, so to speak), the second is when there are higher levels of parental investment by both parents. Women, through evolution, are predisposed to look for investors (men who will help provide and care for children). In some species, males are highly promiscuous and invest nothing in the care of children, in other species, males take on greater childcare roles and monogamy is also more common. Theorists argue that the human species swings from one model to the other depending on the sex ratio. When there are more men than women—the K of the model—men exhibit more aggressive behavior (because they are competing with each other for fewer women), and females have selection power so more monogamy results because they select men who exhibit parental investment traits. When there are fewer men than women—the r of the model—men tend to emphasize activities of propagation and do not exhibit much parental investment; females cannot demand monogamy, so there are more disrupted families, divorce, and unsupervised children.[111] Authors have applied the r/K theory to the African-American community; because so many young men are in jail or prison, the sex ratio favors the pattern of propagation and weak parental investment on the part of men. Rowe also applies the r/K selection factor theory to common forms of theft and violent crimes.[112]

Raine looks at biological theories of criminal psychopathy and includes evolutionary theory, genetics, neurochemistry, neuropsychology, brain imaging, psychophysiology, and cognitive deficits in his explanation.[113] The approach taken is that serious, recidivistic criminality is a psychological disorder, and other correlates have biological and socio-biological bases.

He argues that there are two genetic predispositions—a selfish gene (promoting self even at the sacrifice of others) and one of altruism (sacrificing self for others), and provides examples of both in the animal kingdom as well as in humankind. Raine argues that crime is an evolutionary adaptation of the first type of genetic inheritance. Further, he argues, similarly to others, that females are controlled by social influences that act to suppress criminal choices; therefore, those women who do commit crime can be predicted to show more significant biological influences than male samples of delinquent/criminals, using twin studies and adoption studies that showed women had higher concordance rates than men.

Vila offers a comprehensive "paradigm" of criminology that includes biological factors, sociological factors, and evolutionary ecological interactions.[114] The approach is too broad to do justice to here, and does not explicate in detail evolutionary and biological constructs that are associated with criminality/delinquency. He attempts to include all disparate threads of explanation into a cohesive whole that includes both explanatory power as well as prevention suggestions. Vila, unfortunately, does not explicate the sex/gender differential, thus his prevention suggestions do not take advantage of the explanatory and preventive potential of women's lower crime rates.

Ellis and Walsh review evolutionary theories, including those above, that are crime specific (i.e., theories regarding rape and homicide), as well as more general theories (sex selection and the r/K selection theory).[115] In a more detailed explication of the r/K theory and how it related to crime and delinquency, they propose that r men (those who have high drives for propagation and low parental investment) would also be more criminal.[116] The authors point out that such theories are new and need further development, but that they at least explain how crime (i.e., victimizing others) may stem from a "reproductive niche" that ensures the presence of victimizers in society.

Biosocial theories are interesting, challenging, and speculative. They place humans back into the animal kingdom and do not presume that human behavior is less subject to evolutionary controls because of some unique characteristics of the species. Obviously, the theorists do not mean to imply that individuals consciously make these choices based on evolutionary rationales. Nor, one assumes, do they mean to imply that rationality and learning cannot moderate evolutionary pressures. One does not, however, necessarily have to agree with all or even part of the theories described above to accept biological influences of criminal choices.

CONCLUSION

Arguments will continue regarding the validity (or value) of biological theories. It is important to differentiate criticism that objectively points to scientific and methodological weaknesses, and criticism that is political and polemical. Unfortunately, at times it is hard to tell one from the other since it appears that reviewers have a tendency to present findings in the light most favorable to one's point of view.[117]

However, certain conclusions seem reasonably agreed upon. The first conclusion is that there is no question sex and age (and more arguably race) are the strongest correlates of crime, and they are biological constructs. Second, there is no comparison between the biological theories of Lombroso and other early positivists and those biological researchers today[118] who look at extremely complicated connections between hormones, brain chemistry, and other physiological processes that affect personality traits and/or learning abilities, that then create a predisposition toward (not a determination of) delinquent/criminal choices. Finally, all biological theorists and many sociological theorists now agree that biology and environment work together to create the probability of delinquent/criminal choice. In the final chapter we will propose one more additional element to the understanding of criminal choice and conclude with a discussion concerning the policy implications of a sex-based understanding of crime.

NOTES

[1]   Lombroso believed that some criminals were "born criminals" who were evolutionary mutants—more primitive than modern man, and diagnosed by physical atavistic qualities (such as excessive facial hair or heavy musculature), in addition to their criminality.

[2]   In the United States, for instance, African-Americans are disproportionately represented in crime statistics, as are Hispanics and Native Americans. However, in other countries, the racial minority in that country typically represents disproportionate figures in crime statistics. Furthermore, in the United States, crime patterns vary and, more interestingly, the minority population in any given state or region is disproportionately represented in crime statistics. Further, where those populations become the majority, crime patterns shift (indicating sociological factors are at work).

[3]   One could argue that sex is a continuum since some individuals may be born with both sex organs, or a statistically abnormal mix of sex hormones, furthermore, all individuals experience different levels of sex hormones. However, given certain normal distributions of sex hormones, most individuals fall within the range of their sex.

[4]   See Rafter (1988).

[5]   As this chapter was being writtten, ABC presented a special on sex differences and Gloria Steinem and Bella Abzug were asked about research that had uncovered sex differences in very young children in play preferences as well as the way the brain worked

(ABC, January 16). They argued that even infants are socialized differently, thus accounting for differences in toddlers, and more importantly, that such research *should not be done*; that it was anti-woman and should not be supported by public monies.

[6]   1994.

[7]   Andrews and Bonta (1994, 128-129).

[8]   At least one adoption study, however, did provide interesting information relevant to a discussion of sex differences in criminality. Bohrman (1996) reports that in an adoption study of 862 men and 913 women born between 1930 and 1950 that were adopted at an early age, men were more likely, in both the parents groups and the adoptees group, to be arrested (12.8% of adopted men arrested, 2.9% of women; of the biological parents 29% of men and 6.4% women were arrested), or alcoholic (16.1% of the male adoptees were compared to 2.4% women; of the biological parents 34% men and 4.6% mothers were alcoholic). The most interesting finding, however, was that: "21% of 39 criminal men had at least one biological parent with petty criminality (i.e., criminality and no alcohol abuse). By comparison, the risk of petty criminality in the biological parents of the criminal women was more than double that of their male counterparts (50 versus 21% . . .)" (1996, 105). It is not clear what, if anything, this means. Perhaps it can be argued that because socialization tends to tolerate delinquency/criminality among men, biological transmission of operative factors is diffused by a more general tendency toward delinquent choices.

[9]   Walsh (1991, 136) refers to the syndrome as Premenstrual Dysphoric Disorder and points out that while all women may experience to greater or lesser degrees what is commonly referred to as premenstrual syndrome; only a very few women suffer from Premenstrual Dysphoric Disorder.

[10]   Walsh (1995a, 83).

[11]   Mann (1984b, 67-69) reviews the literature on PMS and female criminality related to "generative" phases of women—pregnancy and menopause. She reviews studies and chronicles the problems with such studies, including such things as subjective reporting (subjects' feelings of irritability are used as a measure), identifying the PMS-related cycle as covering almost the whole month, the fact that most women have inconsistent cycles, small samples, and often prison samples. Even though these studies find a correlation between "aggressive acts" and the onset of menses Mann points out that this does not necessarily relate to criminality, and the methodology is too weak to draw any conclusions.

[12]   Another sex-specific theory involves the idea of "lactational insanity." Historically infanticide was a crime legally committed only by women and those who committed such a crime received fairly mild sanctions (early courts often recognized social and economic reasons for such murders). Sometimes they were acquitted by reason of lactational insanity, a mental illness suffered only by women and only immediately after birth, which was believed to be somehow related to the biological processes of birth and lactation. The modern-day explanation of this fairly rare syndrome is post-partum depression. While all women experience some mental and behavioral effects of the massive hormonal changes the body endures during pregnancy and birth, some women experience more extreme hormonal effects with accompanying behavioral effects, including at times delusions and suicidal ideation.

[13]   Maccoby and Jacklin (1974, 242-243).

[14]   Tedeschi and Felson (1994, 26).

[15]   Mednick et al. (1987, 243-250), also see Mednick and Christiansen (1977).

16   Olweus (1987), also see Eysenck and Gudjonsson (1989).

17   Walsh (1991).

18   Walsh (1995a, 85).

19   Walsh (1995a, 85). One interesting aspect of this field of research is that many of these studies were conducted in Scandanavian countries. It is intriguing to consider whether cultural differences would affect study results. Two hypotheses related to culture and biology are diametrically opposed: the first would propose that if culture does act to increase or decrease aggressive behavior, then those countries that discourage aggressive behavior would have samples that show a stronger correlation between testosterone and aggression (because biology is overcoming culture), and those cultures that allow and/or encourage aggression would not show a strong correlation because culture overshadows biological differences. The second hypothesis, however, would utilize the testosterone as a "permissive effect" and predict that those cultures that allowed or encouraged aggression would show a stronger correlation between aggression and testosterone.

20   Mednick, Moffitt, and Stack (1987).

21   Denno (1990, 14).

22   Denno (1990, 14).

23   Walsh (1991, 139).

24   Walsh (1995a, 89).

25   1995, 90.

26   1987, 202.

27   Eysenck and Gudjonsson (1989, 135) and Walsh (1991, 140).

28   Walsh (1991, 140).

29   Wilson (1993, 127).

30   Walsh (1995a, 50-54), also see Ellis (1991).

31   Walsh (1995a, 54).

32   Walsh (1991a, 141).

33   Sandhu and Satterfield (1987).

34   Eysenck and Gudjonsson (1989, 129).

35   1990, 15.

36   Denno also cites Silberg et al. (1996, 78) and Farrington, et al. (1990) as supporting these findings. Silberg et al. (1996, 78-83) differentiates conduct disorder and ADD in childhood, however there does seem to be a group that overlaps both categories. The strongest predictor of membership in one of the groups was mother's diagnosis of major depression, anxiety disorder, panic disorder, phobia; interestingly, the fathers' diagnosis of same was not as strong a predictor.

37   1990, 17. Similarly, Moffitt (1990) reports that in a longitudinal study in New Zealand, it was found that delinquents had significantly lower verbal skills, auditory verbal memory, interspatial analysis, and visual-motor integration in elementary school. Such early evidence of cognitive deficits indicates that it is not simply a delinquent "lifestyle" and/or

drug use that causes subsequent lower cognitive abilities, there may be problems at birth that affect the child early in school.

[38]   Wilson (1993, 165).

[39]   Moffitt (1990, 112) concludes that delinquents consistently show an IQ deficit of about eight points.

[40]   1989, 53.

[41]   1994, 131-135.

[42]   Raine (1993, 233).

[43]   1990, 47.

[44]   1990, 49.

[45]   Denno notes: "Highly significant differences existed in comparisons for select reading and language achievement tests. For example, twice as many violent offenders than nonoffenders scored in the bottom third . . . of the Biosocial project sample for Total Reading achievement" (1990, 51).

[46]   See Kohlberg (1981). Also, moral development stages will be more fully explored in the next chapter.

[47]   1990, 56. Denno found that the correlation between low test scores and some offenses were significant for women even when it was less significant or showed no significance for men.

> Significant results with nonindex offenders may be due to the relatively high frequency of their offenses and the fact that some misbehaviors that may be quite minor for males (e.g., truancy and disorderly conduct) are a sign of considerably more misbehavior when conducted by females (1990, 51).

Although the meaning is not entirely clear, what is probably meant by this statement is that certain behaviors are more tolerated for boys than girls; girls, thus, are socially controlled and generally do not engage in them as often; thus, the correlation between girls who do and measures of intelligence would be expected to be higher (low intelligence prevents socialization). The correlation for boys would not be as strong because more boys would feel social support or at least tolerance toward such behavior and, thus, engage in it. However, the offenses mentioned are actually those that have a reduced sex differential, so the finding and the proposed explanation may not be entirely satisfactory.

[48]   1990, 65.

[49]   1990, 94.

[50]   See Eysenck (1977).

[51]   Caspi et al. (1994).

[52]   Caspi et al. (1994).

[53]   Farrington and West (1993).

[54]   Caspi et al. (1994).

[55]   Raine (1993, 93).

[56]   1993, 229.

[57]   1993, 290.

[58]   Eysenck and Gudjonsson (1989, 140).

[59]   1995b.

[60]   Walsh (1995b).

[61]   1989, 44.

[62]   1989, 55.

[63]   1989, 55.

[64]   1997.

[65]   These authors also discuss endorphins more generally, and offer a partial explanation for drug addiction.

> . . . activation of the dopamine synapse in the nucleus accumbens is intrinsically pleasurable, and processes that increase dopamine transmission at this synapse are strongly reinforced. The reason humans and other animals find amphetamines, cocaine, nicotine, morphine, heroin, and their synthetic derivatives intrinsically rewarding is becasue, through different processes, these drugs increase neurotransmssion at this synapse. Drugs have this effect because they activate a naturally occurring neurophysiological process. It is also true that behavior that increases the level of endorphins also activates this reward process, resulting in a "neurophysiological high." It has been established that high levels of endorphins are strongly associated with challenging and/or risky behaviors, and there is significant variation among people regarding the strength of this relationship (Wood et al. 1997, 345).

[66]   Eysenck and Gudjonsson (1989, 126).

[67]   Eysenck and Gudjonsson (1989, 131).

[68]   Tedeschi and Felson (1994, 363).

[69]   Eysenck and Gudjonnson (1989, 7).

[70]   1990. Her data is the Philadelphia Biosocial Project; a longitudinal study of 1,000 individuals born between 1959 and 1966 that was drawn from a larger medical study. These individuals were followed from birth through early adulthood, and all manner of data were collected, including clinical visits, home visits, medical data, and juvenile data. The sample utilized for analysis was composed of 987 individuals—487 males and 500 females—all African-American. Of those in the sample, 22 percent had at least one police contact prior to age 18 (31% of males and 14% of females). These percentages are lower than a general sample of juveniles in Philadelphia at the same time and the authors speculate that it might have been that the continued formal attention to these families protected children from social influences. It is possible, then, that biological influences would take on greater importance because of the reduced power of social influences. Findings indicate that 17 percent of male offenders and 10 percent of the females could be defined as "chronic" offenders, committing two to four offenses (1990, 43). The mean level of seriousness of offenses was nearly 2.5 times greater for males than for females (1990, 43).

[71]   1990, 19.

[72]   1990, 107.

[73]   1990, 107. Also see Moffitt (1990, 111).

[74]   Also see Denno (1988).

[75]   Denno argues:

> Gender differences in behavior can also locate sociological and develop-
> mental effects. In general, developmental and biological factors are more
> strongly associated with female delinquency for two reasons: Females are
> less affected physically than males by environmental influences, and
> females are relatively more socialized to conform to social and cultural
> norms. In other words, females who become delinquent or violent gener-
> ally have more biologically related difficulties than males because serious
> female aggression is highly abnormal conduct (Denno, 1990, 27).

Not all portions of this explanation are clear. First, it is possible that the first sentence
should read "sex" differences rather than "gender" differences, since the idea seems to be
that biological differences interact with the social environment. Second, why are females
less affected physically by environmental influences? This finding refers, one assumes, to
the idea that female delinquents' home lives are usually worse than those of their male
counterparts, the argument is therefore that social dysfunction must be greater before a
girl turns to delinquency. However, one could also argue that boys are more likely to be
delinquent regardless of home life. Arguably, certain developmental and biological factors
are "more strongly associated with female delinquency" because the general influences of
biology act to disincline women to criminality.

[76]   1990, 86.

[77]   1990, 92.

[78]   1990, 125.

[79]   Widom (1984), also see Widom and Ames (1988).

[80]   See, for instance, Moffitt (1990).

[81]   1991, 1995.

[82]   1991, 142.

[83]   1991, 176-178.

[84]   1995, 55.

[85]   Probably due to women's physiology—the birth canal had to accommodate bipodal
mobility; therefore, babies have a smaller, "squishier" head than those of other mammals.

[86]   1995, 59 (notes omitted).

[87]   1995, 63.

[88]   Interestingly, his observation might be applied to child-rearing practice differences: some
argue that boys are picked up less and experience less "cuddling" than girls during early
stages of infancy and through toddler years. This socialization difference might, then,
interact, with the biological sex difference to create differences in male and female learning capacities.

[89]   1995, 73.

[90]   1995, 78.

[91]   One might also apply such a theory to those who live in distressed neighborhoods with a constant barrage of violence, chaos, and fear.

[92]   1995a, 91.

[93]   1995a, 82.

[94]   Walsh (1995a, 82).

[95]   1995, 82 (notes omitted).

[96]   1995, 87.

[97]   Walsh points out that, almost always, Margaret Mead's work is cited as "evidence" that sex differences are largely cultural. However, her work has been heavily criticized by anthropologists and Mead herself believed in the importance of biological differences (1995a, 135). He also discusses the social experiments that took place in Israeli kibbutzes where both sexes shared work equally, marriages and nuclear family attachments were discouraged, and children were raised in gender-neutral daycare centers. Kibbutz research showed that subsequent generations reverted to sex-role behaviors of monogamy, and women wanted to be with their children, eventually nuclear family arrangements re-emerged with parents taking over much of the childcare responsibilities (1995, 135).

[98]   The r/K selection factor will be discussed again in a later section; it postulates that when there are fewer men than women, men will be promiscuous, undependable, and not engage in long-term relationships. When there are more men than women there is more monogamy (since women get to choose, they will choose men who show cues of dependability).

[99]   For instance, several researchers dispute any biological causal factor in the race/crime correlation because the criminal justice system most probably is racist (i.e., makes decisions based on race), victimization data also show disproportional levels of minorities, and that the race differential (the number of African-Americans arrested compared to the number of whites) has increased since the 1940s (Gottfredson and Hirschi, 1990, 150-151; Akers, 1997, 46-47).

[100]   Gora (1982, 13).

[101]   See, for instance, Renzetti and Curran (1992). Sobel (1978) argued against any sex differences by using one study of how two siblings born with external female genitalia were raised as girls but were biologically boys (because they had internal testes). According to Sobel, the girls suffered no psychological problems with continuing to be raised as girls, therefore: "[this study casts] serious doubt on the validity of extrapolations from biology to female behavior" (1978, 270). The case study was used as evidence that one's sex-role identity is largely a function of socialization rather than biology. While case studies are fascinating, the experience of one set of siblings is not sufficient to rebut the great weight of other evidence on the side of sex-differentiated physiological and behavioral differences. Sobel also uses Mead and clinical studies to show that women are likely to be aggressive in certain social settings (1978, 273). Again, however, these findings can be argued against as well. The laboratory settings that elicited aggressive behavior by women were highly artificial, and other settings that were mentioned as evidencing aggressive behavior by women were such that other factors may be partially responsible for the behavior (i.e., the example of a mother protecting her children merely points out and supports her nurturance and child-orientation, not an intrinsic aggressiveness).

[102]   See, for instance, Belknap (1996, 9), Morris (1987, 42), Messerschmidt (1993, 7), and Smart (1995, 18).

[103]   Gottfredson and Hirschi (1990) also heavily criticize the methodology of biological studies, and conclude that if done correctly, the significance found would be reduced to nothing. Raine (1993, 65), in turn, criticizes Gottfredson and Hirschi's critique of biological/genetic theory; arguing that their criticism of Mednick's study that combined a first sample with a second larger sample as not a true replication could also be applied to many other social tests. Raine proposes that Gottfredson and Hirschi ignored many other studies and concentrated on only three. He also points out that they argue the weakness of genetic studies, but that this criticism does not also apply to biological theory that postulates measurable differences (regardless of inheritance). Raine argues that there are more than 100 studies of electrodermal activity in violent and psychopathic offenders; brain injury, and prenatal or postnatal influences on brain development.

Trasler (1987, 10) criticizes evidence of Eysenck's theory linking extraversion to criminality. Mednick et al. (1987, 10) also find that Eysenck's theory of extraversion has little empirical support; when prisoners are compared to controls, their scores of extraversion are sometimes higher, but sometimes not, and in any case differences tend to be slight. Much of the argument concerns methodology, i.e., measurements of low cortical arousal, measures of delinquency or criminality, measures of aggressiveness. As discussed in the first chapter, defining constructs such as aggression is difficult, as is developing some accurate and valid measure of it. There are also scientific arguments concerning the tests of cortical arousal.

[104]   1998, 87.

[105]   Andrews and Bonta (1994, 130).

[106]   1988, 183.

[107]   1988, 42. There is evidently a similar pattern to infanticide regardless of culture. More likely to kill are young women versus older mothers, unmarried versus married, and those without support versus those with support. The authors also point out that the killing almost always occurs in the first phase of attachment between mother and child before any bonding has taken place (during the first several hours after birth). In fact, the largest percentage of all child killings are infanticide and the number of children killed by mothers drops tremendously after the first several days of life. Contrary to popular belief that a woman who kills her baby must be a "monster" and "unnatural," they argue that for the first hours or even days there is an assessment period and the emotional feelings toward the child may start with indifference; only after several hours or even days does "mother-love" emerge, which is described as individualized love (feeling that the child is uniquely wonderful) (1988, 72).

[108]   1988, 201. Further, they argue that marriages with exceptionally high age disparities—in either direction—have homicide rates more than four times as high as that prevailing in marriages with a smaller age gap (1988, 209).

> Men do not easily let women go. They search out women who have left them, to plead and threaten and sometimes to kill. . . . Among legally married, cohabiting Canadian spouses in 1974-1983, a man was almost four times as likely to kill his wife as to be killed by her (404 cases vs. 107); among estranged couples, he was more than nine times as likely to kill her as she him (119 vs. 13) . . . The rare case of a woman killing her estranged husband is likely to be a case of self-defense against a man who will not let her be (1988, 219).

[109]   Explained by Wilson (1993, 169).

[110]   Walsh (1995a, 175; notes omitted).

[111]   Walsh (1995a, 146); also see Ellis (1987a).

[112]   1996.

[113]   1993.

[114]   1994.

[115]   1997.

[116]   ". . . criminal and antisocial behavior is the human version of a low parental investment reproductive strategy. If this theory is true, criminals should be deceptive, irresponsible, and opportunistic in almost everything they do, and if genes are a major cause of this behavior, it would likely begin to manifest itself early in life. Theoretically, cad males will use just about any tactic that works to coax, trick, and/or force numerous females to copulate, including thievery to acquire resources quickly, and will then shirk all long-term investment in offspring" (1997, 247).

[117]   It is accepted that this review is no different in this regard.

[118]   Such as Denno (1988, 1990, 1994), Fishbein (1990), Walsh (1991, 1995a, 1995b), and Ellis and Hoffman (1990), among others.

Sex Differences and Moral Development: Toward an Integrated Understanding of Crime and Crime Prevention

9

<table>
<tr><td>

Objectives

</td></tr>
<tr><td>

- Become familiar with moral development research and how women and men may tend to have different perceptions regarding morality.

- Understand how these differences may have their origin in biological differences.

- Understand how these differences may affect criminal predisposition.

- Apply what we know about women's and men's crime rates to policy decisions regarding crime and punishment.

</td></tr>
</table>

As discussed in the last chapter, evidence supports the idea that certain biological traits, more common to men, result in men's higher propensity to commit crime. These biological factors, however, are mediated through environmental influences, such as sex-role socialization. In the first part of this chapter, one other sex/gender difference is presented—morality, or more precisely, the construct of moral development as we can measure it through psychological testing. Whether these differences exist at all is one question; and, if they do exist, whether they originate through socialization or biological differences is a different and separate question. There is controversy over each question.

Maccoby looked at play differences between boys and girls. She concluded that boys play in larger groups, boys play rougher, there is more fighting in boys' play, boys' encounters tend to be oriented around issues of dominance and a formation of a pecking order, and boys' language is to establish dominance and gain attention. Girls, on the other hand, place a stronger emphasis on taking turns, friendships are more intense, girls interact in smaller cliques, girls' language is used for cooperation, and criticism tends to be veiled. Even boys will exclude hyper-aggressiveness, however, and bullying boys are excluded from peer groups.[1]

In a very general way, the playground, then, is a precursor of the adult world, and the different experiences of men and women in that world. The play of boys, emphasizing as it does, dominance and activity, is more likely to lead to antisocial choices than the play of girls, which emphasizes cooperation and affinity.[2]

THE MORAL DEVELOPMENT OF MEN AND WOMEN

Piaget[3] and Kohlberg[4] are the two most dominant theorists in the area of moral development. The basic assumption of this work is that moral development and cognitive development is positively correlated. Only when the child develops cognitive abilities that move from concrete to abstract thinking, are they able to grasp moral concepts, such as altruism. Kohlberg developed a stage theory of moral development; that is, everyone goes through certain stages of understanding moral concepts related to their cognitive abilities. These stages are described below.

Stage 1. Obedience to authority and avoidance of punishment are the elements of moral reasoning. Associated with a young child, what is right is what parents say is right. What is wrong is what is punished. There is little independent thought regarding right and wrong, and an egoistic view of the world prevails.

Stage 2. There is still a strong egoistic element to morality. What is right is what feels good to self. There is, however, awareness of relativism, that is, what feels good may be different to different people. There is some commitment to exchange and reciprocity.

Stage 3. This is the good boy-good girl orientation. Role modeling is a major mechanism for shaping values and behavior. Actions are judged by intent as well as consequences.

Stage 4. Morality is associated with doing one's duty and showing respect for authority. Maintaining the social order is seen as the sum result of moral rules.

Stage 5. There is recognition of legalistic agreement in the social order and that the social order may be an arbitrary creation at any particular point in time. "Majority rules" is a rule of morality.

Stage 6. This is the conscience or principles-based orientation. Social universality and consistency are the themes that are used to determine moral decisions.[5]

Offenders, compared to non-offenders in similar age groups, tend to cluster in Stages 1 and 2, whereas most non-offender adults tend to cluster in Stages 3 and 4. Few people evidently reach the higher stages. Individuals progress from lower stages when they are raised in environments that do include higher-level reasoning, when they are made responsible for their moral choices, and when they are challenged in their moral beliefs. Morality, then, stems purely from reasoning. A more rational, reasonable, intelligent person will be one who is more moral than someone without those qualities.

Kohlberg's theory has not been without its critics. There are arguments that the theory is culturally biased and presents a Western orientation to ethics that probably does not represent other cultures. In fact, it has been shown that individuals from other cultures do not test in the same way as those raised in Western cultures that have a Greek/Roman philosophical tradition. Another criticism is that the stage sequences are sex-biased. That is, the assumption that individuals progress through the stages as given, and that the highest stages represent a more developed morality may be true only for men, not women.

This criticism arose primarily from the work of Carol Gilligan, a colleague of Kohlberg, who found that women tended to cluster in Stage 3, while men clustered in Stage 4.[6] Women, in other words, tend to base their moral decisions on relationships and needs, while men base their moral decisions on principles and laws. Gilligan noted that Piaget's early research documented differences between how boys and girls played, but the differences were not relevant to his study and he ignored them. Observed differences in girls' play included girls' greater tolerance, a greater tendency toward innovation in solving conflicts, greater willingness to make exceptions to rules, and lesser concern with legal elaborations (rules).[7]

Gilligan proposes that women do not exhibit a *lower* morality, they represent a *different* morality; one that is inconsistent with the Western philosophical tradition, and more consistent with some Eastern religions. Gilligan explains:

> The moral imperative that emerges repeatedly in interviews with women is an injunction to care, a responsibility to discern and alleviate the "real and recognizable trouble" of this world. For men the moral imperative appears rather as an injunction to respect the rights of others and thus to protect from interference the rights to life and self-fulfillment.[8]

In her research, she found that only a portion of women exhibited a relationship-based or needs-based moral reasoning, but almost no men did. She found that when resolving moral dilemmas, most people (about two-thirds) focused on either a care or a justice concern; but almost every male who had a focus, focused on justice while women were split (one-third focused on care, one-third on justice, one-third had no focus).[9] She concluded that because both women and men are socialized in this country to Western philosophy, it is not surprising that many women adopt such reasoning and display it when asked to resolve a moral dilemma. Another interesting finding of her research was that when sensitized to the approach (to utilize factors of relationships and needs in resolving dilemmas), both women and men could adopt and utilize the reasoning adequately.[10]

Some critics of Gilligan complain that she has merely provided a scientific veneer for the age-old stereotype that women are more nurturing, caring, and "nicer" than men. Smart, for instance, was concerned that Gilligan's work represented a "slide into socio-biology" "which merely puts women back into their place."[11] Held, in a discussion concerning Gilligan's work as well as other research that identified sex differences also worried.

> We should be constantly on guard for misuses of such ideas, as in social roles that determine that women belong in the home or in educational programs that discourage women from becoming, for example, mathematicians. Yet, excessive fear of such misuses should not stifle exploration of the ways in which such claims may, in some measure, be true.[12]

Other criticism is methodological. Gilligan criticizes moral development research that uses all male samples and then applies the results to women; however, her research used abortion as the moral dilemma. Later research allowed subjects to choose their own dilemmas. Arguably abortion is a particular moral dilemma that may be perceived differently by women and men and is uniquely a woman's decision, thus accounting for the differences observed in resolving the moral dilemma. Choosing one's own personal dilemma may also introduce unknown variables into men's and women's choice of moral resolution. The idea that the type of dilemma affects the manner of moral reasoning seems a legitimate concern deserving of further study.[13]

However, her work is perfectly consistent with other work in philosophy and psychology. For instance, Chodorow developed a model of development that described differences between men and women as resulting from the relationship of both with their mother.[14] Female children maintain a connection and identity with their mother, thus developing traits of "responsibility, care, and promotion of peace and love." Boys, however, develop by psychological separation from the mother. This explains women's tendency to "connect" rather than disengage, to be sensitive to others, and to be nurturing. The ideal of masculinity, however, is autonomy. She also points out that the very tasks of caring for children and others may promote a caring approach to life. The responsibility of feeding, clothing, and comforting helps to develop a loving relationship. This psychological development would also predict that women would define morality in ways that protected and emphasized human relationships.

Noddings' work in philosophy, is also consistent with Gilligan's findings. She proposes a different "caring" approach that emphasizes needs over rights. Since females live through relationships, connectedness is valued, while men value rationality, women value care.[15] Considering Gilligan's findings, it would be predicted that Noddings is a woman—and she is. Feminist ethics has been discussed more generally as: grounded in a feminist perspective, challenging traditional "masculinist" moral assumptions, reinterpreting the importance of women's role as caregiver, emphasizing the importance of particularity, connection and context, and reinterpreting moral agency and altruism.[16]

One interesting correctional intervention that utilized Kohlberg's stage development theory provides support for Gilligan's assumptions.[17] In two Connecticut prisons, Scharf and Hickey created the elements of a therapeutic community, but employed Kohlberg's reasoning approach to guide the development and implementation of the group meetings. Participation in their program was correlated with a significant increase in stage scores. Scharf and Hickey discovered that offenders could improve their stage scores, typically by about a stage and one-half.[18]

These researchers found that the groups, formed with exactly the same intent and structure, developed very differently: ". . . in the female groups there were many exchanges of feelings and attitudes toward both staff and other inmates, whereas the male groups dealt almost exclusively with cottage conflicts and tensions." Women's group meetings took on the characteristics of a family model where individuals provided mutual support, while the men's groups were more political: "In the female model cottage, women commonly held hands. When a female inmate received a setback in her life, other inmates consoled her while she cried. Such support was almost nonexistent in the male program."[19] Further, the authors observed that: ". . . the men had a political consciousness strikingly absent among the women."

> These male and female differences evolved into radically different interpretations of the Just Community ideal. . . . over time, we came to call these two variations the communitarian and political approaches of the program. The communitarian (women's) program assumed a solidarity between inmates and staff.[20]

The authors did not attribute these differences solely to sex differences, they speculated that other factors were at work, such as the personality of the respective leaders, situation elements, and other factors. However, their findings are perfectly consistent with what we would expect from men and women, given Gilligan's findings.

Biology or Socialization?

If one accepts the notion that women and men view morality differently, the next question is, "Why?" Are there biological influences that "pre-wire" women to be more caring and affiliative, or are the differences observed purely the result of socialization? In the previous chapter, several findings indicated that the differences in moral reasoning are not simply environmen-

tally caused. Women's brains develop in such a way that predicts more integrative, communicative perceptions will emerge. Brain chemistry indicates
that women may be more sensitive to emotional cues. Women's reproductive
realities demand an evolutionary preference for "caring" responses. Of course,
socialization plays a large part as well. Girls are taught to be "nice," while boys
are taught to be "strong." Even with the massive social changes that have taken
place in the last 30 years, these patterns have not changed substantially.

Throughout history, women have always been believed to have a different moral sense than men; however, the specific view of women has changed
from time to time. Early Greeks, for instance, viewed women as amoral (like
children). This belief was still dominant in Lombroso's work. A competing
view, however, was that women were better than men—morally, at least.
Women were viewed in pre-Jacksonian America, as the keepers of the hearth,
and the guardians of societal morality. Morris and Gelsthorpe use an 1891
quote to exemplify this belief:

> The most obvious answer is that they are better morally. The care
> and nurture of children has been their lot in life for untold cen-
> turies; the duties of maternity have perpetually kept alive a certain
> number of unselfish instincts; these instincts have become part and
> parcel of woman's natural inheritance, and, as a result of possess-
> ing them to a larger extent than man, she is less disposed to
> crime.[21]

Morris and Gelsthorpe use this quote critically to argue that women have historically been stereotyped as a "Madonna" figure and this stereotyping con-
stricts them and has no scientific validity. Interestingly, though, the quote is
remarkably close to current findings from biological and psychological
research; only some of which have been reviewed in the last chapter. The fact
that the same views were also expressed in 1891 does not necessarily make
them wrong.

There is strong resistance to the idea that women are "naturally" predisposed to a moral orientation that is relationship-based and results in less criminality among women than men. Messerschmidt,[22] for instance, criticizes Steffensmeier and Allen's argument that women's moral choices constrain them
from behavior that could be harmful to others: "Because women are bound
more intimately into a network of interpersonal ties, their moral decisions are
more influenced by empathy and compassion, and this ethic of care constructs nonviolence and suggests that serious predatory crime is outside
women's moral boundaries."[23] Messerschmidt argues that these authors
"ignore the fact that there exists no scholarship that demonstrates that the
greater conformity of women is a function of their special virtues."[24] To arrive
at the conclusion that there is no scholarship that indicates women and men
have different virtue (morality) is to completely ignore the work of Gilligan,
Chodorow, and many others.

Messerschmidt then uses examples of female gang members to show that women are not always empathetic and nurturant. For example, he provides a quote from a girl gang member gloating about "fucking up" another girl and exhibiting pride in how bad the victim looked. He argues that a theory that proposes women are more naturally caring and empathetic would have to see this gang member as "simply defective and freakish, not authentically female." One might respond, however, that his use of language acts to sensationalize the opposing view and detract from a neutral discussion of the meaning of such violence. The girl does represent a "freakish" view of violence if one uses "freakish" in a purely statistical sense instead of the connotation of stigma that Messerschmidt implies. How many women in the United States or any other country would endorse such a view (but how many men)? The girl is also "defective"—if one uses the term in a value neutral way rather than the condemnatory tone that Messerschmidt places upon it. Such a glorification of violence is not healthy—either emotionally for the individual expressing it, or societally. Is the girl "authentically female"?—of course, but she is a female that most probably has grown up in a societal environment that endorses and encourages violent responses, one that provides no hope or support for the future; and a familial environment that devalued her worth, and quite possibly subjected her to emotional neglect and physical and/or sexual abuse. Why could such an environment not overcome a "natural" predisposition to caring and empathy?

Other research that explores the role of the conscience in criminal decisionmaking may not necessarily focus on sex/gender differences, but is relevant to this discussion. For instance, Trasler assumes that criminal choices result from inadequacies in the functioning of conscience. One's conscience develops through a process of learning—parents or others teach what is right and wrong and the child internalizes the lessons through feelings of guilt and shame. Eventually, external punishments are not necessary to deter wrong behaviors, the individual's internal conscience will be sufficient since the individual will avoid the behavior to avoid the guilt and shame.[25] Wilson and Hernnstein emphasize classical as well as operant conditioning in criminal choice, and view conscience as a punisher.[26] They explain that those who have trouble learning are more resistant to social conditioning and thus would have to have more enriched parental influences to develop a conscience. Arbuthnot and Faust provide some reasons why the socialization of the family may fail to establish moral guidelines (and conscience) in the individual.

- Inconsistencies in terms of why parents reinforce certain actions and in terms of the roles and amounts of responsibility they permit the children in the family.

- Limitations in the reasoning skills of the parents themselves.

- A lack of sufficient cognitive awareness or sensitivity on the part of the parents to respond to their children at a level that the children can appreciate and that will advance the child's reasoning abilities.[27]

If it is true that men are more likely to emphasize rules and women are more likely to emphasize relationships, their beliefs about right and wrong may be different. If their beliefs about right and wrong are different, it is at least possible that their conscience will be sensitive to different behaviors and the guilt and shame that is supposed to deter criminal choice will operate differently for men than for women.

Also, if conscience develops through attachments (i.e., one must have an emotional connection in order for the learning to take place consistently and effectively), and biological research indicates that men are "pre-wired" for autonomy, and psychological literature suggests that the male sex-role identity develops through separation; then, arguably men would be predisposed to have more difficulty developing a conscience. Further, other biological research indicates that men may be more prone to learning disabilities, which would also imply greater difficulty in social conditioning. What is being developed here, of course, is the idea that men are predisposed to crime because of biological, psychological, and socialization influences that act as barriers to the development of a conscience—and women's biological, psychological, and socialization influences are congruent with and, indeed, strengthen the development of a conscience.

Morash is one of the few that address sex/gender differences in morality and delinquency/criminality.[28] Morash points out that a strict reading of Kohlberg would imply that men should commit less crime than women (because they have higher scores). Then she discusses the possibility that the key to explaining lower crime rates for women may be "empathy." That is, their clustering on the relationship stage may imply a higher priority on empathy and caring for others; that, in turn, acts to insulate them against criminal choices: "The construct that is a likely candidate as the girls' special achievement involves affective empathy—the capacity to share the feelings of another person."[29] She cites a wide range of findings that indicate that adolescent girls are more likely to display affective empathy than boys.

> Because empathy and a recognition of oneself as a cause of another person's distress is often translated into guilt, and because both empathy and guilt are highly related to prosocial behavior . . . girls "may have a more highly developed affective base for prosocial behavior than do males." By this logic, girls would have a more highly developed affective motivation to avoid delinquent behavior that hurts other individuals—although, consistent with empirical research, they would not be expected to differ in levels of involvement in victimless offenses, such as the status offenses and drug and alcohol use.[30]

Morash points out, therefore, that conscience may be derived from different mechanisms in men and women. While women's conscience may be engaged through empathy (feeling sorry about hurting a victim), men's may be more likely to be engaged over issues of rulebreaking/lawbreaking or higher order principles of morality (such as altruism). Since few of us evidently reach the higher stages, men's consciences tend to be keyed to Stage 4 concerns: rules and laws. Further, women's affiliation-based conscience may be more crime/delinquency preventative than one based on rules or laws.[31]

Of course there are women who do commit crimes. There could be several explanations: first, is the simple fact of human variability within groups. For every predisposition or statistical probability there are those who deviate—in biological characteristics as well as psychological or sociological. Second, it may be that those women who commit crime are more likely to come from backgrounds that are so dysfunctional, they overcome biological predispositions to develop an affiliative conscience.

In a slightly different argument, their crime might represent a type of misapplied need for affiliation. Gilfus, for instance, looks at crime by women as often a type of caring (they commit crime for someone or get involved in crime through relationships).[32] She speculates why female criminals also tend to experience a high likelihood of abuse by partners by arguing that childhood neglect and abuse may "socialize women to adopt a tenacious commitment to caring for anyone who promises love, material success, and acceptance." Arnold also speculates on the caring component of women's crime. She reports on interviews with African-American women in prison who report that they started to steal at a young age to get things for their younger brothers and sisters.[33] Obviously, this speculation that women's criminal motivations are different and more consistent with an affiliative conscience is rudimentary and does not apply to all women offenders.

It is, of course, not necessary to the above argument to conclude that men are never affiliative or cannot develop an affiliation-based conscience. Renzetti and Curran point out that fathers who have had primary care of children said such experience made them "more sensitive, less self-centered, and more complete as human beings."[34] The point is that if men are raised with traditional sex-role definitions, their law-abidingness comes from a decision to not break the rules, rather than a decision that to do so would hurt or damage someone. If they are raised in an environment that sensitizes them to care, then they can and do adapt that type of moral reasoning, as those male subjects in Gilligan's research did.

One may choose to accept the findings from biological research (that finds brain chemistry differences predispose women to emphasize affiliation), psychological research (that proposes gender identification leads to "connectness" and affiliation for women and autonomy for men), or sociological research (that argues girls are socialized to be more sensitive to others while boys are socialized to be self-oriented) to conclude that there may be tendencies in the way men and women view morality that might affect their criminality. Or one might decide that there are interactions between biological predispositions, psychological development, and socialization influence to create these differences.

Application of Moral Development Theory and "Feminine" Justice

As mentioned before, there are examples of correctional interventions that apply Kohlberg's stage theory to offender populations. Findings indicate that such interventions can raise the moral stage scores of offenders. Of course, stage scores are not necessarily related to behavior. In fact, there is only weak evidence that stage scores and behavior are related and many other factors influence behavioral decisions.[35] It is exceedingly difficult to measure how beliefs influence behavior; attempts to measure such an interaction have extreme problems of validity and meaning discussed in the first chapter.[36] However, there are fairly consistent findings that delinquents and offenders exhibit lower scores and that their scores can be raised. Cognitive approaches target the reasoning of offenders and provide opportunities (typically in groups or classroom settings) for offenders to challenge their thinking and be exposed to higher level reasoning.[37]

Even more common cognitive approaches are consistent with the idea that offenders need to change their thinking patterns relating to such things as egocentricity and responsibility.[38] Laufer and Day[39] and Pollock[40] review correctional interventions that utilize a moral development approach. These interventions are directed to those who have already come to the attention of the criminal justice system. More effective intervention, of course, could occur before thinking patterns are set. The theorists who employ longitudinal research have consistently maintained that crime prevention seems to be linked to early childhood development and better parenting practices.

Leahy[41] shows how parenting practices can affect the development of moral judgment in children. Specifically, he found that parental practices that emphasized unilateral respect or that were nonnurturant were related to a lower level of moral judgment. Farrington[42] reviews studies of early intervention efforts affecting long-term delinquency and mentions that, for instance, head start programs lead to better school performance and long-term reductions in delinquency. Andrews and Bonta[43] look at studies that identify links between egocentrism and delinquency, and review intervention efforts that indicate it is possible to improve empathy and decrease egocentrism among school children thereby preventing some amount of delinquency. Other research finds a correlation between single-parent households and delinquency, especially for boys, and some authors speculate that what might be occurring is the single parent has less time to "parent," meaning to provide supervision and to teach moral values.[44] While it is no doubt true that supervision has something to do with the higher potential for delinquency, it is also possible that something more is at work here (especially if the findings regarding daughters are true). What may happen in single-mother homes is that supervision levels are lower (a working mother without help is simply less able to provide the surveillance and control that two parents could provide); but also, the male child must separate from her as part of sex identity formation and has no male role model (father) to follow, therefore turning to the street for such models. This is consistent with Chodorow and earlier theories, such as Parsons'. The themes here are definitely not groundbreaking—most would agree that all things being equal (i.e., no violence or abuse, emotional neglect or belittlement from either parent and a relatively healthy interaction between them), children are better off with two parents for emotional and moral development.

"Feminine Justice"

Obviously the idea of a feminine or masculine justice is simply a rhetorical device to isolate and emphasize principles. There is increasing literature and thought, however, that indicate different approaches to justice exist: while some characteristics might be defined as more consistent with Gilligan's "different voice" or Noddings' idea of "caring," others are more typical of the Western Judeo-Christian tradition of retribution and rights. The "feminine" justice idea has been proposed by a number of writers.[45]

"Restorative justice" for instance is a current theme of many different types of programs. However, they all have in common the idea of meeting needs rather than merely punishing. Many approaches emphasize that restoration must address both the victim and the offender. The other major theme is including the offender in the community, rather than excluding the offender from the community. This would include having the offender be involved in restoring the victim and, in general, keeping the offender as part of the community.

"Peacekeeping justice" is another similar approach. Quinney argues that: ". . . the criminal justice system in this country is founded on violence. It is a system that assumes that violence can be overcome by violence, evil by evil . . . This resistance [to crime] must be in compassion and love, not in terms of the violence that is being resisted."[46] McDermott connects peacemaking justice ideas and "feminine justice," as well as other threads of feminist thought.[47] She identifies the following principles as representing some of the thoughts of peacemaking justice:

- Without loving and compassionate individuals, we cannot achieve justice and peace.

- We are tied to other human beings and also to the environment.

- The nonviolent ethic is one of responsiveness (compassion, forgiveness, and love). From love and compassion flow understanding, service, and justice.

- Responsiveness requires equality.

- The nonviolent ethic of human responsiveness assumes that human action is motivated by emotion as well as reason, and that knowledge is both rational and emotional.[48]

Others have also described the idea of peacemaking justice.[49] One related concept is the idea of reintegrative shaming. Low-crime societies, according to Braithwaite, are characterized by communitarianism and interdependency, largely because these societies are able to employ "shaming" as a method of behavior control.[50] Braithwaite argues that shaming still has a place—even in modern, industrialized society. In fact, he argues that individuals have more roles and interdependencies today and, thus, more opportunity to be "shamed" within each of these respective roles (i.e., family member, worker, friend, and so on).[51]

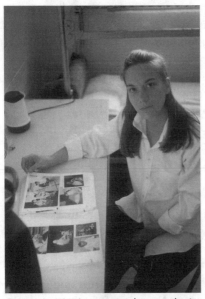

Restorative justice approaches emphasize that restoration must address both the victim and the offender. *Photo credit: Mark C. Ide.*

There are obvious connections between the idea of reintegrative shaming and the sex/gender differences discussed above and in other portions of this book. Braithwaite also notes the sex/gender differential in crime and explains it by the greater interdependency of females upon families and then spouses. He cites studies that indicate females are significantly more concerned about labeling than males; girls and women may care more about what others think: "Reintegrative shaming in the family is more effective with girls because, as suggested by the control theory literature on female delinquency, they are more attached to their parents, and more concerned to be respected by their parents, than are boys."[52] While men may react to confrontation about criminal behavior with rage, women will be more likely to feel shame, especially in those cultures that promote an ideal of masculinity that encourages unconnectedness and unconcern for others.

It is not necessary for our purposes to identify and isolate differences between the feminine justice idea, peacekeeping justice, restorative justice, or reintegrative shaming. The point is that they all tend to view a "caring" approach as different from the retributive or punitive approach of our traditional justice system, and therefore, intentionally or not, recognize a different morality that might be defined as "feminine."

Wilson: The Moral Sense

Some of those interested in answering questions of criminality have rediscovered the relevance of morality to such inquiries. Wilson, for instance, proposes an innate "moral sense" that transcends historical or cultural influences, arguing that all societies abhor murder, incest, and abandoning children.[53] Further, sentiments of sympathy, fairness, self-control, and duty seem to be prevalent across all cultures. He argues that some of these themes have been removed from the moral arena in today's culture, and we suffer for it: "But self-control is today much less likely to be defined as a moral question than is sympathy or equity, even though many problems of contemporary society, including smoking, drug addiction, predatory sexuality, and much street crime are at root problems of impulsivity."[54]

Wilson argues that criminality is immorality, and immorality is largely the result of impulsiveness combined with aggressiveness and a lack of empathy. Wilson concludes that there is a biological basis to immorality through the traits of impulsivity and aggression.[55]

> Just what this heritable trait [impulsivity] may be is far from clear. Among the leading candidates are some of the neurotransmitters (the chemical messengers of the brain), especially dopamine and serotonin, and the enzyme, monoamine oxidase, that flushes used neurotransmitters out of the gap between brain cells. People with low levels of monoamine oxidase (MAO) tend to be more impulsive than people with high levels of that enzyme, suggesting that the stimulation they receive from dopamine flowing from one brain cell to another is not ended by MAO.[56]

Continuing the argument, he proposes that self-control comes from a conscience, and a conscience develops through attachment: "Conscience, like sympathy, fairness, and self control, arises not out of repressed lust and rage but out of our innate desire for attachment, and thus it acquires its strongest development when those attachments are the strongest."[57] He argues that this desire and need for attachment is innate: "That desire is evident in the instinctively prosocial behavior of the newborn infant and in the instinctively caring response that parents make to that behavior."[58]

The relevance of sex/gender differences and Gilligan's work on moral development to Wilson's theory is obvious, and he describes her findings and others.[59] Wilson argues that the innate aggressiveness of men, and the psychological development of women that emphasizes relationship-building rather than dominance, are responsible for observed behavioral differences.

> Through prolonged involvement in play where sustaining relationships is more important than managing dominance, girls tend to acquire both a moral orientation that emphasizes caring and harmony and a non-hierarchical orientation toward the organization of common undertakings.[60]

He points out that cultural differences can also be observed. Asian business-men seek more consensus building, they are more likely to approve of pro-tective business practices, and do not emphasize rights and contractual oblig-ations in the same manner as Western business. However, gender differences exist similarly in all cultures, indicating that sex differences exist apart from culture.[61] Wilson proposes the differences in morality as follows—women will respond to issues of distributive justice with equality, men with equity; concerning issues of human suffering, women will respond with empathy (sympathy), and men with solutions.[62] It is not inconsistent with his proposi-tion (although he did not propose this directly) that when confronted with issues of criminal justice, women will respond with restorative or peace-keeping justice solutions, and men will respond with retributive justice.

One might quibble with Wilson's facts and some of his arguments.[63] In fact, contrary to his use of incest as an example of behavior that is cross-cul-turally abhorrent, incest has been documented as culturally acceptable in cer-tain societies, and his evidence that infanticide is exceptional is not extreme-ly persuasive since female infants have been the recipients of culturally accepted infanticide historically as well as fairly recently. He ends his chapter on gender differences with barely a mention of domestic violence, the greater general aggressiveness of men, other evidence of moral differences in women, or making much of the connection between relationship differences between men and women and morality and crime.

He might also be criticized for proposing a theory biased by Western ego-centrism (similar to those who criticized Kohlberg), since his chapter on uni-versalism basically describes Western philosphical thought in the emphasis on equality and freedom. One might even describe some portions of his dis-cussion as sexist; he continually refers to *men* as free, and *man* as enjoying freedoms; in fact, the female pronoun is not used at all throughout the whole chapter. However Wilson's work provides much evidence that the sex/gen-der differential in criminal behavior can be understood through accepting certain biological, as well as culturally induced, differences.

Naffine: The Feminist View

Naffine presents a different integrated view of gender, morality, and crime. She de-emphasizes any biological component, and instead offers a decidedly feminist worldview. This is an extremely insightful, critical view of traditional and current criminological theory. She also reviews Western philo-sophical thought and defines it as essentially misogynistic. As far back as the Greeks, women's morality was devalued as arising from their inferiority and weakness rather than from any essential moral nature. Immanuel Kant (1724-1804) identified morality with rationality, and since women were not per-ceived as rational, their morality was perceived to arise through their emotion and weaker nature. Most historical perceptions of women portrayed them as amoral, as children, and unmasculine in their lack of rationality and display-ing emotion rather than reason.[64]

Naffine argues that these views of women run as a thread throughout ear-lier criminology theories. For instance, she argues that Cohen discounted altruism as inconsistent with the American pursuit of success; and Suther-land, who bemoaned the lack of emphasis on altruism in American society and identified this lack as a factor in the prevalence of crime, failed to recog-nize the similarity of altruism with his description of "niceness" as part of the socialization of girls. Sutherland and Cressey cite, as an example of coopera-tive living, pre-modern China, but make no comment regarding the spirit of cooperation in women in their own society.[65] Naffine argues that this blind-ness to gender, even when it is central to an argument such as altruism or cooperativeness, was evidence of the theorists essential sexism and their unwillingness to grant that women's law-abidingness should have been an integral part of their study: "With the single word 'niceness,' the lawfulness of women is reduced to a vapid thing. It is a matter of absence of choice (super-vision) and conditioning (into anti-criminal behavior patterns). It is stripped of any positive moral content."[66]

Naffine also notes that Parsons identified the women's role in moral development as one of socializing men. She argues that he saw the mother's role as to socialize the next generation, including the socialization of ethical behavior, but instead boys see the "goodness" of mothers as weak (since the dominant society disvalues her) and therefore rebels against niceness creat-ing the "strong tendency for boyish behavior to run in antisocial . . . direc-tions."[67] She further notes that Parsons viewed Western society as suffering from a negative association between moral behavior and femininity, and since femininity is viewed as weakness, societal definitions devalue moral behavior as well.[68]

Naffine proposes that a fruitful avenue of exploration is hinted at in the findings of control theory and Gilligan.[69] Women are more conforming than men, but that conformance does not necessarily arise from dependency, help-lessness, and weakness; rather, like Hirschi's original descriptions of the con-forming male, women can be hardworking, responsible, and rational in their pursuit of goals. Adding Gilligan's findings, women generally are more tied into relationships and care about others' needs. Their commitment is not nec-essarily to principles but to dependent children. Naffine worries that this premise may be attacked because it accepts that women are different from men in their compassion and their conception of morality. Indeed, many fem-inists do reject the notion that women are essentially different from men, but after a careful consideration of the research, the conclusion is extremely hard to argue against.

SO WHAT? POLICY IMPLICATIONS

Perhaps every work should be required to end with a chapter titled: So what? In criminological inquiry, hopefully the "so what?" has something to do with crime prevention. The thesis of this book is that criminological theorizing has been handicapped because it has been largely a male enterprise. Early male theorists had a thinly veiled attraction to their delinquent subjects, not surprisingly since the delinquent represents hypermasculinity and men and women both respond to the allure because this culture socializes us to see masculine characteristics as ideal.

Delinquency and crime hurt people. Graffitti damages. Theft destroys trust. Physical assaults and robbery result in injury. The most pristine white-collar crime still has a victim; even indirectly. Crime is not "glamorous" (as Cohen described it), it is not fun (at least not for everyone concerned), and it is not romantic (as the media portrays it). We have a surfeit of crime because American culture is still largely masculine: more than 40 years after Cohen described girls as everything contrary to the American culture of success.

Feminists have added immeasurably to the understanding of how dominant and traditional criminology ignored one-half of the population, but in many of their attempts to rectify the situation they were too quick to assume that women could be just like men, given half a chance. Simon and Adler were the strongest proponents of the view that men and women were equal in their motivation and inclinations toward crime, given equal opportunities, but even the more radical/critical feminists seem to defend women's right and ability to be as "bad" as men.[70]

Feminists and many others vociferously resist findings from biological research, including those related to sex differences, probably because of the legacy of those views and the potential for abuse.[71] Unfortunately, biological theories that found "natural" differences have been wrong in the past, so it is obviously an understandable position to take that today's biological theories could be no more correct than Lombroso's theory that criminal women were biological mutants, or some of the other ridiculous presumptions throughout the early 1900s. However, it may be just as ridiculously wrong to argue against biological differences. After all, no one seriously argues some biological differences, e.g., that women menstruate, that they get pregnant, give birth, lactate, and that all these bodily functions come with attendant hormonal and other physical changes. Why would it be inconsistent to assume that there are also brain chemistry differences that have evolved to ensure the survival of the species?

There are little data to indicate that women do act exactly like men, in any culture. This does not mean that they are "naturally" as society represented them. Historically, criminal women were demonized, then viewed as helpless. The cultural ideas regarding appropriate femininity continue to change. Feinman wrote:

> Beliefs concerning women's role and place, stemming from Judeo-Christian theology, are deeply rooted in our culture. Women who conform as pure, obedient daughters, wives, and mothers benefit men and society; the Madonna's are honored. Women who do not conform threaten men and society; the whores are punished.[72]

It could be argued, however, that the ideal of femininity is changing. One might conclude that today's society views women as perfectly capable in economic and social spheres. However, these views are never homogenous. In the same time period that we have women generals and politicians, we have a Southern religious group that has mandated that followers subscribe to the Bible's teaching that women "submit" to their husband.[73] Modern sex-role theory is beyond the scope of this book; the point made here is that images of women are not reality, but in reacting against old sex-role images, we should not ignore true differences.

Listening to the voices of women themselves—whether they be gang members, women in prison, or even other women in the system (such as police officers or correctional officers)—one comes to the conclusion that women's worldviews continue to be different from men's. Babies still seem to be more important to most (but not all) women, and the fiercest gang member and female police officer may have this in common. Women do seem to talk about relationships more. They do seem to be more attuned to others. They seem to feel more guilt regarding their crimes.

Furthermore, it may be a waste of energy to continue to argue about the relative influences of biology and environment. Most of the researchers in the field recognize that both play a part; even strongly sociological researchers, albeit a bit grudgingly, admit some influence. Note that most research has now come to some agreement that delinquency/criminality originates in childhood (most typically), that it stems from biological predispositions (such as poor conditionability and low impulse control), as well as familial influences (poor discipline, neglectful or abusive parenting), and that social factors (poverty, racism, presence of social disorganization) exacerbate these pre-conditions and lead to a greater likelihood of delinquency/criminality.

One current "catalog" of the factors in crime offers the following:

- A history of early childhood problem behaviors and poor parental child-rearing techniques, harsh and inconsistent discipline, school failure, failure to learn moral reasoning, empathy, and problem-solving.

- Certain neurotransmitter imbalances such as low serotonin, hormone imbalances such as high testosterone, central nervous system deficiencies such as frontal or temporal lobe dysfunction, and autonomic nervous system variations such as unusual reactions to anxiety.

- The presence of alcohol and many illegal drugs, as well as some toxins such as lead, head injuries, pregnancy, or birth complications.

- Personality characteristics such as impulsivity, insensitivity, physical or nonverbal orientation, and risktaking.

- Thinking patterns that focus on trouble, toughness, smartness, excitement, fate, and autonomy, and an exaggerated sense of "manliness."

- Chronic physiological arousal and frequent experience of negative emotions.

- Association with others who are engaged in and approve of criminal behavior.

- Weaker attachments to people, less involvement in conventional activities, less to lose from committing crime, and weaker beliefs in the moral validity of law.[74]

Additionally, they cite a number of structural factors:

- Economic modernization and development create higher rates of property crimes, due to routine activities and criminal opportunities.

- Economic inequality is associated with higher rates of violence.

- Cultures that emphasize the goal of material success at the expense of adhering to legitimate means.

- Neighborhoods with poverty, frequent residential mobility, and family disruption.

- Poverty, urban environments, racial discrimination, and social isolation.

- Media dissemination of techniques and rationalizations that are favorable to law violation.

- Societal stigmatization of deviants.

- Societies wherein some people control others have higher crime rates than societies in which people control and are controlled by others in approximately equal amounts.[75]

Thus, this list, like several others, includes biological, familial, and societal influences. As stated previously, most criminologists today accept some amount of biological influence in crime causation, and there is widespread agreement that the "answer" to crime must be found in an integrated theory that addresses predeterminors, structural constraints, and opportunity factors. In fact, the only contribution to the discussion added by our review herein has been to (hopefully) more clearly explicate the role of sex and gender in the predisposing conditions that lead to delinquency or criminality.

Paradigms and Policy Implications

Recall that the first chapter discussed the influence of values and paradigms on social science research. Paradigms and beliefs also affect policies. It will be the contention of this final section that beliefs and attitude shifts concerning women have been detrimental, at least insofar as the criminal justice system is concerned. Historically, women experienced perhaps less formal punitive treatment from the justice system, unless she was a promiscuous juvenile.[76] Treatment is also related to race: evidently white women are likely to be diverted to private treatment facilities while African-American, Hispanic, or Native American women are formally institutionalized. Historically, most adult women were less likely to be incarcerated; however, today that is not the case. Women are much more likely to be incarcerated today than in the past.[77]

Treatment of women by the formal justice system has changed, arguably, because of a change in the image of women. If public perception has adopted the idea that women can be just as bad as men, then it is predictable that criminal women will be sentenced as such. Yet if one looks closely, their crimes, criminal motivations, and histories are not the same. Women in prison are more likely to be drug addicted, they are more likely to have been sexually and physically victimized, more likely to be responsible for small children, and more likely to be in prison for a non-violent crime.[78]

It appears that women are now viewed like men, and this equalization has translated to policy—but this policy is not helpful to women offenders, nor to society. There is arguably nothing essentially redeeming nor rehabilitative about a prison sentence. In fact, women have historically had lower recidivism rates than men, even though they received more so-called lenient treatment. One might argue that the increased tendency to use incarceration instead of other correctional alternatives will lead to more entrenched female criminality, as well as ripple effects for the children of women in prison.

There is also the possibility that women will be punished and controlled because of their role in reproduction. Early eugenics movements targeted women in broad social policies designed to control population growth of "undesirables."[79] This may be happening again, given the recent proposals to tie welfare benefits to agreements not to have children, incarcerating drug-using women because they are pregnant, and making women take Norplant as a condition of probation. These issues are extremely controversial; the balance between the legal rights of mother and child are extremely problematic and central to some of the policies. For instance, Norplant has been suggested only for those women who consistently abuse their children despite various forms of formal sanctions. While reproductive freedom is something that is essential to a free democracy, it is understandable why some would believe that an individual who cannot seem to change her behavior should not have any more children—at least during the period of punishment.[80] Similar arguments attach to the issue of imposed drug treatment or criminal penalties for women who abuse drugs during their pregnancy. One observation that can be made, however, is that typically the absolute "worst case" is used as an example. While there are women who use drugs throughout the course of their pregnancy and do not care about the effects of such drugs on their infant, there are also women who try to stop or at least reduce their drug use, frantically look for treatment alternatives, and are provided no assistance from the state. Both women may be subject to any severe criminal penalties imposed against drug-using mothers.

Retributive versus Restorative Justice

As mentioned before, two competing orientations to justice are retribution and a "kinder, gentler" justice that emphasizes restoration and community. A retributive (punitive) orientation that accounts for the increase in imprisonment, the increasing numbers of waivers to adult courts and lowering the age when such waivers can take place, the rapidity with which we execute, and the tendency to apply harsher and harsher sentences—even capital punishment—to drug offenders. Contrarily, there is also a trend for restorative justice and peacekeeping justice solutions—mediation, victim-offender restitution conferences, community conferencing, and so on—that promote caring rather than retribution.[81]

The increasing incarceration of women is an example of the former; halfway houses for women with their children is an example of the latter. There is good evidence to indicate that offenders are more likely to respond to those interventions that promote affiliation rather than those that stigmatize and banish. Research also indicates that early intervention is more efficacious than punishment. The very same social policy implications emerge from biological research, longitudinal research, the general theory of crime, and the social support theory. In order to reduce crime, families need to be strengthened. This involves broad societal policies that allow all families to earn a living wage and avoid the stress and disintegration of the family unit that poverty creates. Racism must be addressed since it blocks opportunities, creates different treatment by the formal law enforcers, and promotes segregated housing that acts to isolate and polarize communities. State intervention in the family is essential when that family is dysfunctional—however, it must be done better than it has been done in the past. Children must be saved when parents are abusive or neglectful, but the "cure" (foster or institutional care) cannot be worse than the "cause." As many policymakers and researchers are pointing out, we will spend money on the same group of children—we can spend money early when there is some chance to give them the skills and emotional support necessary to become productive citizens, or we can spend it later on probation, juvenile institutions, and prisons.

Wright and Wright argue that a punitive response to juvenile crime is counterproductive and resources should be directed to early prevention efforts.[82] They propose that social policy decisionmakers should direct resources to help in the following areas: prenatal and early childhood health care, early intervention, comprehensive family policy, family treatment for troubled youth, and parent training. They also point out, however, the potential dangers of state intervention and the possibility that help may result in worse results than no help. Thus, they argue for programs that address the family structure and help to strengthen the family, as opposed to those that direct attention to the individual child, which may potentially stigmatize and lead to self-fulfilling prophecies.[83] Other evidence exists that early programs, such as violence prevention programs in school, can help to reduce delinquency and crime rates.[84]

Some current policy decisions are contrary to the conclusions of this review of literature. Increased imprisonment is unlikely to help reduce criminal choices in any long-term way (although obviously it acts to incapacitate). Furthermore, it rarely makes the individual a better person. Some recent commentators argued that orphanages or congregate care facilities for children born into welfare families would help solve the problem of welfare in the United States. That solution flies in the face of all literature on early bonding and attachment (and incidentally arises from a mistaken belief that welfare is being disproportionately abused in the United States). Sending welfare mothers to work with no provisions made for good child care will probably lead to the delinquency of their children, given the research concerning the correlation between delinquency and single heads of households. Sending more women to prison rather than using community alternatives also disrupts families and affects children.

What is needed to reduce crime is to emphasize and encourage "feminine" values. Messner and Rosenfeld[85] argue that the American dream of financial riches with little emphasis on legitimate ways to achieve it, and the devaluation of non-economic functions, the family, and other institutions has created the crime problem. They argue that large-scale social changes are necessary to shift cultural emphases to the family. Interestingly, nowhere in this book are sex/gender issues discussed, although, obviously, there is a connection between the point that the culture devalues family life. One might argue that our culture devalues family because it devalues women.

Vaux, as well, argues for large-scale societal changes to provide more social support for the family, and through the family, the individual.[86] This argument goes even further than our isolated interest in crime and argues that social support is the key element in health, recovery, mental health, and coping. Social support includes intimate relationships, social networks, and communities, and social support helps to provide emotional support and task assistance, as well as the mechanism to share values, expectations, social contacts, and information.[87] Cullen also believes that the lack of social support is criminogenic, and increasing social support would be a crime preventative.[88]

Each of Cullen's propositions comes with an obvious plan for action: "The more support a family provides, the less likely it is that a person will engage in crime" involves giving assistance to families so that they may provide support. It is an interesting test of the idea that social support will reduce crime.[89]

Walsh discusses the necessity for improving prenatal and perinatal care, hospital practices that encourage early mother-child bonding, and family leave policies that assist the family to provide for the early attachment needs of infants.[90] According to authors who propose them, these are crime-control strategies because they increase the likelihood of children developing healthy attachments. From the infant to the elderly, research shows that humans need attachments and are healthier when they care for and are cared for by others. Not at all coincidentally, this description, unfortunately, describes more women's lives than it does men's.

CONCLUSION

Wilson and Herrnstein propose that a theory of crime ought to fit the following facts:

- Crime is committed disproportionately by males.

- Crime is perpetrated disproportionately by 15-to-25-year-olds.

- Crime is committed disproportionately by unmarried people.

- Crime is committed disproportionately by people living in large cities.

- Crime is committed disproportionately by people who have experienced high residential mobility and who live in areas characterized by high residential mobility.

- Young people who are strongly attached to their school are less likely to engage in crime.

- Young people who have high educational and occupational aspirations are less likely to engage in crime.

- Young people who do poorly at school are more likely to engage in crime.

- Young people who are strongly attached to their parents are less likely to engage in crime.

- Young people who have friendships with criminals are more likely to engage in crime themselves.

- People who believe strongly in the importance of complying with the law are less likely to violate the law.

- Placement in the bottom of the class structure increases the rates of offending.

- Crime rates have been increasing.[91]

Other than the last statement, these correlates are still present. Many are speculating on the reasons behind the apparent recent decrease in crime. In 1996, the National Criminal Victimization Survey reported that violent crime was down 10 percent and the rate of property crime fell by eight percent. Decreases are also reported in the Uniform Crime Reports and have been for the last several years. Some attribute this to the increased use of prisons, some to the demographic age group known as the "baby boom" aging out of crime, some to the better economy, other explanations may be target hardening and better police protections. The macro-level explanations for crime rates will always be speculative—there are simply too many variables that may affect criminal activity.

This book has set out to address only the first fact that Wilson and Herrnstein mentioned; however, the reader may have found relevant data to address other correlates to criminal choice as well. Certain consistencies and connections have become clear: sex differences predispose men to be more likely to have low arousal levels and poor conditionability. They are more subject to learning disorders, such as ADD and hyperactivity. They are more likely to have poor impulse control, and also exhibit greater aggressive tendencies. Women, on the other hand, generally have higher verbal skills and thus are better at communication and sensitive to emotional cues. They are engaged in reproductive tasks (pregnancy and lactation) that require them to be other-directed. It is not a stretch to consider that evolution has influenced affiliative traits to be predominant in the female of the species because it would be essential that mothers want to care for their young (i.e., nurse them and make sure they are safe), while it is not necessarily essential for fathers to do so. Thus, women and men are "naturally" different in their predispositions and personality constructs; women are generally more affiliative and men are more autonomous.

Prosocial choices stem from self-control and self-control is most probably influenced by a conscience. Developing a healthy conscience may be due to having loving, caring attachments that also provide discipline. Because of a variety of sex differences in *general*, the *predisposition* of men and women leads to a greater likelihood that men will choose crime, especially victim-harming crime. Placed in social settings where violence is tolerated, social networks are weak, and formal social supports are non-existent, men are more likely than women to make criminal choices; however, women in such environments are more likely than those women who live in more supportive environments to make criminal choices.

To prevent crime, we should increase the affiliation capacity of at-risk youth, meaning the capacity to empathize and care for others—in effect this means we need to make men think and act more like women—at least insofar as moral development is concerned. We can do this by improving the economics that hold families together, providing medical and social services that will ensure healthy development (including parenting training if necessary). We should remove children from resistantly abusive homes, and, provide schooling that accepts and nurtures children, and helps children learn to negotiate and communicate rather than fight and victimize. For those already involved in lawbreaking, official intervention should emphasize restorative rather than retributive goals to reduce the likelihood of future offending. Offenders should be provided opportunities to increase their "caring capacity" through victim restitution, community service, and moral development opportunities rather than be subject to experiences that encourage violence and egocentricism (as do most prisons and juvenile institutions in the United States). Instead of ignoring the sex differences of crime and different tendencies, we can use these facts to understand how to reduce crime.

NOTES

[1]   Maccoby (1985, 270).

[2]   1985, 275. Maccoby notes that some "studies generally find no sex difference in cooperation, sharing, or offering help and sympathy" but argues that these studies used laboratory settings with contrived situations, rather than the naturalistic environment of children at play.

[3]   1965.

[4]   1976, 1981.

[5]   Kohlberg (1976).

[6]   Gilligan (1982).

[7]   Gilligan (1987, 22).

[8]   1982, 19.

[9]   1987, 26.

[10]   Also see Gilligan (1990) and Gilligan et al. (1991).

[11]   1989, 75.

[12]   Held (1987, 114).

[13]   Rothbart, Hanley, and Albert (1986).

[14]   Chodorow (1978).

[15]   Noddings (1984).

16   Cole and Coultrap-McQuin (1992, 3).

17   Scharf and Hickey (1976); also see Hickey and Scharf (1980).

18   Hickey and Scharf (1980, 92).

19   1980, 93.

20   1980, 95.

21   Morris and Gelsthorpe (1981, 52).

22   1997.

23   Steffensmeier and Allen (1988, 73).

24   1997, 67.

25   1980, 10.

26   1985, 35.

27   Arbuthnot and Faust (1981, 10).

28   Morash (1983).

29   1983, 394.

30   1983, 394 (notes omitted).

31   Consider: discussions with offenders in the criminal justice system provide striking patterns of "blaming" among male offenders that target others (either friends who "snitched" on them, or police officers who lied regarding evidence). The outrage expressed by these offenders is that others broke the *rules,* and the fact that there might be a victim somewhere rarely enters the conversation.

32   1992, 86.

33   1995.

34   1992, 156.

35   Arbuthnot and Faust (1981, 101).

36   See, for instance, Menard and Elliott (1994).

37   See, for instance, Gibbs et al. (1976), Arbuthnot (1984), Arbuthnot and Faust (1981), and Arbuthnot and Gordon (1988).

38   Ross, Fabiano, and Ewles (1988), for instance, propose a reasoning-based intervention that teaches offenders to modify impulsive, egocentric thinking. The intervention includes social skills training, lateral thinking (creative problem solving), critical thinking, assertiveness training (teaching nonaggressive, socially appropriate ways to obtain outcomes), negotiations skills training, interpersonal cognitive problem solving (to teach thinking skills for solving interpersonal problems), social perspective training (to teach how to recognize and understand other people's feelings), role-playing, and modeling.
      Walters (1990) argues that criminals have eight thinking patterns that excuse selfish, impulsive behavior:

    1.   mollification (laying blame for irresponsibility on external sources)

    2.   cutoff (the ability to ignore deterrents)

3. entitlement (the idea that one deserves a fun time, a possession, sexual satisfaction, etc.)

4. power orientation (the glorification of strength)

5. sentimentality (a kind of emotional rather than rational reaction to life's possibilities)

6. superoptimism (unrealistic beliefs regarding future schemes)

7. cogntive indolence (mental laziness)

8. discontinuity (difficulty in seeing the connection between actions and consequences).

He proposes cognitive interventions to address these thinking errors, and in this way, is similar to Ross, and other cognitive approaches.

[39] 1983.

[40] 1991.

[41] 1981.

[42] 1991.

[43] 1994.

[44] Wilson (1993, 178) reviews the evidence that boys raised in single-parent (single-mother) headed households are more likely to be delinquent, do poorly in school, and other socialization factors; this association has been observed even when income is controlled (however, no study has been able to run comparisons against father-headed households because there are so few of them). Statistics indicate, interestingly, that girls are not any more likely to be delinquent when raised by a single mother. Wright and Wright (1994, 195-196) find that delinquency is 10 to 15 times more common in single-parent households and review the evidence regarding potential causal factors. They conclude that higher delinquency may result from reduced parental supervision and control, increased susceptibility to peer pressure, poor economic conditions, and/or living in high-crime neighborhoods.

[45] See Heidensohn (1986), Carlen (1989), Daly (1994a, 1994b), McDermott (1994), and Chesney-Lind and Pollock (1995).

[46] Quinney (1991, 12).

[47] 1994.

[48] McDermott (1994, 24).

[49] Gold, Braswell, and McCarthy (1991) and Braswell (1990). Braithwaite (1989, 1993) discusses the impact of "reintegrative shaming" and bringing morality back into punishment. He believes that labeling theory was partially correct as it applied to non-reintegrative shaming efforts of society—by stigmatizing and banishing the offender, the community sets in motion the probability of reoffending. Low-crime societies, according to Braithwaite, are those that utilize community responses to deviance; reintegrative shaming makes the offender responsible for his or her actions, but does not exclude them (a type of accept the person, not the offense approach): "A culture impregnated with high moral expectations of its citizens, publicly expressed, will deliver superior crime control compared with a culture which sees control as achievable by inflicting pain on its bad apples" (1989, 10).

Braithwaite makes the point that reintegrative shaming is consistent with traditional theories of crime. For instance, control theory addresses the notion that those who are bound by "bonds" to society, including attachment, will be less likely to deviate. He argues that attachment and commitment are necessary but not sufficient factors for crime prevention; the added component is that socializers (parents, teachers, etc.) must use these attachments for reintegrative shaming, in effect he is arguing that parenting must include using the relationship to induce guilt and shame over bad behavior, thereby (hopefully) establishing good behavior. This is not too different from learning theory, or even the general theory of crime. Braithwaite argues that shaming is effective only under a family model that also includes approval and love. He cites child development studies that show authoritarian families (using coldness and strictness) and permissive families (characterized by warmth and leniency) were less successful at socialization than authoritative families (described as using warmth and strictness) (1989, 36).

Whether these findings can be abstracted to a societal level is intriguing. He argues that most forms of punishment (banishment, mutilation, killing) are examples of disintegrative shaming, as is modern punishment that banishes the offender to prison and, in effect, invites the offender to feel sorry for himself or herself. Japan is used as an example of a culture that uses shame to control behavior (1989, 61).

[50]   1989, 86.

[51]   1993.

[52]   Braithwaite and Daly (1994, 190).

[53]   1993, 18.

[54]   1993, 86.

[55]   1993, 87.

[56]   1993, 87.

[57]   1993, 108.

[58]   1993, 127.

[59]   For instance, evidently women are more likely to share equally (and men are more likely to share equitably, i.e., take a bigger proportion when they did more work) when it was an ongoing relationship, although there were no differences observed when the task was done with strangers. The conclusion was that women put more emphasis on relationships than rules or justice. Other research cited by Wilson included the finding that as early as age two, girls talk more about feelings and have stronger friendships; boys respond to conflict with fights, girls with social ostracism (1993, 180-181).

[60]   1993, 187.

[61]   1993, 189.

[62]   1993, 188.

[63]   In a point that is admittedly perhaps more a matter of intelletual debate than importance he states that: "In its worst forms, radical individualism is mere self-indulgence; in its best forms it is a life governed by conscience and a cosmopolitan awareness. In its worst forms, extreme communalism is parochial prejudice; in its best forms, it is a life governed by honor and intimate commitments" (1993, 246). It seems that emphasis could be better described here: one might argue that radical individualism is based on rights, duties, rules, universalism, and democracy—in other words, the individualistic approach is gov-

erned by *duty* not *sympathy*. Desert rather than need is emphasized; therefore, the extreme would be "I've got mine, you get yours" unless there is some duty to provide. Extreme communalism would be based on sympathy, commitment, familial connections—in fact, the ideal extends family connections to whole society. The negative side is that individual will is subsumed and utilitarianism prevails. The self-indulgence he mentions as the side effect of extreme individualism is really the absence of either individualism or communalism, since the truly self-indulgent individual would not live up to responsibilities or care for others. Individualism may be the "masculine" model and communalism may be a "feminine" model of human relations, but they both come with moral consequences that Wilson perhaps does not explicate as clearly as he could.

[64]   Naffine (1981, 1987).

[65]   Naffine (1987, 41).

[66]   Naffine (1987, 41).

[67]   Parsons (1954, 306).

[68]   Naffine (1987, 46). Naffine's general critical treatment of Parsons seems somewhat unfair since he did not seem to subscribe to the idea of femininity as weakness, he only pointed out the societal definition, and his observations continue to seem valid.

[69]   1987, 131.

[70]   Naffine (1987, 23), for instance, seems to waver between recognizing the essential differences of men and women, and the argument that women, given similar opportunities, would commit similar crimes. Her only support for the latter view, however, was self-report delinquency studies of minor misbehaviors, truancy, and drinking—hardly evidence of serious victimizing behavior.

[71]   Walsh (1995a, 13) argues that:

> Those who reject the encroachment of biology into sociology envision the ghosts of the likes of Lombroso, Spencer, the eugenicists, and the social Darwinists, along with Hitler's hordes of racial purists, marching silently in the data. Because these folks drank from the same well as modern biosociologists, it does not mean that the well is poisoned.

[72]   1986, 15.

[73]   Southern Baptist announcement, Summer 1998.

[74]   Vold, Bernard, and Snipe (1998, 323).

[75]   1998, 329.

[76]   Chesney-Lind (1997) documents the juvenile system's concern for female sexuality. Family courts and women's courts were methods of social control over immigrant and working-class girls. These girls were incarcerated when they appeared promiscuous, and subjected to physical exams to discover if they were virgins. Juvenile systems continue to be more concerned with wayward girls (Chesney-Lind, 1997, 69).

[77]   Chesney-Lind and Pollock (1995). Chesney-Lind (1997, 147) points out that between 1985 and 1994, women's arrests increased 36.5 percent but their imprisonment increased 202 percent.

[78]   See, for instance Pollock (1998).

[79]   Rafter (1988).

[80]   Bartrum (1992).

[81]   See, for instance, Umbreit (1997, 1998) and Braithwaite and Daly (1994).

[82]   1994.

[83]   1994, 191.

[84]   Evidence Builds: Youth Violence Prevention Programs Working (1997).

[85]   1994.

[86]   1988.

[87]   1988, 20.

[88]   1994.

[89]   Chamlin and Cochran found that there was an inverse relationship between the amount of giving to the United Way and property and violent crime rates (1997).

[90]   1991.

[91]   1985, 44-47.

Bibliography

Adler, F. (1975). *Sisters in Crime: The Rise of the New Female Criminal.* New York, NY: McGraw-Hill.

Adler F. (1981). *The Incidence of Female Criminality in the Contemporary World.* New York, NY: New York University Press.

Adler, F. and R. Simon (eds.) (1979). *The Criminology of Deviant Women.* Boston, MA: Houghton Mifflin Company.

Adler, P. (1993). *Wheeling and Dealing: An Ethnography of an Upper-Level Dealing and Smuggling Community,* Second Edition. New York, NY: Columbia University Press.

Ageton, S. (1983). "The Dynamics of Female Delinquency 1976-1980." *Criminology* 21, 4: 555-584.

Agnew, R., F. Cullen, V. Burton, T.D. Evans, and R.G. Dunaway (1996). "A New Test of Classic Strain Theory." *Justice Quarterly* 13, 4: 682-703.

Akers, R. (1994/1997). *Criminological Theories: Introduction and Evaluation.* Los Angeles, CA: Roxbury.

Akers, R. (1996). "Is Differential Association/Social Learning Cultural Deviance Theory?" *Criminology* 34, 2: 229-247.

Akers, R.L. (1973/1985). *Deviant Behavior: A Social Learning Approach.* Belmont, CA: Wadsworth.

Akers, R.L. (1991). "Self-Control as a General Theory of Crime." *Journal of Quantitative Criminology* 7, 2: 201-211.

Alarid, L.F., J. Marquart, V. Burton, F. Cullen, and S. Cuvelier (1996). "Women's Roles in Serious Offenses: A Study of Adult Felons." *Justice Quarterly* 13, 3: 431-454.

Albanese, J. (1993). "Women and the Newest Profession: Females as White Collar Criminals." In C. Culliver, *Female Criminality: The State of the Art,* pp. 119-131. New York, NY: Garland.

Alleman, T. (1993). "Varieties of Feminist Thought and Their Application to Crime and Criminal Justice." In R. Muraskin and T. Alleman, *It's a Crime: Women and Justice,* pp. 3-43. Englewood Cliffs, NJ: Prentice-Hall.

257

Allen, J. (1988). "The Masculinity of Criminality and Criminology: Interrogating Some Impasses." In M. Findlay and R. Hogg (eds.), *Understanding Crime and Criminal Justice,* pp. 1-23. Sydney, Australia: Law Book Company.

Allen, J. (1989). "Men, Crime and Criminology: Recasting the Questions." *International Journal of the Sociology of Law* 17: 19-39.

American Correctional Association (1990). *The Female Offender: What Does the Future Hold?* Washington, DC: St. Mary's.

Anderson, T.L. and R.R. Bennett (1996). "Development, Gender, and Crime: The Scope of the Routine Activities Approach." *Justice Quarterly* 13, 1: 31-56.

Andrews, D.A. and J. Bonta (1994). *The Psychology of Criminal Conduct,* Second Edition. Cincinnati, OH: Anderson Publishing Co.

Andrews, D.A. and J.S. Wormoth (1989) "Personality and Crime: Knowledge Destruction and Construction in Criminology." *Justice Quarterly* 6: 289-309.

Anglin, M.D. and Y. Hser (1987). "Addicted Women and Crime." *Criminology* 25, 2: 359-398.

Arbuthnot, J.B. (1984). "Moral Reasoning Development Programmes in Prison: Cognitive-Developmental and Critical Reasoning Approaches." *Journal of Moral Education* 13, 2: 112-122.

Arbuthnot, J.B. and D. Faust (1981). *Teaching Moral Reasoning: Theory and Practice.* New York, NY: Harper and Row.

Arbuthnot, J.B. and D. Gordon (1988). "Crime and Cognition: Community Applications of Sociomoral Reasoning Development." *Criminal Justice and Behavior* 15, 3: 379-393.

Arneklev, B.J., H. Grasmick, C. Tittle, and R. Bursik (1993). "Low Self-Control and Imprudent Behavior." *Journal of Quantitative Criminology* 9: 225-247.

Arnold, R. (1995). "The Processes of Victimization and Criminalization of Black Women." In R. Price and N. Sokoloff (eds.), *The Criminal Justice System and Women,* pp. 136-146. New York, NY: McGraw-Hill.

Arrigo, B. (1995). "The Peripheral Core of Law and Criminology: On Postmodern Social Theory and Conceptual Integration." *Justice Quarterly* 12, 3: 447-472.

Austin, R. (1982). "Women's Liberation and Increases in Minor, Major, and Occupational Offenses." *Criminology* 20: 407-430.

Bagley, K. and A. Merlo (1995). "Controlling Women's Bodies." In A. Merlo and J. Pollock (eds.), *Women, Law and Social Control,* pp. 135-155. Boston, MA: Allyn and Bacon.

Bainbridge, W.S. and R.D. Crutchfield (1983). "Sex Role Ideology and Delinquency." *Sociological Perspectives* 26: 253-274.

Bandura, A. (1977). *Social Learning Theory.* Englewood Cliffs, NJ: Prentice-Hall.

Barkan, S. (1997). *Criminology: A Sociological Understanding.* Upper Saddle River, NJ: Prentice-Hall.

Barlow, H. (1991). "Explaining Crimes and Analogous Acts, or the Unrestrained Will Grab at Pleasure Whenever They Can." *The Journal of Criminal Law and Criminology* 82: 229-242.

Bartrum, T. (1992). "Birth Control as a Condition of Probation—A New Weapon in the War Against Child Abuse." *Kentucky Law Review* 80: 1037-1050.

Bartusch, D.R., D.R. Lynam, T.E. Moffitt, and P.A. Silva (1997). "Is Age Important? Testing a General Versus a Developmental Theory of Antisocial Behavior." *Criminology* 35, 1: 13-47.

Baskin, D. and I. Sommers (1993). "Females' Initiation Into Violent Street Crime." *Justice Quarterly* 10, 4: 559-583.

Baskin, D. and I. Sommers (1998). *Casualties of Community Disorder: Women's Careers in Violent Crime.* Boulder, CO: Westview Press.

Baskin, D., I. Sommers, and J. Fagan (1993). "The Political Economy of Female Violent Street Crime." *Fordham Urban Law Journal* 20, 3: 401-417.

Beck, A. and D. Gilliard (1995). "Prisoners in 1994." *Bureau of Justice Statistics Bulletin.* Washington, DC: U.S. Dept. of Justice.

Becker, H. (1963). *Outsiders: Studies in the Sociology of Deviance.* New York, NY: Free Press.

Belknap, J. (1996). *The Invisible Woman: Gender, Crime, and Justice.* Belmont, CA: Wadsworth.

Benson, M.L. and E. Moore (1992). "Are White-Collar and Common Offenders the Same? An Empirical and Theoretical Critique of a Recently Proposed General Theory of Crime." *Journal of Research in Crime and Delinquency* 29, 3: 251-72.

Bentham, J. (1843/1970). "The Rationale of Punishment." In R. Beck and J. Orr (eds.), *Ethical Choice: A Case Study Approach,* pp. 326-340. New York, NY: Free Press.

Bertrand, M. (1969) "Self Image and Delinquency: A Contribution to the Study of Female Criminality and Women's Image." *Acta Criminologica* (Jan.): 74-83.

Bishop, C. (1931). *Women and Crime.* London, England: Chato and Windus Press.

Bishop, D. and C. Frazier (1992). "Gender Bias in Juvenile Justice Processing: Implications of the JJDP Act." *Journal of Criminal Law and Criminology* 82, 4: 1162-1186.

Blank, R. (1993). *Fertility Control: New Techniques, New Policy Issues.* New York, NY: Greenwood Press.

Block, A. (1980). "Searching for Women in Organized Crime." In S. Datesman and F. Scarpetti, *Women, Crime and Justice,* pp. 192-214. New York, NY: Oxford University Press.

Block, G. and J. Goode (eds.) (1996). *Genetics of Criminal and Antisocial Behavior.* New York, NY: John Wiley and Sons.

Bloom, B., M. Chesney-Lind, and B. Owen (1994). "Women in California Prisons: Hidden Victims of the War on Drugs." Report. San Francisco, CA: Center on Juvenile and Criminal Justice.

Blum, A. and G. Fisher (1978). "Women Who Kill." In I.L. Kutash, S.B. Kutash, and L.B. Schlesinger (eds.), *Violence: Perspectives on Murder and Aggression,* pp. 187-197. San Francisco, CA: Jossey-Bass.

Blumstein, A., J. Cohen, and D. Farrington (1988a). "Criminal Career Research: Its Value for Criminology." *Criminology* 26: 1-35.

Blumstein, A., J. Cohen, and D. Farrington (1988b). "Longitudinal and Criminal Career Research: Further Clarifications." *Criminology* 26: 57-74.

Blumstein, A., J. Cohen, and P. Nagin (1983). *Research on Sentencing, Vol. 1.* Washington, DC: National Academy Press.

Blumstein, A., J. Cohen, J. Roth, and C. Visher (1986). *Criminal Careers and Career Criminals* (2 Vols.). Washington, DC: National Academy Press.

Bohrman, M. (1996). "Predispositions to Criminality: Swedish Adoption Studies in Retrospect." In M. Rutter (ed.), *Genetics of Criminal and Antisocial Behavior.* Chichester, England: John Wiley and Sons.

Bottcher, J. (1995). "Gender as Social Control: A Qualitative Study of Incarcerated Youths and Their Siblings in Greater Sacramento." *Justice Quarterly* 12, 1: 33-57.

Bourgois, P. and E. Dunlap (1993). "Exorcising Sex-for-Crack: An Ethnographic Perspective from Harlem." In M. Ratner (ed.), *The Crack Pipe as Pimp,* pp. 97-132. Lexington, MA: Lexington Books.

Bowker, L. (1978). *Women, Crime and the Criminal Justice System*. Lexington, MA: Lexington Books.

Bowker, L. (ed.) (1981). *Women and Crime in America*. New York, NY: MacMillan.

Box, S. and C. Hale (1983). "Liberation/Emancipation, Economic Marginalization, or Less Chivalry: The Relevance of Three Theoretical Arguments to Female Crime Patterns in England and Wales, 1951-1980." *Criminology* 22, 4: 473-497.

Boyd, C. and D. Mast (1993). "Addicted Women and their Relationship with Men." *Nursing and Mental Health Services* 21, 2: 10-13.

Braithwaite, J. (1989). *Crime, Shame and Reintegration*. Cambridge, UK: Cambridge University Press.

Braithwaite, J. (1993). "Shame and Modernity." *The British Journal of Criminology* 33: 1-18.

Braithwaite, J. and K. Daly (1994). "Masculinities, Violence, and Communitarian Control." In T. Newburn and E. Stanko (eds.), *Just Boys Doing Business: Men, Masculinities, and Crime,* pp.189-213. London, England: Routledge.

Braswell, M. (1990). "Peacemaking: A Missing Link in Criminology." *The Criminologist* 15, 1: 3-5.

Bridges, G.S. and G. Beretta (1994). "Gender, Race and Social Control: Toward an Understanding of Sex Disparities in Imprisonment." In G.S. Bridges and M.A. Myers (eds.), *Inequality, Crime, and Social Control*, pp. 158-175. Boulder, CO: Westview Press.

Brown, B. (1986). "Women and Crime: The Dark Figures of Criminology." *Economy and Society* 15: 355-402.

Brown, L.M. and C. Gilligan (1992). *Meeting at the Crossroads: Women's Psychology and Girls' Development*. Cambridge, MA: Harvard University Press.

Browne, A. (1987). *When Battered Women Kill*. New York, NY: Free Press.

Browne, A. and K. Williams (1989). "Exploring the Effect of Resource Availability and the Likelihood of Female Perpetrated Homicides." *Law and Society Review* 23: 75-94.

Brownstein, H., B. Spunt, S. Crimmins, P. Goldstein, and S. Langley (1994). "Changing Patterns of Lethal Violence by Women: A Research Note." *Women and Criminal Justice* 5, 2: 99-118.

Bunch, B.J., L.A. Foley, and S.P. Urbina (1983). "Psychology of Violent Female Offenders: A Sex-Role Perspective." *The Prison Journal* 63, 3: 66-79.

Bureau of Justice Statistics (1994a). *Women in Prison*. Washington, DC: U.S. Dept. of Justice.

Bureau of Justice Statistics (1994b). *Domestic Violence: Violence Between Intimates, 1994.* Washington, DC: U.S. Dept. of Justice.

Bureau of Justice Statisics (1995). *Bulletin: Prisoners in 1994.* Washington, DC: U.S. Government Printing Office.

Bureau of Justice Statistics (1997a). "Felony Sentences in State Courts, 1994." Washington, DC: U.S. Dept. of Justice.

Bureau of Justice Statistics (1997b). "Prisoners in 1996." Washington, DC: U.S. Dept. of Justice.

Bureau of Justice Statistics (1997c). "Correctional Populations in the U.S., 1995." Washington, DC: U.S. Dept. of Justice.

Bureau of Justice Statistics (1997d). "Lifetime Likelihood of Going to State or Federal Prison." Washington, DC: U.S. Dept. of Justice.

Burgess, R. and R. Akers (1966). "A Differential Association-Reinforcement Theory of Criminal Behavior." *Social Problems* (Fall)14: 128-147.

Bursik, R.J. and H.G. Grasmick (1993). *Neighborhoods and Crime: The Dimensions of Effective Community Control.* New York, NY: Lexington Books.

Burton, V.S. and F.T. Cullen (1992). "The Empirical Status of Strain Theory." *Journal of Crime and Justice* 15, 2: 1-30.

Burton, V.S., F.T. Cullen, T.D. Evans, and R.G. Dunaway (1994). "Reconsidering Strain Theory: Operationalization, Rival Theories, and Adult Criminality." *Journal of Quantitative Criminology* 10: 213-239.

Byrne, J.M. and R.J. Sampson (eds.) (1986). *The Social Ecology of Crime.* New York, NY: Springer-Verlag.

Cameron, M. (1964). *The Booster and the Snitch.* New York, NY: Free Press.

Campbell, A. (1981). *Girl Delinquents.* Oxford: Basil Blackwell.

Campbell, A. (1984). *The Girls in the Gang.* New York, NY: Basil Blackwell.

Campbell, A. (1990). "Female Participation in Gangs." In R. Huff (ed.), *Gangs in America,* pp. 163-182. Newbury Park, CA: Sage.

Campbell, A. (1993). *Men, Women and Aggression.* New York, NY: Basic Books.

Canter, R. (1982). "Sex Differences in Self-Report Delinquency." *Criminology* 20: 373-393.

Canter, R. (1982). "Family Correlates of Male and Female Delinquency." *Criminology* 20: 149-167.

Cao, I., A. Adams, and V. Jensen (1997). "A Test of the Black Subculture of Violence Thesis: A Research Note." *Criminology* 35, 2: 367-379.

Carlen, P. (1983). *Women's Imprisonment: A Study in Social Control.* London, England: Routledge and Kegan Paul.

Carlen, P. (1985). *Criminal Women: Autobiographical Accounts.* Cambridge, UK: Polity.

Carlen, P. (1989). "Feminist Jurisprudence—Or Woman-Wise Penology." *Probation Journal* 36, 3: 110-114.

Caspi, A., T. Moffitt, P. Silva, M. Stouthamer-Loeber, R. Krueger, and P. Schmutte (1994). "Are Some People Crime-Prone? Replications of the Personality-Crime Relationship Across Countries, Genders, Races, and Methods." *Criminology* 32: 163-195.

Cernkovich, S.A. and P.C. Giordano (1979). "A Comparative Analysis of Male and Female Delinquency." *Sociological Quarterly* 20: 131-45.

Chambers, C., K Hinesley, and M. Moldestad (1970). "Narcotic Addiction in Females: A Race Comparison." *International Journal of the Addictions* 5: 257-278.

Chamblin, M. and J. Cochran (1997). "Social Altruism and Crime." *Criminology* 35, 2: 203-228.

Chapman, J. (1980). *Economic Realities and the Female Offender.* Lexington, MA: Lexington Books.

Chavkin, W. (1990). "Drug Addiction and Pregnancy: Policy Crossroads." *American Journal of Public Health*, 80, 4: 483-487.

Chesney-Lind, M. (1973). "Judicial Enforcement of the Female Sex Role." *Issues in Criminology* 8, 2: 51-69.

Chesney-Lind, M. (1978). "Chivalry Reexamined: Women and the Criminal Justice System." In L. Bowker, *Women, Crime and the Criminal Justice System,* pp. 197-225. Lexington, MA: Lexington Books.

Chesney-Lind, M. (1980). "Rediscovering Lilith: Misogyny and the 'New' Female Criminal." In C.T. Griffiths and M. Nance (eds.), *The Female Offender,* pp. 1-35. Burnaby, BC: Simon Fraser University, Criminology Research Centre.

Chesney-Lind, M. (1986). "Women and Crime: The Female Offender." *Signs; Journal of Women in Culture and Society* 12, 1: 78-96.

Chesney-Lind, M. (1993). "Girls, Gangs and Violence: Reinventing the Liberated Female Crook." *Humanity and Society* 17: 321-344.

Chesney-Lind, M. (1997). *The Female Offender: Girls, Women and Crime.* Thousand Oaks, CA: Sage.

Chesney-Lind, M. and J. Pollock (1995). "Women's Prisons: Equality with a Vengeance." In A. Merlo and J. Pollock, *Women, Law and Social Control,* pp. 155-177. Boston, MA: Allyn and Bacon.

Chesney-Lind, M. and R. Sheldon (1992). *Girls, Delinquency and Juvenile Justice.* Pacific Grove, CA: Brooks/Cole.

Chesney-Lind, M., A. Rockhill, N. Marker, and H. Reyes (1994). "Gangs and Delinquency: Exploring Police Estimates of Gang Membership." *Crime, Law and Social Change* 21: 201-228.

Chilton, R. and S. Datesman (1987). "Gender, Race, and Crime: An Analysis of Urban, Arrest Trends, 1960-1980." *Gender and Society* 1: 152-171.

Chodorow, N. (1978). *The Reproduction of Mothering.* Berkeley, CA: University of California Press.

Christie, N. (1993). *Crime Control as Industry.* London, England: Routledge.

Cloward, R.A. (1959). "Illegitimate Means, Anomie, and Deviant Behavior." *American Sociological Review* 24: 164-176.

Cloward, R.A. and L.E. Ohlin (1960). *Delinquency and Opportunity.* New York, NY: Free Press.

Cohen, A. (1955). *Delinquency in Boys: The Culture of the Gang.* New York, NY: Free Press.

Cohen, A. (1965). "The Sociology of the Delinquent Act: Anomie Theory and Beyond." *American Sociological Review* 30: 5-14.

Cohen, L. and M. Felson (1979). "Social Change and Crime Trends: A Routine Activity Approach." *American Sociological Review* 44: 588-608.

Cohen, L. and B. Vila (1996). "Self Control and Social Control: An Exposition of the Gottfredson-Hirschi/Sampson-Laub Debate." *Studies on Crime and Crime Prevention* 5, 2: 125-151.

Cole, E.B. and S. Coultrap-McQuin (1992). *Explorations in Feminist Ethics.* Bloomington, IL: Indiana University Press.

Cornish, D.B. and R.V. Clarke (eds.) (1986). *The Reasoning Criminal: Rational Choice Perspectives on Offending.* New York, NY: Springer-Verlag.

Covington, J. (1985). "Gender Differences in Criminality Among Heroin Users." *Journal of Research in Crime and Delinquency* 22: 329-353.

Cowie, J., B. Cowie, and E. Slater (1968). *Delinquency in Girls.* London, England: Heinemann.

Craven, D. (1996). *Female Victims of Violent Crime.* Bureau of Justice Statistics. Washington, DC: U.S. Dept. of Justice.

Crew, B.K. (1991). "Sex Differences in Criminal Sentencing: Chivalry or Patriarchy?" *Justice Quarterly* 8, 1: 60-78.

Crites, L. (1976). *The Female Offender.* Lexington, MA: DC Heath.

Crites, L. and W. Hepperle (1987). *Women, the Courts and Equality.* Newbury Park, CA: Sage.

Crittenden, D. (1990, Jan. 25). "You've Come a Long Way, Moll." *Wall Street Journal,* p. A14.

Cullen, F.T. (1984). *Rethinking Crime and Deviance Theory: The Emergence of a Structuring Tradition.* Totowa, NJ: Rowman and Allenheld.

Cullen, F.T. (1994). "Social Support as an Organizing Concept for Criminology: Presidential Address to the Academy of Criminal Justice Sciences." *Justice Quarterly* 11, 4: 528-559.

Cullen, F.T., K.M. Golden, and J.B. Cullen (1979). "Sex and Delinquency: A Partial Test of the Masculinity Hypothesis." *Criminology* 17, 3: 301-327.

Culliver, C. (1993). *Female Criminality: The State of the Art.* New York, NY: Garland.

Curran, D. (1983). "Judicial Discretion and Defendant's Sex." *Criminology* 21: 41-58.

Curry, G.D., R.A. Ball, and R.J. Fox (1994). *Gang, Crime and Law Enforcement Recordkeeping.* Washington, DC: National Institute of Justice.

Daly, K. (1987a). "Discrimination in the Criminal Courts: Family, Gender, and the Problem of Equal Treatment." *Social Forces* 66, 1: 152-175.

Daly, K. (1987b). "Structure and Practice of Familial-Based Justice in a Criminal Court." *Law and Society Review* 21, 2: 267-290.

Daly, K. (1989a). "Gender and Varieties of White Collar Crime." *Criminology* 27, 4: 769-794.

Daly, K. (1989b). "Rethinking Judicial Paternalism: Gender, Work-Family Relations, and Sentencing." *Gender and Society* 3: 9-36.

Daly, K. (1989c). "Neither Conflict Nor Labeling Nor Paternalism Will Suffice: Intersections of Race, Ethnicity, Gender, and Family in Criminal Court Decisions." *Crime and Delinquency* 35, 1: 136-168.

Daly, K. (1994a). *Gender, Crime, and Punishment*. New Haven, CT: Yale University Press.

Daly, K. (1994b). "Gender and Punishment Disparity." In G.S. Bridges and G. Beretta, *Inequality, Crime, and Social Control*, pp. 117-133. Boulder, CO: Westview Press.

Daly, K. and R. Bordt (1995). "Sex Effects and Sentencing: An Analysis of the Statistical Literature." *Justice Quarterly* 12, 1: 141-168.

Daly, K. and M. Chesney-Lind (1988). "Feminism and Criminology." *Justice Quarterly* 5: 497-538.

Daly, M. and M. Wilson (1983). *Sex, Evolution and Behavior*, Second Edition. Cambridge, MA: MIT Press.

Daly, M. and M. Wilson (1988). *Homicide*. New York, NY: Aldine de Gruyter.

Danner, T., W. Blount, I. Silverman, and M. Vega (1995). "The Female Chronic Offender: Exploring Life Contingency and Offense History Dimensions for Incarcerated Female Offenders." *Women and Criminal Justice* 6, 2: 45-64.

Datesman, S. and F. Scarpetti (eds.) (1980a). *Women, Crime and Justice*. New York, NY: Oxford University Press.

Datesman, S. and F. Scarpetti (1980b). "Female Delinquency and Broken Homes." In S. Datesman and F. Scarpetti (eds.), *Women, Crime and Justice*, pp. 129-150. New York, NY: Oxford University Press.

Datesman, S., F. Scarpetti, and R. Stephenson (1975). "Female Delinquency: An Application of Self and Opportunity Theories." *Journal of Research in Crime and Delinquency* 12: 107-132.

Dawson, J. (1994). "Murder in Families." Bureau of Justice Statistics Special Report. Washington, DC: U.S. Dept. of Justice.

Decker, S., R. Wright, A. Redfern, and D. Smith (1993). "A Woman's Place is in the Home: Females and Residential Burglary." *Justice Quarterly* 10: 143-162.

DeKeseredy, W. and M. Schwartz (1996). *Contemporary Criminology*. Belmont, CA: Wadsworth.

DeKeseredy, W., D. Saunders, M. Schwartz, and S. Alvi (1997). "The Meaning and Motives for Women's Use of Violence in Canadian College Dating Relationships: Results from a National Survey." *Sociological Spectrum* 17, 2: 199-222.

DeHaan, W. (1990). *The Politics of Redress: Crime, Punishment, and Penal Abolition*. Boston, MA: Unwin Hyman.

Dembo, R., L. Williams, and J. Schmeidler (1993). "Gender Differences in Mental Health Service Needs Among Youths Entering a Juvenile Detention Center." *Journal of Prison and Jail Health* 12: 73-101.

Denno, D. (1988). "Human Biology and Criminal Responsibility: Free Will or Free Ride?" *University of Pennsylvania Law Review* 137: 615-671.

Denno, D. (1990). *Biology and Violence: From Birth to Adulthood*. New York, NY: Cambridge University Press.

Denno, D. (1994). "Gender, Crime, and the Criminal Law Defenses." *Journal of Criminal Law and Criminology* 85, 1: 80-180.

Denzin, N. (1990). "Presidential Address on the Sociological Imagination Revisited." *Sociological Quarterly* 31: 1-22.

Deschenes, E. and D.M. Anglin (1992). "Effects of Legal Supervision on Narcotic Addict Behavior: Ethnic and Gender Influences." In T. Mieczkowski (ed.), *Drugs, Crime and Social Policy*, pp. 167-196. Needham, MA: Allyn and Bacon.

Dobash, R., R. Dobash, M. Wilson, and M. Daly (1992). "The Myth of Sexual Symmetry in Marital Violence." *Social Problems* 39: 401-421.

Donziger, S. (ed.) (1996). *The Real War on Crime*. New York, NY: Harper Perennial.

d'Orban, P.T. (1979). "Women Who Kill Their Children." *British Journal of Psychiatry* 134: 560-571.

(The National) Drug Control Strategy (1997). Washington, DC: U.S. Government Printing Office.

Drug Use Forcasting: Annual Report: 1996 (1997). National Institute of Justice Research Report. Washington, DC: U.S. Dept. of Justice.

Dunlap, E., B. Johnson, and L. Maher (1997). "Female Crack Sellers in New York City: Who They Are and What They Do." *Women and Criminal Justice* 8, 4: 25-55.

Eagly, A. and V. Steffen (1986). "Gender and Aggressive Behavior: A Meta-Analytic Review of the Social Psychological Literature." *Psychological Bulletin* 100: 309-330.

Eaton, M. (1986). *Justice for Women: Family, Court and Social Control*. Philadelphia, PA: Open University Press.

Elliott, D. and S. Ageton (1980). "Reconciling Race and Class Differences in Self-Reported and Official Estimates of Delinquency." *American Sociological Review* 45: 95-110.

Elliott, D. and D. Huizinga (1983). "Social Class and Delinquent Behavior in a National Youth Panel." *Criminology* 21: 149-177.

Ellis, L. (1987a). "Criminal Behavior and r/K Selection: An Extension of Gene-Based Evolutionary Theory." *Deviant Behavior* 8: 149-176.

Ellis, L. (1987b). "Religiosity and Criminality from the Perspective of Arousal Theory." *Journal of Research in Crime and Delinquency* 24: 215-232.

Ellis, L. (1987c). "Relationships of Criminality and Psychopathy with Eight Other Apparent Behavioral Manifestations of Sub-Optimal Arousal." *Personality and Individual Differences* 8: 905-925.

Ellis, L. (1991). "Monoamine Oxidase and Criminality: Identifying an Apparent Biological Marker for Antisocial Behavior." *Journal of Research in Crime and Delinquency* 28: 227-251.

Ellis, L. and H. Hoffman (eds.) (1990) *Crime in Biological, Social and Moral Contexts*. New York, NY: Praeger.

Ellis, L. and P.D. Coontz (1990). "Androgens, Brain Functioning and Criminality: The Neurohormonal Foundations of Antisociality." In L. Ellis and H. Hoffman (eds.), *Crime in Biological, Social and Moral Contexts*, pp. 162-193. NY: Praeger.

Ellis, L. and A. Walsh (1997). "Gene-Based Evolutionary Theories in Criminology." *Criminology* 35, 2: 229-276.

English, K. (1993). "Self Reported Crime Rates of Women Prisoners." *Journal of Quantitative Criminology* 9: 357-382.

Erez, E. (1989). "Gender, Rehabilitation and Probation Decisions." *Criminology* 27: 307-327.

Erez, E. (1992). "Dangerous Men, Evil Women: Gender and Parole Decision-making." *Justice Quarterly* 9, 1: 106-121.

Evans, T.D., F. Cullen, V. Burton, R.G. Dunaway, and M. Benson (1997). "The Social Consequences of Self-Control: Testing the General Theory of Crime." *Criminology* 35, 3: 475-503.

"Evidence Builds: Youth Violence Prevention Programs Working." *Injury Control Update* 2, 2: 1-12.

Ewing, C. (1987). "Battered Women Who Kill." Lexington, MA: Lexington Books.

Eysenck, H.J. (1977). *Crime and Personality.* London: Routledge.

Eysenck, H.J. and G.H. Gudjonsson (1989). *The Causes and Cures of Criminality.* New York, NY: Plenum.

Fagan, J. (1994). "Women and Drugs Revisited: Female Participation in the Cocaine Economy." *Journal of Drug Issues* 24: 179-225.

Fagan, J. E. Piper, and M. Moore (1986). "Violent Delinquents and Urban Youths." *Criminology* 24: 439-471.

Faludi, S. (1991). *Backlash: The Undeclared War Against Women.* New York, NY: Crown.

Farnworth, M. (1984). "Male-Female Differences in Delinquency in a Minority-Group Sample." *Research in Crime and Delinquency* 21, 3: 191-212.

Farnworth, M. and R. Teske (1995). "Gender Differences in Felony Court Processing: Three Hypotheses of Disparity." *Women & Criminal Justice* 6, 2: 23-44.

Farrington, D.P. (1996). "The Explanation and Prevention of Youthful Offending." In J.D. Hawkins, *Delinquency and Crime: Current Theories.* New York, NY: Cambridge University Press.

Farrington, D.P., R. Loeber, and W.B. Van Kammen (1990). "Long-Term Criminal Outcomes of Hyperactivity-Impulsivity-Attention Deficit and Conduct Problems in Childhood." In L. Robins and M. Rutter (eds.), *Straight and Devious Pathways from Childhood to Adulthood*, pp. 62-82. New York, NY: Cambridge University Press.

Farrington, D.P., L.E. Ohlin, and J.Q. Wilson (1986). *Understanding and Controlling Crime: Toward a New Research Strategy.* New York, NY: Springer-Verlag.

Farrington, D. and A. Morris (1983). "Sex, Sentencing and Reconviction." *British Journal of Criminology* 23, 2: 229-248.

Farrington, D. and D. West (1993). "Criminal, Penal and Life Histories of Chronic Offenders: Risk and Protective Factors and Early Identification." *Criminal Behavior and Mental Health* 3: 492-523.

Federal Bureau of Investigation. *Crime in the United States, 1994.* Washington, DC: U.S. Dept. of Justice, U.S. Government Printing Office.

Federal Bureau of Investigation. *Crime in the United States, 1995.* Washington, DC: U.S. Dept. of Justice, U.S. Government Printing Office.

Feinman, C. (1976). "Imprisoned Women: A History of the Treatment of Women Incarcerated in New York City, 1932-1975." Unpublished doctoral dissertation.

Feinman, C. (1980/1986). *Women in the Criminal Justice System,* Second Edition. New York, NY: Praeger.

Feinman, C. (1992). *The Criminalization of a Woman's Body.* New York, NY: Haworth Press.

Felson, R. (1996). "Big People Hit Little People: Sex Differences in Physical Power and Interpersonal Violence." *Criminology* 34, 3: 433-452.

Felson, R.F. and J. Tedeschi (1993). *Aggression and Violence: Social Interactionist Perspectives.* Washington, DC: American Psychological Association.

Female Offenders in the Juvenile Justice System: Statistics Summary. (1996). Office of Juvenile Justice and Delinquency Prevention. Washington, DC: U.S. Dept. of Justice.

Fenster, C. (1981). "Societal Reaction to Male-Female Co-Defendants: Sex as an Independent Variable." *California Sociologist* 4: 219-232.

Feyerhern, W. (1981a) "Gender Differences in Delinquency Quantity and Quality." In L. Bowker, *Women and Crime in America,* pp. 82-93. New York, NY: Macmillan.

Feyerhern, W. (1981b) "Measuring Gender Differences in Delinquency Self Reports v. Police Contacts." In M. Warren, *Comparing Female and Male Offenders.* Beverly Hills, CA: Sage.

Figueira-McDonough, J. (1985). "Gender Differences in Informal Processing: A Look at Charge Bargaining and Sentence Reduction in Washington, DC." *Journal of Research in Crime and Delinquency* 22: 101-133.

Figueira-McDonough, J., W.H. Barton, and R.C. Sarri (1981). "Normal Deviance: Gender Similarities in Adolescent Subcultures." In M.Q. Warren (ed.), *Comparing Female and Male Offenders,* pp. 17-45. Beverly Hills, CA: Sage.

Figueira-McDonough, J. and E. Selo (1980). "A Reformulation of the 'Equal Opportunity' Explanation of Female Delinquency." *Crime & Delinquency* 26: 333-343.

Finley, N. and H. Grasmick (1985). "Gender Roles and Social Control." *Sociological Spectrum* 5: 317-330.

Firestone, S. (1970). *The Dialectic of Sex: The Case for Feminist Revolution.* New York, NY: Bantam Books.

Fishbein, D. (1990). "Biological Perspectives in Criminology." *Criminology* 28: 27-75.

Fletcher, B., L. Shaver, and D. Moon (1993). "Women Prisoners: A Forgotton Population." Westport, CT: Praeger.

Freedman, E. (1981). *Their Sisters' Keepers: Women's Prison Reform in America, 1830-1930.* Ann Arbor, MI: University of Michigan Press.

French, L. (1978). "The Incarcerated Black Female: The Case of Social Double Jeopardy." *Journal of Black Studies* 8: 321-335.

French, L. (1983). "A Profile of the Incarcerated Black Female Offender." *The Prison Journal.* 63, 2: 80-87.

Freud, S. (1968/1933). "Some Psychical Consequences of the Anatomical Distinction Between the Sexes." In S. Freud, *Sexuality and the Psychology of Love.* New York, NY: Collier Books.

Friedman, J. and D. Rosenbaum (1988). "Social Control Theory: The Salience of Components by Age, Gender, and Type of Crime." *Journal of Quantitative Criminology* 4: 363-381.

Fullilove, M., A. Lown, and R. Fullilove (1992). "Crack'hos and Skeezers: Traumatic Experiences of Women Crack Users." *The Journal of Sex Research* 29, 2: 275-287.

Gauthier, D. and W. Bankston (1997). "Gender Equality and the Sex Ratio of Intimate Killing." *Criminology* 35, 4: 577-600.

Gelsthorpe, L. and A. Morris (1990). *Feminist Perspectives in Criminology.* Philadelphia, PA: Open University Press.

Ghali, M. and M. Chesney-Lind (1986). "Gender Bias and the Criminal Justice System: An Empirical Investigation." *Sociology and Social Research* 70: 164-171.

Gibbons, D. (1989). "Personality and Crime: Non-Issues, Real Issues, and a Theory and Research Agenda." *Justice Quarterly* 6: 311-323.

Gibbons, D. (1994). *Talking About Crime and Criminals.* Englewood Cliffs, NJ: Prentice-Hall.

Gibbs, J. and D. Giever (1995) "Self Control and Its Manifestation Among University Students: An Empirical Test of Gottfredson and Hirschi's General Theory." *Justice Quarterly* 12, 2: 231-256.

Gibbs, J., L. Kohlberg, A. Colby, and B. Speicher-Dubin (1976). "The Domain and Development of Moral Judgment: A Theory and Method of Assessment." In J. Meyer (ed.), *Reflections on Values Education,* pp. 19-20. Waterloo, Ontario: Wilfrid Laurier University Press.

Gilfus, M.E. (1992). "From Victims to Survivors to Offenders: Women's Routes of Entry into Street Crime." *Women & Criminal Justice* 4, 1: 63-90.

Gilligan, C. (1982). *In a Different Voice: Psychological Theory and Women's Development.* Cambridge, MA: Harvard University Press.

Gilligan, C. (1987). "Moral Orientation and Moral Development." In E.F. Kittay and D.T. Meyers (eds.), *Women and Moral Theory,* pp. 19-23. Savage, MD: Rowman and Littlefield.

Gilligan, C. (1990). "Joining the Resistance: Psychology, Politics, Girls and Women." *Michigan Quarterly Review* 29, 4: 501-536.

Gilligan, C., A. Rogers, and D. Tolman (1991). *Women, Girls and Psychotherapy: Reframing Resistance.* New York, NY: The Haworth Press, Inc.

Giordano, P.C. (1978). "Research Note: Girls, Guys and Gangs: The Changing Social Context of Female Delinquency." *Journal of Criminal Law and Criminology* 69, 1: 126-132.

Giordano, P.C. and S.A. Cernkovich (1979). "On Complicating the Relationship Between Liberation and Delinquency." *Social Problems* 26: 467-481.

Giordano, P., S. Cernkovich, and M.D. Pugh (1986). "Friendships and Delinquency." *American Journal of Sociology* 91: 1170-1202.

Glueck, S. and E. Glueck (1934). *Five Hundred Delinquent Women.* New York, NY: Alfred A. Knopf.

Goetting, A. (1988). "Patterns of Homicide Among Women." *Journal of Interpersonal Violence,* 3: 3-19.

Gold, J., M. Braswell, and B. McCarthy (1991). "Criminal Justice Ethics: A Survey of Philosophical Theories." In M. Braswell, B. McCarthy, and B. McCarthy (eds.), *Justice, Crime and Ethics,* pp. 3-25.

Goldstein, P. (1979). *Prostitution and Drugs.* Lexington, MA: Lexington Books.

Gora, J.G. (1982). *The New Female Criminal: Empirical Reality or Social Myth?* New York, NY: Praeger.

Gottfredson, M.R. and T. Hirschi (1986). "The True Value of Lambda Would Appear to be Zero: An Essay on Career Criminals, Criminal Careers, Selective Incapactation, Cohort Studies and Related Topics." *Criminology* 24, 2: 213-234.

Gottfredson, M.R. and T. Hirschi (1987). "The Methodological Adequacy of Longitudinal Research on Crime." *Criminology* 24: 581-614.

Gottfredson, M.R. and T. Hirschi (1988). "Science, Public Policy, and the Career Paradigm." *Criminology* 26: 37-56.

Gottfredson, M.R. and T. Hirschi (1990). *A General Theory of Crime.* Stanford, CA: Stanford University Press.

Gould, M. and R. Kern-Daniels (1977). "Toward a Sociological Theory of Gender and Sex." *American Sociologist* 12: 182-189.

Gove, W.R. (1994). "Why We Do What We Do: A Biopsychosocial Theory of Human Motivation." *Social Forces* 73: 363-394.

Gove, W.R. and C. Wilmoth (1990). "Risk, Crime, and Neurophysiological Highs: A Consideration of Brain Processes that May Reinforce Delinquent and Criminal Behavior." In L. Ellis and H. Hoffman (eds.), *Crime in Biological, Social, and Moral Contexts,* pp. 261-293. New York, NY: Praeger.

Grant, B. and G.D. Curry (1993). "Women Murderers and Victims of Abuse in a Southern State." *American Journal of Criminal Justice* 16, 2: 73-84.

Grasmick, H.G., N.J. Finley, and D.L. Glaser (1984). "Labor Force Participation, Sex-Role Attitudes and Female Crime." *Social Science Quarterly* 65: 703-718.

Grasmick, H.G., C.R. Tittle, R.J. Bursik, and B.J. Arneklev (1993). "Testing the Core Empirical Implications of Gottfredson and Hirschi's General Theory of Crime." *Journal of Research in Crime and Delinquency* 30, 1: 5-29.

Greenwood, V. (1981). "The Myth of Female Crime." In A. Morris and L. Gelsthorpe (eds.), *Women and Crime,* pp. 73-87. New York, NY: Cambridge University Press.

Griffith, J.E. (1984). "Evidence of Unidimensionality of Locus of Control in Women Prisoners: Implications for Prisoner Rehabilitation." *Journal of Offender Counseling, Services and Rehabiliation* 9, 1-2: 57-69.

Gruhl, J., S. Welch, and C. Spohn (1984). "Women as Criminal Defendants: A Test for Paternalism." *Western Political Quarterly* 37: 456-467.

Hagan, J. (1989). *Structural Criminology.* New Brunswick, NJ: Rutgers University Press.

Hagan, J. (1995). *Delinquency in the Life Course.* Greenwich, CT: JAI Press.

Hagan, J. and A. Palloni (1986). "Toward a Structural Criminology: Method and Theory in Criminological Research." *Annual Review of Sociology* 12: 431-449.

Hagan, J., A.R. Gillis, and J. Simpson (1985). "The Class Structure of Gender and Delinquency: Toward a Power-Control Theory of Common Delinquent Behavior." *American Journal of Sociology* 90: 1151-1178.

Hagan, J. and R. Peterson (1995). *Crime and Inequality*. Stanford, CA: Stanford University Press.

Hagan, J. and N. O'Donnel (1978). "Sexual Stereotyping and Judicial Sentencing: A Legal Test of the Sociological Wisdom." *Canadian Journal of Sociology* 3: 309-319.

Hagan, J., J. Simpson, and A.R. Gillis (1979). "The Sexual Stratification of Social Control." *British Journal of Sociology* 30: 25-38.

Hagan, J. J. Simpson, and A.R. Gillis (1987). "Class in the Household: A Power-Control Theory of Gender and Delinquency." *American Journal of Sociology* 92: 788-816.

Hagan, J. J. Simpson, and A.R. Gillis (1988). "Feminist Scholarship, Relational and Instrumental Control, and a Power-Control Theory of Gender and Delinquency." *British Journal of Sociology* 39: 301-336.

Hahn, N. (1980). "Too Dumb to Know Better: Cacogenic Family Studies and the Criminology of Women." *Criminology* 18, 1: 3-25.

Harmon, R.B., R. Rosner, and M. Wiederlight (1985). "Women and Arson: A Demographic Study." *Journal of Forensic Sciences* 30, 2: 467-477.

Harris, A.R. (1977). "Sex and Theories of Deviance." *American Sociological Review* 42: 3-16.

Harris, M.G. (1988). *Cholas: Latino Girls and Gangs*. New York, NY: AMS Press.

Hartnagel, T.F. (1982). "Modernization, Female Social Roles, and Female Crime: A Cross-National Investigation." *Sociological Quarterly* 23, 4: 477-490.

Hawkins, J.D. (1996). *Delinquency and Crime: Current Theories*. New York, NY: Cambridge University Press.

Heidensohn, F. (1968). "The Deviance of Women: A Critique and an Enquiry." *British Journal of Sociology* 19: 160-175.

Heidensohn, F. (1985). *Women and Crime*. London, England: Macmillan.

Heidensohn, F. (1986). "Models of Justice: Portia or Persephone? Some Thoughts on Equality, Fairness and Gender in the Field of Criminal Justice." *International Journal of the Sociology of Law* 14, 3-4: 287-298.

Heidensohn, F. (1994). "From Being to Knowing: Some Issues in the Study of Gender in Contempoary Society." *Women & Criminal Justice* 6, 1: 13-39.

Held, V. (1987). "Feminism and Moral Theory." In E.F. Kittay and D.T. Meyers (eds.), *Women and Moral Theory,* pp. 111-128. Savage, MD: Rowman and Littlefield.

Henriques, Z. (1995). "African American Women: The Oppressive Intersection of Gender, Race and Class." *Women and Crime* 7, 1: 67-80.

Hickey, E. (1997). *Serial Murderers and their Victims*, Second Edition. Belmont, CA: Wadsworth.

Hickey, J. and P. Scharf (1980). *Toward a Just Theory of Corrections*. San Francisco, CA: Jossey-Bass.

Hill, G. and M. Atkinson (1988). "Gender, Familial Control, and Delinquency." *Criminology* 26: 127-147.

Hill, G. and E. Crawford (1990). "Women, Race, and Crime." *Criminology* 28: 601-623.

Hill, G.D. and A.R. Harris (1981). "Changes in the Gender Patterning of Crime, 1953-77: Opportunity vs. Identity." *Social Science Quarterly* 62: 658-671.

Hindelang, M. (1979). "Sex Differences in Criminal Activity." *Social Problems* 27: 143-156.

Hindelang, M. (1981). "Variations in Sex-Race-Age-Specific Incidence Rates of Offending." *American Sociological Review* 46: 461-474.

Hirsch, M.F. (1981). *Women and Violence.* New York, NY: Van Nostrand Reinhold.

Hirschi, T. (1969). *Causes of Delinquency.* Berkeley, CA: University of California Press.

Hirschi, T. (1994) "Family." In T. Hirschi and M. Gottfredson, *The Generality of Deviance,* pp. 47-69. New Brunswick, NJ: Transaction Publishers.

Hirschi, T. (1996). "Theory Without Ideas: Reply to Akers." *Criminology* 34, 2: 249-256.

Hirschi, T. and M. Gottfredson (1987). "Causes of White Collar Crime." *Criminology* 25: 949-974.

Hirschi, T. and M. Gottfredson (1993). "Commentary: Testing the General Theory of Crime." *Journal of Research in Crime and Delinquency* 30, 1: 47-54.

Hirschi, T. and M. Gottfredson (1994). *The Generality of Deviance.* New Brunswick, NJ: Transaction Publishers.

Hirschi, T. and M. Gottfredson (1995). "Control Theory and the Life-Course Perspective." *Studies on Crime and Crime Prevention* 4: 131-142.

Hoffman, P.B. (1982). "Females, Recidivism, and Salient Factor Score: A Resarch Note." *Criminal Justice and Behavior* 9, 1: 121-125.

Hoffman-Bustamante, D. (1973). "The Nature of Female Criminality." *Issues in Criminology* 8: 117-136.

Howe, A. (1994). *Punish and Critique: Toward a Feminist Analysis of Penality.* London, England: Routledge.

Hser, Y., D. Anglin, and M. Booth (1987a). "Sex Differences in Addict Careers: Addiction." *American Journal of Drug and Alcohol Abuse* 13: 155-157.

Hser, Y., D. Anglin and M. Booth (1987b). "Sex Differences in Addict Careers: Initiation of Use." *American Journal of Drug and Alcohol Abuse* 13: 231-251.

Hser, Y., D. Anglin, and C. Chou (1992). "Narcotics Use and Crime Among Addicted Women: Longitudinal Patterns and Effects of Social Intervention." In T. Mieczkowski (ed.), *Drugs, Crime and Social Policy,* pp. 197-221. Needham, MA: Allyn and Bacon.

Huling, T. (1994). "Breaking the Silence" (Internal Report). March 4. New York, NY: Correctional Association of New York.

Huling, T. (1995). "Women Drug Couriers." *Journal of Criminal Justice* 9, 4: 14-20.

Humphries, D. (1993). "Mothers and Children, Drugs and Crack: Reactions to Maternal Drug Dependency." In R. Muraskin and T. Alleman (eds.), *It's a Crime: Women and Justice,* pp. 130-146. Englewood Cliffs, NJ: Prentice-Hall.

Humphries, D., J. Dawson, V. Cronin, P. Keating, C. Wisniewki, and J. Eichfeld (1992). "Mothers and Children, Drugs and Crack: Reactions to Maternal Drug Dependency." *Women and Criminal Justice* 3: 81-99.

Inciardi, J. (1980). "Women, Heroin and Property Crime." In S. Datesman and F. Scarpetti, *Women, Crime and Justice,* pp. 214-223. New York, NY: Oxford University Press.

Inciardi, J., D. Lockwood, and A. Pottieger (1993). *Women and Crack-Cocaine.* New York, NY: Macmillan.

Inciardi, J. and A. Pottieger (1986). "Drug Use and Crime Among Two Cohorts of Women Narcotics Users: An Empirical Assessment." *Journal of Drug Issues* 16: 91-106.

Inciardi, J., A. Pottieger, and C. Faupel (1982). "Black Women, Heroin and Crime: Some Empirical Notes." *Journal of Drug Issues* 12, 3: 241-50.

James, J. (1976). "Motivations for Entrance into Prostitution." In L. Crites (ed.), *The Female Offender,* pp. 177-206. Lexington, MA: Lexington Books.

Jankowski, M.S. (1991). *Island in the Street: Gangs and American Urban Society.* Berkeley, CA: University of California Press.

Jensen, G.F. (1988). "Mainstreaming and the Sociology of Deviance: A Personal Assessment." In S.H. Aiken, K. Anderson, M. Dinnerstein, J.N. Lensink, and P. MacCorquodale (eds.), *Changing Our Minds: Feminist Transformations of Knowledge,* pp. 77-89. New York, NY: State University of Albany Press.

Jensen, G.F. (1996). "Comment on Chamblin and Cochran." *Criminology* 34, 1: 129-134.

Jensen, G. and D. Brownfield (1986). "Gender, Lifestyles, and Victimization: Beyond Routine Activity." *Violence and Victims* 1: 85-99.

Jensen, G.J. and R. Eve (1976). "Sex Differences in Delinquency: An Examination of Popular Sociological Explanations." *Criminology* 13: 427-448.

Jensen, G.F. and L. Westphal (1998) "Gender and Conformity: Submission versus Reasonable Choices" (Response to Tittle's Control Balance Theory). Paper presented at the Academy of Criminal Justice Sciences Meeting.

Joe, K. and M. Chesney-Lind (1993). "Just Every Mother's Angel: An Analysis of Gender and Ethnic Variations in Youth Gang Membership." Paper presented at the American Society of Criminology Meeting.

Joe, K. and M. Chesney-Lind, M. (1995). "Just Every Mother's Angel: An Analysis of Gender and Ethnic Variations in Youth Gang Membership." *Gender and Society* 9, 4: 408-430.

Jones, A. (1980). *Women Who Kill.* New York, NY: Holt, Rinehart and Winston.

Jones, M., D. Offord, and N. Abrams (1980). "Brothers, Sisters, and Antisocial Behavior." *British Journal of Psychiatry* 136: 139-145.

Jurkovic, G. (1980). "The Juvenile Delinquent as a Moral Philosopher: A Structural Developmental Perspective." *Psychological Bulletin* 88: 709-727.

Kanowitz, L. (1969) *Women and the Law.* Albuquerque, NM: University of New Mexico Press.

Katz, J. (1988). *Seductions of Crime: Moral and Sensual Attractions of Doing Evil.* New York, NY: Basic Books.

Kauffman, H.M. (1993). "In Search of the 'New Violent Female Offender' in Hawaii." Unpublished Honors Thesis, University of Hawaii at Manoa. Cited in M. Chesney-Lind (1997). *The Female Offender: Girls, Women and Crime.* Thousand Oaks, CA: Sage.

Keane, C., P. Maxim, and J.J. Teevan (1993). "Drinking and Driving, Self-Control, and Gender: Testing a General Theory of Crime." *Journal of Research in Crime and Delinquency* 30: 30-46.

Keeney, B. and K. Heide (1994). "Gender Differences in Serial Murderers: A Preliminary Analysis." *Journal of Interpersonal Violence* 9, 3: 383-398.

Keeney, B. and K. Heide (1995). "The Latest on Serial Murderers." *Violence Update* 4, 3: 1-4.

Kelley, B., D. Huizinga, T. Thornberry, and R. Loeber (1997). "Epidemiology of Serious Violence." Juvenile Justice Bulletin. Washington, DC: U.S. Dept. of Justice, Office of Justice Programs.

Kempinen, C. (1983). "Changes in the Sentencing Patterns of Male and Female Defendants." *Prison Journal* 63: 3-11.

Kermode, J. and G. Walker (eds.) (1994). *Women, Crime and the Courts in Early Modern England.* Chapel Hill, NC: The University of North Carolina Press.

Ketner, L. and J. Humphrey (1980). "Homicide, Sex Role Differences and Role Relationships." *Journal of Death and Dying* 20: 379-386.

Kittay, E.F. and D.T. Meyers (eds.) (1987). *Women and Moral Theory.* Savage, MD: Rowman and Littlefield.

Klein, D. (1973). "The Etiology of Female Crime: A Review of the Literature." *Issues in Criminology* 8, 2: 3-30.

Klein, D. and J. Kress (1976). "Any Women's Blues: A Critical Overview of Women, Crime and Criminal Justice." *Crime and Social Justice* 5: 34- 45.

Kohlberg, L. (1976). "Moral Stages and Moralization: The Cognitive Development Approach." In T. Lickona (ed.), *Moral Development and Behavior: Theory, Research and Social Issues,* pp. 31-53. New York, NY: Holt, Rinehart and Winston.

Kohlberg, L. (1981). *The Philosophy of Moral Development.* San Francisco, CA: Harper and Row.

Konopka, G. (1966). *The Adolescent Girl in Conflict.* Englewood Cliffs, NJ: Prentice-Hall.

Kratcoski, P. and L.D. Kratcoski (1982). "The Relationships of Victimization Through Child Abuse to Aggressive Delinquent Behavior." *Victimology* 7: 199-203.

Krohn, M.D., J.P. Curry, and S. Nelson-Kilger (1983). "Is Chivalry Dead? An Analysis of Changes in Police Dispositions of Males and Females." *Criminology* 21: 417-437.

Kruttschnitt, C. (1982a). "Respectable Women and the Law." *The Sociological Quarterly* 23: 221-234.

Kruttschnitt, C. (1982b). "Women, Crime and Dependency." *Criminology* 19, 4: 495-513.

Kruttschnitt, C. (1983). "Race Relations and the Female Inmate." *Crime & Delinquency* 29, 4: 577-592.

Kruttschnitt, C. (1984). "Sex and Criminal Court Dispositions: The Unresolved Controversy." *Journal of Research in Crime and Delinquency* 21, 3: 213-232.

Kruttschnitt, C. (1985). "Legal Outcomes and Legal Agents: Adding Another Dimension to the Sex-Sentencing Controversy." *Law and Human Behavior* 9: 287-303.

Kruttschnitt, C. and M. Dornfeld (1993). "Exposure to Family Violence: A Partial Explanation for Initial and Subsequent Levels of Delinquency?" *Criminal Behavior and Mental Health* 3: 61-75.

Kruttschnitt, C. and D. Green (1984). "The Sex Sanctioning Issue: Is It History?" *American Sociological Review* 49: 541-551.

Kruttschnitt, C., D. Ward, and M.A. Sheble (1987). "Abuse-Resistant Youth: Some Factors that May Inhibit Violent Criminal Behavior." *Social Forces* 66: 501-519.

Lahey, K. (1985). "Until Women Themselves Have Told All They Have to Tell." *Osgoode Hall Law Journal* 23, 3: 519-541.

Laub, J. and M. Joan McDermott (1985). "An Analysis of Serious Crime by Young Black Women." *Criminology* 23, 1: 81-98.

Laub, J. and R. Sampson (1993). "Turning Points in the Life Course: Why Change Matters to the Study of Crime." *Criminology* 31: 301-326.

Lauderback, D., J. Hansen, and D. Waldorf (1992). "Sisters Are Doin' It for Themselves: A Black Female Gang in San Francisco." *The Gang Journal* 1: 57-72.

Laufer, W.S. and J.M. Day (eds.) (1983). *Personality Theory, Moral Development, and Criminal Behavior*. Lexington, MA: Lexington Books.

Leahy, R.L. (1981). "Parental Practices and the Development of Moral Judgment and Self Image Disparity During Adolescence." *Developmental Psychology* 17, 3: 580-594.

Lemert, E. (1951). *Social Pathology: A Systematic Approach to the Theory of Sociopathic Behavior*. New York, NY: McGraw-Hill.

Leonard, E. (1982). *Women, Crime and Society: A Critique of Theoretical Criminology*. White Plains, NY: Longman.

Lepowsky, M. (1994) "Women, Men, and Aggression in an Egalitarian Society." *Sex Roles* 30: 199-211.

Levin, J. and J. Fox (1993). Female Serial Killers. In C. Culliver (ed.), *Female Criminality: The State of the Art*, pp. 119-131. New York, NY: Garland.

Lewis, D. (1981). "Black Women Offenders and Criminal Justice: Some Theoretical Considerations." In M. Warren (ed.), *Comparing Female and Male Offenders*, pp. 89-105. Beverly Hills, CA: Sage.

Loeber, R. and M. LeBlanc (1990). "Toward a Developmental Criminology." In M. Tonry and N. Morris (eds.), *Crime and Justice: A Review of Research, Vol. 12*, pp. 375-473. Chicago, IL: University of Chicago Press.

Lombroso, C. and W. Ferrero (1958/1894). *The Female Offender*. New York, NY: Philosophical Library.

Lombroso, C. and W. Ferrero (1972/1895). *The Criminal Man*. Montclair, NJ: Patterson-Smith.

Longshore, D., S. Turner, and J. Stein (1996). "Self-Control in a Criminal Sample: An Examination of Construct Validity." *Criminology* 34, 2: 209-227.

Lujan, C. (1995). "Women Warriors: American Indian Women, Crime and Alcohol." *Women & Criminal Justice* 7, 1: 9-33.

Lykken, D.T. (1995). *The Antisocial Personalities*. Hillsdale, NJ: Lawrence Erlbaum.

Lynch, M., J. Huey, J.S. Nunez, B. Close, and C. Johnston (1992). "Cultural Literacy, Criminology, and Female-Gender Issues: The Power to Exclude." *Journal of Criminal Justice Education* 3, 2: 187-203.

Lyng, S. (1990). "Edgework: A Social Psychological Analysis of Voluntary Risk Taking." *American Journal of Sociology* 95: 851-886.

Lytton, H. (1990). "Child and Parent Effects in Boy's Conduct Disorder: A Reinterpretation." *Developmental Psychology* 26: 683-697.

Maccoby, E. (1985). "Social Groupings in Childhood: Their Relationship to Prosocial and Antisocial Behavior in Boys and Girls." In D. Olweus, J. Block, and M. Radke-Yarrow (eds.), *Development of Antisocial and Prosocial Behavior: Theories, Research and Issues,* pp. 263-285. Orlando, FL: Academic Press.

Maccoby, E. and C. Jacklin (1974). *The Psychology of Sex Differences*. Stanford, CA: Stanford University Press.

MacKinnon, C. (1983). "Feminism, Marxism, Method and the State: Toward Feminist Jurisprudence." *Signs* 8, 2: 635-658.

MacKinnon, C. (1987). *Feminism Unmodified: Discourses on Life and Law*. London, England: Harvard University Press.

Maher, L. (1990). "Criminalizing Pregnancy—the Downside of a Kinder, Gentler Nation?" *Social Justice* 17, 3: 111-135.

Maher, L. (1992). "Punishment and Welfare: Crack Cocaine and the Regulation of Mothering." *Women & Criminal Justice* 3: 35-70.

Maher, L. and R. Curtis (1992). "Women on the Edge of Crime: Crack Cocaine and the Changing Contexts of Street-level Sex Work in New York City." *Crime, Law and Social Change* 18, 3: 221-258.

Maher, L. and K. Daly (1996). "Women in the Street Level Drug Economy: Continuity or Change?" *Criminology* 34, 4: 465-498.

Mann, C.R. (1984a). "Race and Sentencing of Female Felons: A Field Study." *International Journal of Women's Studies* 7: 160-172.

Mann, C.R. (1984b). *Female Crime and Delinquency*. Tuscaloosa, AL: University of Alabama Press.

Mann, C.R. (1988). "Getting Even? Women Who Kill in Domestic Encounters." *Justice Quarterly* 5, 1: 34-46.

Mann, C.R. (1993). *Unequal Justice: A Question of Color*. Bloomington, IN: Indiana University Press.

Marshall, I.H. (1982). "Women, Work, and Crime: An International Test of the Emancipation Hypothesis." *International Journal of Comparative and Applied Criminal Justice* 6, 1: 25-37.

Matsueda, R. (1989). "The Dynamics of Moral Beliefs and Minor Deviance." *Social Forces* 68: 428-457.

Maxfield, M. (1987). "Lifestyle and Routine Activity Theories of Crime: Empirical Studies of Victimization, Delinquency and Offender Decision Making." *Journal of Quantitative Criminology* 3: 275-282.

McClain, P.D. (1982). "Black Females and Lethal Violence: Has Time Changed the Circumstances Under Which They Kill?" *Omega* 13: 13-25.

McCord, J. and L. Otten (1983). "A Consideration of Sex Roles and Motivations for Crime." *Criminal Justice and Behavior* 10: 3-12.

McDermott, M.J. (1994). "Criminology as Peacemaking, Feminist Ethics and the Victimization of Women." *Women & Criminal Justice* 5, 2: 21-42.

McLeod, E. (1982). *Women Working: Prostitution Now*. London, England: Croom-Helm.

McLeod, M. (1984). "Women Against Men: An Examination of Domestic Violence Based on an Analysis of Official Data and National Victimization Data." *Justice Quarterly* 1: 171-194.

McLeod, R. (1995, October 17). "Number of Single Parent Families Continues to Increase, Report Says." *Austin American Statesman*, p. A2.

Mead, G.H. (1934). *Mind, Self and Society*. Chicago, IL: University of Chicago Press.

Mead, M. (1963). *Sex and Temperament in Three Primitive Societies*. New York, NY: William Morrow.

Mealey, L. (1995). "The Sociobiology of Sociopathy: An Integrated Evolutionary Model." *Behavioral and Brain Sciences* 18: 523-599.

Mednick, S. and K. Christiansen (1977). *Biosocial Bases for Criminal Behavior*. New York, NY: Gardner.

Mednick, S.A., T.E. Moffitt, and S.A. Stack (eds.) (1987). *The Causes of Crime*. New York, NY: Cambridge University Press.

Menard, S. and D. Elliott (1994). "Delinquent Bonding, Moral Beliefs, and Illegal Behavior: A Three Wave Panel Model." *Justice Quarterly* 11, 2: 173-188.

Merlo, A. (1993). "Pregnant Substance Abusers: The New Female Offender." In R. Muraskin and T. Alleman, *It's a Crime: Women and Justice*. Englewood Cliffs, NJ: Prentice-Hall.

Merlo, A. (1995). "Female Criminality in the 1990s." In A. Merlo and J. Pollock, *Women, Law and Social Control*, pp. 119-135. Boston, MA: Allyn and Bacon.

Merton, R. (1938). "Social Structure and Anomie." *American Sociological Review* 3, 6: 672-682.

Messerschmidt, J. (1986). *Capitalism, Patriarchy, and Crime: Toward a Socialist Feminist Criminology*. Totowa, NJ: Rowman & Littlefield.

Messerschmidt, J. (1993). *Masculinities and Crime: Critique and Reconceptualization of Theory*. Lanham, MD: Rowman and Littlefield.

Messerschmidt, J. (1997) *Crime as Structured Action: Gender, Race, Class and Crime in the Making*. Thousand Oaks, CA: Sage.

Messner, S.F. and R. Rosenfeld (1994). *Crime and the American Dream*. Belmont, CA: Wadsworth.

Messner, S.F. and R.J. Sampson (1991). "The Sex Ratio, Family Disruption, and Rates of Violent Crime: The Paradox of Demographic Structure." *Social Forces* 69: 693-713.

Miller, B., W. Downs, and D. Gondoli (1989). "Delinquency, Childhood Violence, and the Development of Alcoholims in Women." *Crime & Delinquency* 35: 94-108.

Miller, E. (1985). *Street Woman*. Philadelphia, PA: Temple University Press.

Miller, S.L. and C. Burack (1993). "A Critique of Gottfredson and Hirschi's General Theory of Crime: Selective (In)Attention to Gender and Power Positions." *Women and Criminal Justice* 4, 2: 115-34.

Miller, W. (1958). "Lower Class Culture as a Generating Milieu of Gang Delinquency." *Journal of Social Issues* 14: 5-19.

Miller, W. (1980) "Molls." In S. Datesman and F. Scarpetti, *Women, Crime and Justice*, pp. 238-254. New York, NY: Oxford University Press.

Moffitt, T.E. (1990) "The Neuropsychology of Juvenile Delinquency: A Critical Review." In M. Tonry and N. Morris, *Crime and Justice: A Review of Research, Vol. 12*, pp. 99-171. Chicago, IL: Chicago University Press.

Moffitt, T.E. (1993). "Adolescence-Limited and Life-Course Persistent Antisocial Behavior: A Developmental Taxonomy." *Psychological Review* 100: 674-701.

Moffitt, T.E. and S.A. Mednick (1988). *Biological Contributions to Crime Causation*. Dordrecht, Netherlands: Martinus Nyhoff.

Moore, J. (1991). *Going Down to the Barrio: Homeboys and Homegirls in Change*. Philadelphia, PA: Temple University Press.

Moore, J. and J. Hagedorn (1996). "What Happens to the Girls in the Gang?" In R.C. Huff (ed.), *Gangs in America*, Second Edition, pp. 205-218. Thousand Oaks, CA: Sage.

Morash, M. (1983). "An Explanation of Juvenile Delinquency: The Integration of Moral Reasoning Theory and Sociological Knowledge." In W.S. Laufer and J.M. Day (eds.), *Personality Theory, Moral Development, and Criminal Behavior*, pp. 385-414. Lexington, MA: Lexington Books.

Morash, M. (1986). "Gender, Peer Group Experiences and Seriousness of Delinquency." *Journal of Research in Crime and Delinquency* 23: 43-67.

Morash, M. and M. Chesney-Lind (1991). "A Reformulation and Partial Test of the Power Control Theory of Delinquency." *Justice Quarterly* 8: 347-377.

Morgan, P. and K.A. Joe (1996). "Citizens and Outlaws: The Private Lives and Public Lifestyles of Women in the Illicit Drug Economy." *Journal of Drug Issues* 26, 1: 199-218.

Morgan, P. and K.A. Joe (1997). "Uncharted Terrain: Contexts of Experience Among Women in the Illicit Drug Economy." *Women and Criminal Justice* 8, 3: 85-109.

Morris, A. (1987). *Women, Crime and Criminal Justice*. Malden, MA: Basil Blackwell.

Morris, A. and L. Gelsthorpe (1981). "False Clues and Female Crime." In A. Morris and L. Gelsthorpe, *Women and Crime*, pp. 49-70. New York, NY: Cambridge University Press.

Morris, R. (1964). "Female Delinquency and Relational Problems." *Social Forces* 43: 82-88.

Moulds, E. (1980). "Chivalry and Paternalism: Disparities of Treatment in the Criminal Justice System." In S. Datesman and F. Scarpetti (eds.), *Women, Crime and Justice*. New York, NY: Oxford University Press.

Mrazek, P. and D. Mrazek (1987). "Resilience in Child Maltreatment Victims: A Conceptual Exploration." *Child Abuse and Neglect* 11: 357-366.

Mukherjee, S. and R.W. Fitzgerald (1981). "The Myth of Rising Female Crime." In S.K. Mukherjee and J.A. Scutt (eds.), *Women and Crime,* pp. 127-166. Winchester, MA: George Allen and Unwin.

Mukherjee, S.K. and J.A. Scutt (eds.) (1981). *Women and Crime.* Winchester, MA: George Allen and Unwin.

Nachson, I. and D. Denno (1987). "Violent Behavior and Cerebral Hemisphere Function." In S.A. Mednick, T.E. Moffitt, and S.A. Stack (eds.), *The Causes of Crime,* pp. 185-213. New York, NY: Cambridge University Press.

Naffine, N. (1981). "Theorizing About Female Crime." In S.K. Mukherjee and J.A. Scutt (eds.), *Women and* Crime, pp. 70-91. Winchester, MA: George Allen and Unwin.

Naffine, N. (1987). *Female Crime: The Construction of Women in Criminology.* Boston, MA: Allen and Unwin.

Nagel, I. (1981). "Sex Differences in the Processing of Criminal Defendants." In A. Morris and L. Gelsthorpe, *Women and Crime,* pp. 104-124. New York, NY: Cambridge University Press.

Nagel, I. (1983). "The Legal/Extralegal Controversy: Judicial Decisions in Pre-trial Release." *Law and Society Review* 17: 481-575.

Nagel, I.H. and J. Hagan (1983). "Gender and Crime: Offense Patterns and Criminal Court Sanctions." In M. Tonry and N. Morris (eds.), *Crime and Justice: An Annual Review of Research, Vol. 14,* pp. 91-144. Chicago: University of Chicago Press.

Nagel, S. and L. Weitzman (1971). "Women as Litigants." *The Hastings Law Journal* 23, 1: 171-198.

Nagin, D.S. and D.P. Farrington (1992a). "The Stability of Criminal Potential From Childhood to Adulthood." *Criminology* 30: 235-60.

Nagin, D.S. and D.P. Farrington (1992b). "The Onset and Persistence of Offending." *Criminology* 30: 501-523.

Nagin, D.S., D.P. Farrington, and T.E. Moffitt (1995). "Life-Course Trajectories of Different Types of Offenders." *Criminology* 33, 1: 111-139.

National Institute of Justice (1997). *Drug Treatment Needs Among Adult Arrestees in Baltimore: Research Preview.* Washington, DC: U.S. Dept. of Justice, U.S. Government Printing Office.

Noddings, N. (1984). *Caring: A Feminine Approach to Ethics and Moral Education.* Berkeley, CA: University of California Press.

Norland, S. and N. Shover (1977). "Gender Roles and Female Criminality." *Criminology* 15, 1: 87-104.

Ogle, R., D. Maier-Katkin, and T. Bernard (1995). "A Theory of Homicidal Behavior Among Women." *Criminology* 33, 2: 173-189.

Olweus, D. (1987). "Testosterone and Adrenaline: Aggressive Antisocial Behavior in Normal Adolescent Males." In S.A. Mednick, T.E. Moffitt, and S.A. Stack (eds.), *The Causes of Crime,* pp. 263-283. New York, NY: Cambridge University Press.

Ouellet, L. J., W.W. Wiebel, A.D. Jimenez, and W.A. Johnson (1993). "Crack Cocaine and the Transformation of Prostitution in Three Chicago Neighborhoods." In M. Ratner (ed.), *The Crack Pipe as Pimp,* pp. 69-95. New York, NY: Lexington Books.

Parisi, N. (1982). "Exploring Female Crime Patterns: Problems and Prospects." In N.H. Rafter and E.A. Stanko (eds.), *Judges, Lawyer, Victim, Thief*, pp. 111-129. Boston, MA: Northeastern University Press.

Parsons, T. (1949). *Essays in Sociological Theory.* New York, NY: Free Press.

Parsons, T. (1954). *Essays in Sociological Theory (Revised).* Glencoe, IL: Free Press.

Paternoster, R. and R. Brame (1997). "Multiple Routes to Delinquency? A Test of Developmental and General Theories of Crime." *Criminology* 35, 1: 49-80.

Patterson, G. (1993). "Orderly Change in a Stable World: The Antisocial Trait as a Chimera." *Journal of Consulting and Clinical Psychology* 61: 911-919.

Patterson, G., B. DeBaryshe, and E. Ramsey (1989). "A Developmental Perspective on Antisocial Behavior." *American Psychologist* 44: 329-335.

Pearson, P. (1997). *When She Was Bad: The Myth of Innocence.* New York, NY: Viking Press.

Pettiway, L. (1987). "Participation in Crime Partnerships by Female Drug Users: The Effects of Domestic Arrangements, Drug Use, and Criminal Involvement." *Criminology* 25: 741-766.

Phillips, A. (1987). *Feminism and Equality.* Oxford, England: Basil Blackwell.

Piaget, J. (1965). *The Moral Judgement of the Child.* New York, NY: Free Press.

Pike, L. (1876). *A History of Crime in England.* London, England: Smith, Edler and Co.

Piquero, A. and S. Tibbetts (1996). "Specifying the Direct and Indirect Effects of Low Self-Control and Situational Factors in Offenders' Decision Making: Toward a More Complete Model of Rational Offending." *Justice Quarterly* 13, 3: 481-510.

Poe-Yamagata, E. and J. Butts (1996). *Female Offenders in the Juvenile Justice System.* Pittsburgh, PA: National Center for Juvenile Justice.

Polakowski, M. (1994). "Linking Self-and Social Control with Deviance: Illuminating the Structure Underlying a General Theory of Crime and its Relation to Deviant Activity." *Journal of Quantitative Criminology* 10, 1: 41-78.

Pollak, O. (1950). *The Criminality of Women.* Philadelphia, PA: University of Pennsylvania Press.

Pollock, J. (1978). "Early Theories of Female Criminality." In. L. Bowker, *Women, Crime and the Criminal Justice System*, pp. 25-57. Lexington, MA: Lexington Books.

Pollock, J. (1998). *Counseling Women Offenders.* Thousand Oaks, CA: Sage.

Pollock-Byrne, J. (1990). *Women, Prison and Crime.* Pacific Grove, CA: Brooks/Cole.

Pollock-Byrne, J. (1991). "Moral Development and Corrections." In M. Braswell, B. McCarthy, and B. McCarthy (eds.), *Justice, Crime and Ethics*, pp. 221-237.

Pollock-Byrne, J. and A. Merlo (1991). "Against Compulsory Treatment: No Quick Fix for Pregnant Substance Abusers." *Criminal Justice Policy Review* 5: 79-99.

Portillos, E. and M.S. Zatz (1995). "Not To Die For: Positive and Negative Aspects of Chicano Youth Gangs." Paper presented at the American Society of Criminology Meeting. Cited in M. Chesney-Lind (1997) *The Female Offender: Women, Girls and Crime.* Thousand Oaks, CA: Sage.

Quicker, J. (1983). *Homegirls: Characterizing Chicana Gangs.* San Pedro, CA: International Universities Press.

Quinney, R. (1973). *Critique of Legal Order: Crime Control in a Capitalist Society.* Boston, MA: Little, Brown.

Quinney, R. (1991). "The Way of Peace." In A. Pepinsky and R. Quinney (eds.), *Criminology as Peacemaking,* pp. 3-13. Bloomington, IN: Indiana University Press.

Raeder, M. (1993). "Gender Issues in the Federal Sentencing Guidelines." *Journal of Criminal Justice* 8, 3: 20-25, 56-58, 60-63.

Rafter, N. (1985). *Partial Justice: Women in State Prisons, 1800-1935.* Boston, MA: Northeaster University Press.

Rafter, N. (1988). *White Trash: The Eugenics Family Studies, 1877-1919.* Boston, MA: Northeastern University Press.

Raine, A. (1993). *The Psychopathology of Crime: Criminal Behavior as a Clinical Disorder.* San Diego, CA: Academic Press.

Rankin, J.H. and E.L. Wells (1990). "The Effect of Parental Attachments and Direct Controls on Delinquency." *Journal of Research in Crime and Delinquency* 27: 140-165.

Rasche, C. (1974). "The Female Offender as an Object of Criminological Research." *Criminal Justice and Behavior* 1: 301-320.

Redl, F. and H. Toch (1979). "The Psychoanalytic Perspective." In H. Toch (ed.), *Psychology of Crime and Criminal Justice,* pp. 183-197. New York, NY: Holt, Rinehart & Winston.

Reed, G. and P.C. Yeager (1996). "Organizational Offending and Neoclassical Criminology: Challenging the Reach of a General Theory of Crime." *Criminology* 34, 3: 357-382.

Reiss, A. and M. Tonry (eds.) (1986). *Communities and Crime.* Chicago, IL: University of Chicago Press.

Reiss, A. and J.A. Roth (eds.) (1993). *Understanding and Preventing Violence.* Washington, DC: National Academy Press.

Renzetti, C. and D. Curran (1992/1995). *Women, Men and Society,* Second Edition. Boston, MA: Allyn and Bacon.

Richards, P. (1981). "Quantitative and Qualitative Sex Differences in Middle-Class Delinquency." *Criminology* 18: 453-470.

Richards, P. and C. Tittle (1981). "Gender and Perceived Chances of Arrest." *Social Forces* 59: 1182-1199.

Rosenau, P. (1992). *Post-Modernism and the Social Sciences: Insights, Inroads, and Intrusions.* Princeton, NJ: Princeton University Press.

Rosenbaum, M. (1981). *Women on Heroin.* New Brunswick, NJ: Rutgers University Press.

Rosenbaum, J.L. (1987). "Social Control, Gender, and Delinquency: An Analysis of Drug, Property, and Violent Offenders." *Justice Quarterly* 4,1: 117-132.

Rosenbaum, J. (1989). "Family Dysfunction and Female Delinquency." *Crime & Delinquency* 35, 1: 31-44.

Rosenbaum, J.L. (1993). "The Female Delinquent: Another Look at the Role of the Family." In R. Muraskin and T. Alleman, *It's a Crime: Women and Justice,* pp. 399-417. Englewood Cliffs, NJ: Prentice-Hall.

Rosenbaum, J.L. and J.R. Lasley (1990). "School, Community Context, and Delinquency: Rethinking the Gender Gap." *Justice Quarterly* 7: 493-513.

Rosenbaum, K. (1980). "Female Deviance and the Female Sex Role: A Preliminary Investigation." In S. Datesman and F. Scarpetti (eds.), *Women, Crime and Justice,* pp. 106-127. New York, NY: Oxford University Press.

Ross, R., E. Fabiano, and C. Ewles (1988). "Reasoning and Rehabilitation." *International Journal of Offender Therapy and Comparative Criminology* 32, 1: 29-35.

Rothbart, M., D. Hanley, and M. Albert (1986). "Gender Differences in Moral Reasoning." *Sex Roles* 15, 11/12: 640-655.

Roundtree, G.A., B. Mohan, and L.W. Mahaffey (1980). "Determinants of Female Aggression: A Study of a Prison Population." *International Journal of Offender Therapy and Comparative Criminology* 24, 3: 260-269.

Rowe, D.C. (1996). "An Adaptive Strategy Theory of Crime and Delinquency." In J.D. Hawkins (ed.), *Delinquency and Crime: Current Theories,* pp. 268-315. New York, NY: Cambridge University Press.

Rowe, D.C. and D.P. Farrington (1997). "The Familial Transmission of Criminal Convictions." *Criminology* 35, 1: 177-196.

Rowe, D.C., A.T. Vazsonyi, and D.J. Fannery (1995). "Sex Differences in Crime: Do Means and Within-Sex Variation Have Similar Causes?" *Journal of Research in Crime and Delinquency* 31, 1: 84-100.

Rushton, J.P., D. Fulker, M. Neale, D. Nias, and H. Eysenck (1986). "Altruism and Aggression: The Heritability of Individual Differences." *Journal of Personality and Social Psychology* 50: 1192-1198.

Rutter, M. (ed.) (1996). *Genetics of Criminal and Antisocial Behavior.* New York, NY: John Wiley and Sons.

Rutter, M., D. Quinton, and J. Hill (1990). "Adult Outcome of Institution Reared Children: Males and Females Compared." In L. Robins and M. Rutter, *Straight and Deviant Pathways From Childhood to Adulthood,* pp. 135-158. New York, NY: Cambridge University Press.

Sagatun, I. (1993). "Babies Born with Drug Addiction: Background and Legal Responses." In R. Muraskin and T. Alleman, *It's a Crime: Women and Justice,* pp. 118-130. Englewood Cliffs, NJ: Prentice-Hall.

Sampson, R. (1986). "Crime in Cities: The Effects of Formal and Informal Social Control." In A. Reiss and M. Tonry, *Understanding and Preventing Violence.* Washington, DC: National Academy Press.

Sampson, R. (1987). "Urban Black Violence. The Effect of Male Joblessness and Family Disruption." *American Journal of Sociology* 93: 348-382.

Sampson, R. and W.B. Groves (1989). "Community Structure and Crime: Testing Social-Disorganization Theory." *American Journal of Sociology* 94: 774-802.

Sampson, R.J. and J.H. Laub (1991). "Crime and Deviance Over the Life Course: The Salience of Adult Social Bonds." *American Sociological Review* 55: 608-627.

Sampson, R. and J. Laub (1993). *Crime in the Making: Pathways and Turning Points Through Life*. Cambridge, MA: Harvard University Press.

Sampson, R. and J. Lauritsen (1990). "Deviant Lifestyles, Proximity to Crime, and the Offender-Victim Link in Personal Violence." *Journal of Research on Crime and Delinquency* 27: 110-139.

Sampson, R. and J. Wooldredge (1987). "Linking the Micro- and Macro-Level Dimensions of Lifestyle-Routine Activity and Opportunity Models of Predatory Victimization." *Journal of Quantitative Criminology* 3: 371-393.

Sanchez, J. and B. Johnson (1987). "Women and the Drugs-Crime Connection: Crime Rates Among Drug Abusing Women at Rikers Island." *Journal of Psychoactive Drugs* 19, 2: 200-216.

Sandhu, H. and D. Allen (1969) "Female Delinquency: Goal Obstruction and Anomie." *Canadian Review of Sociology and Anthropology* 5: 107-110.

Sandhu, H. and H. Satterfield (1987). "Childhood Diagnostic and Neurophysiological Predictors of Teenage Arrest Rates: An Eight Year Prospective Study." In S.A. Mednick, T.E. Moffitt, and S.A. Stack (eds.), *The Causes of Crime*, pp. 146-168. New York, NY: Cambridge University Press.

Scharf, P. and J. Hickey (1976). "The Prison and Inmates Conception of Legal Justice: An Experiment in Democratic Education." *Criminal Justice and Behavior* 3, 2: 207-222.

Schur, E. (1971). *Labeling Deviant Behavior: Its Sociological Implication*. New York, NY: Harper and Row.

Schur, E. (1984). *Labeling Women Deviant: Gender, Stigma and Social Control*. New York, NY: Random House.

Schwartz, M. (1987). "Gender and Injury in Spousal Assault." *Sociological Focus* 20: 61-75.

Schwartz, M.D. Milovanovic (eds.) (1994). *The Intersection of Race, Gender and Class in Criminology*. New York, NY: Garland.

Schwartz, M. and D. Friedrichs (1994). "Postmodern Thought and Criminologial Discontent: New Metaphors for Understanding Violence." *Criminology* 32, 2: 221-246.

Schweber, C. and C. Feinman (1985). *Criminal Justice Politics and Women: The Aftermath of Legally Mandated Change*. New York, NY: Haworth Press.

Sellin, T. (1938). *Culture Conflict and Crime*. New York, NY: Social Science Research Council.

Seydlitz, R. (1991). "The Effects of Age and Gender on Parental Control and Delinquency." *Youth and Society* 23: 175-201.

Shaffer, E.C., C.G. Pettigrew, D. Bout, and D.W. Edwards (1983). "Multivariate Classification of Female Offenders MMPI Profiles." *Journal of Crime and Justice* 6: 57-65.

Shaw, C. (1951). *The Natural History of a Delinquent Career*. Philadelphia, PA: Albert Saifer.

Shaw, C. and H. McKay (1934/1972). *Juvenile Delinquency and Urban Areas*. Chicago, IL: University of Chicago Press.

Shichor, D. (1985). "Male-Female Differences in Elderly Arrests: An Exploratory Analysis." *Justice Quarterly* 2, 3: 399-414.

Siegel, L. (1989) *Criminology*. St. Paul, MN: West Publishing Co.

Sikes, G. (1997). *8 Ball Chicks: A Year in the Violent World of Girl Gangsters.* New York, NY: Anchor Books (Doubleday).

Silberg, J., J. Meyer, A. Pickles, E. Simonoff, L. Eaves, J. Hewitt, H. Maes, and M. Rutter (1996). "Heterogeneity Among Juvenile Antisocial Behaviors: Findings From the Virginia Twin Study of Adolescent Behavioral Development." In M. Rutter (ed.), *Genetics of Criminal and Antisocial Behavior,* pp. 76-87. New York, NY: John Wiley and Sons.

Silverman, I. and S. Dinitz (1974). "Compulsive Masculinity and Delinquency: An Empirical Investigation." *Criminology* 11: 498-515.

Simon, R.J. (1975a). *Women and Crime.* Lexington, MA: DC Heath.

Simon, R.J. (1975b). *The Contemporary Woman and Crime.* Monograph in the Crime and Delinquency Issues Series. Washington, DC: National Institute of Mental Health.

Simon, R.J. (1976). "Women and Crime Revisited." *Social Science Quarterly* 4: 658-663.

Simon, R.J. and S. Baxter (1989). "Gender and Violent Crime." In N. Weiner and M. Wolfgang (eds.), *Violent Crime, Violent Criminals*, pp. 171-197. Beverly Hills, CA: Sage.

Simon R.J. and J. Landis (1991). *The Crimes Women Commit, The Punishments They Receive.* Lexington, MA: Lexington Books.

Simon, R. and N. Sharma (1979). *The Female Defendant in Washington, DC: 1974 and 1975.* Washington, DC: Institute for Law and Social Research.

Simpson, S. (1989). "Feminist Theory, Crime and Justice." *Criminology* 27, 4: 605-631.

Simpson, S. (1991). "Caste, Class, and Violent Crime: Explaining Differences in Female Offending." *Criminology* 29, 1: 115-135.

Simpson, S. and L. Elis (1995). "Doing Gender: Sorting Out the Caste and Crime Conundrum." *Criminology* 33, 1: 47-81.

Singer, S.I. and M. Levine (1988). "Power-Control Theory, Gender, and Delinquency: A Partial Replication with Additional Evidence on the Effects of Peers." *Criminology* 26: 627-647.

Smart, C. (1976). *Women, Crime and Criminology: A Feminist Critique.* London, England: Routledge and Kegan Paul.

Smart, C. (1979). "The New Female Criminal: Reality or Myth?" *British Journal of Criminology* 19, 1: 50-59.

Smart, C. (1989). *Feminism and the Power of the Law.* New York, NY: Routledge.

Smart, C. (1995). *Law, Crime and Sexuality: Essays in Feminism.* Thousand Oaks, CA: Sage.

Smith, C. and T. Thornberry (1995). "The Relationship Between Childhood Maltreatment and Adolescent Involvement in Delinquency." *Criminology* 33, 4: 451-481.

Smith, D.A. (1979). "Sex and Deviance: An Assessment of the Major Sociological Variables." *Sociological Quarterly* 20: 183-195.

Smith, D. and R. Paternoster (1987). "The Gender Gap in Theories of Deviance: Issues and Evidence." *Journal of Research in Crime and Delinquency* 24: 140-172.

Smith, D. and C. Visher (1980). "Sex and Involvement in Deviance/Crime: A Quantitative Review of the Empirical Literature." *American Sociological Review* 45: 691-701.

Snell, T. and D. Morton (1994). *Women in Prison: Special Report.* Washington, DC: Bureau of Justice Statistics.

Sobel, E. (1978). "The Aggressive Female." In E. Sobel, *Violence: Perspectives on Murder and Aggression,* pp. 267-285. San Francisco, CA: Jossey-Bass.

Sommers, I. and D. Baskin (1992). "Sex, Race, Age and Violent Offending." *Violence and Victims* 7: 191-202.

Sommers, I. and D. Baskin (1993). "The Situational Context of Violent Female Offending." *Journal of Research in Crime an Delinquency* 30: 136-162.

Sparks, R.F. (1979). "Crime as Business and the Female Offender." In F. Adler and R.J. Simon (eds.), *Criminology of Deviant Women,* pp. 171-183. Boston, MA: Houghton Mifflin Company.

Spohn, C. and J. Spears (1997). "Gender and Case Processing Decisions: A Comparison of Case Outcomes for Male and Female Defendants Charged with Violent Felonies." *Women & Criminal Justice* 8, 3: 29-59.

Spohn, C., J. Gruhl, and S. Welch (1985). "Women Defendants in Court: The Interaction Between Sex and Race in Convicting and Sentencing." *Social Science Quarterly* 66: 178-185.

Spohn, C., J. Gruhl, and S. Welch (1987). "The Impact of Ethnicity and Gender of Defendants on the Decision to Reject or Dismiss Felony Charges." *Criminology* 25: 175-192.

Spunt, B., H. Brownstein, S. Crimmins, and S. Langley (1994). "Female Drug Relationships and Murder." Report to the National Institute on Drug Abuse. Washington, DC: Government Printing Office.

Steffensmeier, D. (1978). "Crime and the Contemporary Woman: An Analysis of Changing Levels of Female Property Crime, 1960-75." *Social Forces* 57: 566-584.

Steffensmeier, D. (1980). "Sex Differences in Patterns of Adult Crime, 1965-1977: A Review and Assessment." *Social Forces* 58, 4: 1080-1108.

Steffensmeier, D. (1981). "Patterns of Female Property Crime, 1960-1975: A Postscript." In L. Bowker (ed.), *Women and Crime in America,* pp. 59-65. New York, NY: Macmillan.

Steffensmeier, D. (1983). "Organization Properties and Sex-Segregation in the Underworld: Building a Sociological Theory of Sex Differences in Crime." *Social Forces* 61: 1010-1043.

Steffensmeier, D. (1989). "On the Causes of White-Collar Crime: An Assessment of Hirschi and Gottfredson's Claims." *Criminology* 27: 345-358.

Steffensmeier, D. (1993). *National Trends in Female Arrests, 1960-1990: Assessment and Recommendations for Research.* Unpublished paper.

Steffensmeier, D. and E.A. Allen (1988). "Sex Disparities in Arrest by Residence, Race, and Age: An Assessment of the Gender Convergence/Crime Hypothesis." *Justice Quarterly* 5: 53-80.

Steffensmeier, D., E.A. Allen, and C. Streifel (1989). "Development and Female Crime: A Cross-National Test of Alternative Explanations." *Social Forces* 68, 1: 262-283.

Steffensmeier, D. and M. Cobb (1981). "Sex Differences in Urban Arrest Patterns, 1934-1979." *Social Problems* 29: 37-50.

Steffensmeier, D. and J. Kramer (1980). "The Differential Impact of Criminal Stigmatization on Male and Female Felons." *Sex Roles* 6, 1: 1-27.

Steffensmeier, D., J. Kramer, and C. Streifel (1993). "Gender and Imprisonment Decisions." *Criminology* 31, 3: 411-446.

Steffensmeier D. and C. Streifel (1992). "Time-Series Analysis of the Female Percentage of Arrests for Property Crimes, 1960-1985: A Test of Alternative Explanations." *Justice Quarterly* 9: 77-103.

Steffensmeier D. and C. Streifel (1993). "Trends in Female Crime, 1960-1990." In C. Culliver, *Female Criminality: The State of the Art,* pp. 63-101. New York, NY: Garland.

Steffensmeier, D. and R.H. Steffensmeier (1980). "Trends in Female Delinquency." *Criminology* 18, 1: 62-85.

Steffensmeier, D. and R. Terry (1986). "Institutional Sexism in the Underworld: A View from the Inside." *Sociological Inquiry* 56: 304-323.

Steinmetz, S. (1978). "The Battered Husband Syndrome." *Victimology* 2: 499-509.

Straus, M. and R. Gelles (1986). "Societal Change and Change in Family Violence from 1975-1985 as Revealed by Two National Surveys." *Journal of Marriage and the Family* 48(Aug.): 465-480.

Straus, M., R. Gelles, and S. Steinmetz (1980). *Behind Closed Doors.* Garden City, NY: Anchor Books.

Sutherland, E. (1939). *Principles of Criminology.* Philadelphia, PA: Lippincott.

Sutherland, D. and D. Cressey (1960/1966). *Principles of Criminology (revised).* Philadelphia, PA: Lippincott.

Sykes, G. and D. Matza (1957). "Techniques of Neutralization: A Theory of Delinquency." *American Sociological Review* (December): 664-670.

Taylor, C. (1993). *Girls, Gangs and Drugs.* East Lansing, MI: Michigan State University Press.

Taylor, I., P. Walton, and J. Young (1973). *The New Criminology.* New York, NY: Harper and Row.

Tedeschi, J. and R. Felson (1994). *Violence, Aggression and Coercive Actions.* Washington, DC: American Psychological Association.

Temin, C.E. (1973). "Discriminatory Sentencing of Women: The Argument for ERA in a Nutshell." *Criminal Law Review (Winter)*: 358-372.

Thomas, W.I. (1969/1923). *The Unadjusted Girl.* Monclair, NJ: Patterson Smith.

Thornberry, T. (1987). "Toward an Interactional Theory of Delinquency." *Criminology* 25: 863-891.

Thornberry, T. (1994). *Violent Families and Youth Violence. Fact Sheet.* Office of Juvenile Justice and Delinquency Prevention, Washington, DC: U.S. Dept. of Justice.

Thorne, B. (1993). *Gender Play: Girls and Boys in School.* New Brunswick, NJ: Rutgers University Press.

Thrasher, F.M. (1927). *The Gang.* Chicago, IL: University of Chicago Press.

Tittle, C. (1991). "Review of a General Theory of Crime, by Michael R. Gottfredson and Travis Hirschi." *American Journal of Sociology* 96: 1609-1611.

Tittle, C. (1995). *Control Balance: Toward a General Theory of Deviance*. Boulder, CO: Westview Press.

Tittle, C. (1998). "Comments on Papers Concerning Control Balance Theory." Paper presented at the Academy of Criminal Justice Sciences Meeting.

Toch, H. (1969/1992). *Violent Men: An Inquiry into the Psychology of Violence*. Washington, DC: American Psychological Association. (get new edition)

Tong, R. (1984). *Women, Sex and the Law*. Totawa, NJ: Rowman and Littlefield.

Tonry, M. (1995). *Malign Neglect: Race, Crime, and Punishment in America*. New York, NY: Oxford University Press.

Tonry, M., L. Ohlin, and D. Farrington (1991). *Human Development and Criminal Behavior: New Ways of Advancing Knowledge*. New York, NY: Springer-Verlag.

Townes, B.D., J. James, and D.C. Martin (1981). "Criminal Involvement of Female Offenders: Psychological Characteristics Among Four Groups." *Criminology* 18, 4: 471-480.

Trasler, G. (1987). "Some Cautions For the Biological Approach to Crime Causation." In S.A. Mednick, T.E. Moffitt, and S.A. Stack (eds.), *The Causes of Crime*, pp. 7-25. New York, NY: Cambridge University Press.

Triplett, R. and L. Meyers (1995). "Evaluating Contextual Patterns of Delinquency: Gender-Based Differences." *Justice Quarterly* 12, 1: 59-83.

Tronto, J. (1987). "Beyond Gender Differences to a Theory of Care." *Signs: Journal of Women in Culture and Society*. 12: 644-663.

Tuana, N. (1993). *The Less Noble Sex: Scientific, Religious, and Philosophical Conceptions of Woman's Nature*. Bloomington, IN.: Indiana University Press.

Umbreit, M. (1997). "Victim-Offender Dialogue: From the Margins to the Mainstream Throughout the World." *The Crime Victim Report* (July/August): 35-36.

Umbreit, M. (1998). "Impact of Victim-Offender Mediation in Canada, England and the United States." *The Crime Victim Report* (Jan/Feb): 83-70.

Vaux, A. (1988). *Social Support: Theory, Research, and Intervention*. New York, NY: Praeger.

Vedder, C. and D. Somerville (1970). *The Delinquent Girl*. Springfield, IL: Thomas.

Vila, B. (1994). "A General Paradigm for Understanding Criminal Behavior: Extending Evolutionary Ecological Theory." *Criminology* 32: 311-359.

Visher, C. (1983). "Gender, Police Arrest Decision, and Notions of Chivalry." *Criminology* 21, 1: 5-28.

Vold, G., T. Bernard, and J. Snipes (1998). *Theoretical Criminology*. New York, NY: Oxford University Press.

Walsh, A. (1991). *Intellectual Imbalance, Love Deprivation and Violent Delinquency: A Biosocial Perspective*. Springfield, IL: Charles C Thomas.

Walsh, A. (1995a). *Biosociology: An Emerging Paradigm*. Westport, CT: Praeger.

Walsh, A. (1995b). "Genetic and Cytogenetic Intersex Anomalies: Can They Help Us to Understand Gender Differences in Deviant Behavior?" *International Journal of Offender Therapy and Comparative Criminology* 39: 151-166.

Walsh, A. and J. Beyer (1987). "Violent Crime, Sociopathy and Love Deprivation Among Adolescent Delinquents." *Adolescence* 22: 705-717.

Walsh, A. and T.A. Petee (1987). "Love Deprivation and Violent Juvenile Delinquency." *Journal of Crime and Justice* 10, 2: 45-61.

Walters, G.D. (1990). *The Criminal Lifestyle: Patterns of Serious Criminal Conduct.* Newbury Park, CA: Sage.

Walters, G.D. (1992). "A Meta-Analysis of the Gene-Crime Relationship." *Criminology* 30: 595-613.

Walton, P. and J. Young (1998). *The New Criminology Revisited.* London, England: Macmillan.

Ward, D., M. Jackson, and R. Ward (1979). "Crimes of Violence by Women." In F. Adler and R. Simon (eds.), *The Criminology of Deviant Women,* pp. 114-138. Boston, MA: Houghton Mifflin Company.

Warren, M.Q. (1979). "The Female Offender." In H. Toch *Psychology and Criminal Justice,* pp. 444-469. Prospect Heights, IL: Waveland Press.

Warren, M.Q. (1981). *Comparing Female and Male Offenders.* Beverly Hills, CA: Sage.

Warren, M.Q. and J. Rosenbaum (1986). "Criminal Careers of Female Offenders." *Criminal Justice and Behavior* 13, 4: 393-418.

Weis, J.G. (1976). "Liberation and Crime: The Invention of the New Female Criminal." *Crime and Social Justice* 6: 17-36.

Weisheit, R. (1984). "Female Homicide Offenders: Trends Over Time in an Institutionalized Population." *Justice Quarterly* 1, 4: 471-489.

Weisheit, R. and S. Mahan (1988). *Women, Crime and Criminal Justice.* Cincinnati, OH: Anderson Publishing Co.

Welch, M. (1997). "Regulating the Reproduction and Morality of Women: The Social Control of Body and Soul." *Women and Criminal Justice* 9, 1: 17-38.

Wellisch, J., M. Prendergast, and J.D. Anglin (1994). *Drug Abusing Women Offenders: Results of a National Survey.* National Institute of Justice. Research in Brief. Washington, DC: U.S. Dept. of Justice.

Wellisch, J., M. Prendergast, and J.D. Anglin (1996). "Needs Assessment and Services for Drug-Abusing Women Offenders: Results from a National Survey of Community-Based Treatment Programs." *Women and Criminal Justice* 8, 1: 27-61.

White, H.R., E Labouvie, and M. Bates (1985). "The Relationship Between Sensation-Seeking and Delinquency: A Longitudinal Analysis." *Journal of Research in Crime and Delinquency* 22: 197-211.

Widom, C. (1979). "Female Offenders: Three Assumptions About Self-Esteem, Sex-Role Identity, and Feminism." *Criminal Jusitce and Behavior* 5, 1: 365-382.

Widom, C. (1981). "Perspectives of Female Criminality: A Critical Examination of Assumptions." In A. Morris and L. Gelthorpe (eds.), *Women and Crime,* pp. 33-48. Cambridge, England: University of Cambridge Institute of Criminology.

Widom, C. (1984). *Sex Roles and Psychopathology.* New York, NY: Plenum Press.

Widom, C.S. (1989a). "Child Abuse, Neglect, and Violent Criminal Behavior." *Criminology* 27: 251-271.

Widom, C. (1989b). "Does Violence Beget Violence? A Critical Examination of the Literature." *Psychological Bulletin* 106: 3-38.

Widom, C. (1991). "Avoidance of Criminality in Abused and Neglected Children." *Psychiatry* 54: 162-174.

Widom, C. (1995). *Victims of Childhood Sexual Abuse-Later Criminal Consequences.* NIJ: Research in Brief. Washington, DC: U.S. Dept. of Justice.

Widom, C. and A. Ames (1988). "Biology and Female Crime." In. T. Moffitt and S. Mednick, *Biological Contributions to Crime Causation,* pp. 308-331. Boston, MA: Martinus Nijhoff.

Wilbanks, W. (1980). "Female Homicide Offenders in the U.S." *International Journal of Women's Studies* 6: 302-310.

Wilbanks, W. (1986). "Are Female Felons Treated More Leniently by the Criminal Justice System?" *Justice Quarterly* 3, 4: 518-532.

Williams, F. and M. McShane (1988). *Criminological Theory.* Englewood Cliffs, NJ: Prentice-Hall.

Williams, F.P. III and M.D. McShane (1998). *Criminology Theory: Selected Classic Readings,* Second Edition. Cincinnati, OH: Anderson Publishing Co.

Wilson, J. (1993) *The Moral Sense.* New York, NY: Free Press.

Wilson, J. and R. Herrnstein (1986). *Crime and Human Nature.* New York, NY: Simon and Schuster.

Wilson, N.K. (1981). "The Masculinity of Violent Crime: Some Second Thoughts." *Journal of Criminal Justice* 9, 2: 111-123.

Wilson, N.K. and C.M. Rigsby (1975). "Is Crime a Man's World? Issues in the Exploration of Criminality." *Journal of Criminal Jusitce* 3, 2: 131-139.

Wolfgang, M.E., T.P. Thornberry, and R.M. Figlio (eds.) (1987). *From Boy to Man, From Delinquency to Crime.* Chicago, IL: University of Chicago Press.

Wonders, N. (1996). "Determinate Sentencing: A Feminist and Postmodern Story." *Justice Quarterly* 13, 4: 611-648.

Wood, P.B., W.R. Gove, J.A. Wilson, and J.K. Cochran (1997). "Nonsocial Reinforcement and Habitual Criminal Conduct: An Extension of Learning Theory." *Criminology* 35, 2: 335-366.

Wood, P.B., B. Pfefferbaum, and B.J. Arneklev (1993). "Risk-Taking and Self-Control: Social Psychological Correlates of Delinquency." *Journal of Crime and Justice* 16, 1: 111-130.

Worral, A. (1990). *Offending Women.* New York, NY: Routledge.

Wright, R.A. (1992). "From Vamps to Tramps to Teases and Flirts: Stereotypes of Women in Criminology Textbooks, 1956 to 1965 and 1981 to 1990." *Journal of Criminal Justice Education* 3, 2: 224-242.

Wright, R. (1995). *The Biology of Violence.* New York, NY: Vintage.

Wright, K. and K. Wright (1994). "A Policy Makers Guide to Controlling Delinquency and Crime Through Family Interventions." *Justice Quarterly* 11, 2: 190-206.

Young, V. (1980). "Women, Race and Crime." *Criminology* 18: 36-34.

Young, V. (1986). "Gender Expectations and Their Impact on Black Female Offenders and Victims." *Justice Quarterly* 3, 3: 305-327.

Zager, M.A. (1994). "Gender and Crime." In T. Hirschi and M.R. Gottfredson (eds.), *The Generality of Deviance*, pp. 71-79. New Brunswick, NJ: Transaction Publishers.

Zietz, D. (1981). *Women Who Embezzle or Defraud: A Study of Convicted Felons*. New York, NY: Praeger.

Zingraff, M. and R. Thompson (1984). "Differential Sentencing of Women and Men in the U.S.A." *International Journal of the Sociology of Law* 12: 401-413.

Zingraff, M., J. Leiter, K. Myers, and M. Johnson (1993). "Child Maltreatment and Youthful Problem Behavior." *Criminology* 31: 173-202.

Zingraff, M., J. Leiter, M. Johnson, and K. Myers (1994). "The Mediating Effect of Good School Performance on the Maltreatment-Delinquency Relationship." *Journal of Research in Crime and Delinquency* 31: 62-91.

Name Index

Abzug, B., 218
Adler, F., 22, 81, 84, 97, 148, 151, 164-167, 242
Adler, P., 51, 52, 75
Agnew, R., 125
Akers, R., 8, 9, 21, 22, 124-126, 163, 224
Akers, R.L., 119, 125, 126, 127, 191
Alarid, L.F., 41, 80
Albanese, J., 38
Albert, M., 250
Alleman, T., 141, 162, 163
Allen, D., 126
Allen, E.A., 45, 84, 97, 149, 232, 251
Allen, J., 140
Alvi, S., 221
Ames, A., 223
Anderson, T.L., 186
Andrews, D.A., 106, 111, 124, 125, 197, 204, 219, 225, 236
Anglin, D., 75, 76, 79
Anglin, D.M., 76
Anglin, M.D., 54, 76, 79
Arbuthnot, J.B., 233, 251
Arrigo, B., 20

Bagley, K., 77
Bandura, A., 110
Bankston, W., 43
Barkan, S., 21
Bartrum, T., 255
Bartusch, D.R., 190
Baskin, D., 25, 41, 54, 76, 79
Baxter, S., 166
Beccaria, C., 104
Becker, H., 122
Belknap, J., 163, 224
Bell, 77
Bennett, R.R., 186

Bentham, J., 104, 124
Beretta, G., 99
Bernard, T., 42, 163, 194, 214, 254
Bertrand, M., 161
Bishop, C., 164
Bishop, D., 91, 99
Blank, R., 76, 77
Block, A., 37, 45
Bloom, M., 54, 76
Blum, A., 27
Blumstein, A., 190, 192
Bohrman, M., 219
Bonta, J., 160, 111, 124, 124, 197, 204, 219, 225, 236
Booth, M., 75, 76, 79
Bordt, R., 91, 94, 99
Bottcher, J., 138, 161
Bowker, L., 75
Box, S., 166
Boyd, C., 75
Braithwaite, J., 238, 252, 253
Brame, R., 185, 194
Braswell, M., 252
Bridges, G.S., 99
Browne, A., 31, 43
Brownfield, D., 194
Brownstein, H., 42
Buck, C., 77
Bunch, B.J., 160
Burack, C., 183
Burgess, R., 119, 126
Bursik, R.J., 187
Butts, J., 63
Byrne, J.M., 194

Cameron, M., 45
Campbell, A., 64, 67, 68, 78, 79, 99
Carlen, P., 144, 162, 164, 252

Marshall, I.H., 149, 166
Martin, D.C., 76
Mast, D., 75
McCarthy, B., 252
McDermott, M.J., 237, 252
McKay, H., 112, 187
McLeod, E., 164
McLeod, M., 22, 43
McLeod, R., 166
McShane, M., 3, 5, 20, 21, 124
Mead, G.H., 122
Mead, M., 224
Mednick, S., 177, 219
Mednick, S.A., 219, 220, 225
Menard, S., 251
Merlo, A., 49, 77, 79, 86, 98
Merton, R., 113, 114
Messerschmidt, J., 142, 153, 154, 163, 166,
    224, 232, 233
Messner, S.F., 247
Miller, E., 166
Miller, S.L., 183
Miller, W., 70, 78, 113, 125
Moffitt, T.E., 190, 220, 221, 223
Moore, J., 78, 79
Morash, M., 155, 234, 235
Morgan, P., 75
Morris, A., 90, 93, 99, 140, 145, 162, 224,
    232, 251
Morris, R., 21, 116, 126
Morton, D., 75
Moulds, E., 98
Mukherjee, S., 86
Myers, K., 62, 77

Nachson, I., 201
Naffine, N., 21, 115, 121, 126, 139, 140,
    161, 162, 240, 241, 253
Nagel, I., 93, 99
Nagel, I.H., 90, 98, 99
Nagel, S., 89, 98
Nagin, D.S., 190
Noddings, N., 230, 231, 237, 250
Norland, S., 165

O'Donnel, N., 90
Ogle, R., 42
Ohlin, L., 189, 190
Ohlin, L.E., 114, 115, 116, 170
Olweus, D., 220

Parsons, T., 134, 135, 136, 160, 237, 241,
    253
Paternoster, R., 185, 194

Pearson, P., 41
Phillips, A., 163
Piaget, J., 109, 228, 229
Pike, L., 159
Piquero, A., 186
Poe-Yamagata, E., 63
Pollak, O., 15, 18, 19, 22, 24, 37, 84, 88,
    124, 131, 140, 164, 165
Pollock, J., 75, 96, 124, 139, 159, 160, 236,
    252, 254
Pollock-Byrne, J., 77
Portillos, E., 78
Pottieger, A., 75, 76

Quetelet, L.A.J., 112
Quicker, J., 66, 67, 78, 79
Quinney, R., 117, 237, 252

Raeder, M., 95
Rafter, N., 76, 218, 255
Raine, A., 204, 205, 217, 221, 225
Rasche, C., 139
Redl, F., 124
Reed, G., 191
Reiss, A., 34, 40, 44, 187, 194
Renzetti, C., 224, 235
Rigsby, C.M., 21
Rosenau, P., 20
Rosenbaum, J., 133
Rosenbaum, J.L., 133
Rosenbaum, K., 56, 76, 161
Rosenbaum, M., 49, 50, 51 75
Rosenfeld, R., 247
Ross, R., 251, 252
Roth, J., 190
Roth, J.A., 34, 40, 44
Rothbart, M., 250
Rowe, D.C., 190

Sagatun, I., 77
Sampson, R., 174, 175, 176, 178, 185, 187,
    190, 192, 194
Sampson, R.J. 194
Sanchez, J., 76
Sandhu, H., 126, 220
Satterfield, H., 220
Saunders, D., 22
Scarpetti, F., 77, 160, 166
Scharf, P., 231, 251
Schur, E., 122, 127
Schwartz, M., 3, 20, 22, 43, 124
Schweber, C., 100
Sellin, T., 125
Sharma, N., 89, 98

Subject Index

Abortion, 10, 230
Abuse
 child, 32-34, 133, 160, 164
 elderly, 32-34
 physical, 30, 68
 sexual, 30, 69, 143
ADD (Attention Deficit Disorder) (also
 includes hyperactivity) 173, 202-203,
 210, 249
Adoption studies, 191, 219
African-American
 families, 152, 216
 women, 72-74, 90, 91, 235
Age effect, 180
Aggression, 25, 110, 135, 177, 192, 199,
 205, 212, 220, 224, 225, 239
Alcohol(ism), 8, 29, 32, 35, 53, 73, 133
Altruism, 228, 231, 235, 241
Arson, 26-27
Assault, 41
Attachment, 13, 14, 120, 156, 234, 239

Biological approaches, 21, 177
 differences (between men and
  women), 7, 154, 180
 influences
 predispositions, 8, 132
 theories, 8, 130-132, 191, 195-215,
  225
Biosocial (theories), 162, 177, 215-218
Body-type theories, 195
Boot camps, 41
Brain
 chemistry, 206, 207, 232, 235, 242
 differences, 200-202
 lateralization, 200-201, 210

Broken homes, 3, 5, 13, 14, 32, 116, 131,
 133, 160, 173
Burglary, 36

Career criminal, 189, 190, 191, 194
Chicago School, 112, 187
Child abuse, 32-34. *See also* Abuse
Chivalry hypothesis, 52, 60, 84, 87-97
 declining, 94-97
Classical theory, 104, 105, 111, 185, 187
Cognitive development, 109
Compulsive masculinity (theory), 134-136
Conflict Tactics Scale, 31
Conscience, 233, 234, 235, 239, 249
Control theory, 13, 120-122, 127, 176, 180,
 241
Control-balance theory, 156-158
Correlation, 13, 14
"Crack," 51, 52, 75
"Crack babies," 58, 59
Crime(s)
 "dark figure" of, 24, 37
 juvenile. *See* Delinquency
 organized, 37-39
 property, 23, 36-39, 82-83, 117
 rates, 15, 23, 214
 violent, 12, 23, 24-35, 62, 77, 82, 110
 white-collar, 16, 37-39, 178, 181, 191
Critical criminology, 10, 117-118
Cross-cultural comparisons (of crime), 149
Cross-sectional research, 169, 189
Cultural deviance theory, 112

Delinquency, 6, 8, 47, 60-63, 77, 154, 172,
 174, 179
Developmental theories, 109, 194. *See also*
 Life-course development theories

297